OUT OF TIME

Why Football Isn't Working!

Alex Fynn and Lynton Guest

SIMON & SCHUSTER

LONDON·SYDNEY·NEW YORK·TOKYO·SINGAPORE·TORONTO

For Peter, Nicola and Michelle
and
Anne Fynn

———————

First published in Great Britain by Simon & Schuster Ltd, 1994
A Paramount Communications Company

Simon & Schuster Ltd
West Garden Place
Kendal Street
London W2 2AQ

Simon & Schuster of Australia Pty Ltd
Sydney

A CIP catalogue record for this book is available from the British Library.

ISBN 0–671–71220–9

Typeset in 11/13 Melior
by Florencetype Ltd, Avon
Printed and bound in Great Britain by
Butler & Tanner Ltd, Frome and London

Acknowledgments

This book could not have been produced without the help of many people who deserve thanks. It will be obvious that much of the material was gained through first hand experience of working with the football authorities, television companies and a number of clubs, not just in the UK but around the world. It is not certain whether Graham Kelly, Lennart Johansson, Glen Kirton, Trevor Phillips et al will appreciate thanks for their inadvertent contribution but they have them anyway.

Much more of the book was based on research and interviews and many people gave willingly of their time. It will rapidly become apparent to any reader how important their input was. They include Alan Smith and his anonymous England team-mate, Erik Thorstvedt, Glenn Hoddle, Liam Brady, Frank Worthington, Peter Osgood, Malcolm Allison, David Dein, Ken Bates, Bernie Coleman, Irving Scholar, Charles Hughes, Peter Storrie, Simon Inglis, David Hill, Jean-Claude Dassier, Trevor East, Steve Davies, Stuart Mutler, Guido Tognoni, Morris Keston, Mel Goldberg, Graham Smith, Dennis Roach, Mel Stein, Dennis Campbell, Chris Belt, Freddie Fletcher, Mark Rooney, Jim Cadman, Martin George and Barrie Pierpoint. Special thanks to Steve Allatt, Malcolm Berry, Mike Simmonds, David Willacy, Martin Duffield, Peter Hughes, John Morton and Adrian Riddiford, all involved with the English Schools Football Association, for their help in understanding the world of schools and youth football.

Working as a consultant to a television series called Masters Of The Game brought an enhanced perception of European football. This is reflected in the book mainly in the form of quotes taken from some of the interviews, particularly that of Silvio Berlusconi. Thanks are therefore due to Johan Op de Beeck of Multimedia, as they are to Chris Nawrat, Tony Allaway, Nick Pitt and their former colleague on the *Sunday Times,* Jason Tomas, who gave the opportunity to espouse theories on how reform throughout Europe could take place. Extra thanks at least to Jason for his encouragement in the early stages and to Colin Malam of the *Sunday Telegraph* for hour upon hour of enlightening football conversation.

A past president of the Football League once reminded journalists of their station in life when he told them brusquely; 'You guys only know what we choose to tell you.' Such narrow-minded opinions go some way towards explaining why the football authorities continue to make such a cock-up of things. Many pundits know far more than that and they have much to contribute beyond the reporting of events. A huge debt of gratitude is owed to the following for their friendly and expert advice: Norman Fox, Patrick Barclay, Giancarlo Galavotti, David Lacey, Joe Melling, the indefatigable Brian Glanville, Chris Lightbown, Louise Taylor, Kevin McCarra, Archie MacPherson, Neil Duncanson, David Grice, Paul Gardner, Don Peretta, Bill Brewster, Philip Cornwall, Andrew Shields and Tony Cook. A special thank you also to Richard Keys and BSkyB's Footballer's Football Show, which is essential viewing for any serious student of the game.

Kevin Morton and Gerald O'Connell provided important media insights and analysis, as did Mike Jones, and Steve Jenkins. Steve and Alasdair McNabb, helped with the compilation of the appendices. Graham Snowdon, Duljit Guram and Stephen Booth asked for advice on a dissertation on football and business which was part of their degree. Any help they received was more than balanced by the help they gave.

Friends and colleagues who gave vital support include Peter Suchet, Steve Mono, Gareth Coombs, Mark King, Geoff Bougarde, Laurence Harris, Colin Spencer, Michael Moreton, Darren Epstein, David 'First-to-the-Ball' Forrester, Pat Barker, Neil Aslett and Justin Barnes. Sonia Medin and the ladies in the Business Development Unit at Saatchi & Saatchi provided much needed background information as did Tony Myers, Richard Lewis, Rob Bagchi, Dominic Bercelli, David Luxton, Dan Jackson and Andrew Roberts at John Gaustad's Sportspages in London who allowed the shop to be used as a library rather than the wonderful book store it is.

Claire Coleman, Jacqui Long, Kate Blockley and Rhoda Fynn did invaluable typing of the background material and Rhoda also had the onerous task of transcribing many of the recorded interviews. Alban Lloyd helped with Italian translations while Anil Jindal saved the situation when deadline day approached by providing emergency computer back-up when the Amstrad was out of use.

Special thanks to all at Simon & Schuster particularly Martin Fletcher, Jenny Olivier, Jessica Cuthbert-Smith, Jacquie Clare and freelance editor extraordinaire, Caroline North. We hope their faith in the project is rewarded.

Finally, a big thank you to Bill Maynard for a great night out at Leicester which showed how football supporters should be treated and to the many fans of all clubs who were always ready with their opinions.

Alex Fynn & Lynton Guest
London: October 1993

Contents

Introduction

On February 24 1993, the whole nation mourned the death of Bobby Moore, who at the age of 51 had been stricken by cancer. The outpouring, in about equal measures of grief and affection, was a testimony to the high regard in which Moore was held, not only in the UK but throughout the world. Anybody who had seen him play could not have been anything but immensely impressed with both his ability and the way he used it. According to Pele, the greatest footballer the world has yet produced, Moore was the best defender he ever faced.

The high level of emotion was all the more moving for its spontaneity. Moore had been out of the headlines for many years and had not held a job inside the game since he retired as a player in 1976, apart from a couple of years when he managed non-league Oxford City and third division Southend United. There were natural feelings of loss at the premature death of a hero but beyond that, there was a recognition that in life, football had not repaid its debt to Moore by endeavouring to keep him in the game and utilising his knowledge and renown.

Bobby Moore was one of a long line of great players who, if they possess little aptitude for management or coaching, are continually lost to the game. There is no well-defined route by which they can be used to the benefit of the next generation. Bobby Charlton, another who, unlike his brother Jack, was not cut out for management, developed his own coaching clinics and was lucky enough to be invited to become a director of Manchester United. Moore could easily have been offered a similar position at West Ham, the club he captained to FA Cup and European success. Alternatively, he could have been given an ambassadorial role by the FA or the Sports Council or a job in the development of the national team. Compare the treatment of Moore to that of one of his opponents on that famous day in 1966. Franz Beckenbauer, when he retired, was courted by the German Football Federation which sought to keep him in the game. Then, with no managerial experience, Beckenbauer was put in charge of the German national team and won the World Cup.

Bobby Moore could point to a long list of achievements in football. The greatest of them came when he captained England's World Cup winning team, which on July 30 1966, beat West Germany 4–2 to bring the trophy to England for the only time. What followed was a golden age for British football. Bobby Charlton was named European Footballer Of The Year, soon to be followed by George Best. If these were at the top of the bill, there existed just below them a plethora of true international stars, such as Jimmy Greaves, Denis Law, Johnny Giles and Ian St John. Not only that, there were any number of immensely gifted youngsters who were about to make their mark; Frank Worthington, Peter Osgood, Rodney Marsh and Charlie George to name but four. These players, however, became the lost generation, never properly used by England.

In the wake of the World Cup success, attendances in the English League shot up dramatically – in 1966–67 by almost two million in the first division alone. Moreover, English clubs suddenly began to do consistently well in European competitions and within a few short years the English began to dominate Europe at club level.

However, after the euphoria of 1966 and a worthy display in the 1970 Mexico World Cup, the English national team began to flounder. What characterised the decline more than anything else was a lack of leadership to find out what was going wrong and any serious attempt to put it right. The clubs continued to be successful but – often made up of as many Welsh, Scots and Irish as English players – did not have the same impact on the game's popularity across the board in England as did success for the national team.

In 1990, after two decades of spectacular failure, England once again did well in the World Cup, only losing in a semi-final penalty shoot-out to the eventual winners, Franz Beckenbauers' Germany. Moreover, England had produced a new star – Gazza – who had shown what he could do on the greatest stage of all. The team also had other crowd pleasers like Chris Waddle and world class performers like Des Walker and David Platt. In addition, Gary Lineker was at the peak of his powers. Italia '90 proved to be England's best performance since 1966.

Crowds all over the country flocked to see Gazza, Lineker, Platt et al in the season after Italia '90. Attendances in the English first division rose by three quarters of a million. There were other reasons for celebration after the 1990 World Cup. Manchester United won the Cup Winners Cup in 1991, the first season back in European competitions following the ban on English clubs after the Heysel tragedy in 1985. Even more pleasing, the England team was on course to qualify for the 1992 European Championships in Sweden under new manager, Graham Taylor. But the seeds of self-destruction had already been sown. One month after the World Cup in 1990, the English first division chairmen voted to increase the size of the division from twenty, where it had been for two years, to twenty-two, with effect from the 1991–92 season. Many believed that one reason England had done so well in Italy was because of the reduced commitments at home in a 38-game league. Now, not only would top players be playing more league games, there were also extra games in Europe with which to contend.

Apart from the issue of the number of games, there were other instances of quite stupefying ineptitude which were about to engulf the English game. In the culmination of a battle that had raged for most of the 1980s, the Football League was all but destroyed as the first division created their own Premier League. The FA, which initiated the breakaway, was itself sidelined in all the important decisions concerning the new league and within a year played no part whatever in its operation. Instead of creating one all-powerful body, which was the FA's original intention, there were now three completely separate power-centres; the FA, the new Premier League and the rump of the old Football League. Far from the national team being placed at the top, it once again has to exist in a system in which no-one can be sure what the real priorities are.

The television deal signed by the Premier League and the FA was another mind-boggling decision in the face of what could have been achieved at the time. Along with the money BSkyB provided, the deal took top-level live football away from mainstream domestic television, thus making it available only to a minority. Television has also killed off Saturday as the day of focus when the whole nation, not just football supporters, was actively interested in the progress of games, both League and FA Cup. If anyone has doubts as to how important football has become to television in the 1990s, the financial performance of BSkyB immediately before and after the company signed its football contracts with the FA and the Premier League should dispel them. In the year prior to the football contract, BSkyB made an operating loss of £40 million. In the first year of the contract, that loss became an operating profit of £61.3 million (interest charges on past loans, mainly made by BSkyB's parent company, News Corporation, which would have wiped out the profit, were waived).

Despite the new appetite for football on the part of the public after Italia '90, most fans continued to be exploited through high prices and poor facilities. The requirements of the Taylor Report were complied with, but grudgingly, with clubs continually trying to evade their responsibilities.

This catalogue of misjudgment culminated in England's dismal failure in the European Championships in 1992 and the team's struggle to qualify for the 1994 World Cup. When the England team is successful, the English game is concomitantly healthy. The FA, charged with the responsibility of building on this strong base, has failed miserably in its task. In doing so, the governing body has made it more difficult for the England team to achieve success. At the same time, the FA's failure to act within the European body, UEFA, has resulted in qualification regulations being instituted which will make it far harder for English clubs in Europe. Meanwhile, great changes are taking place at the European level as a new breed of entrepreneur, led by Italian media-king Silvio Berlusconi, forces UEFA to reassess some of its most fundamental tenets.

The thrust of this book is an attempt to demonstrate that football and football fans, be they participants, supporters at grounds or television viewers, deserve a better deal from the game's leaders than they are currently getting. The game is riddled with what is at best incompetence, at worst corruption throughout its various levels. Only through a complete overhaul, rather than the cosmetic alterations that have so far masqueraded as fundamental change, can the true potential of English football be realised.

The omens are not good. While the really sharp operators are forcing major changes in Europe and further afield, the English authorities appear to have finally run out of time. This book seeks to show why the system must be challenged *now* and suggests how the situation can be saved before the whistle blows time on all of us.

1

Back to the Future

With Graham Taylor and England at the European Championships in Sweden: summer 1992

> *'I expect to win. Let me do the worrying, that's what I'm paid for. You get your feet up in front of the telly, get a few beers in and have a good time.'*

> England manager Graham Taylor's advice to the nation before the 0–0 draw with Denmark in the 1992 European Championships.

As the UEFA official approached the touchline wielding his two numbered boards, the England supporters were momentarily uplifted to see that another out-and-out striker, in the shape of Alan Smith, was about to enter the fray. At last, the largely ineffectual tactical formation which had blighted England's second-half display against Sweden would have to be abandoned. Optimism, however, soon gave way, first to disbelief, then to anger, as it became clear that the board the UEFA official was holding to indicate the player about to be substituted was emblazoned with the number 10. The man Smith was going to replace was Gary Lineker.

The following day, amid the gloom engendered by England's 2–1 defeat and elimination from the European Championships, Graham Taylor attempted to justify and explain, not only his decision to take off Lineker when the score was 1–1 (with almost 30 minutes left to play) but also the lamentable performances of the English squad throughout the tournament. Taylor's starting line-up had already mystified many, not least for the inclusion of David Batty at right

back and the exclusion of Trevor Steven, who arguably had
been one of England's few successes in the two no-score
draws against Denmark and France earlier in the Championships. Despite these handicaps, England had dominated the
first half against Sweden, with David Platt operating effectively in a forward-cum-midfield role behind Gary Lineker.
The team, however, still needed to rely on good fortune when
the referee waved away Sweden's penalty appeals after Batty
characteristically clattered in to Tomas Brolin. Nevertheless,
England could have been three up at the interval but for two
blatant misses by Tony Daley.

'The Swedes,' Taylor insisted afterwards, 'were more
English than the English. They played the kind of football we
see in our League – hitting long balls into us, bypassing the
midfield. We couldn't cope with it. We have been overtaken by
other countries possessing more physical strength.' Quite how
that accounted for the stunning winning goal, instigated and
finished by the smallest man on the pitch, Brolin, Taylor failed
to reveal. The move leading to the goal seemed to be the very
antithesis of the English game. Brolin won the ball wide on the
left, took it in to the England penalty area after exchanging
precise, first-time passes with Ingesson and Dahlin, then
unleashed a shot on the run which flashed past Chris Woods
before the goalkeeper had time to react. It was, Taylor implied,
the sort of goal you can see every week in the Football League.

As for the Lineker substitution, Taylor claimed that he
was 'trying to get Gary one more game' (to equal and perhaps
surpass Bobby Charlton's goalscoring record of 49 – Lineker
had 48). England, according to Taylor, were not holding
up the ball for long enough to enable midfield support to
get forward, and Smith could perform this task better
than Lineker. More curious even than this explanation of
the manager's reasoning was his comment that 'we could
have done with half-time not arriving', after which he added
with a shrug, 'but you have to have half-time'. The idea
of Taylor trying Canute-like to keep the referee's whistle at
bay was perhaps the least ridiculous image conjured up
by this bizarre statement.

Although it coincided with the interval, Swedish manager
Tommy Svensson's astute decision to take off the ineffective
Anders Limpar, who plays in the English League every week,

and replace him with the strong-running Johnny Ekstrom, who doesn't, could have been taken at any time. England's defeat stemmed from their complete inability to cope with the new tactics the Swedish substitution brought. With Ekstrom's eye for goal, Sweden's attack became far more threatening and the confidence of their midfield players noticeably increased. Neither Taylor nor his team sought to adjust their own formation in order to nullify the new threat and as Sweden gained the initiative the English defence collapsed. After all the confident words that had accompanied the build-up to the tournament, England's failure to impose themselves on the competition was best summed up by the man still holding the goalscoring record, Bobby Charlton, who was obviously exasperated with what had gone on. 'Whatever happened to football?' he asked the millions watching on television. 'You know, passing, that sort of thing.'

One of the team recalled later that in the dressing room immediately after the game, 'Graham Taylor was bitterly disappointed', particularly at 'how we caved in when they came at us'. It was as if the manager now thought he had acted against his better judgement in the tactics he used and he talked reverently about Ireland and how Leeds and Arsenal had got the blend just about right between playing football and not being 'passy-passy'. He pointed to a more direct style that might serve England better in international football, 'because that's the way the majority of teams play in England'. The die appeared to have been cast.

In the more public forum of his press conference, Taylor reiterated his theme and claimed to have a good idea of what his selection would be for the forthcoming World Cup qualifying campaign. 'I can see a team in my mind,' he mused. Even more enigmatically, he hinted at the style of play this 'team of the mind' would employ. 'Working with the England team and seeing this particular tournament has confirmed a lot of what I always thought to be the case,' he said. '[It's] something a lot of people are not prepared to admit and don't like.' Discerning Taylor's meaning had become like trying to understand the utterings of the Delphic oracle. Apparently, Taylor meant that England should play a more direct game, utilising traditional English strength's such as the long ball and an old-fashioned, big centre forward.

The pressures on international football managers have undoubtedly intensified in the modern era, in parallel with the extended role of the media. In England, the criticism suffered by team bosses of other countries is compounded by the unrelenting scrutiny of the tabloid press. Former England international Steve Coppell, commenting on Sweden 1992, wrote of the effect this phenomenon had had on his contribution to the 1980 European Championships in Italy: 'My chief tormentor was Mick Channon. His criticism made me feel that I was letting myself, my family and my country down. I was frightened to play. I vowed at that stage that I would never be a cynical old pro who made a living criticising other players.'

The press occasionally tempers its abuse with an element of perverse humour, such as the *Sun*'s succinct headline after the Swedish defeat: SWEDES 2, TURNIPS 1, which was followed up the next day by a surreal caricature showing Taylor as a sort of half-man, half-vegetable creature reminiscent of 1960s science fiction comics. Outrages such as these might not bother some personalities, but in other, more introspective types they induce a certain paranoia, evidenced by an increasing abhorrence of press conferences. Taylor, despite being perceived as someone who knew how to deal with the media and despite all the advance warnings meted out to Bobby Robson during his occupation of the job, seemed unprepared for the sort of vitriol his predecessor had endured.

There had been confrontations with the media in the past, notably when Taylor was forced to suffer severe recriminations over his selection policy for the two European Championship qualifying games against the Republic of Ireland. In the first he dropped Paul Gascoigne in favour of Gordon Cowans, while in the return match at Wembley he played three central defenders in the first half before Tony Adams was substituted and the side reverted to a more orthodox pattern. To make matters worse, the manager proceeded to compare goalkeeper David Seaman unfavourably with his predecessor, Peter Shilton. Seaman was so upset by the criticism that he asked Taylor for an explanation. Whether or not he received a satisfactory answer, what is not in dispute is that Seaman's form dipped so drastically after the incident that by the time the European

Championships started in Sweden he was no longer regarded as the main contender for the England goalkeeper's jersey, which now belonged to Chris Woods. As Taylor's honeymoon period came to an end, paranoia over what the media might say next began to set in.

Once in Scandinavia the condition took hold with a vengeance. Instead of allowing his assistant, Lawrie McMenemy, who was employed precisely to fill this kind of public relations role, to take the worst of the flak, Taylor waded in himself with both feet. In an interview with the BBC's Des Lynham, the England boss castigated the mild-mannered anchorman for daring to ask Gary Lineker the previous day how the manager was feeling. In a subsequent outburst, Taylor went on to ask a bemused BBC reporter, David Davies, 'How do you want me to be? I'll be anything you want me to be. If you want me to be happy, I'll be happy – if you want me to be sad, I'll be sad, how do you want me to be? If you want me to be relaxed, I'll be relaxed, how do you want me to be?' It was as if he were rehearsing for one of Ingmar Bergman's least accessible Swedish movies. In order not to appear biased, the manager gave a repeat performance to an embarrassed Jim Rosenthal on ITV.

After his team's second 0–0 draw, against France, Taylor, knowing what to expect, got his retaliation in first. 'You sit in front of people,' he said, 'and straight away you feel you have to defend this and defend that. But what do I have to defend?' By the time he left Sweden, Taylor even felt betrayed by the so-called 'number ones', favoured football correspondents who were accepted into the inner sanctum. The following September, when they were together in one place again to watch a World Cup qualifying game between Norway and San Marino, Taylor refused to talk to any of the pressmen at all, although he had recovered his earlier poise somewhat by the time of the friendly match against Spain two weeks later. Unfortunately for Taylor, he had left several hostages to fortune. The most notable was the removal of Gary Lineker from the action against Sweden.

Graham Taylor made Lineker his captain, and it was an obvious choice: a footballer whose record stands comparison with the very best; a striker whose ratio of goals to games in top-class international football is bettered in the last forty years only by Gerd Muller of West Germany. Yet Taylor's relationship with Lineker had its darker side. It could, of course, have been that the manager was looking ahead to that post-Lineker period when a new combination would be needed to spearhead the attack. Lineker had announced several months before Sweden that he would retire from the national team after the tournament as a consequence of his transfer to Grampus 8 of the newly formed Japanese professional League. What Taylor really needed to find in the short term, however, was an effective partner for Lineker up front. Unfortunately, the manager seemed diverted from the task and felt it necessary on occasion to publicly criticise Lineker's contribution, particularly in the pre-Sweden friendly against Brazil, in which the captain missed a penalty. Eventually, Lineker ran out of time to break Bobby Charlton's record, although Taylor's act of substitution against Sweden brought not one more game, but probably one less.

Gary Lineker played under a number of different managers during his career in Europe: the volatile Jock Wallace; the more introverted characters Gordon Milne, Howard Kendall and Peter Shreeves; and the talented and driven personalities Terry Venables and Johan Cruyff. None had experienced the problems that Graham Taylor seemed to find in the man he made captain of England. Cruyff had forced him to play on the wing for Barcelona and had publicly expressed doubts about his ability, yet Lineker's response was to do everything he could to prove Cruyff wrong. The culmination of Lineker's efforts came when he provided the cross which led to the goal that won the Cup-winners' Cup for Barcelona in 1989. And it was Lineker who ensured that England qualified for Sweden by scoring a late equaliser in Poland in a game in which he looked about as likely to score as he did against Sweden. In the Swedish game it was Lineker, finding space wide on the right, who again executed the cross from which David Platt put England ahead. When he was substituted, he threw his captain's armband to the ground in what, for Lineker, was the ultimate show of disgust.

Among the watching millions, the only people not surprised by the withdrawal of the England captain were the occupants of the England bench. One of those sitting there that evening claimed that Taylor had been 'having a go' at

Lineker from early in the game. All this suggests that Taylor's failure to get the best out of his main asset, and his inability to get along with the person described by the *Spur* fanzine as 'The Nicest Man on Earth', revealed an aspect of the manager's personality hitherto unseen. Could it be that unlike Helmut Schoen with Franz Beckenbauer and Beckenbauer himself with Lothar Mathaus; unlike Rinus Michels with Johan Cruyff and later Ruud Gullit; unlike Michel Hidalgo with Michel Platini, Taylor did not wish to relinquish control to a leader or outstanding player on the pitch?

There is support for this explanation of the rift between manager and captain. Taylor made some mild comments concerning Lineker's performance against the Republic of Ireland in March 1991, when he had been in charge for only eight months. That summer Lineker temporarily left an England tour party to play for Tottenham in Japan. Although he missed one international against New Zealand, the captain came back for the next game against Malaysia and scored four goals. Nonetheless, the incident rankled with Taylor, who believed that Lineker had gone to Japan to further his transfer negotiations with Grampus 8, a charge which Lineker vehemently denied. Most of the rancour, though, probably emanated from the friendly international against France at Wembley, when, to general consternation, Lineker was relegated to the substitutes bench from the start.

Lineker himself thought that if he was an automatic selection for Sweden (as he was led to believe), then the most pressing problem was to find an effective striking partner. Against France, Taylor decided to experiment with an untried duo, David Hirst and Alan Shearer. The manager told Lineker the news two days before the game in a conversation in the captain's car. Lineker, at a low ebb due to his son's continuing illness, felt the way he was told was insensitive. While sitting behind the manager on the England bench during the first half, Lineker made some casual remarks criticising the way the team was playing. Taylor overheard and was upset. Nevertheless, during the interval he adopted the line of thinking Lineker had been advocating, without acknowledging his input. The tactics were changed and Lineker replaced Hirst, scoring the second goal in an improved display, and England ran out 2–0 winners.

Taylor thought that Lineker, through his agent, Jon Holmes, had manipulated the press over the captain's feelings of disappointment at being left out against France, Holmes painting Lineker as whiter than white while the manager emerged as the villain. The final straw came after Lineker's penalty miss against Brazil, when Taylor claimed, in a thinly veiled reference to his captain: 'When somebody is almost a national institution, it's almost as if you can't touch them. I'm not into all that. Looking at it realistically, we could argue that we played Brazil with ten men.'

Although Taylor and Lineker became estranged, the manager has often gone out of his way to encourage the senior professionals to speak their minds. One member of the squad revealed that Taylor 'encouraged dialogue and liked to get feedback'. Moreover, according to the same player, 'In team meetings, Gary Lineker, Stuart Pearce and Des Walker would always have something to say and people like Gary had a lot more international experience than himself [Graham Taylor]. He accepted that and that's what he put across the whole time.' Either Taylor was only paying lip-service to the views of his more experienced players or he genuinely believed he was taking them on board. Whatever the case, it has been claimed that Lineker occasionally strayed from pre-planned tactics, which, if true, is likely to incense any manager, let alone one under such intense pressure as Graham Taylor.

The widespread condemnation of Taylor's decision to substitute Lineker in the match against Sweden seemed to engender a change of heart in the manager when he spoke about the matter after announcing his first post-Lineker squad for the friendly international against Spain the following September. In an interview, again with the BBC's David Davies, Taylor went out of his way to explain how his feelings concerning the incident had changed. 'It's easy to be wise after the event,' he said. 'I regret taking Gary off because I think the interpretation of that [action] has gone beyond football, as if it was something personal. It would have been better if I hadn't done that but at the time I was making a football decision purely based on trying to win a football match. Now I'm quite happy if people disagree with my decision on football grounds, but for people to interpret it as a personal decision that I should end somebody's career – a magnificent England career – in that way, that hurts. So if I hadn't done that I wouldn't have had that accusation thrown at me.'

If Taylor could have wound back the clock, then, he would have made a non-footballing decision in order to avoid the brickbats.

It was left to Lineker to put the matter in perspective with his response to Taylor's interview. 'I never thought for a moment it was personal,' he said. 'I just wish he regretted it because he thought I might have got a goal.'

According to his team-mates, Lineker was astonished at being substituted and will probably, like Jimmy Greaves, who suffered a similar fate under Alf Ramsey, always feel that Taylor made the wrong decision, although Greaves' omission from the 1966 World Cup team had happier consequences for the side. Unlike Ramsey, whose gamble with Geoff Hurst and Roger Hunt paid off when his team won the World Cup, Taylor's ploy of bringing on Alan Smith to 'hold the ball up' completely backfired. Even Alan Smith, the man who replaced Lineker, thought it 'strange that he [Taylor] brought off one forward instead of putting another one on'. Taylor's conclusion that the Sweden match was 'not Lineker's type of game' was one that hardly anybody could understand, let alone agree with. The effect the substitution had on the opposition was as dramatic as the one it had on the English fans. The departure of their most dangerous opponent gave the Swedes the belief that they could win and there was visible delight on their faces once they realised their eyes were not deceiving them.

Apart from Lineker, Taylor had not selected other experienced internationals for Sweden. Bryan Robson, despite his age and injury record, had no obvious successor and Chris Waddle had helped Marseille to the European Cup final in 1991 with some breathtaking performances. Both had been discarded in unusual circumstances. Robson announced his retirement from international football immediately after being left out of the squad for the vital qualifying match in Poland in November 1991, while Waddle incurred Taylor's wrath first by criticising his tactics and then when he failed to tell him that he actually wanted to play. Speaking to the French sports newspaper, *L'Equipe*, before the England–France game at

Wembley in February 1992, Taylor said: 'From what I've been told, he [Waddle] has decided to end his international career. Moreover, he is better suited to French football than to English football.' It is barely credible that an international manager would act on third-party advice without finding out for himself. It seems Taylor just waited for Waddle to put the record straight.

This mountain and Mohammed business seemed an endemic part of the manager's make-up when the situation was repeated with Peter Beardsley. After a successful season for Everton (15 goals in 42 First Division games), Beardsley was allowed to drift from the international scene. Having played for the England 'B' team against the CIS in April, Beardsley told Lawrie McMenemy that since he had won 49 caps he felt he had nothing to prove and therefore didn't want to play for the 'B' team in the future. Beardsley never made himself unavailable for Sweden but Taylor thought he had, and once again a misunderstanding was allowed to persist as no direct exchange of views on the subject ever took place. So the man whom David Pleat, the experienced Luton Town manager, claimed had 'carried Howard Kendall's side to respectability', and who was the most effective of Gary Lineker's striking partners (they played with each other in 33 internationals – 15 won, 13 drawn, 5 lost, scoring 32 goals between them, 26 by Lineker) was destined not to grace the Swedish stage. Compare Taylor's behaviour to that of Franz Beckenbauer when he was the German manager to the brilliant but wayward Bernd Schuster, whom Beckenbauer continually cajoled, to no avail, to come and perform for his country in the 1990 World Cup.

Speaking about the selection policy after the Swedish tournament, Lawrie McMenemy said. 'I'm not sure many people would have disagreed with the nineteen we had there' (Mark Wright withdrew after the deadline for replacements had passed). That statement drew derision. To lose Paul Gascoigne, John Barnes and four right backs (Paul Parker, Rob Jones, Lee Dixon and Gary Stevens) through injury was certainly terrible luck for all concerned, but it cannot excuse the lack of a replacement right back in the squad. The experienced David Bardsley, for instance, could have been chosen. He had played over a hundred League games for QPR and had previously played under Taylor at Watford.

Taylor, in his public comments, often expressed the opinion that the step up to international level might be too big for some players. This didn't stop him from using almost fifty in his first two years, a record worthy of Don Revie at his most profligate. Alan Smith said: 'He had a set of players, more than just twenty, that he had given international exposure to and he felt that even if they had only played one game, that would be to their benefit and he really didn't want to call upon players outside that circle.' Another type of player who found favour with Taylor was one who could be considered versatile. Alan Smith again: 'The thing he always stressed to us was that we underestimated ourselves in that we can't adapt like the continentals. He tried to encourage us to adapt and play in different positions and different systems.'

Keith Curle, Trevor Steven, Andy Sinton and David Batty were considered by Taylor to fit this mould, so they were played out of position when the manager thought it necessary. Lawrie McMenemy cited this prerequisite as the reason for not taking to Sweden the First Division's top goalscorer, Ian Wright (29 goals in 38 League games for Crystal Palace and Arsenal). 'Our reasoning was, particularly Graham,' he said, 'that you are looking for people in a squad who, if possible, can be flexible and play in more than one position, because you've got to play so many games in a short period of time. If Gary Lineker hadn't been there, Ian Wright would have been a certainty, but we didn't expect we'd ever play the two of them together in a team.'

It was a view the management would live to regret as they became disenchanted with Lineker. After Sweden, Taylor told Tony Francis of *The Sunday Times*: 'With hindsight, perhaps I should have substituted him [Lineker] against France [the 0–0 draw in the Championships]. Gary will admit he had not been as sharp as we'd have liked. In training his shots were hitting the bar or rebounding off the goalkeeper. I got it into my head that he was in a rut.' So Taylor condemned Ian Wright to a summer at home, paved the way in his own mind for the substitution of Lineker against Sweden (having toyed with the idea against France), but left himself with no real alternative since the one player who, according to the manager, could fill Lineker's role was left behind in England.

By getting rid of Bobby Robson's old guard, Bryan Robson, Waddle and Beardsley, by failing to ensure he had a reserve right back, and by leaving out Ian Wright, the argument that Taylor did the best he could with the players available is totally destroyed.

The manager's tactical formations were as worrying as his selection policy. Before the tournament in Sweden Taylor said that a flat back four had not won anything for England for twenty-six years. Thus his choice of a sweeper-orientated defence came as no surprise. However, once Mark Wright was injured, the sweeper system had to be abandoned. Wright could fill the role because he is in Taylor's view, unique among English central defenders in being able to bring the ball out of defence. The Dutch, Germans and the Danes would never have contemplated changing their systems because of the unavailability of one man. Indeed, the Danish manager, Richard Moeller Nielsen, demonstrated this to perfection. He did not select Jan Molby of Liverpool because having Molby in the side meant making him the focal point of the team's attacking strategies, which was not how Moeller Nielsen wanted to play. Michael Laudrup of Barcelona, arguably Denmark's most gifted player, made himself unavailable because he did not fancy the running and tackling back that was expected of him. Instead of using the talents of Molby and Laudrup, Moeller Nielsen built a team based on a simple but fluid tactical formation, so that serious injuries to Bent Christiansen and Henrik Andersen were absorbed with the minimum of disruption. Individuals were changed, not the shape of the team. Moeller Nielsen proved that a good technique and the ability to carry out a tactical plan were far more important than the extended preparation that England employed.

A club manager has, in the main, to build a team and its tactics around the players at his disposal, unless he is lucky enough to be able to spend large sums of money on the players of his choice. A national manager, on the other hand, can select a system, then pick the players to carry it out. Sadly for England, this was a lesson Graham Taylor failed to learn. In a total of 270 minutes of action in Sweden, England played with a flat back four and with a sweeper. The midfield went from five to four and eventually two. In attack Taylor used no wingers, one winger and two wingers, while Lineker was first the lone spearhead then part of a duo, but never with the same personnel twice in succession. David Platt was used both in midfield and up front with Lineker. Trevor Steven played in midfield, was moved to right back, then dropped. Nigel Clough, one player who might have unhinged opposing defences with his clinical passing style and could have provided Lineker with the chances he so desperately required, was never allowed anywhere near the action.

On the other hand, in the second half of the Swedish match, Neil Webb was asked to get the ball forward quickly, even at the expense of accuracy, hence the choice of Alan Smith to hold it up until reinforcements could arrive: except that the ball hardly ever reached Smith and the cavalry was conspicuous by its absence. Finally, ludicrously, there was the use of international novices like Keith Curle, Andy Sinton and David Batty, all out of position at right back, while the squad contained a brace of international-class left backs in Pearce and Dorigo. Dorigo was actually asked by Taylor to play on the right but refused because of a previous unhappy experience playing there with Leeds. This state of affairs surely made a mockery of Lawrie McMenemy's theory of flexibility.

The lasting impression of England's contribution to the competition in Sweden is one of incompetence on a scale not experienced since the last time the tournament was held, in Germany in 1988, when Bobby Robson's side lost all three of their games. Despite the careful preparations, the England players were left unable to cope with a simple tactical alteration by an opposing side which would be easily beaten by Germany just four days after they had humbled England. England, for their part, were simply not on the right wavelength.

None of this, of course, meant that there was the slightest likelihood of Taylor losing his job. On the contrary, vigorous noises of support emanated from the Football Association, particularly from Peter Swales, chairman of both Manchester City and the FA's International Committee, which appoints the England manager. Swales claimed, somewhat paradoxically surely, that his faith in Taylor had not only been maintained by events in Sweden, but had been reinforced.

Some weeks later, the hierarchy of the Football Association met for their annual summer meeting at a hotel in the idyllic setting of Lake Windermere. For the first time in the history of such gatherings, the England manager delivered a report on the progress of his regime. Taylor spoke for about twenty minutes, confining himself to a review of England's showing in Sweden. Beforehand, FA chairman Sir Bert Millichip announced that no questions would be allowed. Taylor, far from apologising for the national humiliation, actually claimed credit for his team's performance, which he insisted was better than most European Championship showings since England finished third in 1968. He reminded his audience that Bobby Robson had lost all three matches in 1988 and failed even to qualify for the finals in 1984. Moreover, he continued, Don Revie's side had not qualified in 1976 and England were eliminated by the Germany of Muller, Netzer and Beckenbauer in 1972. That left, according to Taylor, only Alf Ramsey's world champions, who had performed creditably in 1968, and one other tournament in which England had fared slightly better than in 1992: Ron Greenwood's campaign in Italy in 1980. Although once again the team had had to pack its bags after the first round, the Championships had at least brought one victory, a 2–1 win against Spain in the final group match.

Observing the courtesies, the assembled councillors polite-ly clapped at the conclusion of Taylor's report. More than one councillor was of the opinion that had Sir Bert Millichip not quashed any thoughts of questioning, Taylor could well have been given a rough ride. When news of the meeting surfaced, the press were quick to portray Taylor's reception as a round of applause from out-of-touch old-age pensioners. Under a headline proclaiming BERT'S BUFFOONS MUST BE MAD TO SUPPORT TAYLOR, Brian Clough wrote in his column in the *Sun* that he was 'appalled' and suggested that Peter Swales was 'over the bloody hill'. Good copy indeed, though it obscured the true nature of the proceedings.

By the time the new season kicked off, Graham Taylor was having second thoughts about some of the things he had said at the height of the pressure in Stockholm. Admitting that his own performance had been below the standard he had set, he said: 'I expected better from myself.' A new dimension to the manager's character slowly began to emerge, however, as his very real grievances against the excesses of the tabloids appeared to make him see persecution everywhere. He claimed that he had been misrepresented after the Sweden match. He denied suggesting that he wanted to change to a long-ball game, claiming that this was a position assigned to him by an unfair press. 'It is nonsense, misleading nonsense,' he blasted. 'I am stuck with the label, I suppose. The fact that I finished second to Liverpool playing in a totally different style when I was manager of Aston Villa appears to count for nothing. It is a cross I will have to bear for the rest of my professional life.'

The manager now seemed to be trying to rewrite history. He also said: 'On the day after our exit from the European Championships I talked about the way Sweden had pushed four players up against us and got the ball to them. I said we simply could not handle it. But I never mentioned anything about the long ball or direct football.' Although his original remarks were somewhat ambiguous, this was not how either the players or the journalists on the receiving end of his diatribes remembered it.

Taylor's reference to his time at Aston Villa was interesting, for although no one can take away his achievement of galvanising a somewhat moribund club, bringing it into the First Division and finishing second, there is another aspect to his tenure at Villa Park which is less complimentary. Taylor's Villa had indeed taken the First Division by storm, playing, in the main, a direct passing game. They reached the top of the table at the perfect time as the season approached its climax. The momentum was theirs as Liverpool faltered. Then Taylor bought Tony Cascarino, a big, tall centre forward, from Millwall. But this emphasis on the long-ball game failed, and Liverpool stole the Championship from under Taylor's nose.

Given such a catalogue of ineptitude in Sweden, the question arises as to whether any of this could have been fore-seen when Taylor was appointed. The general consensus at the time was favourable: Taylor was admired as a good com-municator and, after his period at Villa Park, as a modern, successful manager. These are qualities not to be dismissed lightly. What Taylor achieved at the clubs he managed, Lincoln, Watford and Villa, and with individual players like

John Barnes, deserves the highest praise. There were few, if any, real competitors if this was the criterion. But did his record, impressive though it undoubtedly was, equip him to be manager of the national team? After all, none of his sides had actually won anything and his experience of European club football was limited to one season with Watford.

Some months before Sweden, Taylor was guest of honour at an England Schoolboys international at Wembley. Afterwards, in the banqueting suite, a buffet was served to about two hundred visitors invited by the organisers of the match, the English Schools Football Association. For a brief moment Taylor managed to get a cup of tea into his hands but it never made the short journey to his lips. He was besieged by the eager throng which bombarded him with questions and requests for his autograph. If Taylor was put out it didn't show for an instant. The England manager was courtesy personified as he dealt with every question and signed every programme and piece of paper thrust at him. He showed particular consideration towards the youngsters. It was as impressive and dignified a display as any diplomat could have mustered and Taylor never did get his refreshment. Taylor's bearing at this gathering showed why the FA found him so attractive. Here was a man who, possessed a natural charm and displayed a real liking for people, a man who knew what was expected of him and could be relied upon to do his duty.

When the job falls vacant, the responsibility for appointing a new England boss lies with the International Committee of the FA. This committee has never been able to shake off the embarassment associated with the ill-starred tenure of Don Revie, which ended in disgrace when Revie broke the news, through the *Daily Mail*, that 'the job is no longer worth all the aggravation' and he was off to the United Arab Emirates. Although some members of the International Committee have changed, most seem to have been around since before the flood. Sir Bert Millichip, for instance, was a member of the committee that sacked Alf Ramsey and appointed Don Revie over twenty years ago. Both the committee and the FA councillors still feel the stigma of the Revie era and they were determined that never again would anyone be employed as England manager if there were the slightest indication of a suspect temperament. Therefore, after Revie, rather than opt for the managers with the best track record (Brian Clough and Bob Paisley), they went for 'Uncle' Ron Greenwood, who, they felt, would restore dignity to the post. If there is one thing that Ron Greenwood, Bobby Robson and Graham Taylor have in common it is their conspicuous loyalty to their employers. To the FA, this was a far more important attribute than the ability to win a major tournament. The thought of another Alf Ramsey was, for them, too much to bear. Ramsey, after all, had the temerity to dismiss the views of everyone except himself and was openly contemptuous of FA councillors. His single-minded approach might have won England the World Cup but it also cost him his job when results started to go against him in the qualifying competition for the 1974 tournament.

When candidates for the England job were being scrutinised in 1990 events had made it more imperative than ever for the next occupant of the job to be considered safe, someone who wouldn't rock the boat. The Hillsborough disaster of 1989 and the report of Lord Justice Taylor which followed it had forced a largely reluctant English game down the road of change. There were those in football, however, who recognised that the Taylor Report, and the government pressure on football to 'speak with one voice', presented an opportunity for which they had been awaiting for years. Forces were about to coincide which would leave the various component parts of the football world at each other's throats and leave the way open for internecine warfare unprecedented in the game's history.

England's injury situation leading up to Sweden was also, as Taylor pointed out, a severe blow. Other countries suffered one or two, most notably Germany, who lost Lothar Mathaus before the tournament and Rudi Voeller after half an hour of their first game, but England's casualty list went far beyond anyone else's. Yet this did not happen by accident. It is a perennial problem of the English game and is getting worse. The British professional footballer plays extremely competitive matches twice a week throughout the season, is often sent out to play when not fully recovered from injury, and, with the ever-increasing pace and aggression of the English game, is generally burnt out by the end of the season, which is of course exactly the time when international tournaments take place. When at last the FA decided to bite this particular bullet in their 'Blueprint for the Future of Football', which proposed a new Premier League of eighteen clubs in order to help the national team, the idea was firmly stamped on by an alliance of vested interests whose enthusiasm for the England team was not a priority to say the least.

The effects of the English system are not only felt at the highest levels. Whatever happens at the top is imitated below and there is now a general consensus that there are too many matches throughout the game. The most frightening consequence is that doctors attending new inductees in to the FA School of Excellence at Lilleshall have been alarmed to find ever-increasing numbers of youngsters suffering from serious long-term injury problems. Already this has meant that careers have been finished before they have begun.

So, although Graham Taylor contributed to his own down-fall in a number of ways – the inability to get the best out of Lineker and his amazing substitution, leaving talented players at home and the constant switching of tactics and personnel – his main encumbrance was the system bequeathed to him by a Football Association with its mind on other things. It is doubtful whether any England manager could have produced a winning team under the constraints built into the job. Perhaps a Terry Venables, a Jack Charlton (who manages to motivate his Irish team, most of whom play in the same League as their English counterparts), or, in an earlier era, a Brian Clough, might have achieved more. But they remain individualistic and uncompromising characters, and would probably have criticised their masters unmer-cifully for their failure to provide a structure which actually helped the national team. Such forceful personalities were anathema to the FA and it was no surprise when the 1990 shortlist consisted of Taylor, Joe Royle and Howard Kendall, good, but 'safe' men whom the FA felt it could control. Of these, only Kendall had extensive managerial experience of European football, which was probably what in the end precluded him from the job.

Those running English football deserve to be on the receiv-ing end of equal if not greater wrath than that meted out to Graham Taylor, who at least has the excuse of having to work in an imperfect system. It was they who possessed the power to change the game for the better. Instead, petty squabbles, empire building, and sheer incompetence were the order of the day. As ever, this would result in the English game going its own way, unmindful of developments elsewhere. The fact that all this would leave the England team firmly marooned in the backwater it has occupied since 1970 mattered little to those who stood to gain most from the future they had shaped. Worse still, a great confidence trick was about to be perpetrated on the football public, and nothing would be allowed to stand in its way.

2

Blueprint for Chaos

The way opens for reform, but what sort of reform do the FA have in mind?

> *'The Blueprint mixes radicalism and realism and I believe that if the vision it embodies is matched in its subsequent implementation it will come to be regarded as a landmark in the history of football.'*

> Graham Kelly, chief executive of the Football Association, at the launch of his Blueprint, June 19 1991.

> *'A document full of contradictory statements and half-baked ideas.'*

> When Saturday Comes.

> *'[The] Blueprint is a way for the leading clubs to seize virtually all the money, leaving the remaining clubs to wither and, for some, to die.'*

> Gordon Taylor, chief executive of the Professional Footballers Association.

The telephone call was all the more welcome for being so unexpected. Alex Fynn, by using his position as a director of the UK's largest advertising agency, Saatchi and Saatchi, had for some years been expounding his philosophy concerning the marketing, indeed the very future, of football. Until now, those in officialdom had shown little inclination to take his views seriously enough to act on them. Yet here, on the other end of the line, was the Football Association itself requesting a meeting to discuss the issues about which Fynn had been talking to anyone who would listen. Pessimistic about whether the FA really would at last get to grips with the game's severe structural problems, but intrigued that they had seen fit to consult him, Fynn arranged to meet FA chairman Bert Millichip, chief executive Graham Kelly, and director of coaching and education Charles Hughes in Kelly's office at the FA's Lancaster Gate headquarters.

Alex Fynn's career had taken off when he joined a fledgling advertising agency, which at that time packed all its employees into one room and appeared to Fynn to be more like a comedy film, *Carry On Advertising*, than a serious business. However, that company, Saatchi and Saatchi, was to become the biggest advertising agency in the world and Fynn prospered with its growth, becoming first a director, then, in 1987, deputy chairman of the UK operation. Fynn was originally brought in to handle the account of the Health Education Council. In 1982 he decided to see if the HEC were interested in becoming sponsor of Tottenham Hotspur, believing that the nature of the sponsor's message (anti-smoking) would force the television authorities to relax the ban that existed at that time on the sponsor's name appearing on players' shirts in televised games. The deal fell through when Ossie Ardiles and Ricky Villa were discovered having a surreptitious post-match fag. However, one positive outcome was that Fynn struck up a relationship with the club. Out of this came an advertising campaign designed to boost attendances and sell season tickets. Despite using the legendary grandmother and Tottenham supporter Mrs Ridlington, alongside Glenn Hoddle, to support the contention that 'This Saturday Spurs will be fielding 30,000 against QPR – make sure you're one of the team', the campaign had a short life. This was partly because Tottenham had a wretched season in the League, and partly because some players complained to the club's management that they were fed up with the fans' taunt that they were playing like old women and should be substituted by Mrs R.

More important than the campaign was the dialogue Fynn established with Tottenham's then chairman, Irving Scholar, and the interest Scholar showed in some of Fynn's ideas on how the game should be marketed. For the next two years the discussions between the two remained largely theoretical (Fynn unfairly maintained that Scholar often asked his advice but never took it. Fynn once mentioned this to the manager at the time, Terry Venables. Venables laughed and said 'You're doing better than me, mate. I can't get a word in edgeways'), but events which would give them substance were about to unfold.

Irving Scholar's take-over of Tottenham Hotspur in 1982 had come about for two reasons. First, the club had got into terrible financial trouble over rebuilding work and was heavily in debt. Second, the structure of football clubs had changed little since the nineteenth century and even a big name like Tottenham was vulnerable in the face of a determined predator such as Scholar. Once he gained control, Scholar took Tottenham down a new path of rampant commercialism which would precipitate his ignominious departure in 1991. Back in the early 1980s, however, Scholar was seen as the prophet of a brave new world for English football, one in which the big clubs would realise their potential and become rivals, not of the smaller teams of the First Division, but of the giants of continental Europe. In Scholar's mind, Tottenham had more in common with Milan than Coventry City.

Scholar found allies among the élite of the English game, who felt they were being held back by the archaic ways of the Football League. Scholar joined the League's television sub-committee where, along with Robert Maxwell, he attempted, unsuccessfully, to secure more money from television.

By 1985 he had come to the conclusion that the only solution was for the big clubs to force the League into whole-sale reforms. He once again approached Alex Fynn to write a proposal which could form the basis of such a change. Fynn's plan, which envisaged a smaller First Division, regional football in the lower divisions and a pyramid structure with the England team at the top, caused a stir but the revolution failed to happen when the rest of the Football League agreed a new voting system which put more power into the hands of the First Division. A reduction in the size of the First Division, to twenty clubs, plus the introduction of play-offs to decide some promotion and relegation issues, were the results of the deal. Most significantly, home clubs were allowed to keep 100 per cent of gate receipts, instead of sharing them with the away club. This meant that big pay-days for smaller clubs when they played the likes of Manchester United became a thing of the past, and therefore the new system accelerated the process, which had been going on since the abolition of the maximum wage, whereby the rich clubs became richer and the poor clubs poorer. The one public success of the limited reforms was the play-off system, which draws large crowds, not only to the play-off matches themselves but also to what Ken Bates, chairman of Chelsea, who were involved in the first play-off series, said were previously 'meaningless semi-friendly matches played from February onwards'. When the final matches were moved to Wembley and played over the course of a bank holiday weekend, they became even more popular. Although the purists will always doubt their equitability, the old system, according to Bates, 'has gone forever'.

Despite the success of the play-offs, the changes that took place seemed mere tinkering when set against football's problems at the time. The English game took a considerable battering in the mid 1980s. The Heysel, Bradford and Birmingham disasters, hooliganism, and a general perception of football as a declining sport led to falling gates, no television exposure and a downturn in the game's image and appeal. In a dispute over money, the television companies were telling whoever would listen that football was on the way down and snooker was now more popular on television. Ken Bates relates what happened next. 'They [ITV and BBC] said, we will give you £3.1 million, or whatever the figure was, and I said no. I said, "I'll tell you what, you reckon football doesn't appeal very much . . . I can understand that it must be a risk for you . . . Why don't we give you soccer and you just pay us a percentage of your advertising? If you're doing badly, we'll suffer with you."

'Jonathan Martin [the BBC's head of sport] said he couldn't do that because they didn't have advertising. I said, "No problem, you just pay us on your viewing figures, which you claim you get when you try to convince us how much cleverer you are than ITV." Bloody silence . . . If they'd done that, BSkyB wouldn't have been in existence today. They're so bloody stupid they cut their own throats.'

In the end Bates' revolutionary idea was not acted upon, there was no televised football for half a season and the game had to accept less money from television than it had previously rejected when it came back on to the screens around the turn of the year.

The trend in continental Europe, however, was exactly the opposite to what was happening in England, as large amounts of money flooded into the game from new television deals. But by 1988, when a new television contract in England was about to be negotiated, violence seemed to be on the wane and football was again on the rise, and for the first time there was competition among the television companies for the rights to screen games. The Football League's commercial department, under a former sales manager of Beechams, Trevor Phillips, with support from the FA's head of external affairs, Glen Kirton, wanted to sign with the new satellite service, British Satellite Broadcasting, but this plan ran into sustained opposition from the big clubs, who believed they would suffer financially from any deal with BSB as sponsors and advertisers would not pay the amounts those clubs expected if their games could not attract the mass audience that terrestrial television brought.

The big clubs, represented on the Management Committee of the Football League by Philip Carter, who as well as being chairman of Everton was also president of the League, and David Dein, vice-chairman of Arsenal, threatened to break away and form their own league. Irving Scholar, having been defeated in his attempt to gain a place with them on the Management Committee, prompted from the sidelines, along with, among others, Manchester United chief executive Martin Edwards. The threat was effective as the rest of the Football League caved in and supported a deal with ITV, which not only gave the big clubs the largest slice of television fees they had ever had, but also ensured that the smaller clubs virtually disappeared from the nation's television screens. Under the terms of the new contract, ITV, which had previously shared costs of less than £3 million per season with the BBC, would pay £11 million in the first season of the deal, rising to £18 million a season over the course of the next four years.

The big clubs had got what they wanted, but would have to

pay a heavy price. Carter and Dein were thrown off the Management Committee and Carter was replaced as president of the League by Bill Fox of Blackburn Rovers, a staunch opponent of everything the big clubs stood for. Ken Bates explained why they felt so strongly. 'We tried to get them [BBC and ITV] to bid against each other and [they] refused point-blank,' he said. 'Then later on they put the same tender in. So then we announced we were going to do a deal with BSB. Then Greg Dyke [head of ITV Sport] does a back-door deal with David Dein. They wouldn't come through the front door and put a fair bid in. David Dein was a member of the Management Committee [and] Philip Carter was the president of the Football League. If you convert it to business terms it was the chairman and one of the directors of the company.'

The backlash had begun. Some club chairmen, led by Ken Bates and Ron Noades of Crystal Palace, claimed that their clubs needed to play more games to make ends meet. With clubs already playing in the FA Cup, League Cup and the Full Members' Cup, top English players were now playing two highly competitive games every week of the season, and sometimes the schedule was even more hectic. No other League in the world (except in Scotland) made such demands on its best players. Nevertheless, the Bates-Noades argument succeeded and in 1990 it was decided that the First Division would go back to twenty-two clubs. Only David Dein voiced strong opposition and only Arsenal, Manchester United and Tottenham voted against the increase (Ron Noades claimed that Irving Scholar decided how to vote by tossing a coin). Although most commentators now agreed that there was too much football, the opposing camp had its vociferous advocates, none more so than Ken Bates, who said: 'If you listen to Arsenal and Manchester United, all they are saying [is that] it's a disadvantage for them competing in Europe. What is really being said is that we should reduce the number of games so that the less successful clubs should have even fewer matches which give them even less revenue, which will condemn them perpetually to being poor while the so-called Big Five perpetuate their stranglehold on soccer ... I am always told the argument in favour of it [a smaller First Division] is that there would be less football played, which would improve the quality of the game. Well, my answer is, that is bullshit . . . The most ardent advocates of smaller divisions can't wait to jump on an aeroplane and get jet-lagged on the other side of the world, either because the directors want an all expenses paid booze-up or they want to get the money that's on offer.'

The shenanigans of the club chairmen notwithstanding, the rehabilitation of the English game was given a shot in the arm when the England team made it to the semi-finals of the World Cup in Italy in 1990. It had been almost twenty-five years since England had reached such dizzy heights in an international tournament and the whole nation was brought together on a wave of emotion. If ever there was a moment when the national team demonstrated football's hold over the country's imagination, this was it. The time was now propitious for change, and moves were once again afoot at the highest levels to instigate a reorganisation of the English game. The impetus for change was the vast amount of money needed to convert grounds to all-seat stadia in line with the Taylor Report into the Hillsborough disaster, estimated at £600 million. There were also calls by the government for football to 'speak with one voice' if the game wanted to receive help in the form of rebuilding subsidies from the public purse.

The rivalry between the Football Association and the Football League goes back to the origins of organised football itself. No one knows the true roots of football, except that examples of humans kicking some kind of round object with their feet can be found as far back as the first civilisations. It was in mainland Britain, however, that the sport we know today was devised. During the sixteenth and seventeenth centuries it was a pursuit for the lower orders of rural society. In *King Lear*, Shakespeare used the term 'football player' as an insult, attaching the adjective 'base' as the most natural description of the species. The modern game was codified in the nineteenth century but by then had been taken up by the public schools, universities and the officer class of the armed services. The organisation these bodies set up to regulate the game was the southern-based Football Association, which along with the first proper competition, the FA Cup, and the first international match, against Scotland, was established in

1872. The national body was mirrored at local level by county associations which affiliated to the national organisation. The winners of the FA Cup in its formative years show just how the game which would engulf the world had been taken over by the English upper classes and was, in the spirit of the era, amateur in nature. They include Oxford University, the Royal Engineers, Old Carthusians (from Charterhouse School), Old Etonians and the embodiment of the amateur ideal, Wanderers, who won the Cup on five occasions between its inception in 1872 and 1879.

The game had not been entirely forsaken by its earlier practitioners, however. The industrial revolution, which created the huge British working class, saw football once again established among the masses, both in England and Scotland. These people, who were denied access to the rarefied atmosphere of the public schools and the universities, developed football along different, club-based lines. Gradually, these clubs came to represent whole towns and cities, particularly the boom cities of the midlands and north. Their location also meant that money was generated, and almost overnight a whole industry sprang up, servicing a variety of needs, from the employment of professional players to the design and manufacture of turnstiles, terracing and stands. The FA would have preferred to have ignored the upstarts but they couldn't. The clubs were free to enter the FA Cup since there was nothing in the rule book to stop them and a professional club, Blackburn Rovers, won it in 1884, just twelve years after the competition was instituted. From that moment, the professionals dominated the FA Cup and no amateur side ever won the trophy again.

The financial and playing power of the professional clubs, added to the class and regional divide, set the two sections of football in England apart. The same was true in Scotland, but the separation north of the border was never quite as pronounced. The two parts of the game did, however, have one thing in common. They played by the same rules and these rules had become the 'property' of the FA. The professional clubs were, at this stage, no more than a loose federation at best but that situation did not last long. Within three years of Blackburn winning the FA Cup, twelve professional clubs formed a league, the first such national competition ever, and called themselves the Football League. The formation of the League had much to do with money. Professional players, the creation of grounds in which to play and other pressing cost increases meant that regular fixtures were needed to justify the outlay. The FA did not formally object to the proposed League – in fact they were happy not to have to dirty their hands with its organisation, although in true authoritarian style they kept control of disciplinary matters.

The structure of the modern FA retains links with its Victorian past. All the factions which formed the amateur game were from the ruling class and expected to have their say. A Council of these vested interests was formed which not only still exists today but has expanded to over ninety members. It is the Council that has the formal power to take all the important decisions concerning English football. While other bodies, such as the English Schools Football Association and the various leagues, including the Football League, that have come into existence over the last hundred years or so have gained representation on the Council, bodies such as county FAs and the military still retain their rights of voting and it is fair to say that without support from their direction, changes in football in this country cannot be made.

There are other connections with the past that continued to haunt relationships between the two bodies until the Premier League began in 1992. The FA was never constituted in a way that recognised football as a spectator sport. It was made up entirely of participants and officials. The organisation was probably completely surprised at the success of the FA Cup with the public and was not concerned with making any money beyond what it needed to organise itself. The League, being concerned with money from the outset, understood the need to accommodate supporters. This did not mean it treated them well: on the contrary, it subjected them to conditions similar to those that factory employers provided for their workers, the barest minimum. However, the clubs always understood that in the absence of a benefactor or some other means of generating income the paying spectator was their life-blood.

It was for these historic reasons, bound up as they were with the peculiar social relations that permeated the nation, that two separate bodies, each with their own power base and interests, developed in England. The FA, in charge of rules and discipline, owner of the FA Cup and responsible for the national team, was nominally the body in overall control, but it had allowed a significant area of the game to achieve autonomy from the beginning and would find it difficult to rein in the power it had let go. A century later, this was why the government felt the need to ask the game to 'speak with one voice'. In the early years, it must have seemed to the FA that the League was a small, northern, working-class organisation which would never achieve the kind of success that soon came its way. It was not long, however, before the clubs, in addition to dominating the FA Cup, supplied most of the players for the national team. Thus the FA was forced to recognise that it depended on these clubs and it was terrified of the consequences should it alienate them. To this day, it is the clubs who determine their own future. It was the Football League, for instance, not the FA, that stopped the English champions, Chelsea, from entering the inaugural European Cup in 1955–56. As ever, it was the wilful action of a club (admittedly one of the country's biggest) in support of its manager that forced the League to back down. Manchester United, or more accurately, Matt Busby, insisted they compete in the European Cup the following season. For most of the debate, the FA refused to intervene.

The conservative and narrow attitude of the FA not only precluded it from having any positive influence on the fledgling Football League but also ensured that it failed to comprehend developments in other areas of the game. One of these was its burgeoning international popularity. The FA refused to become a founder member of FIFA (Fédération Internationale de Football Association), subsequently the world governing body, and after belatedly joining, resigned in a huff over the definition of amateur status and missed playing in the first three World Cups (1930, 1934 and 1938). As custodian of the game's code, the FA did not see that anything could be learned from abroad. In other countries, the national associations (generally 'federations') either directly control and organise the professional league (as in Germany), or there is an established chain of command with the federation calling the shots (as in France). The tensions induced by the schism in England, epitomised by the perennial club-versus-country debate, persisted until the Hillsborough disaster and the Taylor Report. If they wanted government money to implement Taylor, something had to give. By the 1990s, after over a hundred years of uneasy alliance, there were at last moves afoot to end the dichotomy once and for all.

Aware that the FA was intending to flex its muscles over the professional game, commercial director Trevor Phillips and the League's chief executive, Arthur Sandford – known as 'The Invisible Man' because of his low profile – laboured throughout the summer of 1990 to produce a plan for change that would seize the initiative from the FA. By October they were ready to go public and their proposal was unveiled in a document entitled 'One Game, One Team, One Voice', which called for the League and the FA to have equal representation on a new joint board which would take overall control of the English game. League president Bill Fox was on hand to make sure that the proposal was discussed by the game's supreme rule-making body, the FA Council, of which he was also a member. Fox believed that the Council would consider the plan seriously. 'We have been told to expect their response to it after a meeting in January,' he said. While much of the League's document was up for negotiation, the crucial issue was equal representation on the new joint board. 'It has to be a fifty-fifty split,' Fox maintained. 'It just can't work any other way.'

   The Phillips-Sandford plan would virtually denude the FA Council of its power to control change, which would reside in the new joint board, so a very careful lobbying exercise would have to take place if it was to stand any chance of success. But apart from the expected opposition from within the Council, there was also another faction at the FA which would not countenance change if it meant a diminution of its power base.

Robert Henry Graham Kelly came to the Football Association by a route which in a previous generation would have been inconceivable. The son of a Blackpool tram driver, he trained as an accountant, worked for Barclays Bank and played football as an amateur goalkeeper for Blackpool's 'A' team before joining the Football League's accounts department in 1968. 'I was in love with the game and when the chance came to work in it I jumped at it,' he recalled. 'I was a complete fanatic – I went everywhere to watch football.' Five years later, Kelly had risen to become assistant to the League's autocratic leader, Alan Hardaker, who took the League into battle with anybody who disagreed with his view that the Football League was the most important body in the game.

For instance, Hardaker believed that professional players were unworthy of the money demanded by the chairman of their association, Jimmy Hill, who sought to abolish the maximum wage of £20 per week in 1961 – 'I wouldn't hang a dog on the word of a professional footballer,' he argued. Equally at home fighting the FA, he added a fresh perspective to the crucial 1973 World Cup qualifying tie against Poland, which England had to win in order to reach the finals in West Germany. As the nation hyped itself up for the big game, Hardaker remarked: 'It's a football match, not a war . . . if we do lose, the game is not going to die. It will be a terrible thing for six weeks and then everyone will forget about it.'

When Hardaker eventually retired in 1979, Graham Kelly became the new secretary. His regime was completely opposite to that of his predecessor. Hardaker's all-consuming style of confrontation was replaced by a more reflective and diligent approach, in which good housekeeping became the order of the day. Kelly was smart enough not to try to emulate the Hardaker manner. As he said himself, 'I learned how not to do some things from Alan.' One of Kelly's assets is his self-effacing, dry humour which can be disconcerting to someone unaware of this trait. Kelly tells a story of a match when he was playing in goal for Blackpool's 'A' team. On his side that day was Emlyn Hughes, later to become captain of Liverpool and England. 'Emlyn . . . put his arm round me in that inimitable fashion of this after we'd lost 4–0 and said, "Graham, you'll always be a banker." At least I think that's what he said.'

In place of the Hardaker brashness, Kelly worked quietly in the background, leaving the high profile to others. Throughout his years as League secretary he assiduously built up contacts throughout the game. When the secretary of the Football Association, Ted Croker, retired in 1988, it was Kelly who was the surprise choice to succeed him. It was the first time anyone had moved from such a high position in the League to a similar post at the FA. In fact, Kelly's title was upgraded from general secretary to chief executive, and he became the most powerful man in the English game.

When Kelly arrived at Lancaster Gate, the days of running the organisation like a gentleman's club were numbered. The isolation that followed the Heysel disaster was about to end and the rumblings of discontent within the big clubs, and the old division between the Football League and the Football Association could not continue. If Kelly had expected a quiet life he was to be disillusioned with a vengeance when ninety-six people were killed in a crush at the Leppings Lane end of the Hillsborough ground in Sheffield at the FA Cup semi-final between Liverpool and Nottingham Forest in 1989, just weeks after he had taken up his new position. All the years of neglect, of treating supporters as if they were merely turnstile fodder, came to a head in the wake of the tragedy.

Kelly was propelled into the national arena as it fell to him to express the feelings of those who ruled the game and to tell the nation what they were going to do to make sure nothing like Hillsborough could ever happen again. 'It cannot be denied,' wrote Clive White in *The Times*, 'that his chubby, permanently glum face which appeared daily on our television screens throughout the Hillsborough tragedy was an uninspiring sight.' Had a similar disaster happened on the continent, it was likely that some senior people in the FA would have ended up in the dock facing criminal charges, but in Britain these things are handled differently and the public was assuaged by the Taylor Report, which called for far-reaching change, including making grounds all-seat.

The Taylor Report was the greatest catalyst for change the English game had yet seen. As Kelly's thoughts began to coalesce, he heard of rumblings coming from the League. In a moment of realism not often seen in the higher echelons of football, he determined to produce a plan which would completely reorganise the game from top to bottom. Underlying his thoughts was the premise that the position of the FA at the pinnacle of the English game could be maintained only if its power were extended to incorporate the clubs of the Football League.

In December 1990, two months after the Phillips-Sandford proposal was produced, Kelly announced to journalists at a lunch in London that he was working on his own plan, which would form a 'Blueprint for the Future of Football', the details of which would be forthcoming in the next six months. 'Concern has been felt,' he emphasised, 'about the fifty-fifty split [in the League's plan].' Kelly's proposals would be wide-ranging and would include stadia, television, sponsorship, coaching, junior football, health, refereeing standards and the laws of the game. Another idea, which had also appeared in the League's document, was that England should make a bid to stage either the 1996 European Championships or the 1998 World Cup. Kelly announced that Charles Hughes, the FA's national director of coaching and education, was to be appointed to the post of director of the project.

Charles Hughes is a much-maligned figure within football. A small, earnest man in his late fifties with the air of the school-master he once was (prior to joining the FA he was head of PE at a northern grammar school), he reputedly told an American coaching symposium that 'Brazil have got it all wrong'. This led to his portrayal as the arch-exponent of the long-ball theory. He joined the FA's coaching department in 1964 and, after managing the England amateur and Olympic teams, was appointed national director of coaching and education in 1989. His ideas, based on painstaking research, are expounded in his book *The Winning Formula*, in which he describes himself as a football purist. He defends his criticism of Brazil by arguing that 'if they allied their level of skill to the right strategies, we would all be in trouble'. The right strategies, in Hughes' view, are direct play in attack and the pressing game in defence.

Although Hughes had used his analytical skills in coming to his opinion, there were many who thought their value was akin to those of a deckchair attendant on the Titanic. It was certainly an ill-considered comment, given the relative success rates of the Brazilian and English national teams. As he had survived the savaging he encountered over his ideas, which didn't seem to bother him at all, Kelly reasoned that Hughes was the best possible person to lead the Blueprint team and ought to be more than capable of coping with whatever hostility came his way.

There are also many within the FA who view Hughes as

someone who has assiduously built up a power base at Lancaster Gate by riding roughshod over any opposition. According to this opinion, Kelly had no option, if he wanted to challenge football's status quo, but to give Hughes a major say, otherwise Hughes would have been more than able to quash the proposal from within.

Change was needed in just about every area but change would cost money which football simply did not possess. Pleas to the government produced some help, chiefly through a reduction in the pools betting levy, which would release £20 million per year, but anything further was dependent on football putting its house in order. With the lack of any firm commitment from Whitehall, Kelly realised that the only way to generate the necessary funds was to revitalise the FA's commercial operations, which had hitherto been conducted on an ad hoc basis. This area had been the province of Glen Kirton, whose title of head of external affairs was a catch-all for a multitude of responsibilities. Kirton's route to the top of the game came through the FA's press office and media relations is his speciality. He had also had his fingers burned in 1988 when he supported the BSB bid for football but had been outmanoeuvred, like everyone else, by the big clubs. Subsequently, he was passed over for the job of chief executive when Kelly was preferred. There was little love lost between Kirton and Hughes, and when Kelly realised he would need commercial expertise, he suggested that Hughes should fix a meeting with Alex Fynn.

The meeting was convened on January 24 1991 in Kelly's office. By that time, it was clear that the FA Council, contrary to Bill Fox's expectations, would not discuss the Sandford-Phillips plan until Kelly's own proposals had been finalised. The longer the delay continued, the further the League's ideas receded into the background.

At the January meeting, Kelly, Millichip and Hughes wanted to know what the prospects were for increased commercial income and how much it could turn out to be. Fynn took some little time to settle into his stride, mainly due to mild embarrassment because he had forgotten to change out of his driving shoes (an old pair of black casuals even a tramp would disown). Gradually though, he got his thoughts together and began to talk about ways in which increased revenues could be achieved. Reiterating his long-held views, Fynn told the trio that the League needed restructuring; that there should be a smaller First Division, and the professional game should alter its club-based nature to an approach recognising the importance of the England team, which should be at the top of a new pyramid structure alongside the top clubs. Success for the national team, he said, and a smaller First Division were interdependent. If this change were implemented, large amounts of new money could be found from television, based on an increase in the number of live televised League games from eighteen to thirty-four. Kelly and Millichip said little but Hughes was full of questions. One odd note was that none of the three seemed to have realised the England team was suffering unnecessarily through too many club games. 'Tell me again,' Hughes said when this opinion was outlined.

It was at this point that Hughes dropped his bombshell. The FA, he declared, were ready to encourage a new Premier League comprising eighteen clubs which would break away from the First Division. The Football League had gone too far with its own plans, the FA could never countenance power-sharing and the time had come to sweep away the cobwebs of a hundred years. The FA would run the new League, thus marginalising the trouble-making Football League forever.

At the conclusion of the meeting, Fynn had occasion to visit the lavatory and was startled to find Kelly accompanying him. He was relieved to discover that Kelly merely wanted to tell him discreetly that thirty-four live games on television were more than could be accommodated. It was decided that Fynn should be brought on to the Blueprint working party to advise on commercial considerations. He was sworn to secrecy on the matter of the Premier League.

The first major meeting of the Blueprint working party took place at Lancaster Gate on February 5 1991. Papers had been prepared on coaching, sports medicine, the role of county associations, referees, supporters (under the agenda heading of crowd control) and education. Outside the working party, but parallel to it, the management consultants, Peat Marwick, were developing what became known rather grandly as the National Plan for Stadia. Fynn ended up attending both sets of discussions since his commercial forecasts were more and more coming to be seen as necessary to underwrite the cost of implementing the Blueprint. Amazingly, because the few who knew about the Premier League were subject to a vow of confidentiality, those producing plans for the future were unaware that revolution was about to take place.

While work on the Blueprint pressed ahead, Graham Kelly had the task of killing off the Phillips-Sandford plan from the Football League. The League had representation on the FA Council which, although small, was enough to ensure the plan would be discussed. Since it appeared before Kelly's Blueprint, it seemed that the League was taking the initiative, and indeed the plan had received encouraging support from the Sports Minister, Robert Atkins. Some furious lobbying took place to ensure first that the proposal was not put to a Council vote until the Kelly camp had gained time to muster its forces, and secondly that the whole idea would be overwhelmed by the sheer comprehensiveness of the Blueprint. Realistically, there was always little likelihood that the League's plan would be accepted since it took from the Council most of its power.

In many ways, the League played into Kelly's hands by continuing to insist on the fifty-fifty split. At first, Bill Fox believed that the support of Robert Atkins was enough to get the plan accepted and little lobbying took place to garner support within the FA Council. The League, in fact, were totally unprepared for Kelly's response and hurriedly contrived a new strategy when they heard about the Blueprint and the mounting campaign against their own plans. A series of regional presentations to sell their proposals to FA councillors was arranged. Unfortunately, this had the opposite effect, alienating more than it converted. Phillips, Sandford and Fox exhorted their audience to accept their proposals, veering from a promise of increased wealth to dire threats about what would happen if the plan were rejected. The presentations, Kelly said later, 'went down like half a dozen lead balloons'.

Kelly's response to the presentations was to point out that the League's own governing body, the Management Committee, had rarely been able to agree about anything and there was no guarantee that it would accept these proposals.

Since Kelly, through his time at the League, had intimate knowledge of the way the organisation worked, it was a telling criticism, and one that was never properly answered. The two architects of 'One Game, One Team, One Voice', Trevor Phillips and Arthur Sandford, seemed to give up the fight for their plan and it was finally thrown out by the FA Council in April. At the same time the Council gave its blessing to the Blueprint and to the concept of an FA Premier League, subject to the new League's details coming back for a further vote once they were agreed. Trevor Phillips seemed the most disillusioned with the outcome, saying: 'By asking to share power with the FA we kicked a sleeping dog. It is now up on its feet and barking at us and whether it goes back to sleep in the sun or bites us is the sixty-four-thousand-dollar question.' In truth, Phillips already knew the answer. In the wake of subsequent events, Arthur Sandford, The Invisible Man, would leave his position some months later with a handsome pay-off. Phillips, on the other hand, despite his disappointment, saw the writing on the wall and decided to fight a different battle. Both men nevertheless accused the FA of stealing their clothes. 'Every single item they propose', said Phillips, 'is a rehash of things we put together last year for the good of football.'

By the time the Blueprint working party was midway through its task at the beginning of April 1991, news of the proposal for a Premier League was released. Predictably, it caused a storm. The FA Council approved the idea in principle on April 8, by which time the League's own plan was finished. At least with the Premier League out in the open at last, Alex Fynn could offer a realistic financial analysis of the FA's commercial future. The resultant figures, prepared by a Saatchi and Saatchi subsidiary, Zenith Media, indicated that current FA income could be trebled, while the total football could earn from marketing could be as high as £100 million per year. The analysis was presented to a special meeting of the FA's Executive Committee on April 30. Fynn's pitch was simple. This amount of revenue could be attained only by central control of all commercial matters and the negotiations with third parties had to be conducted by experts. Not unnaturally, Fynn thought they should be handed over to Saatchi and Saatchi.

Television income, according to Fynn, could go through the roof. Thirty live games a season of the Premier League plus a highlights programme would bring in over £30 million. No title sponsorship was envisaged for either the Premier League or the FA Cup, but a mix of World Cup-style sponsors and suppliers, with broadcast sponsorship on the commercial television channels, was suggested as the preferred route to riches.

Fynn's projections ran into opposition during the meeting. Glen Kirton, in charge of the FA's existing commercial arrangements but excluded from Blueprint discussions up to that point due to his frosty relationship with project director Charles Hughes, was most severe in his criticism. Fynn, after all, was interfering in what should have been Kirton's domain. One telling point that Kirton raised was what he regarded as an over-optimistic estimate of merchandising income. Fynn himself had realised that merchandising was the least supportable of his arguments and had produced what was really an open-ended estimate. Kirton's observation was, paradoxically, more a criticism of his own efforts in the commercial arena as the future use of FA symbols and crests was circumscribed by existing and, it could be argued, unsatisfactory, contracts. A lively debate ensued after which Fynn believed he had fully answered the criticism. The committee asked him to leave the room while they discussed the matter among themselves.

Sitting outside, Fynn could hear quite distinctly what was being said (is this the reason few secrets can be kept at the FA?). So audible was the debate that after a while Fynn felt acutely embarrassed, but try as he might – by going to the toilet and wandering into the adjacent Council chamber (there was a partition separating it from the room where the meeting was taking place) – it was impossible to get away from the animated discussions. Some of the criticism contained a personal element. Jack Wiseman, a director of Birmingham City and a senior FA councillor, recalled being on the receiving end of Fynn's high-pressure salesmanship for one of the books he had co-written, *The Secret Life Of Football*. Then Jim Thompson, chairman of Maidstone United, opined that the commercial estimates could not be taken seriously as Fynn had allowed only a few hundred pounds for presentation purposes rather than several thousands. Moreover, he vehemently objected to the premise that regionalisation of the lower divisions would increase commercial income. Glen Kirton picked up the point about Fynn's fee. Kirton doubted the need for Fynn's expertise, particularly if his merchandising evaluation was anything to go by. This led to general scepticism. Maybe Fynn sang a nice song, but could he deliver? In his defence, Charles Hughes asked rhetorically: 'Well, hasn't he sold himself to us?'

When Fynn was eventually invited back into the meeting, he was able to dismiss Thompson's and Kirton's arguments, much, it seemed, to the pleasure of Bert Millichip. Fynn thought he would leave the meeting with the appointment of Saatchi and Saatchi as commercial advisors to the FA. He should not have expected so much and was disappointed when he was informed that any decision in this regard would have to be referred back to a meeting of the Commercial Committee. At this gathering it was decided to recommend to Graham Kelly that Saatchi and Saatchi be appointed to renegotiate the FA's television contract and find sponsorship for the FA Cup. The recommendation was, however, never implemented by Kelly and Fynn was left to work on the commercial section of the Blueprint without knowing where his input would lead.

On June 20 1991, the FA's 'Blueprint for the Future of Football' was issued amid much fanfare. Within its 119 pages were a broad range of proposals which made it the most important document on the administration of English football since a report by Sir Norman Chester in 1983. That report, Sir Norman's second for the Football League, had been rejected, resulting in the sickly state of health in which football found itself in 1991. The new Blueprint's key elements were: a revised structure to aid the coaching of young players; the establishment of an international Sports Institute in conjunction with Loughborough University; a research programme to bring in fresh criteria for referees; increased commitment to English influence overseas via coaching, touring and a Commonwealth Cup; the creation of a new National Supporters Association with a seat on the Football Licensing Committee, a government quango which had the power to close football grounds; and the implementation of the National Plan For Stadia, which would encourage ground-sharing in order to produce eleven stadia with capacities in excess of 30,000 and at least four which could seat over 40,000 (needed for any application to stage the European Championships or the World Cup).

Predictably, many of these worthy points were lost as the Premier League and its concomitant commercial revenue estimates grabbed all the headlines. The Premier League was set to begin with twenty-two clubs, to be reduced to eighteen by the 1996–97 season. There would be promotion and relegation from and to the Football League, which would comprise twenty-two clubs in the new First Division, with twenty-four in each of the Second and Third Divisions. Regionalisation was discussed as a possibility at the lower levels of the Football League and the Vauxhall Conference. Candidates for the Premier League would also have to meet off-field criteria, such as financial targets and stadia seating at least 20,000 supporters. No Premier League fixtures would be allowed at weekends prior to England games in the European Championships and World Cup.

For commercial purposes, the three key properties under FA control would now be the Premier League, the FA Cup and the England international team. A centralised marketing strategy would provide the necessary finance to tackle the problems of the game's development. The gross value of the properties was estimated at £112 million for season 1992–93. Arthur Sandford, unusually, was particularly fiery in his dismissal. 'I call on Graham Kelly,' he said, 'to openly publish the exact breakdown of these figures for all to see.' The FA, somewhat lamely, replied that it couldn't do that for fear of damaging its negotiating position. In truth the FA was scared witless as it had abdicated all responsibility in this area to Alex Fynn, who wrote the commercial section of the Blueprint in its entirety. If Fynn had chosen to talk about £52 million or £212 million, it would have been accepted with the same alacrity.

For once all sections of the media were united in their scorn for the estimate, a response which threatened to undermine the Blueprint as a whole. £112 MILLION SELL-OUT screamed the *Daily Mirror* over a double-page spread. The *Guardian* called the figures 'a load of old codswallop'. The efforts of the press were helped by Trevor Phillips and Glen Kirton, who did their best to discredit the figures. The most optimistic estimate they could come up with was £45 million a year.

Unfortunately, the search for hidden gold tended to devalue the Blueprint's other recommendations. Arthur Sandford could not help but agree with much of the document because, as he put it, 'many of the proposals are simply lifted from our document, "One Game, One Team, One Voice".' He was, however, totally opposed to the Premier League, which he thought was divisive and élitist. A similar objection was forthcoming from Gordon Taylor, chief executive of the Professional Footballers Association, who said: 'They [the FA] seem to be looking after the interests of the few without looking after the majority, with the big clubs taking most of the money.' Perhaps the most vehement criticism came from Craig Brewin, chairman of the Football Supporters Association (FSA), who indignantly pointed out that 'the Blueprint contains loquacious praise for the achievements of the FSA and other supporters organisations . . . but then goes on to state that the FA will establish its own organisation'. It appears that when the FA expanded the crowd control section to encompass supporter relations, no one saw any reason to involve real fans. This element was left in the hands of sociologists from the Sir Norman Chester Centre for Football Research at Leicester University. Similarly, Gordon Taylor took the FA to task for its claim that the Blueprint was 'conceived and produced inside the game' because 'neither the Football League nor the PFA – the two main professional bodies – had any input'.

The FA were in for a rough ride from the League representatives on the FA Council when it met for its annual summer meeting at the Palace Hotel in Torquay the following week. This meeting was originally scheduled for the representatives to vote on the details of the Blueprint but the possibility of legal action over the Premier League was in the air and no vote was taken. Alex Fynn, who was in Torquay to present the thinking behind the commercial recommendations, was asked by Jack Wiseman how the television and sponsorship negotiations were going. Wiseman was surprised to discover that Saatchis had not been officially appointed.

Alex Fynn took the Council through his proposals. By now

they had taken a beating in the press in what seemed like a concerted campaign to discredit his analysis. While the proposal not to seek title sponsorship for the FA Cup was welcomed, and polite applause ensued when Fynn emphasised the opportunity reorganisation could bring to the England team, there were many hostile comments. Bill Fox said he had read Fynn's books and so knew which side Fynn was on – that of the 'big battalions'. Jim Thompson once again complained about regional football for the likes of Maidstone. The most lengthy diatribe came from Gordon McKeag, chairman of both Newcastle United and the Football League's Management Committee, who Fynn thought was ill fitted to lecture him on commercial matters after presiding over the sad decline of the club they both supported.

The First Division representatives were in somewhat of an invidious position as the previous day a number of them had agreed to resign from the Football League. Peter Swales of Manchester City welcomed the decision, which he called a 'very positive move'. Doug Ellis of Aston Villa probably summed up the mood of the meeting when he said: 'If you can get us £112 million, Mr Fynn, you're elected.' To what, Fynn wasn't sure, but he felt afterwards that the tide of opinion was turning away from him and that he was about to become a footnote in the history of the Premier League as the juggernaut mowed down everything in its path.

The 'Blueprint for the Future of Football' was finally approved by the FA Council on February 20 1992. Graham Kelly, the man who had spent so many years in the shadow of Alan Hardaker, had all but destroyed what Hardaker had so painstakingly created, a dominant Football League. In the process, he had given the game the opportunity to revitalise itself at last.

A central plank of the Blueprint was the need for unity within the game. 'A unified approach,' it states, ' . . . is a prerequisite for success in any major enterprise.' The Premier League proposal by itself, however, had caused the greatest disunity even the argument-prone football industry had ever produced. But the fine words of the Blueprint were, in the end, window-dressing, and diverted many from what was really going on. By the end of 1992, of eighty-eight major recommendations contained in the Blueprint, only twenty-four had been implemented, and most of these were technicalities. Of those that were put into practice, many, like the Premier League, were changed beyond recognition. Other major features, such as the proposed Sports Institute with Loughborough University and the National Plan for Stadia, have hardly been heard of since. The one positive outcome of the argument was that England won the right to host the 1996 European Championships. But the Premier League clubs have taken virtually all of the increased commercial income, leaving little for the more worthwhile projects.

Nevertheless, the Blueprint brought Kelly's vision to the attention of both the government at home and the wider world of UEFA and FIFA. And the Football League had been smashed. The fact remains, however, that English football, yet again, missed the opportunity to renew itself, and vision became blurred in the double-dealing and the welter of recrimination which followed in the wake of the most contentious of all the Blueprint recommendations, the formation of the Premier League.

3

The Twenty-Two-Headed Monster

The creation of the Premier League

> *'A historic day for football ... The evolution and management of the game have been in neutral for the last hundred years but today's decision has sent it into overdrive, which should reward all clubs great and small.'*

Arsenal vice-chairman David Dein, on confirmation of the Premier League, September 1991.

> *'It was a lost opportunity [a league of 18 clubs]. I'm getting increasingly embarrassed when people say, what is the difference between the Premier League and the old First Division? I have to face them and say, "Nothing, except there's more money swishing around."'*

David Dein, September 1992.

Those present in the boardroom at Goodison Park, Liverpool, in March 1991, could have been mistaken by some for a rogues' gallery of football's hierarchy. First, there was the soon-to-be-knighted Philip Carter, formerly of the Littlewoods pools and shopping empire, ex-chairman of Everton and now occupying a key position in the government's team to implement its plan for the regeneration of Merseyside. Carter, once chairman of the Football League, had been ignominiously forced to step down because of his role in the 1988 television negotiations which handed control of television rights to ITV. Next was David Dein, vice-chairman of Arsenal, who had been removed from the Management Committee along with

Carter and was held to be responsible, according to his critics, for the sour atmosphere which surrounded ITV's bid for football. Also in attendance was Martin Edwards, chief executive of Manchester United, the man many blamed at the time for the club's failure to recapture the glory days of the past; Graham Kelly, whose low-key response to the Hillsborough disaster was deemed by the media to have been inadequate and Charles Hughes, under attack from all sides for his views on direct football. The only possessors of unblemished public reputations were the then Liverpool chairman, Noel White, and chief executive Peter Robinson. However, within the game there was much resentment of Liverpool's perennial tactic of always going by the book, and as one insider put it, 'letting others do the dirty work, arriving late and then proceeding to drink all the champagne'. Thus Liverpool's views on the meeting's agenda were likely to prove decisive to its outcome.

This diverse though undoubtedly influential crew, was on the verge of taking a decision which would bring about the biggest changes in English football since the formation of the Football League in 1888. The balance of power within the game would now shift for a time towards the Football Association, which, with the connivance of the big club representatives present at Everton, would smash the Football League to smithereens by agreeing to back the break away Premier League under its own direct control.

The road to Goodison had taken David Dein eight years to travel. He had been appointed to the Arsenal board in September 1983 after agreeing to make £300,000 available to the club's coffers and in January 1984 had been made vice-chairman, a position created specially for him. By the early 1980s, Dein had built up and diversified the family business to the point where he was able to indulge himself in his passion for Arsenal. The company for which Dein worked after dropping out of university, Dein Brothers Ltd, had been started by him and his brother in 1965. From its base in Shepherd's Bush it imported exotic fruit and vegetables from around the world. Later, David Dein took the business into commodity broking and, as the London Sugar Company, moved from west London to the altogether plusher confines of Pall Mall, W1. Six years after assuming his place on the

Arsenal board, having devoted ever more time to the club for no recompense, he reorganised his affairs by arranging a management buy-out of the London Sugar Company and moving into Highbury full-time to take charge of Arsenal's building and development programme. When the structure of the club was changed to meet the legal requirements of issuing debenture bonds to pay for redevelopment at the stadium, Dein emerged as the main shareholder and became, to all intents and purposes, Arsenal's new owner. Although opponents of his policies would not agree, this was an instance of an inmate taking over the asylum. A self-confessed 'football nut' but above all an Arsenal fanatic since the day his uncle took him as a six-year-old to see Tommy Lawton power a header into the opposition net, Dein is something of a rarity, a lifelong fan who has realised his most cherished dream, a place on the board of the football club he adores.

It was, in the main, a quiet revolution at Highbury. In his dealings with football's power-brokers, however, Dein was anything but quiet, and to many within the game he became something of a factious figure who had to be stopped at all costs. Despite losing his place on the League's Management Committee, Dein believed that his actions in the 1988 television contract had been vindicated by the increased amounts of money that had since come into the game and he felt he still had much to contribute. Setbacks were there to be overcome, as instanced when he rescued his company from the verge of liquidation in 1987 and turned it once again into a profitable concern. He was determined that football should look to the future and formulated a strategy based on a controversial plan that had been on his mind for some time and was not dissimilar to Alex Fynn's theories on the 'event-like nature' of football matches.

Dein was most interested in how Fynn's ideas on restructuring applied to big clubs like Arsenal, because he believed that if the big clubs were healthy then the rest of football would benefit. It was the sporting equivalent of the 'trickle down' theory of economics. The event-like theory contends that in a forty-two-game First Division, Arsenal versus Liverpool is a national event, likely to generate widespread interest throughout the country. Swindon versus Oldham, however, is a non-event which only matters to the supporters of the two clubs involved and anyone who marked them down for a draw on their pools coupon. At the lower levels of the game, so the theory goes, Torquay versus Exeter is a regional or local event, whereas Torquay versus Carlisle is a non-event. Of course there are always exceptions. If, for instance, Arsenal were playing Oldham needing a win to clinch the title then that game would become a national event. The key to the theory is that the number of 'event games' should be maximised and the number of 'non-event games' minimised. The trouble with the English set-up, according to Fynn, was that at all levels far too many games were played which were non-events.

In Fynn's view, the main prerequisites for achieving a better balance were: a reduction in the size of the First Division; an end to spurious cup competitions, including the League Cup; and regional football in the lower divisions. If these steps were taken, the scarcity value of the game would be restored. The League, FA Cup and the England team would be sacrosanct and Saturdays would regain their pre-eminence as the week's football day. When the England team played, whether in friendlies or international competitions, there would be no top division games and the focus would naturally shift to midweek. The icing on the cake would come for those clubs in European tournaments. The whole theory could be summed up in the concept: less equals more. It was a concept with which some, like Ken Bates, who views football as a 'marginal costing system' (a football club's costs are more or less fixed, so more games equals more profit, or perhaps the difference between extinction and survival), profoundly disagree. Others, like David Dein, embraced the idea wholeheartedly.

With the ITV contract in 1988, which concentrated on televising the big clubs, and with the reduction of the First Division to twenty clubs, David Dein felt that the game had gone some way towards creating a First Division showcase of substance. Ken Bates disagreed. 'We saw Arsenal and Liverpool more times than fucking *Coronation Street*,' he asserted. 'That wasn't an event, it became a pain in the arse.'

For Dein, although he had locked ITV into the big clubs, there still remained the problem of the League's arcane working practices. 'I went to a few League meetings in my first year [at Arsenal],' he said, 'and I was appalled at the way this multi-million pound industry was being run . . . Every time I went to Football League meetings I'd get more depressed.' Dein presented his own restructuring plan to the First Division chairmen in 1986. '[It] actually met with their approval, they could see a lot of sense in it,' Dein claimed, adding, 'but deep down they were not ready to relish the challenge to the other clubs, players' contracts, etc. They didn't have the stomach for the fight so in the end it went on the back-burner.'

The crunch came for David Dein when, in August 1990, Ken Bates, supported by Ron Noades, pushed through the League a motion to return the First Division to twenty-two clubs. To Dein this was madness, but to the smaller clubs of the First Division, more games meant more income, no matter how inconsequential those games were. Changes to the League introduced in 1985 and 1988 had left the First Division with more power, but the First Division was always going to be made up of more smaller clubs than big ones, and if those smaller clubs acted in concert, they could still thwart the ambitions of the big club chairmen. Instead of the likes of Cardiff standing in Dein's way, it was now the likes of Coventry. Given this experience, it is all the more surprising that the mistake was repeated, with more far-reaching consequences, when the Premier League was eventually set up.

'As the years went by,' Dein maintained, 'you could not say that the English game was improving, either on or off the field.' He felt once again that it fell to him to take action. In the past, one of the obstacles in the way of far-reaching change had been the conservative nature of the country's top club, Liverpool, which had always refrained from giving wholehearted support to the reform lobby. However, Liverpool was undergoing change itself and the invincible dynasty seemed to be crumbling – it was soon to be shaken by the sudden departure of Kenny Dalglish. Dein correctly judged that the time was right finally to get Liverpool on board. He set up a meeting with Noel White, then Liverpool's chairman, and asked the question, 'What do we have to do to drive the game forward to the next century, to position ourselves, both at club and international level to compete with the rest of the world?' This was designed to touch the core of Liverpool's emotional claim to be England's leading club, a position that was being eroded, not so much by the challenge of Arsenal or Manchester United, but by the increasing demands of the football programme and the necessity of complying with the Taylor Report in a recession.

Together, White and Dein began to edge towards the idea of a break-away. Whatever happened, the structure of the League could no longer accommodate their ambitions. In addition, the television contract was up for renewal in 1992 and there was serious money to be earned at long last, especially for a showcase First Division. If nothing was done, the League's own restructuring plans would entrench the very power Dein wanted to break if they were adopted by the FA. White suggested that before anything could be accomplished, he and Dein should have a chat with Bert Millichip, the FA chairman. White, an FA councillor, was aware of the opposition within the FA to the League's plans and felt that an alliance of some kind could be put together. So in December 1990 the two men visited Lancaster Gate to discuss their ideas with Millichip, who immediately called in Graham Kelly.

To the surprise of Dein, Kelly was extremely receptive to the duo's ideas. Kelly had decided that in order to head off the challenge of 'One Game, One Team, One Voice', he had to put forward an alternative plan. For any Kelly plan to gain acceptance, there had to be a credible reason for not including the Football League. Dein and White supplied the reason and the centrepiece of Kelly's vision became the proposal for a new Premier League, to be run by the FA.

Armed with the backing of the FA, and feeling much more confident that something could at last be achieved, Dein now saw his task as convincing the other big clubs to support the Premier League plan. After a flurry of phone calls, the fateful meeting at Goodison Park was arranged. On hearing direct from the horse's mouth, in this case Graham Kelly and Charles Hughes, that the FA was four-square behind revolutionary change, the meeting gave unanimous support for the creation of a Premier League. Concluding the meeting, Philip Carter said: 'Well, gentlemen, that seems to be satisfactory. All that remains to do is elect our chief executive.'

On hearing this Charles Hughes was seized by the zeal of loyalty and broke in, 'We already have a chief executive, there.' He pointed at a rather uncomfortable-looking Graham Kelly. However, Kelly said nothing and the opportunity was gone.

In fact, the position of chief executive was something Kelly was not seeking. He realised better than most that the job, particularly in its early phase, would be extremely demanding. Extricating the clubs from the Football League, for instance, would be no easy matter. Moreover, Kelly was more concerned by the wider aspects of reform which his Blueprint would embrace and which he hoped would cement his position as chief executive of an ultimately omnipotent FA. Instead, Kelly introduced a man he had come across in 1987, when the Football League had been trying to avert an earlier break-away. During that time he had worked for six months alongside an accountant from the management consultancy Arthur Young, which had been hired to assess the League's management structure. The man Kelly advocated to carry out the role of chief executive was Rick Parry. Kelly's choice ensured that the two people who had worked out the League's reforms in 1987 were now employed on the other side of the fence. All the arguments the League could muster would be known in advance. It was a true 'double whammy', a ploy designed to induce maximum apoplexy at the League's headquarters at Lytham St Anne's.

Rick Parry had been a good enough footballer to represent Cheshire Schoolboys as a goalkeeper in the 1970s. Trials at Liverpool and Everton followed but the young Parry failed to make the grade as a professional player. He graduated from Liverpool University in 1979 with a degree in maths and joined Arthur Young (later merged to become Ernst and Young) as a sports and leisure management consultant. Arthur Young had worked with the Los Angeles Olympic Committee on the 1984 Games and this experience led to a close involvement in Manchester's bid for the 1992 Olympics, which was doomed to failure. Nevertheless, Parry's association with the Olympic quest led directly to the Football League and Graham Kelly. When Kelly decided that the Premier League assignment called for an independent but experienced man, Parry was, for him, the obvious choice.

Meanwhile, Alex Fynn was proceeding with his analysis of the Premier League's commercial potential for the FA. He persuaded Graham Kelly and Charles Hughes that market research should be undertaken to ascertain the football fans' reaction to such a development. The survey, conducted by Research Services Ltd (RSL), questioned 1,000 adult football supporters who regularly attended games. All twenty First Division grounds were covered. The results showed that opinion was divided equally, 41 per cent to 41 per cent, between support for an eighteen-club First Division and a return to twenty-two (at the time the move back to twenty-two clubs, although agreed, had not been implemented). This was encouraging for the FA because, as the research report stated: 'Since the British public tends to be conservative and will typically support the status quo, the acceptance level of the eighteen-club option should be treated as a positive result.' In addition, supporters of the Big Five (Liverpool, Everton, Manchester United, Arsenal and Tottenham), preferred the eighteen-club scenario by 49 per cent to 34 per cent. Of particular importance was the interdependence, in the fans' eyes, of an eighteen-club First Division and a successful England team. Of those who expressed a preference for an eighteen-team division, 62 per cent said the main reason for their support was that they believed it would allow more time for the England team to get together.

Armed with the knowledge that the supporters of an eighteen-club league were on the same wavelength as himself regarding the national team, Kelly became determined that eighteen clubs would be the price of his total support. At last, the national team could find its rightful place at the head of a pyramid of excellence, alongside a showcase Premier League. A month after RSL delivered its findings, which the FA never made public, the Football League conducted its own survey with Gallup on attitudes towards a break-away Premier League, which not surprisingly found that 'seven out of ten supporters were against it'. Equally unsurprising was the fact that the Gallup survey comprised supporters from all four divisions. The League released the results to the press, which made good copy, but the response had come too late. Alex Fynn had phoned Charles Hughes on the night of April 5 to give him the RSL results, which convinced the FA to put the issue of the Premier League to a vote in the FA Council the following Monday. That meeting, conducted amid enraged hostility from the Football League, approved the concept of an eighteen-club League, although Bert Millichip said afterwards that in the first season of the Premier League, 1992–93, all twenty-two First Division clubs would be involved, with a reduction to eighteen within four years.

The Football League and its rump of clubs was furious. The then managing director of Derby County, Stuart Webb, said the Premier League was motivated entirely by greed. 'It is a classic case,' he said, 'of the rich trying to get richer and the devil take the rest ... I am all for progress – but for everybody, not just a greedy few. And it should be achieved by democratic methods within the structure of the Football League.'

This was now a forlorn hope. The League was having to battle on two fronts. It was fighting to gain acceptance of its own plan and now it had to take on its major clubs. It was a war the embattled League could not possibly win. In fact, the same FA Council meeting which approved the principle of a Premier League also threw out for good the proposals contained in 'One Game, One Team, One Voice'. The Council also voted to disallow a crucial League regulation, number 11, passed after the 1987–88 threats of a break-away, that required clubs to give three years' notice to quit before they could leave the League. League president Bill Fox slammed the vote, saying, 'I don't find it acceptable that the First Division should be hijacked. This will bring all the old aggro to the fore again.'

Bert Millichip would have none of it. 'We are not hijacking the Football League,' he claimed. 'It would be impossible for us to do this unless there is agreement with the clubs.' Graham Kelly had steered the project through the FA Council while Rick Parry worked on the clubs. As Jeff Powell put it in the *Daily Mail* when commenting on Kelly's conversion from obscure League official to executioner-in-chief, 'No more Mr Nice Guy.'

The Council vote had the desired effect on those clubs in the First Division not already signed up for the new League and an unseemly scramble for inclusion began. By the end of June fifteen of them had agreed to give notice of resignation to the Football League. The League retaliated by asking the

High Court to restrain the FA from inducing member clubs to leave the League. On the eve of the FA's annual meeting in Torquay, a comment from Rick Parry gave a clue as to how the balance of power was beginning to shift once again, this time away from the FA and towards the big clubs. 'The will of the clubs and what they want to do is paramount. Whatever the legal outcome, they don't want to stay with the League. If the court action goes against the FA they have agreed to go ahead and form their own League.' Parry went on to say that the clubs were asking the two governing bodies to stop the legal proceedings, in the interests of the game.

In fact Parry had discovered an important truth in his mission to get all the First Division on board, or rather, his original feelings had been confirmed. All rules and regulations concerning the establishment of a Premier League would either have to be imposed by the FA, an unlikely outcome given the FA's reluctance to become engaged in trench warfare, or the Premier League clubs would have to establish their own. If the latter were to be the case, then the clubs would have to operate a one club, one vote system. If that happened the key to power would lie outside both the FA and the big clubs, with the fifteen or so lesser brethren of the First Division. Graham Kelly's response to the threat to go it alone was immediate, though hardly decisive. 'The prospect of an autonomous league would be questionable,' he said. 'We would have to consider all the facts but we would have to ask some very searching questions. If the FA does not sanction a new league, it cannot operate.'

The first problem the nascent league ran into was the issue of twenty-two or eighteen clubs. According to David Dein, 'Ron Noades and Ken Bates pointed out that everyone had building works and therefore we should coincide it [the reduction in numbers] with the Taylor Report [which stipulated that all First and Second Division grounds had to be all-seat by 1994). We [Arsenal] were one of the few clubs that wanted to see an eighteen-club League straight away. I said if that's too radical let's see twenty in 1993–94 so that prior to the World Cup we are down to twenty clubs. This would give the England team more chance.' Dein had the support of the FA but it was rapidly becoming clear that the Bates-Noades axis had considerable leverage, as Rick Parry had realised.

Parry, seeing which way the wind was blowing, further distanced himself from Kelly and the big clubs when he said: 'There is a strong mood that eighteen is too small.' This was too much, even for Kelly, who commented that he and the FA 'would hate the prospect – my feeling has always been that the right figure is eighteen and that twenty-two is too many.' If the price of Kelly's original support for a Premier League had been an eighteen-club entity, the price now of support from the fifteen or so clubs comprising the majority in the new league was the abandonment of the eighteen-club concept, at least for the foreseeable future, and the dropping of other criteria that were contained in the Blueprint, particularly the call for minimum stadia capacities and financial controls. Thus the eighteen-club ideal was lost, partly because the FA, with Kelly receding more into the background, did not fight hard enough for it; partly because of the influence exerted by the bulk of First Division clubs and partly because pragmatism was always going to win out over idealism.

David Dein recalled the argument. 'The clubs didn't want to lose another two home fixtures. It was a short-term view as usual in football. Meanwhile, they would receive [through the sale of television rights] wealth beyond possible measure.' The repercussions of the argument would rumble on, gather pace, and engulf just about every aspect of the new league's operations as the organisation, which was not even legally formed, degenerated into the kind of faction fighting that had characterised the old Football League.

A majority of clubs now believed that they should go for autonomy, in order to be in control of their own destiny. David Dein saw the FA as an ally rather than a threat. 'There was a good deal of kudos to being part of the FA,' he said. 'We would be working directly with the governing body to drive the game forward.' Dein was virtually a lone voice, however as there was opposition from other clubs which were suspicious of what the alliance with the FA might lead to.

On July 17 1991, the Premier League founder members' agreement was signed, which led to the legal establishment of the League one month later. There was no mention of an eighteen-club ideal. Although the idea of entry criteria was rather woolly, at least it had not disappeared completely. Part of clause 2 of the agreement states: 'There will be entry criteria after an agreed time period.' The agreement also made it clear that all decisions would be taken on a 'one club, one vote basis'. FA control of the new entity had all but disappeared. The new league would be called the FA Premier League but that was about all the say the FA now possessed, and it would not be long before even that meagre consolation was eroded.

Later, Ken Bates explained his strategy at the time. 'When we had the founders' meeting,' he said, 'David Dein was so over the moon at getting his little Premier League and couldn't understand why Ken Bates was being so supportive. We got a few things in there ... He is only now beginning to realise what hit him. One club, one vote, no committees, only self-liquidating working parties, so you had no permanent chance to be in the corridors of power or have committee influence.'

Shortly before the start of the 1991–92 season, the entire First Division gave one year's notice of their intention to resign from the Football League. By then, on July 31, the High Court had ruled that the FA possessed the authority to run a league and therefore (crucially as far as the Premier League was concerned) was within its rights to disallow Football League regulation 11, which required three years' notice. The League was left without a functioning Management Committee as the Premier League club representatives vacated their positions. Totally defeated, the Football League, at first threatening to appeal against the High Court judgement, switched tactics to negotiate for some form of compensation. In reality, the League was paralysed and had to appoint an administrator to run its affairs. It eventually accepted £3 million from the FA and Premier League, half of its claim. For its part in the compensation settlement, the Football League sanctioned the Premier League and revoked regulation 11. The coup was almost complete.

A new and more formidable adversary was about to appear, however, in the shape of Gordon Taylor's Professional Footballers Association (PFA). Taylor had been used in the past to help the Football League avert threatened break-aways, particularly in 1988, and was held in considerable respect throughout football. He had been one of the Premier League's sternest critics and insisted that the stars among his members would refuse to play in the new league if it was to the detriment of those in the lower divisions.

In December, the Premier League took another step towards autonomy by appointing the chairman of Barclays Bank, Sir John Quinton, to the position of part-time, unpaid chairman of the Premier League. Within days, Quinton laid into Gordon Taylor's threats to ballot his members for strike action if the PFA were not included in the decision-making process. Trades unions, according to Quinton, had no right to participate in management. This insensitive view brought even more support for Taylor's position. Quinton had not realised that footballers, unlike bank employees, elicit widespread fondness and their leader, Taylor, was one union representative who could not be dismissed lightly. Meanwhile, the Football League, which had itself often indulged in arguments with the players' union in the past, invited Taylor to become a member of a revamped Management Committee. The issue of the PFA role came to a head over television money. Under an agreement with the Football League, the PFA was entitled to 10 per cent of television revenue, but Taylor had waived half of this sum in 1988 in the interests of unity. Now he insisted that the PFA's full share was essential to secure the future of professional players in the lower divisions.

The threat of a players' strike disrupted the Premier League's negotiations with television. As 1992 began, Taylor decided that if push came to shove, he would definitely ballot his members. Quinton and Parry, meanwhile, tried to portray the players as greedy but this cut little ice with the media and the fans. The PFA had, after all, stepped in to assist ailing clubs, keeping some, such as Northampton and Aldershot, in business when support from the rest of the game had been conspicuous by its absence. Taylor easily destroyed the argument that he was acting out of self-interest. 85 per cent of Division 1 players started in the lower divisions,' he stated, 'and 95 per cent of them finish their playing careers or start in management there.'

With little progress in the early weeks of 1992, and stories circulating of massive amounts of television money in the offing, Taylor sent out ballot papers in February. The players gave their leader massive support and voted to boycott televised matches by 548 votes to 37. The issue began to reveal splits within the new league. While Parry and Quinton, with support from Ken Bates, pushed for a hard line to be taken, some chairmen, including Martin Edwards and Doug Ellis, were meeting with Taylor to hammer out a compromise. Eventually, the Premier League capitulated and Taylor got the deal he was seeking: 10 per cent of the first £10 million, 5 per cent between £10 million and £20 million, 2.5 per cent between £20 million and £30 million and 5 per cent of everything above £30 million, with a minimum guarantee of £1.5 million.

Significantly, the FA sat on the sidelines during the rumpus and played no part in the negotiations. The incident showed once again that it was now the clubs, not the FA, that were dictating events within the Premier League. Only the players were determined enough to stand in their way.

Having secured the existence of the Premier League, Rick Parry was appointed acting chief executive until August. On February 20, the FA Council finally approved the Blueprint, which included the Premier League, but without any commitment to the principle of eighteen clubs. The League was to begin with twenty-two the following August. Parry was convinced that his earlier judgement had been correct. The balance of power within the Premier League now lay with the clubs outside the Big Five. This would be reaffirmed when the new league signed a television contract with BSkyB against the wishes of the top clubs.

Amid the rancour and recriminations, a working structure for the Premier League had to be built. As the ramifications of the television deal with BSkyB spilled over into other arguments, including sponsorship, money, as always, seemed to dominate the agenda of meetings of the Premier League's clubs.

In July, the imminence of a new season and the launch of the Premier League at least concentrated David Dein's mind. Trying to put the bitterness he felt over the television agreement behind him, he pushed for the establishment of a strategy for the new league with a timetable to fulfil agreed objectives. Dein had come to realise, albeit late in the day, that the high hopes that had led him to knock on the FA's door eighteen months before were now just broken dreams. 'I've got to put my hand on my heart and say that there's no difference between us and the old Football League,' he told the club chairmen, 'because we haven't created one.' Dein's disillusionment came to a head at the penultimate meeting of the Premier League, before the big kick-off on August 15. At the end of a long session on July 27, and after the agenda had covered such subjects as the chief executive, sponsorship, television, overseas sales, rules and committees, Dein once again raised what was now recognised as a pet subject of his, criteria.

He wanted, above all, to establish a timetable for an eighteen-club League but he realised he was 'banging my head against a brick wall on this one', because it had been excluded from the founder members' agreement. He also wanted minimum standards introduced for pitches, flood-lights and stadium facilities ('fifty people per urinal, or what-ever the architects tell us'). The standards would also have to include minimum seating capacities 'so that if Cambridge come up they will know what they will have to do'. However, Dein's proposals were summarily dismissed and the meeting abruptly terminated leaving Dein nonplussed. This caused no small amount of satisfaction to a number of the other chairmen, who saw Dein as a troublemaker.

David Dein was not the only prophet in the wilderness. One of Alex Fynn's recommendations in the Blueprint was the creation of a new post at the FA, that of commercial director. It was one of the few proposals that was adopted. The FA advertised the position and received 200 applications, including one from Fynn himself. He and the other 199 need not have bothered, and the man whose commercial knowl-edge had been included in the Blueprint without question did not even rate an interview. The position had been earmarked for Trevor Phillips in a classic case of jobs for the boys.

In this cosy world of ex-Football League employees and consultants (Kelly, Parry and now Phillips), where was the objectivity and strength of character to do what was best for football going to come from? Who could now tell the Premier League chairmen that enough was enough and force them to institute a timetable for getting down to eighteen clubs?

David Dein's view is that 'the FA were simply not strong enough in the early stages. They left it to Parry and that was wrong. They should have been far more involved in every decision-making process. After all, it's their League, they've got a golden share, a right of veto.' The FA, however, weakly acquiesced when it came to what was supposed to be its primary objective, an eighteen-club league. Graham Kelly took the soft option. He told BBC's *Public Eye* programme in May that he was only 'hopeful but not convinced that they [the clubs] agree ... We wanted an eighteen-club top league and we've had to compromise.'

The soft underbelly of English football had been well and truly punctured and it was about to happen all over again. The big clubs, or a majority of them at least, had decided they could rarely get their own way in a straight fight under a one club, one vote system. Neither could they rely on Graham Kelly or Rick Parry for support. It was the ultimate irony that those who had caused the break-away to secure more power for their own views had now been stripped of most of their power within the twenty-two-headed monster they had created.

With acrimony breaking out everywhere, the Premier League limped into operation. The public were somewhat underwhelmed, and in the first few weeks of the season attendances were down, a situation not wholly attributable to reduced capacities at a number of grounds, such as Arsenal, Manchester United and Leeds. The real battle, though, had come over one issue. Rick Parry could hardly have suspected, when he began to hear of the massive amount of money available, that its source would cause more problems than all the other arguments put together. The greatest rift of all came about directly as a result of the deal Parry had recommended to the clubs of the Premier League. The issue that created all the problems was television.

4

Amateur Night in Dixie

The battle for television rights

'We've served up the dinner and they've [the small clubs] eaten it, gravy and all.'

David Dein to Irving Scholar.

'They've taken the cutlery as well.'

Irving Scholar.

'I think that this is the best thing that's happened to football in years.'

Sam Hammam, owner of Wimbledon, after the Premier League agreed to sign a television deal with BSkyB in May 1992.

'This is for the long haul. And the long haul means, in the end, pay-per-view. That is going to be the answer.'

Paul Fox, ex-managing director of Yorkshire Television, on the same deal.

As the inaugural season of the Premier League got underway, confrontations over football matters were becoming as intense in the High Court as they were on any field of play. The law courts in the Strand were a novel, if unwelcome addition to the already numerous football venues of the capital. At the end of September 1992, lawyers representing the Football

Association were once again asking the judiciary to rule in their favour, this time over a dispute with the satellite broadcaster, BSkyB. With the ink barely dry on a five-year contract between the parties, Sky requested an injunction against the FA, accusing its new partner of restraint of trade.

It was a far cry from the eulogies of four months earlier, when Premier League chief executive Rick Parry and chairman Sir John Quinton had extolled the virtues of Rupert Murdoch's television service to the club chairmen and the world. Neither did it bear much relation to the arguments about partnership emanating from Lancaster Gate when the FA signed its other properties, the FA Cup and the England team, to Sky and the BBC in June.

Thirty years ago such litigation would have been inconceivable. Then, televised football was merely a novel way of bringing the game to the attention of a wider public and giving to the committed supporter a chance to view teams other than his own on a regular basis, but the medium did not significantly benefit the game's finances. As the years passed, however, the number of hours devoted to sport by television companies increased. Across Europe, the time allocated more than quadrupled in the decade from 1970. In England, the game's authorities (with a few notable exceptions such as Robert Maxwell, Irving Scholar, David Dein and Ken Bates) took somewhat longer to recognise football's growing interdependence with the small screen, but elsewhere the lessons were absorbed and applied. Following the example shown by the development of televised sport in the USA, first Italy, then France, Germany and Spain all began to insist that television paid more money for football. When this continental movement reached its peak in the latter half of the 1980s, football in England had been forced off the screen for half a season in a dispute over a meagre amount of money – a fraction of the price continental television was paying – and the image of the game was at such an all-time low following the Heysel tragedy that English clubs had been banned from European competitions, thus cutting the nation adrift from the mainstream of European developments. This process gave added impetus to the 'little Englander' mentality with which the football authorities had always been more than a little acquainted.

The dramatic revaluation in television rights began as a consequence of the huge audiences that sport delivered through its major tournaments and events, especially the NFL Superbowl, the World Cup and the Olympic Games. This trend caused advertising agencies, whose research techniques were becoming more sophisticated, to pay closer attention to the football-viewing public than had hitherto been the case. They came to realise that not only mega-events but also domestic football could deliver audiences of high value (free-spending young men) to their clients better than any other type of programming. When, in England, live Sunday football began, the television industry woke up to the fact that what was previously considered a 'dead' time in the schedules could actually draw up to 10 million viewers. Finally, the advent of new delivery systems in the shape of satellite and cable brought competition to a previously complacent marketplace.

In the UK, any idea of competition gave way to a cosy relationship between ITV and the BBC which created a cartel to keep the price paid to football as low as possible. The television companies had been encouraged to establish their ties with each other by the result of another court action, fought between the BBC and ITV in 1979, when an ITV bid organised by Michael Grade for exclusive rights to League matches, known at the time as 'Snatch of the Day', was declared against the public interest.

By the end of the 1980s such considerations were deemed irrelevant. In the world of deregulation, market forces were the name of the game. The new players on the stage, as far as British football was concerned, consisted of Sky and British Satellite Broadcasting (BSB). The entry of these two forced a radical rethink on the part of the traditional broadcasters, the BBC and ITV. The first skirmish took place in 1988, when BSB made an audacious bid for football. ITV came off best then by scooping exclusive rights to League action through some sharp tactics employed by Greg Dyke, the head of ITV Sport. Dyke, assisted by David Dein, Philip Carter, Irving Scholar and Martin Edwards, made an offer to the Big Five which then threatened to sign their own television contract with ITV if the rest of the League voted to accept the BSB bid. At the time League rules made it clear that television deals could only be concluded by agreement of a majority of all ninety-two clubs but the Big Five stuck to their guns and the rest of the League caved in.

There is good reason to believe that the defeat BSB suffered not only cost the company dish sales in the battle with Sky but proved a very public rebuff, causing a sap in morale from which the company never recovered. Two years later, in November 1990, BSB and Sky merged to form a single service, BSkyB. Perhaps merged is too loose a term since there was no question that in all but name, Sky had taken over its rival. Rupert Murdoch's company, News International, owned the biggest stake by far and before long all semblance of the old BSB had disappeared.

One tangible prize which Sky gained from the merger was a football contract of substance. Although BSB had lost out on the Football League deal, the company did manage to acquire, in association with the BBC, the FA Cup and England internationals. The BBC, not having the finance to compete head-to-head with ITV and in danger of being frozen out, made an historic decision to throw in its lot with BSB in order to retain a share of the FA's rights. It was the first time a terrestrial broadcaster had joined forces with one of the rival satellite companies. That watershed decision marked a radical redrawing of the battle lines and was crucial to the outcome of the negotiations when bidding began for the Premier League.

As a consequence of the 1988 ITV deal, it had at last dawned on the vast majority of football club chairmen that television, and the sponsorship and ground advertising revenue that came with it was becoming ever more important to the finances of the game. Before 1988, English football received less than £5 million per season from television. After 1988 the figure rose to over £20 million with every prospect that even this sum could be bettered in the future. However, few in the higher echelons of football appreciated the true extent of the potential: that Sky needed to be available in over 3 million homes to trade profitably; that football could be the catalyst that made the target feasible by 1993; that as a result of satellite growth ITV would lose audience share, particularly among young viewers, and football provided the means to halt the drift; and that the BBC had an emotional commitment to the restoration of the Saturday night highlights programme Match of the Day, which had been the first show to create a mass television audience for the game. Whatever the level of knowledge within football, these trends meant only one thing. A Dutch auction was about to begin.

Trevor Phillips, then commercial director of the Football League, saw what was coming when he launched 'One Game, One Team, One Voice' in 1990: 'For many years,' he said, 'the BBC and ITV operated as a cartel in order to keep the price of football down to a minimum ... It would be unwise and commercially naïve if football were not to apply the same cartel principle in order to keep the price up. With respect to television, football is about to enter an era of unprecedented opportunity but also of great risk, if one is to maintain a balance and ensure that we do not compromise our basic values and beliefs, that paying, attending spectators are an integral part of the event itself. Football as an industry must have a long-term policy with regard to television, not only to ensure that we maximise the commercial opportunities, but more importantly to control the output.'

While Phillips' words would prove to be prophetic, there were others who not only recognised what the future would bring but possessed the power to do something about it. Of these, the most committed was David Dein. Clubs like Arsenal, he reasoned, should no longer have to share television earnings with the likes of Hartlepool because they were catering for different markets and the Hartlepools of this world should plan to be self-sufficient, no longer reliant on hand-outs from above. The logical conclusion to this line of thinking was the break-away Premier League.

Rick Parry had been brought in by Graham Kelly to do the spadework, in particular to extricate the twenty-two First Division clubs from the Football League and write a rule book and constitution, but Parry was not experienced in television negotiations, where a knowledge of the shifting legal and commercial considerations governing rights is essential if a sport is going to achieve the optimum deal. Nonetheless, having been confirmed as chief executive designate, the task of negotiating a contract would eventually fall to him, due to the high level of mutual suspicion generated among the twenty-two chairmen.

David Dein recognised Parry's strengths. 'He did an excellent job [in getting the First Division out of the Football League], that was his forte.' Ken Bates had other reasons for supporting Parry. 'I was instrumental in getting [him] the job,' Bates said, a reference to some dissent within the Premier League about Parry being confirmed as chief executive. 'The fact that he has no experience is absolutely a first-class reason for giving him the job,' the Chelsea chairman continued 'He had no preconceived notions. He was not under the influence of any club chairman. He didn't have any allegiance to any particular club ... He came in with a totally dispassionate manner and I can tell you he does a bloody good job. He's very efficient and that's why some people don't like him. He's not susceptible to being influenced.'

Nonetheless, David Dein was worried that Parry's inexperience would be ruthlessly exposed by the television companies. Initially, his fears were allayed when a working party was set up, comprising Dein, Ron Noades of Crystal Palace and Bill Fotherby, managing director of Leeds, but the group was disbanded after only two sessions (or, as Ken Bates would put it, it liquidated itself). Before its demise, the working party recommended that the Premier League sell one live game per week to a satellite station, and one to a terrestrial broadcaster, with one highlights package also on offer (by coincidence the plan was based on the same schedule Alex Fynn used in his estimate of what the Premier League could contribute to the £112 million which appeared in the FA's Blueprint). However, perhaps because some chairmen had never really forgiven Dein for negotiating the 1988 deal with ITV when he was mandated as a member of the Football League Management Committee to represent the interests of all ninety-two League clubs (though to this day Dein insists the ITV contract benefited the league as a whole by bringing in nearly £50 million over four years), the Premier League chairmen decided to leave negotiations in the hands of their collective chairman, the part-timer Sir John Quinton, and the chief executive, Rick Parry.

While the working party was in existence, Dein, a good friend of Greg Dyke's, entered into informal discussions with ITV. These, according to Dein, were a natural consequence of ITV being the existing contract-holder rather than part of a duplicitous strategy. The discussions gave Dein the impression that co-operation between the various television companies would be difficult. Meanwhile, those long-time opponents of ITV, Ron Noades and Ken Bates, went to see the owner of Sky, one of the world's biggest media moguls, Rupert Murdoch, along with Sky's managing director, Sam Chisholm, and the satellite station's head of sport, Dave Hill, at Murdoch's London apartment just off St James's. Having been served smoked salmon and champagne, Ken Bates came to the point. 'There's no problem about it, Mr Murdoch,' he said. 'We can deliver you English football but we want £50 million a year.'

If Murdoch was taken aback by the figure he didn't let it show. 'Well, yes,' he replied, 'I'm sure you will be able to organise that in good time.' Bates, however, wanted to be clear. 'No,' he stated, 'we want £50 million from the start, the add-ons come later.'

Given that there was no consensus among chairmen, it was understandable that the Premier League decided to go for independent mediation. The problem lay in the personnel selected.

A group of chairmen became seriously concerned as Quinton and Parry went about their task. As David Dein later recalled, 'We had no idea what he [Rick Parry] was thinking. We had no idea he'd got David Plowright [ex-Granada television] on board until much later when negotiations were taking place. I kept saying that the right method should be for all broadcasters to present to us so that we could see what type of production they were going to do, what their scheduling was going to be. It was the most important contract we would make – let them present to us.' Dein's suggestion, however, was brushed aside. He now had to rely on the fact that Parry and Quinton could not finalise a deal without a two-thirds majority vote by chairmen. Parry was detailed to gain as much information as possible on the various bids and to bring them to a meeting of the chairmen for the vote to be taken. He understood his brief to mean that he was in place to analyse all the bids and make a recommendation as to which would be the best to adopt. The way he conducted the bidding process, however, was never defined. The bottom line was that Parry would brief the chairmen, and the chairmen would then vote.

ITV had made it clear that it would bid big money for the

Premier League. The contract of 1988 had proved beyond all doubt to have been a commercial success. Advertisers flocked to *The Match* and some brewers put 20 per cent of their advertising spend into the programme. *The Match* gave advertisers those free-spending young men they craved. No one knew this better than Greg Dyke. Dyke had made his name in television by saving TV-AM from oblivion with Roland Rat, and his coup for football rights in 1988 had cemented his reputation. In 1991, as chief executive of London Weekend Television, he masterminded LWT's bid to retain its ITV franchise. The 1988 football deal was part of his strategy to 'strangle the satellite threat at birth'. If the BBC's response to the challenge that satellite services posed was to seek joint arrangements, ITV, in the shape of Dyke, was completely hostile, and Dyke sought to take on Sky at every turn. Dyke had made enemies, though, by the way he had conducted the 1988 negotiations, one of whom was Ken Bates. 'I was determined to get Greg Dyke,' he revealed.

David Dein, meanwhile, had been examining a revolutionary concept. He had been approached by the Swiss Bank Corporation (SBC) to help produce a proposal, code-named Project Premier, for the Premier League to operate its own television channel beamed from the Astra satellite, the same system used by Sky. Neil Duncanson, head of sport at Chrysalis Television, one of the largest of the country's independent producers, was drafted in to produce a sample week's schedule. Project Premier envisaged a live Premier League game every day of the week except Thursday (thirty-two live games per month) and estimated profits of up to £50 million in 1992–93, predominantly through subscription payments. Dein passed the proposal to Rick Parry but it was never fully debated by the chairman perhaps because it involved a projected cost base of £20 million per year, which would have to be guaranteed by the Premier League.

Exactly what happened with the Swiss Bank Corporation became the subject of another legal dispute, the bank later claiming it was owed over £2 million in fees by the Premier League, which Parry disputed. Whatever the merits of the SBC case, the misunderstanding was just the start of a long line of inconsistencies and confusing decisions which were to characterise the television negotiations. What is not in doubt is that Parry dealt with SBC well into 1992, suggesting to ITV as late as April that the two organisations should get together to offer complementary services.

Just as Alex Fynn had played a crucial role in defining the commercial future for the FA and therefore the Premier League, so Lynton Guest gradually became embroiled in the unfolding events. One afternoon in the summer of 1991, Guest was walking along Ladbroke Grove in west London when he saw a large banner over the entrance to the Earl Percy public house. 'Sportscast Available Here', it read. Intrigued, he made enquiries which eventually led to a meeting with the head of Sportscast, Gerald O'Connell, and an article in the *Sunday Telegraph* about the company. Sportscast was owned by British Aerospace and has since ceased trading, but at the time it was providing a sports television service broadcast by satellite into licensed premises.

O'Connell is one of the unsung heroes of football marketing. In the mid-1980s he invented, along with a colleague, Mark Rooney, the concept of premium-rate sports telephone lines. The business, of which the best known part is Clubcall, was put together with British Telecom despite resistance from football clubs, which could not imagine their supporters paying to make phone calls to find out information about their team. 'We were thrown out of many clubs,' recalled O'Connell, 'and most of the others just couldn't understand how they could make money.' Today, Clubcall, which was bought from BT by the betting shop chain Ladbrokes for £40 million, pays royalties of some £7 million per season to football clubs and no club is now without its own 0898 number.

After Clubcall, O'Connell was poached by British Aerospace, which had won valuable satellite licences from the British government but, as a company with traditions in hardware manufacturing, was not sure what to do with them. Among other ideas, O'Connell came up with the concept of Sportscast. Unfortunately, British Aerospace was soon to suffer from a disastrous rights issue of new shares, which led to the demise of its chairman, Roland Smith (also the chairman of Manchester United plc). As British Aerospace retrenched and concentrated on core activities in response to the company's financial troubles, Sportscast was denied the investment it required and O'Connell left. When Guest interviewed him for the article in the *Sunday Telegraph*, O'Connell asked him a disconcerting question. Having ascertained Guest's affiliations (he is a Leicester City supporter), he said: 'If you were guaranteed to see every Leicester game, home and away, on television, in full but not necessarily live and sometimes at three in the morning, would you pay £10 a month for that service?'

From this came the idea to offer a satellite service which showed every game in the Premier League and Football League in full but in recorded form, thus offering committed supporters access to their club, wherever they lived in the UK. The cost of £10 per month was little more than two calls per week on a Clubcall line. Research showed that there was a core market of 1 million 'must-have' football households. The beauty of the concept was that since it did not encroach on live televised matches, a separate, lucrative deal could be struck with a terrestrial broadcaster for live rights. It was a non-exclusive offer which could produce a total revenue of £100 million in its first year, at least half of which could go straight to the game.

In the months to come Guest would advise the company O'Connell and his partners formed to try to get a share of the television contract, Full Time Communications (FTC). The FTC plan was raised by Guest in a private meeting with Graham Kelly around Christmas 1991. Over mince pies in the chief executive's office, the two discussed not only FTC but the general way in which all negotiations for television would be conducted.

At the beginning of 1992, the bidding began to get underway in earnest. Kelly informed FTC that talks should be conducted with Rick Parry and Glen Kirton, who were representing the Premier League and FA interests respectively. What was becoming increasingly obvious at this stage was that the Football League were well and truly out in the cold and Graham Kelly would not have a significant input into any of the television negotiations.

Trevor Phillips knew well enough what the implications were for his own organisation if the Premier League took the lion's share of the television cake. The rancour engendered by the break-up, however, had left him in a considerably weakened position and relations between the Football League on the one hand and the FA and Premier League clubs on the other had seriously deteriorated. The two governing bodies virtually stopped communicating except where necessary to keep the game functioning (one exception to this was the head-hunting of Phillips for the job of commercial director of the FA while delicate television negotiations were taking place). In order to get the best out of television, football needed to negotiate, as Phillips had pointed out in 1990, as one united body. That view had been confirmed by Alex Fynn and Zenith in their advice to the FA in 1991. There was now not a snowball's chance in hell of it happening.

Despite the emergence of new ideas the real battle was always going to be between ITV and Sky for the Premier League. On January 7 1992, Greg Dyke and ITV's executive director of football, Trevor East, met with Rick Parry and Sir John Quinton at the Barclays Bank head office in the City of London. The irony of the venue will not be lost on supporters of teams then in the Barclays Football League. The meeting was cordial and the two ITV executives left believing they could come up with a winning bid. ITV had every reason to feel confident but in fact Parry was already wavering. Trevor East, moreover, knew Parry had been talking to Sky and was worried. During the meeting, East brought up a newspaper article he had read which claimed that Rupert Murdoch and his companies were in debt to Barclays to the tune of £135 million in the UK and £4 billion worldwide. How, he asked Sir John, can you give out a contract which will increase that debt? Perhaps a more pertinent question would have been: how can you not give it to Sky if it is going to make one of Barclays' most important customers less of a long-term risk? Subsequently, Trevor East said he felt that Parry also had good reason to plump for Sky. If he didn't he would lose the support of Ron Noades, Ken Bates and the rest of the anti-ITV faction within the Premier League. If that happened Parry's chances of getting the chief executive's job on a long-term basis would be reduced to zero.

In February information was leaked to the press that ITV was prepared to offer £20 million a year to the Premier League for a four-year deal, providing the coverage was exclusive.

'We have made a bid and we are confident of winning,' Greg Dyke exclaimed. Exclusivity was one of the central planks of Dyke's strategy. Quite simply, if he had the Premier League, Sky didn't, thus their dish sales would slow down and their sports channel would lack substance. Any co-operation with a satellite company was anathema to ITV, and the events of 1988 had given Dyke the confidence that he could win again.

However, the BBC was making it clear that it could not afford to compete against ITV and Sky by itself. This was manna from heaven for Sky. The one great disadvantage under which the satellite company was labouring was that the number of households able to receive its service was only about 2 million, compared to the 20 million plus who could tune into ITV. Therefore, there were bound to be arguments, particularly from the big clubs, that Sky's level of viewers was too low to maintain the game as a national spectacle and that lucrative sponsorship and advertising deals would be affected if brands did not have the platform of terrestrial television. As Sky had inherited the old BSB-BBC contract, the idea of co-operation between Sky and the BBC was already well established. If Sky could provide the cash and the BBC the national profile, a joint bid could be mounted for the Premier League which could match anything ITV offered. While ITV made the running publicly, Sky and the BBC were getting together to discuss their alliance.

Parry and Quinton had, by March, gained a good idea of the kind of offers they would be receiving. None of the various bids were directly comparable and, as neither man possessed a deep understanding of the medium with which they were dealing, it was decided to call in professional advice. Amazingly, the person who had told them what their product was worth, Alex Fynn, was not even considered. At the time relations between the FA and Saatchi and Saatchi had deteriorated over the former's unwillingness to allow Saatchis to implement its television and sponsorship proposals, the very plans the FA had previously accepted and published in the Blueprint. Instead, Parry and Quinton brought in a company called Academy, owned by another advertising agency, Lowe Howard Spink, to advise on sponsorship, and the former head of Granada Television, David Plowright, to explain the merits of the various television bids.

Plowright was a strange choice. He had presided over the incredible success of Granada over a number of years but had been forced out of the company when deregulation came along and it was having to cut costs. His leaving had been acrimonious to say the least, and he had accused the new regime of being more interested in accounting than making television programmes. How such a person could give an unbiased opinion on a situation in which ITV was involved was a question that never seemed to bother Parry, who failed to inform his chairmen of Plowright's role until it was too late for them to do anything about it.

On March 25, FTC went public, and its offer was described in *The Times* under the headline FOOTBALL OFFERED £500 MILLION IN TV DEAL. Before its involvement, the amount on offer to the Premier League by other broadcasters was in the region of £20 million. Unfortunately, the FTC proposal suffered from two fatal flaws. First, it assumed that a deal could be made with the whole of football. Unless the proposed channel could screen Football League games along with the Premier League, then it could not achieve its objective of making itself desirable to every football fan. Second, there was a widespread suspicion over the financing of the FTC project. No one knew who their backers were or where the money would come from (in fact, FTC had been promised funding from the Saudi Arabian royal family, channelled through Greek and American intermediaries. The promised finance, however, was not in place when Parry and Quinton wanted to move and FTC ran out of time).

Parry and Glen Kirton informed FTC in March that the Premier League and the FA could not negotiate a deal that involved the Football League. The League, so FTC was told, had done everything possible to thwart the FA's plans, so now, according to Kirton, 'We are going to teach them a lesson.' It was clear that the FA and Premier League would conduct negotiations solely on the basis of what was good for them. While the real implications of the FTC concept – that television was entering an era when the uses to which it could be put were set to multiply – never seemed to register with Parry and Kirton, they did realise that they could use the vast amounts of money that FTC research had shown to be available to lever better deals out of Sky, ITV and the BBC.

As the Premier League became embroiled in the threatened players' strike, television took a back seat for a time. During this period, Sky boss Sam Chisholm produced a new offer, this time in conjunction with the BBC, which would bring back *Match of the Day*, the Saturday night highlights programme. Chisholm also introduced a new element, the prospect of further huge amounts of cash from a pay-per-view operation.

There are three main ways a commercial television operation can produce revenue. First, through advertising and on-air (or 'broadcast') sponsorship; second, through subscription payments and third, through a charge for each programme watched (pay-per-view). At the time, Sky's sports channel earned income through advertising (only the film channels were subscription-based). There was some talk of subscription being extended if the company secured the rights to the Premier League, although David Dein claims it was never made clear that a subscription payment would be introduced from the beginning of a contract. Pay-per-view, however, certainly was discussed, and held out as the alternative means by which football could earn the sums forecast by the Swiss Bank and FTC analyses. Parry, who had no experience of pay-per-view, appeared to be mesmerised.

What anyone who understood television could have told him, but of which he remained blissfully unaware until it was too late, was that pay-per-view is not the holy grail it has been held out to be. There is only one market in which it has been introduced on a widespread basis and that is North America. The Sky plan claimed it could eventually put up to sixty matches a season on pay-per-view, whereas all the evidence from North America suggests that pay-per-view works only when an extraordinary event is involved, a heavyweight, world-title boxing bout, for instance. Indeed, NBC's attempt to put a large part of the Barcelona Olympics on to pay-per-view had been a signal failure. NBC never attracted more than 250,000 of the 2 million customers it was looking for and in order to achieve even that level had to slash the rate from $29.95 to $10.95. It should have been a lesson in price sensitivity and scarcity value for football. In the UK, perhaps the semi-finals and final of the FA Cup could tempt fans to pay (in fact the FA Cup final is banned from exclusive transmission on pay-per-view by an Act of Parliament), but it cannot work for the regular fare of league matches. The idea was a non-starter from the outset, yet Parry latched on to it with the tenacity of a pit bull terrier. Moreover, there was a question-mark over Sky's ability to deliver a pay-per-view system to dish-owners with its existing technology, particularly if it also operated a subscription service on the same channel. To get around the problem Sky intends to launch a second sports channel in 1994.

Meanwhile, ITV established a fall-back position for itself by initiating talks with Trevor Phillips at the Football League. The move suggested a lesser degree of confidence in ITV's bid for the Premier League than their bullish public statements led everyone to believe. As the discussions continued, Greg Dyke offered the League £6 million per year for regional coverage of First Division games. This did not stop Trevor East continuing talks with Rick Parry, who, East claimed, told him that he would be supporting the ITV bid. On April 13, Parry invited ITV to meet the Swiss Bank Corporation to see whether the two could work together. The meeting took place two days later but, given ITV's antipathy towards agreements with satellite channels, the chances of the two joining forces were virtually nil. In the event, the most ITV offered by way of co-operation with SBC was to form a working party to study the proposal. Trevor East met Rick Parry in Manchester on April 25 to give him a revised ITV bid, which had been increased to top the £30 million which was now on offer from Sky and the BBC. Almost two weeks later, during which time East had received no news from Parry, the Premier League man rang East to tell him that he still supported the ITV bid. East asked Parry about Sky and claimed that Parry replied: 'Don't worry, they would have to come up with £100 million a year.' East left for a holiday in the Lake District comforted by what he thought was Parry's wholehearted support for ITV.

Sky, for its part, worked up the pay-per-view figures and put them alongside the offer of £30 million. It also introduced the prospect of guaranteed extra income from sponsorship and overseas sales which would make the Premier League the recipient of some £200 million over four years. A meeting of the club chairmen was set for Monday May 18, at which the rival bids would be put before the assembled representatives.

By now, Parry had jettisoned the Swiss Bank and the FTC ideas. FTC was not even informed that the meeting was going to vote on the bids and neither the FTC bid nor the Swiss Bank concept was put to the chairmen for consideration.

The week before the fateful meeting saw a flurry of activity and lobbying. Parry went to Sky headquarters at Livingston in Scotland, where Sky pulled out all the stops to win him over with a comprehensive presentation. He also met Rupert Murdoch. Murdoch personally convinced Parry that he should support the Sky bid and that he, Murdoch, would throw the weight of his newspapers behind Sky's plans. The Murdoch approach must have worked because Parry indicated to Greg Dyke on the Thursday that he was switching his support to Sky. He also informed Dyke of the agreement between Sky and the BBC, which had been concluded the previous week. 'If you're now going to go against us,' Dyke told Parry, 'I will have to resort to going directly to the clubs.' It was a threat to do what Dyke had successfully done in 1988, peel off the top clubs from the rest by promising extensive coverage as well as large amounts of money. Over the weekend Dyke and his team worked to produce a new offer which they would place before the meeting on Monday. Having been informed that Parry was now firmly in Sky's camp, Dyke decided to follow up on his threat by having Trevor East hand an envelope containing the ITV bid to each chairman personally, rather than have Parry present it on ITV's behalf.

East gave the new ITV offer to Parry at 8.20 on the morning of the meeting at the Royal Lancaster Hotel in London. ITV's bid was for £155 million over five years for thirty live games a season, rising to £262 million when overseas sales and sponsorship were added. Soon after, he delivered the same offer to all the Premier League representatives along with a letter of explanation as to why ITV thought its offer the best. What happened next was perhaps the most bizarre incident in the whole sorry tale. After handing out the envelopes, Trevor East was sitting in the hotel lobby reading a newspaper when his attention was drawn to an extremely agitated phone conversation going on almost next to him. The voice he could hear belonged to Alan Sugar, chairman of Tottenham Hotspur plc, the public company of which the football club is a subsidiary. It later transpired that Sugar had been talking to Sam Chisholm of Sky and had told him the details of ITV's new bid. According to evidence East later gave to the High Court, Sugar was obviously having problems in making himself clear. 'You don't seem to understand what I'm talking about,' Sugar shouted down the phone. 'These are the figures, take them down. You'd better get something done. You'd better get someone down here quickly ... Blow them out of the water.'

Just as the significance of the audible side of the conversation was sinking in, East spied Terry Venables, who had left the meeting to see a delegation from Lazio and act out another instalment in the continuing saga of the Paul Gascoigne transfer. East accosted him and complained bitterly about Sugar's phone call. 'Your chairman is giving out our figures,' he said. Venables' reply was unusually terse. 'What the fuck do you expect me to do about it?' he railed as he disappeared towards the lift.

East was still not overly concerned about events in the lobby. He thought that since the meeting had started there was nothing Sky could do to top the ITV bid. What he didn't know was that as the meeting got underway, Parry was in an adjacent room, ostensibly looking through ITV's new offer but in reality receiving yet another revised bid from Sam Chisholm. Chisholm upped Sky's offer to more than £35 million in year one, rising to just under £40 million in year five for sixty live games a season. In addition, the BBC would pay £4.5 million per year for recorded highlights, which, together with anticipated revenue from overseas sales (£8 million a year) and sponsorship (£10 million a year) made a grand total of £304 million over five years. Parry went back into the meeting triumphant.

A discussion ensued during which it became clear that the Premier League was split into three factions. Sam Hammam led one strand of opinion, supported by Parry and Quinton, that the League should accept the offer from Sky. Other smaller clubs were less committed to either bidder but simply looked at the difference in the money between the two. Outright opposition to Sky came from Martin Edwards of Manchester United, Doug Ellis of Aston Villa, Peter Robinson of Liverpool and, most vociferously, from Arsenal's David

Dein. Dein later recalled how the most important talks in the history of negotiations between football and television were conducted. 'When you analyse the offers, they weren't bidding like for like. It's quite astonishing and appalling that we're looking at a contract – a global contract if you take in sponsorship and the overseas sales – in excess of £300 million and there was only one scruffy piece of paper ... without any representatives from the broadcasters, no visual presentations from the executives, and we were supposed to make a decision on nothing more than his [Parry's] verbal presentation. Nobody mentioned that we were going to have two repeats of whole games within twenty-four hours and God knows how many snippets thereafter.'

Dein wanted to put off a vote until the bids could be properly examined, but the momentum was now with Sky. At that stage Alan Sugar once again intervened. It was the first time anyone could remember Sugar attending a Premier League meeting. Tottenham were normally represented by chief executive Terry Venables, but this time Sugar had turned up as well. When Venables was called away, Sugar was left to vote on Tottenham's behalf. Sugar was in a delicate position. As well as being the largest shareholder at Tottenham, he was the chairman of Amstrad Electronics, which manufactured dishes for Sky. Amstrad were going through a rough patch and needed the sales stimulus that a deal with football could bring. It was a clear case of a potential conflict of interests. Far from keeping out of the discussions, however, Sugar produced a paper showing various income levels that pay-per-view television could bring. Only Sky could offer pay-per-view, he told the meeting, and this was an avenue of opportunity football could not pass up. What Sugar did not tell the assembled chairmen was that when he had been in the midst of his battle with Robert Maxwell and Irving Scholar to take over Tottenham, he had been given moral support by Rupert Murdoch. Murdoch had spoken to Sugar, who had requested that, since he was up against a newspaper owner in Maxwell, he needed the backing of the Murdoch press. After the conversation, the take-over of Tottenham was characterised by the way the two biggest selling national newspapers lined up: the *Mirror* for Maxwell, the *Sun* for Sugar.

David Dein called for a vote to disqualify Tottenham from taking part because of Sugar's vested interest in the role of Amstrad as a supplier of BSkyB equipment, but was defeated by the overwhelming majority of 21 to 1. When the argument turned to the loss of ITV's mass audience, Parry pointed to the BBC's part in the contract which would bring back *Match of the Day*. What few seemed to understand was that *Match of the Day* would go out late on a Saturday night, when children were in bed and young adults out on the town. Moreover, returning to some mythical, idyllic past, when everyone watched the BBC on a Saturday night, was never an option in 1992.

Perhaps there were old scores to settle, perhaps the clubs were seduced by the extra money. Whatever the case, the Sky bid was accepted by 14 votes to 6. Amazingly, two clubs abstained. When the news was made public, £7 million was instantly added to Amstrad's valuation on the stock exchange as the company's share price, which had taken a hammering over the preceding months, shot up.

Ken Bates was delirious with pleasure. 'I'm delighted I smashed ITV's monopoly,' he said. 'Whereas in the previous four years David Dein (that is, Arsenal) was making a million pounds plus out of television, I was banking £100 to £150,000 year.' Bates was referring to the fact that the largest part of the rights fees under the ITV contract of 1988 went to the clubs featured in the live games, hence the resentment when ITV concentrated, in the main, on the big clubs. This resulted, according to Bates, in Arsenal 'buying an international player for cash every year to ensure that they would beat me every season'. Bates then revealed the secret agenda behind the television vote. Support for Sky was not entirely dependent on the merits of its case. 'The clubs did the Sky deal,' said Bates, 'because we were determined to smash the Big Five dominance and we were determined to get a fair share of the money ... The whole thing is if the ITV deal had gone ahead the Big Five clubs would have been perpetuated.'

Rick Parry confirmed afterwards that pay-per-view had also been central to the outcome, particularly in dispelling any feelings of uncertainty among the undecided. 'On May 15, Greg Dyke said, "You can't have a pay channel, ITV don't want it,"' Parry revealed. 'Now that meant, as far as I was concerned, ITV were failing to meet one of our fundamental objectives. Our television adviser and I spent the next three days firming up the details [with Sky], then we concluded this was the right route.' There is no question that a number of chairmen, in addition to Rick Parry and Sir John Quinton, are still pinning their hopes on the success of pay-per-view, which is set to be introduced in 1995. When it arrives, Ken Bates for one thinks it 'will be the end of ITV'. The irony is that because pay-per-view is only justifiable for big events, the likelihood is that more event games, such as Arsenal versus Liverpool, will be featured, rather than non-event games such as Oldham versus Chelsea. A move in this direction would be against the spirit of the contract between the Premier League and BSkyB, which views all twenty-two clubs as equal, and indeed would be virtually impossible to sustain given the guarantee that each club will be featured live in a minimum of one home and one away game on Sky.

ITV immediately cried foul and sought an injunction to prevent the deal going through on the grounds that BSkyB had been tipped off about ITV's last-ditch offer and had therefore been able to outbid ITV, which had not been allowed to respond. However, there was no confidentiality clause in ITV's offer and it was not a sealed-bid auction, as some chairmen would have preferred. The court did not find any impropriety in the way the Premier League conducted itself and refused to grant the injunction.

However much criticism could be levelled at the way the matter was handled, there was little sympathy for ITV, which had itself been more than prepared to play hardball in the past, most notably in 1988. 'They have been shamelessly manipulated by the greedy bunch of backsliders in charge of the Premier League,' wrote *When Saturday Comes*, 'but hell will freeze over before we feel even the slightest twinge of sympathy for the ITV sports department.'

David Dein was mortified by the way things had turned out. As the instigator of the Premier League, he had glimpsed a new world which was now crumbling before his eyes. 'It will be seen as a black day for football,' he said. What particularly irked him was that when the vote was taken, few of the twenty-two chairmen had been privy to the behind-the-scenes activity, knowledge of which, he believed, would undoubtedly have changed the outcome. Trevor East, for instance, was convinced that Nottingham Forest supported ITV after having previously explained the bid personally to the club's chairman, Fred Reacher. When East began handing out his envelopes on the morning of May 18, however, there was no Fred Reacher. Eventually, East located two Forest officials, Dave Pullan, the commercial manager, and Paul White, the secretary. White had come straight from the airport following a holiday and had not been briefed by his chairman, so East attempted to explain the complexities of his £262 million offer in a two-minute conversation. In truth, all White really had to go on was £304 million plays £262 million. The full extent of the saturation coverage and the possibility of immediate subscription were not known until much later, so Forest voted with the majority for Sky, only to have second thoughts when it was too late.

When it came to broadcasting sport, there was no doubt that Sky knew its business. Chief executive Sam Chisholm had built his reputation in Australia by taking Channel 9 to market leadership on the back of sports like World Series cricket and Rugby League, and he kept it there for over a decade. According to his colleague of thirteen years, fellow Australian David Hill, Sky's head of sport, Chisholm has 'an innate talent for working out what will make good television'. Both Chisholm and Hill fit perfectly the stereotype of the brash Aussie wheeler-dealer (Hill described FTC's complaints over being ignored by the Premier League as 'the worst case of dummy spitting I've seen in ages').

Having reduced Sky's huge losses – at one point running at over £1 million per day – Chisholm knew the value of subscription for raising revenue another notch. It had been income from the film channels rather than advertising on the general entertainment or sports channels which had turned Sky's fortunes. So he needed little convincing by Hill that without regular, top-class football there was no long-term future for a UK sports channel. Hill himself described football as 'first, second and third' in the ranking of British sport and early on in the life of the sports channel determined that any football was better than nothing. Unable to obtain anything from the Football League, he bought rights to the Full Members' Cup (the Simod, then Zenith Data Systems Cup) in the hope that a competition culminating in a Wembley final would tempt viewers. He also bought the Autoglass Trophy for Third and Fourth Division teams for the same reason. Hill then set about building up a young, professional and enthusiastic team. Another Australian, Gary Davy, was appointed director of programmes, while two ex-BBC men, Roger Moody and Vic Wakeling, ensured a wealth of production experience. They cut their teeth on the cheap-to-produce Zenith and Autoglass matches knowing they had something in hand in respect of production values.

It was the success of the 1992 Cricket World Cup in selling dishes which brought the final evidence, if any were needed, of the contribution sport could make to a television service's success. After that, the whole Sky operation, from Murdoch down, was convinced that the next great leap forward could be taken only with the acquisition of the Premier League. Moreover, a subscription-based audience existed which could enable Sky to outbid ITV.

Two weeks after Sky won the vote, the company made a presentation to the twenty-two clubs. The thrust of its strategy was, according to David Hill, 'to give football a whole new look to a whole new audience – kids, women'. The central plank was the inception of Monday night football, an American concept adapted by Australians for England's national sport. David Hill defended it by saying it was 'extending the weekend. Precisely because football is rooted in society,' he continued, 'Monday night football is going to work.' As part of the 'new look', Sky pledged over ten hours of programming, which Hill claimed was 'worth a fortune in advertising the game'.

If the content of Sky's presentation was somewhat speculative, its style, at least, was committed. Rugby League commercials were shown cut to 'The Boys are Back in Town' and featuring Tina Turner. Sam Chisholm dismissed any notion that this wasn't football by boldly announcing: 'When we play, everyone wins.' Chisholm was in an indulgent mood, promising to sort out Arsenal's Japanese sponsor, JVC, should David Dein's worries about loss of sponsorship and advertising income resulting from Sky's low audiences prove well founded. He evidently believed that if he could assuage these fears then the big clubs would get back in their box.

Despite Chisholm's ebullient performance, there were some things he didn't come clean on at the presentation. These were the imminence of subscription on Sky Sport, which until then had been available free, and the intention to sell on-air, or broadcast sponsorship. Further, the revenue-sharing principle established in Sony's sponsorship of the Rugby World Cup on ITV was ignored by the Premier League when it should have been used as a valuable precedent.

Later, Sam Chisholm revealed a fundamental lack of appreciation for football, a trait which saw Sky introduce dancing girls and fireworks at its televised games. Chisholm suggested changing the points system so that a win by more than one goal would be rewarded with five points. Going on the principle that goals equals excitement equals good television, Chisholm was so terrified of a 0–0 draw that he asked Jon Smith of First Artists, which handles the England players' pool, in his capacity as a FIFA agent, to call Sepp Blatter, FIFA's general secretary. 'Whatever it takes,' Chisholm is reputed to have told Smith, 'bigger goals, smaller goalkeepers, shoot-outs, we've got to get rid of these 0–0 draws.' He must have felt it was a reasonable request as FIFA's President Joao Havelange had himself suggested something similar (as well as dividing the game into four quarters) in order to encourage the major American television networks to broadcast the 1994 World Cup in the USA. Common sense and tradition for once prevailed and both Sky and FIFA had to accept that there really is still some merit in the way football is played.

Shortly before the beginning of the 1992–93 season, BSkyB launched a £5 million advertising campaign, the centrepiece of which was a sixty-second commercial set to Simple Minds' hit 'Alive and Kicking', featuring the proposition 'It's a Whole New Ball Game'. At the same time Sky unveiled the biggest on-air sponsorship package in the UK, with Ford Motors and Foster's Lager, for a combined total of £4.5 million over three years. The promotional weight on the one hand and sponsor income on the other gave the service impetus, even when it was announced that Sky Sport would now be encrypted and only available on subscription. With prices set at £2.99 a month if subscriptions were taken up before the end of August and £5.99 thereafter, Sky correctly estimated that about 1 million homes would subscribe, which would provide enough income to cover the cost of the football contract, although running costs, including production and transponder rental on the Astra satellite, would require a further 250,000 subscribers. A year later, Sky revamped its price structure to dish-holders and the sports channel could be purchased only as part of a package. The cheapest would cost £11.99 a month, which would include other channels such as Nickelodeon (children), Discovery (documentaries and general entertainment), Bravo (old films and television shows), The Family Channel (general entertainment), QVC (home shopping), UK Living (women), and Country Music Television. These channels came in addition to Sky 1 (general entertainment), Sky News, UK Gold (old ITV and BBC shows), The Children's Channel and MTV (contemporary music), which come with all packages.

Two weeks after the deal with the Premier League was agreed, Sky and the BBC pulled off another coup by negotiating a new contract with the FA for England internationals and the FA Cup. The new arrangement, which brought the two contracts into alignment, was worth £75 million to the FA over four years. ITV was left to pick up the pieces with the Football League and the two agreed to the regional deal Greg Dyke had offered earlier in the year. Through this agreement, ITV managed to gain access to the Premier League by including in the contract coverage of the League (Coca-Cola) Cup, which the Premier League clubs had promised to enter in a separate arrangement with the Football League. ITV also secured rights to the European matches of Leeds, Manchester United and Sheffield Wednesday, while the BBC snapped up Liverpool's games in the Cup-winners' Cup. Perhaps taking his eye off the ball for a moment, Rick Parry virtually gave away radio rights to the Premier League to BBC Radio 5. The amount the BBC paid was a paltry £65,000. Zenith Media estimated that at commercial rates the BBC should have paid nearer £1 million.

It was not, then, all plain sailing. One of Martin Edwards' main objections to Sky was the concept of *Monday Night Football*. 'Many of our fans,' he said, 'come from a long way out of Manchester. It would be extremely difficult for them to get here on a Monday night and then come back for a

Wednesday game in the Cup or in Europe.' Some of Edwards' fears were realised in the first week of the 1992–93 season, when Queen's Park Rangers gained widespread sympathy for having no game on the first day of the season and then having to play three games in six days. It wasn't long before *Monday Night Football* was cut back and teams were guaranteed that they would have to play no more than two home fixtures per season on Mondays.

Nevertheless, as Trevor East observed at the end of the season: 'We've had football on nearly every night of the week some weeks and the supporters are expected to put up with that, and that [the overkill] is a serious problem.'

Sky's first task under the new contract was to screen live the 1992 Charity Shield game between Liverpool and Leeds, which, as usual, kicked off the new season in August. This brought a protest from the Scottish FA, which had a full programme of matches on the same day and felt that a televised event from Wembley would affect gates. It was the first time anyone had seriously considered the problems that broadcasting into Scotland could bring. ITV and BBC were able to exclude Scotland from network coverage of English football but Sky was unable to do this since its signal emanates from one source and covers the whole country, rather than from a number of regional transmitters which is the case with terrestrial broadcasters. The Scottish FA's complaint to the English FA drew no official response, although Trevor Phillips, now ensconced in his new job as commercial director of the FA, was quick to defend the right to broadcast. Not impressed, the Scots took their case to UEFA, under article 14 of the UEFA statutes, which gives national football associations the right of veto against any live television transmissions of football, including those being beamed from another territory. The Scottish complaints were noted by UEFA, but such was the backlog of cases and associated appeals following widespread European deregulation in the television industry and the Single European Act, which was brought in precisely to promote cross-border trade within the European Community, that by Christmas the matter had not been investigated. By now the Scots were becoming rather impatient. 'Our gates on the day of the Charity Shield match,' said Jim Farry, chief executive of the Scottish FA, 'were down by 20 per cent. We asked the FA to stop it but they did not oblige. In fact they flagrantly disregarded a written instruction from UEFA to prevent the signal coming in.' Farry went on to insist that the games on Sky on Sundays and Mondays were also having an adverse effect on Scottish attendances. The Scots had long resisted the temptation to sell regular live matches to television in Scotland, although their case was weakened somewhat by a deal struck with BSB in 1988. Farry defended this by saying that the satellite audience in 1988 was miniscule and they would have reviewed the position when the contract came to an end. 'We know that televising football has important implications over the short, medium and long terms,' Farry continued, 'and we think our sister FA in England has got it wholly wrong.' For its part, the English FA, without admitting any liability, moved the kick-off time of the following year's Charity Shield game between Manchester United and Arsenal to 12.30 pm to avoid clashing with the first Saturday of the Scottish League season. Yet another piece of the wedge was driven home as television once again interfered with tradition.

By the end of October, although Sky was claiming a million subscribers to its sports channel, viewing figures were miniscule compared to the numbers which had previously watched on ITV. Whereas before, audiences were attracted in their millions – the average for *The Match* was around 7 million – now they were counted in hundreds of thousands. This mattered to the big clubs who had been used to topping up income from televised games with perimeter advertising worth over £50,000 a game and now had difficulty in making £5,000 from that source. It did not, however, matter to Sky, because success depended on subscription numbers rather than viewers. Neither had the return of *Match of the Day* been the expected panacea, since its viewing figures turned out to be lower than had been hoped, averaging 4 million. ITV con-tributed to the low number of viewers watching *Match of the Day* by screening movies featuring Arnold Schwarzenegger and Clint Eastwood at the same time on Saturday nights. Since ITV had no Premier League football, it had to gain those young male viewers with other programming. Seeing the opportunity to kill two birds with one stone, it decided to schedule the movies against *Match of the Day*. It was a mismatch worthy of a Frank Bruno fight, with the films attracting twice the number of viewers as the revived *Match of the Day*.

Despite all the hype, the deal with Sky relegated the Premier League to a marginal television station just when it needed a national profile to ensure success in its first season. As David Dein put it, 'You can't create heroes on a minority channel.' It also allowed the new First Division clubs to gain exposure on ITV. Moreover, stiffer competition from another source was on the horizon. When the FTC bid was put together, the company approached Chrysalis Television to talk about the production facilities FTC would need if it were successful. At a series of meetings FTC also put forward the idea of following English players in Italy, particularly Paul Gascoigne at Lazio. When it became clear that the FTC bid was not going anywhere, Chrysalis, who had already been involved in making films with Gazza, decided to see whether they could buy the rights to Italian football for screening in the UK. The Italian League had previously been shown on Sky but the contract was about to end. Chrysalis snapped it up and sold two weekly programmes, including a live Serie A match every Sunday, to Channel 4 for £1.6 million.

As a result of the television negotiations, the amount of football available on the small screen increased dramatically. Games were scheduled in competition with each other on rival channels, with each claiming success. Gordon McKeag, chairman of the Football League's Management Committee, actually welcomed the confusion. 'I relish the prospect,' he said, 'that on some Sundays, when there may be a relatively unattractive Premier League match screened to a comparative handful of viewers on Sky, one of our matches could take three times their audience.' If ever there was a case of dog eat dog, this was it.

Not only did McKeag not appreciate that the proliferation of televised football could destroy the scarcity value of the product, he didn't understand television, period. Although he was a director of Newcastle, the first his club knew about the true nature of the new contract with ITV came when ITV informed them that they would be paid a mere £7,900 for the rights to screen a live Division 1 match. Newcastle's chief executive, Freddie Fletcher, responded furiously that the deal was unacceptable, only to be told that McKeag had signed the contract and had all the authority he needed to do so.

'I don't want to say this [in front of ITV],' Fletcher told McKeag, 'but you have bankrupted Newcastle United, and you now seem intent on doing the same to the rest of the Football League. I invite you to resign.' McKeag, to give him credit, was not fazed and replied: 'I reject your offer, Mr Fletcher.' Nevertheless, shortly afterwards, while still chairman of the Management Committee (he would later be elected president of the League following the untimely death of Bill Fox), McKeag was no longer a member of the Newcastle board.

Fletcher then turned his attentions to ITV and told them, 'You've got two courses of action. Either I'll see you in court because I'll issue a writ which will keep us off the screen for two years, by which time we'll be in the Premier Division (he was being a trifle pessimistic as Newcastle subsequently romped away with the First Division), or we can talk about a fairer sum.' Later that day ITV called and subsequently a revised agreement worth £65,000 was signed. A precedent had been established and other regional deals were also renegotiated.

Of all the new programmes, Channel 4's *Football Italia*, often attracting in excess of 2 million viewers, was perceived as the biggest success, although it would be premature to believe that it was going to change the long term viewing habits of soccer fans. Sky sometimes attracted an audience of less than 400,000 and dish sales were down on target, although this was said by Sky to be due to a log-jam in the supply of dishes. The sluggish dish sales could also, however, have been because the sports channel was encrypted from the start of the Premier League. Subscription penetration in homes that already had Sky rose from just under 1 million to 1.6 million – about 50 per cent of all satellite homes – through the season. It was 'the fastest growth of subscription TV in the world', according to Sky's Vic Wakeling, refuting Trevor East's assertion that 'so far it has been an expensive gamble that hasn't paid off'. However, East was forced to admit: 'I don't think there can be any complaints about their coverage of the actual games.' Indeed, the amount of time BSkyB devoted to the celebrations after Manchester United clinched the first Premier League title, including interviews with players, officials and fans, was in marked contrast to ITV's effort the previous season when presenter Elton Welsby had asked the Leeds United manager, Howard Wilkinson, how it felt to win the Championship, only to prevent the flabbergasted Wilkinson from answering because he had to close the show, otherwise there would have been no commercial break before *Bullseye*.

ITV's own coverage of the Football League was patchy. While some regions, Central Television in the midlands, for instance, showed more matches than ever and got regional audiences to rival BSkyB's national figures, others, like Granada, which had a large number of Premier League clubs in its catchment area, showed few. With a smaller number of attractive fixtures ITV began to lose its grip on male viewers while BSkyB showed that a television channel does not need a mass audience to be profitable. In fact, the only regular audience that could be measured in millions (apart from the Italian football on Channel 4) was for *Match of the Day* and even that programme failed to recapture the glory of bygone days. Football in England, despite the money, began to suffer drops in attendances that could not simply be attributed to reduced capacities in grounds converting to all-seat stadia. Perhaps they were also a manifestation of the dangers Trevor Phillips had predicted back in 1990. The whole business certainly left a most unsatisfactory taste and caused a not inconsiderable amount of bitterness. 'It was,' said David Dein, 'like amateur night in Dixie. The way it was presented, the way it was negotiated beforehand, and the way it has subsequently been implemented.'

A strange phenomenon throughout was the non-appearance of football's new invisible man. It transpired that Graham Kelly had taken over the mantle from Arthur Sandford. Kelly, who had begun the whole process, once again receded into the background as the negotiations gathered pace. Kelly was fast becoming the man who initiated change but was often somewhere else when the really important decisions were made. It seemed as if he would rather be anywhere doing anything than looking after the shambles in his own backyard. He could have been FIFA's man in Katmandu for all the influence he exerted over the crucial months of the television negotiations.

Meanwhile, Sky had made a deal with Tottenham to show live the club's friendly home game against Lazio, which was part of the transfer deal for Paul Gascoigne. The FA refused permission for the screening because the match clashed with a programme of Coca-Cola Cup games. Trevor Phillips, who had defended free access to markets when talking about the Charity Shield match, now completed a perfect volte face and defended the FA's right to veto the televising of games as they saw fit. 'It is no basis for trust or alliance,' he said, 'and I know that the other television stations, BBC and ITV, would not have acted in this way. Traditionally, they respect the agreements between football authorities that certain domestic weeks have to be kept free of live football.' But this was a whole new ball game and Sky had moved the goalposts.

That was why, less than two months after they signed a contract, Sky went to the High Court for an injunction against the FA on the grounds of restraint of trade over the Tottenham–Lazio match. It was the fourth High Court hearing in which football had become involved in a little over a year: the Football League and the FA clashed over which organisation's rules were pre-eminent; ITV sought an injunction against the Premier League to stop the Sky deal; the Swiss Bank Corporation issued a writ against the Premier League, claiming over £2 million in unpaid fees; and Sky took the FA to court over the Tottenham–Lazio game. Sky won their case and the FA was left powerless to do anything. To David Hill, the game was not, as the FA claimed, an inconsequential friendly and it was about time UEFA's article 14 was challenged. He was pleased with the outcome, as article 14 was to all intents and purposes declared unlawful. The principle had been established that Sky could, in effect, broadcast live football whenever it liked. In June 1993, as a result of Sky's action and pressure from the European commission, UEFA was forced to overhaul article 14. Henceforth it will merely determine exactly who the rights-holder is, although transmissions are still subject to certain restrictions regarding the day and timing of broadcasts which in effect make the changes cosmetic rather than having any real substance. The power had now passed from ITV to Sky, via a brief interregnum during which the FA in particular looked as if it was going to stand up and be counted.

Sky would certainly claim that its first season televising the Premier League was a success. Manchester United's title win helped, but it is also true that the subscriber had a wonderful choice of football to watch. Those who advocated the Sky deal were pleased with it, not just for the money but for the exposure to a television audience. Ken Bates was especially pleased. 'All the insider deals in smoke-filled back rooms have gone out the window,' he said.

The wheel had turned full circle. For a few short months, football had been in control of its own destiny. But the Swiss Bank bid was never discussed properly, the FTC concept was not built upon or encouraged; co-operation within football, the cornerstone of the Blueprint, was jettisoned at the earliest opportunity and the faction-fighting that had so characterised relations within the old Football League had been transferred to the Premier League, intensifying the conflict in the process. The game was left taking the largest amount of money regardless of the consequences. Those consequences would not take long to reveal themselves.

5

For Love or Money

While the Premier League takes the sponsorship money and runs, the fans are left to pick up the costs of going all-seat

'The new kit was a symbolic abandonment of principles and tradition, and an apocalyptic foretaste of what was to come: the realisation that this was not our beloved football club, a part of our Cockney heritage, but a failing business venture run by a bunch of impecunious wide boys and car salesmen with over-inflated ideas and egos.'

Editorial from the final edition of the West Ham fanzine Fortune's
Always Hiding, *April 1992.*

'The supporters don't matter as far as I'm concerned. They just pay their entrance fee.'

Stan Flashman, chairman, Barnet FC, December 1992.

By the first week of September 1992, with the Premier League barely three weeks old, the simmering disquiet over the television deal exploded into open warfare when Ron Noades stormed out of a meeting of chairmen. Noades, whose early exit was quickly emulated by some of his co-chairmen, was incensed because eight clubs had voted to veto a sponsorship deal for the Premier League with the brewer Bass, which had been negotiated by Rick Parry and was said to be worth £13 million to the League over three years. It emerged that the eight had met beforehand and agreed to vote against the Bass deal, thus making it impossible for Parry to secure the two-thirds majority he needed to ratify the arrangement, despite receiving the support of the remaining fourteen chairmen.

Another departee, Chelsea chairman Ken Bates was, if anything, angrier than his colleague. 'I'm going home to my pigsty,' he reputedly told the meeting, a reference to his farming business in Berkhamsted, Herts, 'where you meet a better class of person.' Once Bates had taken time out to reflect, far from toning down his insults, he became even more bellicose. Writing in the Chelsea programme for the game against Norwich, which took place on the Saturday after the walk-out, he welcomed the East Anglian club as 'one of the Clean Fourteen'. The same article saw Bates launch a ferocious attack against the eight clubs which had thwarted the Bass sponsorship, singling out David Dein for special treatment. 'It would appear,' he insisted, 'that a small number of club chairmen, or in the case of Arsenal, their vice-chairman, believe that they have some God-given right to an advantage – an unfair advantage – over their fellow members. One wonders why this is so, is it their arrogance that presumes such greatness? Could it be that their insecurity – or inferiority complex is such that it can only be assuaged by a continual attempt to best their betters – or is it straight-forward cheating because that's the only way they know to play the game?' Not content with that diatribe, Bates followed up with more of the same. 'Make no mistake,' he warned, 'the Premier League will be run free from graft, corruption, cheating or other unfair practices. Clubs will accept being beaten on the field, even if due to the occasional referee error or linesman's mistake. They will not accept ... the antics of smart-assed, get-rich-quick spivs who want to get an edge over their more honourable competitors.'

Such was the furore generated by the public slanging-match, even Graham Kelly heard about it. Kelly was, of course, abroad, this time on duty with the England team, who were playing a friendly against Spain in Santander. Kelly, despite the distance he was putting between himself and the Premier League in his attempts not to get involved, was forced to leave his comfortable hotel at the crack of dawn to fly back to London for urgent discussions with Rick Parry and Sir John Quinton. In fact, Kelly's decision to depart hastily from Spain came as a result of concerns expressed to him by FA councillors, many of whom, said the chief executive, were 'unhappy about the wrangling'.

The argument, as Bates made clear in his article, stemmed from the non-stop bickering over television, which went back to 1988. The vote against Bass, according to the Chelsea chairman, meant there was a danger of 'destroying what could be a far-sighted dream for the sake of short-sighted greed'. This had happened before, Bates claimed, and the 'more honourable clubs have been forewarned'. Bates regurgitated the argument over the proposed BSB deal four years earlier, which he said was 'frustrated by a small clique of clubs headed by David Dein of Arsenal. The infamous [ITV] deal was signed and in return for ensuring the signing of that contract, certain clubs, including Arsenal, were guaranteed a minimum exposure on TV over the following four years.' Chelsea, said Bates, which had resisted ITV, 'were blacklisted for years because I said football wasn't getting a fair deal out of ITV and BBC and they lied and they cheated when they did their negotiations'. Bates' club indeed had no home TV game from 1986 until 1991, until the attitude of the television companies changed because 'the contract was up for renewal and our vote was thought important'.

After the deal with BSkyB in May 1992, the big clubs were, for the moment, powerless to do anything other than fulminate against what they saw as supreme folly. Then, in early August, a lifeline appeared that gave them a chance to begin a fightback. A number of clubs were offered a ground advertising contract by a Spanish sports marketing company called Dorna, which was prepared to pay them up to £3 million a year. Seven clubs accepted the Dorna bid. They were Arsenal, Liverpool, Everton, Manchester United, Leeds, Nottingham Forest and Aston Villa. Others, such as Sheffield Wednesday, declined Dorna's offer to become the eighth member of a clique given the rather grandiose title of the Platinum Group.

The Dorna issue brought to the surface the lack of a marketing strategy and organisational difficulties which had been papered over by the television contract with BSkyB. The large ITV audiences ensured that featured clubs had become used to huge amounts of money from shirt sponsorship and ground advertising deals. Having beaten the big clubs over television, Rick Parry and the smaller clubs felt they could do the same with sponsorship and advertising. The issue of how much an individual club controlled its own income in these areas and how much should be run centrally on behalf of all was not, however, thrashed out when the Premier League was set up.

It thus became a matter of 'club think' versus 'league think' and disagreements developed over where to draw the line. The debate was complicated by a belief among some chairmen that even if it could be demonstrated that central marketing was theoretically correct, the track record of the football authorities over the years gave few grounds for confidence that the best deals would be negotiated. In the mad scramble to squeeze every last drop of money from television, and because of the way in which Rick Parry assumed control of the negotiations because the clubs were so suspicious of each other, no strategy for dealing with this important issue was ever worked out. Martin Edwards, chief executive of Manchester United, highlighted the problem when he said: 'In the founder members' agreement [of the Premier League], equal shares of TV income were agreed, along with overseas sales and sponsorship. Then, suddenly, centralised advertising hoardings crop up. It takes away an individual club's freedom, it brings in secondary sponsors which devalue your main sponsorship. What is coming next? One kit deal and shirt sponsorship for the whole League?' (For the 1993 season 90 English and Scottish clubs introduced at least one new strip.)

The point Edwards was making was that the Premier League could only go so far towards creating parity between the clubs. While he accepted equal access to television exposure and the money it brought, and sponsorship of the Premier League, he drew the line at handing over ground advertising and club sponsorship. Manchester United as a brand name was worth far more to sponsors and the football public than Wimbledon. Unlike advertising, which people will vehemently deny has any influence on their behaviour, football fans readily identify with the sponsor of their club. In a study published in December 1992, called 'Own Goals, Late Winners: The Verdict on TV Football', advertising researchers Adrian Langford and Richard Hunt revealed that fans are more likely to buy the sponsor's brands than those of a competing company. As an example, they quoted an Aston Villa supporter who said: 'If you were in a position to buy a photocopier, I'd look at Mita [Villa's sponsor] rather than Canon.' It is no wonder, therefore, that Manchester United and the other big clubs wished to preserve their superior status, which they felt would be devalued if Rick Parry introduced his title sponsorship policy with its advertising boards appearing at every Premier League ground. Having shared income from television, Martin Edwards believed he should not have to hand over cash earned directly by his club to others who could not attract such income on their own account.

This, then, was the backdrop against which Rick Parry set out to find sponsors for the Premier League. Although eight to ten were originally sought, following the models of the World Cup and the Olympic Games, as the first season approached it became clear to Parry and the sports marketing company IMG, whose task it was to devise the sponsorship package, that they would be unable to arrange such a large group of sponsors in time for the kick-off. Parry eventually decided to go for broke by offering title sponsorship of the Premier League to one large company, hoping to bring in other secondary or subsidiary sponsors as and when he could. For the main sponsor he came up with the brewers Bass, who wanted to use football to promote one of their brands. The new Jerusalem would henceforth be known as the Carling Premier League.

Alex Fynn had continually banged on to the FA that title sponsorship was wrong in principle as it would undermine the integrity of the competition. A non-sponsored league would have more value to advertisers, both inside the stadium and on television. Graham Kelly appeared to have been converted. 'The integrity and name of the FA Premier League should be sacrosanct,' he said, 'certainly for this season.' Parry was taken aback by the FA's attitude. 'It [the Bass deal] is a fantastic offer,' he said. 'In my opinion Bass represents the ideal sponsor. If clubs decide in favour, any FA objections will be discussed in the right and proper manner. The FA behaviour in this matter has been extraordinary. It would seem to me there have been far more important issues, such as the restriction of the new league to eighteen clubs, which the FA could have chosen to fight.'

The participation of IMG was crucial to the figures Rick Parry had put to the meeting which voted on the television deal in May. Of the £304 million the Premier League was to receive under the contract with BSkyB, £50 million (£10 million per year for five years) was to come from sponsorship. In order to achieve the £50 million, sponsors would have to be offered an advertising package at every Premier League game. None of this was made clear at the meeting in May. Getting anywhere near the £50 million depended on clubs surrendering control of advertising at their grounds to a central agency, in this case IMG, which was never a realistic proposition given the clubs' contractual arrangements with their own sponsors and advertisers. After a few weeks, IMG realised the impossibility of its task and withdrew. It now looked as though this section of the television deal had come apart at the seams.

Furthermore, contrary to Parry's assertion that Bass was the ideal sponsor, he could hardly have made a worse choice. The association with an alcoholic beverage alienated the health lobby and educationalists. The FA was opposed to having any title sponsorship whatsoever, while a further group of clubs, including Liverpool and Nottingham Forest, were already sponsored by drinks manufacturers and so opposed Bass because of a perceived conflict of interests.

By the time of the September meeting the forces opposed to the Bass deal had done enough to prevent the two-thirds majority it required. The seven Platinum clubs were always likely to vote against but an eighth ally was needed. This turned out to be Queens Park Rangers, who were upset over the treatment meted out by BSkyB which had forced them to play three matches in six days after sitting out the first Saturday of the season. When Ron Noades sought an assurance, which was not forthcoming, that the eight had not been acting in concert, he decided to stage his walk-out.

If Ron Noades and Ken Bates were enraged, Rick Parry seemed unnerved by the turn of events. 'The fear of those who walked out,' he said, 'was that the voting system has become a sham because eight clubs can get together and block decisions. I don't see any prospect of the Bass deal being revived. The clubs also rejected a centralised approach to other sponsors because of their own deals. We have a major rift ... The whole concept of one club, one vote is proving unworkable. We have to devise a different way of operating.'

Considering the rules had been in place for only a matter of weeks, this was an extraordinary reaction. Once again, in the rush to find the money he had promised would flow from the BSkyB deal, Parry had overlooked the fact that no consensus had been reached over the ramifications of sponsorship. The problem for Parry was compounded because while he was desperately attempting to impose Bass on the Premier League, Ford Motors and Foster's Lager had linked up with BSkyB to sponsor the station's football programmes and the Premier League would receive nothing of the fee the two companies paid to BSkyB for the privilege. Whether Parry thought that once the BSkyB deal had been railroaded through everyone would acquiesce and the world would be full of sweetness and light is impossible to tell. He certainly seemed slow in realising the strength of feeling among those with whom his actions still rankled.

While feelings did cool off, and to his credit Ron Noades sought to distance himself from the personal attacks on David Dein, there was no immediate prospect, as Rick Parry had predicted, of rescuing the deal with Bass. There was some talk about ostracising or even expelling Arsenal, but the threats were basically empty and those chairmen that advocated them always did so from behind a veil of anonymity. For their part, the Platinum clubs agreed to a deal whereby Lucozade became a sponsor, able to use the Premier League logo on its products and have an advertising board at each Premier League ground, but in which no title sponsorship was involved. All the talk of £10 million a year now seemed like so much fluff.

The lack of a coherent policy over ground advertising and sponsorship not only meant that Premier League clubs would not be receiving the amount they expected from the television contract, it also left them with the urgent task of making up the shortfall themselves. The Premier League was born in 1992 largely because the television contract was up for renewal and the old First Division wanted to be in control of its own destiny before a new contract was signed. In all other respects, however, the timing could hardly have been worse.

Exploiting the new-found status of membership of the Premier League was soon shown to be an illusory exercise. In fact, the status itself was a double-edged sword as the rewards of success were replaced by the fear of failure. The possibility of falling off the Premier League gravy train induced a sustained raid on the transfer market in 1992 – Premier League clubs spent over £30 million in the close season – and a seemingly inexorable rise in wages to keep existing staff happy. All this feverish spending was conducted against a background of the worst recession in the UK economy since the slump of the 1930s, and the compulsory renovation of stadia stipulated by the Taylor Report. Enforced by the government quango, the Football Licencing Authority (FLA), all First and Second Division clubs were required to go all-seat by 1994. Initially Divisions 3 and 4 were to attain the same stage by 1999, but in June 1992 the then minister responsible for sport, Chelsea fan David Mellor, declared that outside the Premier League only clubs with average crowds of over 10,000 would have to close down their terracing. The government had reduced its take from the pools betting levy in 1990 by 2.5 per cent to 40 per cent, which yielded an extra £20 million per year for the Football Trust, but the trust had also to help with other costs such as policing and community projects. Three years later, chancellor Kenneth Clarke announced a continuation in the 2.5 per cent reduction which would release a further £100 million over five years. This new cash was earmarked for lower division clubs. It was a victory for common sense and the responsible advocacy, not of football's authorities, but of the Football Supporters Association.

But for the Hillsborough disaster, it is unlikely that the majority of clubs would have given much thought to the improvement of conditions for spectators. Unlike the cinema industry, which has had to rationalise and adapt to the changing entertainment needs of its customers, football never felt it necessary to go awooing. Even before the Taylor Report imposed its biting financial obligations, most clubs were trading in the red, Micawber-like, hoping that something would turn up to save them from bankruptcy. The wonder is not that Aldershot and Maidstone disappeared in 1992 but that so many clubs continued to survive against massive odds. As 1993 approached, the full blast of the chill wind of penury faced far more clubs as supplies of credit dried up and they confronted the prospect of closure by the FLA if the deadlines were not met. Kenneth Clarke's intervention came just in time.

As for the Premier League clubs, how were they going to find the estimated £200 million that was required? The easy up-front money from television, season tickets, hospitality suites, sponsorship and advertising deals had been blown on players' wages and transfers. The Football Trust offered a maximum rebuilding grant of £2 million to each Premier League club (£1 million for First Division clubs). One interesting feature of the trust's offer was a £4 million grant for a shared stadium. Not surprisingly, there have been no takers so far. So much for the aspirations of the Blueprint and its National Plan for Stadia. Basically, each club had to come up with its own scheme and its own method of finance, and as usual each had the same Pavlovian response – the supporters will pay. Charge higher prices and if possible play more matches as well. It was no surprise that when the Premier League opened for business both Crystal Palace and Chelsea, the arch-exponents of this theory, showed increases on some seat prices of over 50 per cent compared to the previous season. The Football Supporters Association surely got it right when it called the rises effected by every Premier League club, to a greater or lesser extent, 'pure greed'. This was a time when most of football's competitors for the leisure industry pound – cinemas, theatres, rock shows – were either holding down prices or offering a range of discounts.

Particularly insensitive was the treatment meted out to casual fans and away supporters, who were often asked to pay full prices for children because they were not club members. Especially short-sighted was the failure of many clubs to realise that the price hike meant that a large number of fans had no option but to pick and choose which games to attend, with the resultant effect that stadia were half empty for much of the time. With the foresight and consideration of the clubs, fans could have been rewarded for their loyalty by reduced prices, particularly for televised matches, which came with extra income guaranteed. As a gesture to loyal fans it would probably also have been good business. As would be expected with a piecemeal approach such as this, some clubs managed to get it right, some half right, while others got it disastrously wrong.

At Highbury, the old Clock End had already been rebuilt in 1989 to accommodate 53 executive boxes, a sports hall, office and conference facilities. The work was financed by advanced payments for leases on the boxes, although if they could have their time over again, Arsenal would undoubtedly build a double-decker stand with improved facilities for more than the select few in the boxes. Plans for a new stand on the famous North Bank took this into account and were on a grander scale. The new North Bank would cost £16.5 million for 12,000 seats. To pay for it, David Dein and the Arsenal board, having investigated debenture models in the USA and at Glasgow Rangers, decided to institute the Arsenal Bond.

The scheme invited supporters to buy a bond at either £1,500 or £1,100. This would entitle the bond-holder to purchase a season ticket in a designated seat for the next 150 years. The price of season tickets for bond-holders was to be kept down so that sitting in the new stand would be cheaper than the prevailing prices in the East and West Stands. Thus, so the theory went, the capital outlay could be recouped in five years and the bond could be sold at any time. The hope was that demand would outstrip supply and bonds could be traded at a profit, making them an investment. The Bank of Scotland underwrote the scheme and offered loans to supporters who could not afford the asking price, with repayments set at a minimum of £32 per month.

The bond issue was not a runaway success. The North Bank was traditionally the cheapest part of the ground. Its regulars provided the real core of Arsenal's working-class support. Many of them would be unable to afford the £32-a-month repayments on a loan, never mind being able to cough up £1,500 in one go. Still more would probably have been judged a financial risk and would not have qualified for the loan at all. This meant that the bonds were in reality targeted at a different, wealthier clientele. This led to the club facing accusations of attempting to alter its fan base by moving upmarket, thereby forcing out its most committed supporters.

The new North Bank Stand is certainly a magnificent structure, impressive both in design and architecture. Simon Inglis, the author of two outstanding books on stadia, *The Football Grounds of Great Britain* and *The Football Grounds of Europe*, and a member of the Football Licencing Authority, said of it when it was half complete: 'When it is built it will be one of the finest grandstands in the country, possibly one of the best in Europe.' According to Inglis, Arsenal, after they were initially poorly advised, eventually, in conjunction with the respected architect Rod Sheard, 'did everything that could be done for that site. It's a very difficult site to work.' To emphasise his point, Inglis added that 'only a club like Arsenal could build such an expensive and lavish stand ... They have thought nothing of adding something like half a million pounds to the cost to cantilever the upper tier over the lower tier so there isn't a restricted view in the stand.' The facilities on offer in the new stand are just as impressive as the architecture, and include themed food outlets, a crèche and an Arsenal museum. Inglis also pointed out that the cost-per-seat ratio of the new stand was extremely high because of these features. An average cost of good-quality seat installation is about £1,000 a seat. This can go down to £300 at the ground of a smaller club. Highbury's new development cost £1,750 per seat. It was, in many ways, a throwback to the traditional Arsenal way of doing things. In the 1930s, the club built what was then one of the best stadia in Europe, and almost bankrupted itself in the process. Now, whatever the drawbacks of the bond scheme, the new North Bank Stand was not constructed at the expense of the team.

The fact remains, though, that the bond scheme alienated many fans to the point that well into the 1992–93 season, when Highbury should have been packed to the rafters every week as its capacity was reduced to 29,000 while the building work was in progress, gates were down significantly. Sell-out crowds were a rarity, while the average for the previous season was 32,000.

However, when the stand opened for business in August 1993 even some of the so called Luddite fans were forced to admit to its virtues, one of them telling David Dein 'If I have to sit down, this stand is the business. It's the dog's bollocks'. So maybe at the end of the day David Dein's vision of a lavish redevelopment at Highbury will be recognised as being appropriate for a club of Arsenal's standing.

Despite their drawbacks, bond schemes remained an attractive means of raising funds to a number of clubs. In some cases, at Leeds United, for instance, there was meaningful research of fans, local authority participation, the bond-financed development was on a much smaller scale and bond-holders were given substantial discounts on their season tickets. Not only that, Leeds were prepared to do the unthinkable and actually bring a supporter on to the board. The regime at Leeds is certainly to be commended for its forward-looking approach, the more so because for a long period Leeds fans have had an unsavoury reputation. While a full Elland Road can still intimidate opposing teams and their fans, the nastiness that was once the hallmark of Leeds supporters seems to have been replaced by an equally committed but less malevolent attitude. Indeed, the involvement of Leeds fans in the decision-making process supports the observation of Lord Justice Taylor that better behaviour would follow from improved conditions.

Another innovative approach was adopted by Leicester City, a club which could never rank among the élite but which has always thought of itself as being First Division (or Premier League) material. Leicester is one of the country's true yo-yo clubs, alternating between the First and Second Divisions as promotion has been followed by relegation then promotion once more. By the time of the Taylor Report, the club was back in Division 2 and, like everyone else, had to raise millions to make Filbert Street all-seat.

Fortunately, Leicester did not fall into the category of club that had made little or no ground improvements over the years. In the early 1970s a plan was put forward by local businessmen to build a new all-seat stadium with a capacity of 35,000 on the outskirts of the city but the club's directors refused to move home. Looking to deflect criticism of their decision, the board made significant improvements to the Filbert Street ground, including turning most of the terracing into seated areas. Leicester was also among the first clubs in the country to install executive boxes. With a good ratio of seats-to-standing, redevelopment was not going to be as onerous as elsewhere, yet for a smallish club, the £7.5 million it would have to raise was an awful lot of money. The cash was to be spent on an imaginative plan to turn the pitch 90 degrees and build one new stand.

The blueprint for the new stand was rejected by the local council after complaints from residents in the Filbert Street area about its height, which would have blocked out daylight. Going back to the drawing-board, the realignment of the pitch was discarded and a smaller stand designed. The new proposals would cost less, about £5.5 million in total. It was now that Leicester did something unusual for a football club. The board created a new post of marketing director and employed an experienced practitioner, Barrie Pierpoint, who had little interest in the game of football. 'We needed someone who could give the finances of the club a lift,' said chairman Martin George, 'someone who could come up with new ideas which we, as football people, might not have thought about. We decided to make the appointee a director rather than a manager so that all could see that he had the power to make decisions'. Contrast this with Liverpool, where an advertisement for the post of commercial director made the job sound like a glorified shop manager.

Pierpoint found that Leicester, like so many other clubs, really had no idea how to communicate with its customers, the fans. He set about devising a number of schemes so that all those interested in the club could get involved. Commercial operations were completely revamped, in particular the club's merchandising operation. First on the agenda was the club shop. In the season after Pierpoint's arrival its turnover was a meagre £180,000. After his overhaul that total was passed in the first two months of the 1992–93 season and Pierpoint's target income for the season of £750,000 looked, if anything, to be on the conservative side. Part of the reason for the increase was a new policy regarding the sale of replica kits. Until Pierpoint's arrival, Leicester, like most clubs, had franchised out its kit manufacturing deal to a sportswear company, in their case Bukta. This led to the kit being available on local market stalls for less than the club paid for its own stock. Pierpoint set up his own manufacturing deal with a local factory (Leicester is the home of the knitwear and clothing industry) and created a new brand called Fox Leisure Wear. Rather than leave the design to the manufacturer, he canvassed the opinions of the people who would have to wear it, the players and the fans. The result was a reversion to traditional Leicester blue and white and a spectacular sales increase. 'I thought what we were doing was just common sense,' Pierpoint said. 'I didn't realise we were sparking a revolution [against the trend for multi-coloured shirts].'

But perhaps the most original project resulted from the board's decision to link up with the local council to become an integral part of Leicester's entry into the government's City

Challenge scheme, under which funds are made available for the regeneration of inner-city areas. Leicester was one of the winners and the area of the city receiving grant aid includes Filbert Street. This has meant an injection of £250,000 of public money to help pay for a conference and sports centre in the ground's redevelopment.

Pierpoint has also tried to increase Leicester's appeal among the city's large Asian community. 'We are encouraging Asians to come and look at the ground,' he said. 'We are adapting our catering to take account of their tastes and this has led to an increase in support from the Asian community, especially businessmen.' This customer-orientated approach was repeated in other areas, as Pierpoint explained: 'We have created a number of different levels of involvement from the ordinary fan to the successful company. That way we spread the load. We looked at all sections of our potential market and made sure we opened the door to everybody.' Pierpoint's policy of encouraging involvement no matter how much an individual could afford paid instant dividends. Gates were up by 20 per cent in the first few months of the 1992–93 season, against the general trend, although team performances were no better than in the previous season.

All this was accomplished without alienating anybody or affecting the finances on the playing side. 'Since the redevelopment's financing comes from new sources,' Pierpoint maintained, 'the spending power of the manager will not be affected.' It is an approach beyond the wit of many clubs, who generally do not understand marketing and see the commercial side of their operations as an easy number for an ex-player. 'When I go to meetings of clubs' commercial managers,' Pierpoint said, 'I am amazed because at least half the time is spent talking about football rather than marketing.' It is often the case that football people complain when non-football fans become involved. They think that marketing men are taking over the game. If Leicester's experience is anything to go by, football could benefit from more rather than fewer experts in this particular field.

There may have been a revolution, the game may have been under the most intense pressure imaginable because of the Taylor Report, yet by and large supporters were still viewed as at best a necessary evil. Letting supporters anywhere near the seats of power has always been anathema to those who run the game. As a consequence, concerned fans are becoming ever more forthright in their opposition to policies they view as unfair or dangerous. It seems that when they are given the opportunity, fans are more than prepared to respond. When they believe they are being conned, however, they are no longer ready to accept it and in 1992 supporters graphically demonstrated that in the new order of things, if they act together in a just cause, they can be a catalyst for change.

Nowhere is this better illustrated than in the case of West Ham United. Of all the London clubs, West Ham is the one with the deepest roots in its community. Whereas in most areas of the capital you can find a good sprinkling of support for all the bigger clubs – there are south Londoners who support Spurs or Arsenal, for instance, and north Londoners who support Chelsea – inhabitants east of Whitechapel largely favour two clubs. The minnow is Leyton Orient but the vast majority of supporters follow West Ham. West Ham is universally known as a family club, a place where loyalty can be traced through the generations and with which Cockneys young and old feel a special affinity.

This feeling has been nurtured over the years by the relative isolation of the east end from the rest of the metropolis, along with the area's special character and a tradition of playing pure football. 'The underdog mentality is a West Ham thing,' says one supporter. 'They know they're not very good most of the time but it is always a good game. A couple of times a season they're going to absolutely wallop somebody and that's worth all the pain of the four or five months in between.' Despite this feeling, West Ham is a club which, under a number of long-serving managers, produced a stream of class players over the years, many of whom went on to become managers and coaches of renown; a club which developed the famous 'academy' of the 1950s with names like Malcolm Allison, Noel Cantwell, Dave Sexton, Frank O'Farrell and John Bond, a tradition carried on by the great triumvirate of Moore, Hurst and Peters and later by Trevor Brooking and Alan Devonshire (to name but a few).

West Ham's stability was legendary. The Cearns family's involvement goes back to the club's very foundation and between 1902 and 1989 they employed only five managers, Syd King, Charlie Paynter, Ted Fenton, Ron Greenwood and John Lyall. But the board were also famous for their parsimony. For many years they had been living on a shoe-string and getting away with it. To their credit, the Cearns maintained an effective youth policy, but after the acrimonious departure of the last long-serving manager, John Lyall, in 1989, and Lou Macari's short tenure, which was ended because of his alleged involvement in the financial scandal at his previous club, Swindon Town, when Billy Bonds (yet another great club stalwart) took over in 1990, the youth cupboard was bare. Stuart Slater was the last in a long line of home-grown stars and he was soon sold to Celtic. Even with the money from that and other sales, Bonds found the kitty was empty.

The money had not been spent on ground improvements. Upton Park, by the end of the 1980s, was definitely looking its age and its ratio of seats-to-standing was poor. Neither had it been spent on players. The million-pound transfers of Tony Cottee and Paul Ince had put the transfer ledger in credit. Moreover, average gates in those days of well over 20,000 made West Ham one of the top ten best-supported teams, even when they were in Division 2. 'Where has all the money gone?' asked the fanzine, *Fortune's Always Hiding* (*FAH*), in October 1991. 'Unfortunately,' it continued, 'we can't answer that question as the club is owned by a family as old as the hills and twice as secretive. We've never been trusted enough to see accounts of where the millions have gone but unless we do, the board could find itself under increasing pressure to resign.' The Cearns' method of running a football club could not survive the harsh commercial realities that the Taylor Report and the recession had brought about. The time of the old patricians had finally run out.

The Hammers gained promotion from the Second Division in 1990–91 as runners-up. The fans knew as well as Billy Bonds that the team needed to be drastically reinforced if instant relegation was to be avoided. Instead of buying players, the West Ham board introduced a bond scheme to pay for the conversion of Upton Park. West Ham needed to raise over £15 million to go all-seat. Although bond prices, which started at £500, were cheaper than at Highbury, in many other essentials the scheme was identical, even down to the same underwriter, the Bank of Scotland.

There were, however, crucial differences between West Ham and Arsenal. Unlike Highbury, where the bonds would finance the rebuilding of the North Bank only, the West Ham bonds would pay for the conversion of the entire ground. Whoever you were at Upton Park you would in future have to pay in advance for the right to go and support your team. In addition, the threshold of tolerance of West Ham supporters for their team's inadequate performances had been well and truly passed. From day one they knew they would be lucky to survive in the First Division. Trevor Brooking called the squad 'the worst I can remember'. At least Arsenal delivered where it mattered most, by producing a Championship-winning team. As *FAH* succinctly commented, 'The idea of being asked to pay £500 in advance for more of the rubbish we currently have to watch would be funny if it wasn't so unforgivable.'

If ever a board of directors misjudged their customers it was West Ham's now. The response of the fans to the bond scheme was outrage. They felt that the directors were unwilling to put their hands in their own pockets to strengthen the team and were now asking the fans to pay for the redevelopment of the ground. Representatives of the three club fanzines (*FAH*, *Over Land and Sea*, and *On a Mission From God*) met managing director Peter Storrie, who was the public face of the club, and the publicity-shy Cearns family to state their opposition, but although the fans themselves came up with more imaginative ideas to raise money, which envisaged a combination of a share issue, a limited debenture bond scheme and extended season tickets, the board refused to budge from its chosen course. The directors rejected the share issue proposals as unworkable, but the fans believed the real reason was that if a share issue went ahead, the board's control over the club would slip, whereas a bond scheme gave bond-holders no voting rights. 'If the fans are expected to pay for the stadium,' said *FAH*, 'they deserve nothing less than a minimum of two seats on the board.' Writing to North Bank Norman of *FAH*, one West Stand Willy put forward a powerful case against the bond scheme, saying: 'Messrs Cearns and Co. do not wish to dilute their shareholding and place themselves in a position whereby they could lose power. Instead, they want everyone to stump up £500 to improve the ground and therefore increase the value of the assets of the company in which they own shares. They wouldn't get away with this in any other industry or company . . . why should they get away with it at

West Ham United? Would Mr Cearns give me £500 to decorate my house and increase its value, getting nothing in return? Don't even bother to answer that one.'

Eventually the board offered to meet regularly with the representatives of bond-holders, who would form a separate company, but this fell well short of what the fans wanted. 'They [the supporters] feel we [the directors] should be prepared to put up some of the money, and I have some sympathy with that view,' said Peter Storrie. 'The problem is that the time-scale imposed by the Taylor Report is so unrealistic . . . we should have had a longer time to implement it.'

Throughout January and February 1992, the West Ham fans mounted a series of protests at home games. Red cards were issued which, on a given signal, were flashed in unison at the directors' box. The public disaffection culminated in a pitch invasion during a home defeat by Everton on February 29. The scene was described by *Time Out* journalist and West Ham supporter Denis Campbell, who said: 'A young fan picked up the corner flag, placed it on the pitch and sat down . . . that was the catalyst for pandemonium and fans poured on to the pitch and the game was held up for five to ten minutes. The club reacted by ringing the ground with stewards to prevent further pitch invasions, but the protest just wouldn't die down.' In March, a day of joint action against bond schemes was carried out by West Ham and Arsenal fans. A petition was organised which drew 7,500 signatures and a new organisation called the Hammers Independent Supporters Association (HISA) was formed (independent, that is, of the traditional supporters club). Such organisations had already been formed elsewhere, notably at Tottenham, where TISA support was invaluable to the Terry Venables–Alan Sugar take-over, and at Arsenal, where the challenge to the bond scheme has brought about more supporter-friendly policies. HISA's stated objectives included the defeat of the Hammers bond scheme, a campaign against the all-seat requirement of the Taylor Report, and stamping out racist abuse at the ground.

Peter Storrie used HISA's campaign against all-seat stadia to portray them as Luddites, out of step with the times. 'The problem is,' he said, 'that people feel the Taylor Report is going to go away, that if enough people lobby the government it will disappear. It won't. I don't think supporters want to accept the stark reality of the alternative. The North and South Banks will be closed.' At least Storrie was brave enough to face a HISA meeting and some tough questions. There was, however, no meeting of minds.

Storrie tried to couch his argument in terms of loyalty. 'This is something you should do if you care about the club', was his message. A HISA member shot that one down, saying, 'Without being melodramatic about the bonds, people have been very quick and shrewd to realise that issue went right to the heart of football. As fans we were being treated like mugs and football fans are not mugs.' The truth is that fans don't owe anything to their club. It is the club that owes loyalty to its fans. The directors are the privileged custodians of people's dreams and they should not presume to deny supporters their dreams out of ignorance or indifference.

Given the atmosphere, it is not surprising that there was a derisory take-up of bonds at West Ham. Less than 1,000 were sold by the end of the 1991–92 season. While the team slipped towards relegation, the fans stepped up their protests. *FAH* commented: 'It's hard to believe anything positive could come out of such a depressing season but it has, and it's called fan power. We have shown the club that we're not going to take any more and to prove it, we've killed the bond dead. . . . The bond scheme betrayed West Ham as a club run on a lie. The happy family club had slammed the door in the face of fans and betrayed them. As landlords they brought new meaning to the term Rachmanism. They thought we'd give them £15 million to develop the ground in return for a shiny seat and a framed photo.'

In fact the bond scheme wasn't quite dead, but it did look extremely ill. In what seemed a mood of vengeance, the board decided that if the bonds couldn't raise the money then prices would have to go up. At the beginning of the 1992–93 season, West Ham, a relegated club, put up prices by up to 50 per cent. This resulted in a massive stay-away campaign as the renewal rate of season tickets fell by 50 per cent. The first three home fixtures of the new season saw average crowds of just over 13,000, which was 8,000 down on the previous season's average. While the recession, redundancies throughout Newham, Tower Hamlets and the Ford plant at Dagenham, and West Ham games shown live on ITV obviously contributed to the downturn, the main reason by far was the anger and disillusionment on the part of supporters. Embarrassed by the year's events, Martin Cearns stepped down as chairman, to be replaced by Terrence Brown, who became the largest shareholder when he acquired 33 per cent of the club's shares for a figure in excess of £2 million. It had little effect on the protesters. HISA representatives were turning up at the ground before matches, selling merchandise and lobbying for support, and were then going home before the game got underway. They had become full-time away fans, not going to Upton Park at all, and arrangements for their members forced the club to rethink its own pricing policy on travel. Denis Campbell expertly summed up the situation. 'You've really done something when you've pissed off vast numbers of those people who are already so hardened and inured and in some ways have taken pride in their suffering,' he said. 'To push them beyond that point is absolutely astounding and I don't think the club have come to terms yet with the situation.'

The stay-away was a trend many would follow. The crowd for the televised game against Derby – a team with a number of attractive stars – was, at 11,493, the lowest League gate at Upton Park for thirty-five years. This dubious record was broken two weeks later when only 10,326 turned up for the match against Sunderland. If the bond scheme was a disaster, this was even worse and the price hike was quickly abandoned, although not by the whole amount – the reduction was in the region of 25 per cent. Like magic, attendances began to pick up, although the response was patchy. After the Sunderland game (which West Ham won 6–0), when the price reduction was announced, 17,000 showed up to watch the next match against Swindon, even though the reduction had not yet taken effect, while the following home encounter against Notts County attracted only 12,000, which was at least 3,000 below what Peter Storrie had expected. Denis Campbell again: 'It's only by cutting prices that the club are admitting their entire policy of the last year is wrong. There's been no public apology of any sort and I know people who say "they have been taking the mickey out of me and they won't get another penny of my money until they apologise."'

For West Ham the future is bleak. Denis Campbell thinks that 'all the signs are there of what we call the Burnleyisation of West Ham, i.e. everyone loves them and everyone knows their name but they never win anything nowadays and they slip down the divisions and there's a resigned air about it.' The disastrous train of events was probably set in motion at the 1991 FA Cup semi-final. After referee Keith Hackett harshly sent off Tony Gale, thousands of West Ham fans sang their heads off as their team crumbled to a 4–1 defeat against Nottingham Forest. Perhaps the board that day misread the fanaticism, believing that these mugs could be sold anything. But it was precisely because the fans' loyalty was to the institution, not to the players, still less to directors, that they would not put up with the systematic destruction of what they believed in. As supporters, they simply had no choice in the matter. It was part of their lives and they were going to fight for it.

At long last the board was forced to admit that the bond had finally expired. The club's annual general meeting in March 1993 was told that income from the sale of bonds was £750,000 less than it had cost to launch the scheme. Less than 600 of the 19,000 bonds had been sold. Coupled with reduced income from the drop in season ticket sales the club lost £2 million over the season. *Time Out* said the directors 'were defeated because of a well-run, vigorous campaign by the people who care most about their club, the fans'. Against the odds, the team won promotion and were assured of a financial windfall from becoming members of the Premier League. The fans were astonished to find that season ticket prices for their return to the top flight were not to be increased. After the long confrontation, perhaps this gesture indicated that the directors had finally realised that a harmonious relationship with supporters was the only way of securing a decent future for the club.

While all clubs struggled to fund the Taylor Report, the Premier League renewed its quest for more sponsors. After months of furious lobbying, some of it in the media, Rick Parry persuaded enough of the Platinum clubs, including those sponsored by drinks companies, to change their minds about the Bass deal for there to be a realistic chance of resurrecting it. The deal was brought back and finally accepted in February 1993. The voting was 21–1, with only Arsenal voting against. One strange aspect of the deal was that from the 1993–94 season, when the sponsorship was to start, the Premier League was to change its name and would be known as the Carling FA Premiership. The change was requested by the sponsors and showed that even the name of the League, which was proclaimed in the Blueprint, was not sacrosanct. From the sponsorship, each club will receive £137,000 per year in a four-year, £12 million deal.

In Rick Parry's view the offer was simply too good to turn down, but his marketing naïveté was exposed when he declared: 'Bass's commitment shows faith in the Premier League's ability to lead football into a new era.' Of course it showed nothing of the sort. It was just another smart move by a company which knew from its experience in Scotland with its Tennents brand how an increased profile which accompanies football sponsorship is good for business. In the highly competitive beer market a minute percentage shift is all that is required for a substantial sales increase. With Carling spending almost £20 million a year on advertising (£13 million on television), £3 million, while not peanuts, is not a massive amount either. Moreover, the Premier League was still a long way short of the £10 million a year sponsorship income promised in the deal with BSkyB.

So once again the Premier League had taken the money and ran. By doing so it had compromised itself by undermining its inherent value and putting an unnecessary constraint on television. The reason why the Bundesliga in Germany and Calcio in Italy are not sponsored is simply to protect individual club sponsorships (and identity) on the one hand and to enhance the television value of the league as a competition on the other, by delivering to the networks an uncontaminated event. In England, meanwhile, Holsten (Tottenham) now play Carlsberg (Liverpool) in the Carling Premiership, sponsored on television by Ford. With such an approach, the days of the FA Cup as a non-sponsored event are surely numbered. In a parrot-like response, it was was not long before the Football League, whose deal with Barclays was due to end, announced a new sponsor. In a three-year deal worth £3.5 million the League became known as the Endsleigh Insurance League. No doubt the sponsorship will increase awareness of a somewhat obscure company, as with Cornhill's involvement in Test cricket, but with what effect on a 106-year-old Football League, now seemingly in permanent hock to sponsors? When, like Canon, *Today* and Barclays, Endsleigh depart from the scene, they will leave behind a less credible institution than the one that could safely stand unaided for most of its history. Meanwhile, Arsenal, at least, appeared to appreciate the value of its brand name by refusing an extra £500,000 from a brewer, preferring to keep its identity by remaining loyal to its existing sponsor, JVC.

The principle of non-title sponsorship was enshrined in the Blueprint and appeared to have been taken on board when it was reaffirmed by Graham Kelly in September 1992, when the eight clubs blocked the original Bass deal. Now, once again, Kelly stood idly by when, in the words of one chairman, there was 'the sound of money talking'. The new sponsorship was hardly necessary. It came on top of bounteous financial rewards to all Premier League clubs. In addition to the basic television fee of £750,000 and £69,000 for each live participation on BSkyB, plus £7,500 for each recorded appearance on *Match of the Day*, each club was incentivised with a sliding scale of prize-money ranging from £815,000 for the champions to £37,000 for the bottom team. Even Ken Bates accepted that television money had created a more level playing field. 'The great thing about now,' he said, 'is you've got the smaller clubs in the Premier League who are not being forced to sell their players any more, and that's why you saw some funny League positions [in 1992–93] . . . Look at Everton, one of the so-called Big Five. Where are they today without the unfair advantage of TV? Did Liverpool do much this year? "There must be something wrong with football because Liverpool didn't win anything." That's what people are saying. That's bullshit.'

It was at this moment, with all this money coming into the game, that the football authorities decided that they couldn't afford the £80,000 a year it cost to keep the Football Stadia Advisory Design Council (FSADC) going. Established as a central recommendation (number 5) of the Taylor Report, the FSADC was conceived as an attempt to replicate one aspect of a service provided by the Italian Olympic Committee (CONI), which controls all sport in Italy, by providing technical advice and support to architects and engineers at the sharp end of implementing the Taylor Report. These people were able to refer to a number of guides compiled by the FSADC covering seating, sight-lines, roofing, PA systems, facilities for the disabled and, after the government revoked the all-seat edict for the lower divisions, safe terracing.

Unfortunately, the apathy of the FA allowed Football League president Gordon McKeag (elected to that position following the death of Bill Fox), to attack the FSADC. The thrust of his criticism was that if architects and engineers were benefiting from the service, then they and not the football authorities should pay for it. The interdependence between good design, safety and economy never seemed to strike McKeag as a good enough reason for the maintenance of the FSADC. Who needs some smart alec architect pointing out that a recent £500,000 roof extension at Villa Park would need substantial overhauling if good sight-lines were to be guaranteed when extra seating was installed? But it is football fans, not architects, who have to sit in new stadia. Rather than attempting to improve Britain's woeful safety record or positively help the fans get the better accommodation they deserve, the authorities backed out once again, leaving it up to individual clubs like Arsenal and Manchester United to set the standards in the forlorn hope that they will be emulated by everyone else.

Unlike the situation at Charlton Athletic, whose return to The Valley restored the club's soul, and Millwall, who moved to a new purpose-built stadium and leisure complex just down the road from The Den (at the exotically named Senegal Field, which opened in August 1993 with a game against Bobby Robson's Sporting Lisbon), compliance with the Taylor Report almost destroyed West Ham. It certainly broke the emotional bond between club and supporter. It is difficult to see how harmony can be completely restored, despite the new season ticket pricing policy. The regime made just about every mistake possible.

With no guidelines from above, clubs that for years had done little to improve facilities were now in way over their heads. The FA said and did nothing beyond the platitudes of the Blueprint; the Football League was itself in a battle for survival and could hardly be expected to spare the energy; and the Premier League was totally distracted by the mountains of television and sponsorship money that was falling into its lap. The Taylor Report required the clearest thinking and the boldest strategy. Instead, nothing whatsoever has been done by the football authorities to guide clubs at probably the most crucial time in the entire history of English football. The National Plan for Stadia has sunk without trace and nothing has been offered in its place. For supporters, it was a matter of luck whether the directors were, as at Leicester and Leeds, up to the job. If they were not, then supporters themselves would have to battle to save their beloved clubs and, by extension, the game itself, from disintegration. In this almost surreal atmosphere, where incompetence and duplicity had been raised to an art form, Graham Taylor was expected to produce a winning England team.

6

The Great and the Good

The start of Graham Taylor's attempt to get England to the USA in 1994 and how two old boys remind everyone they are still around

'He isn't the new Pele, the new Maradona or the new Cruyff. He is Gascoigne, and you should not want him to be anything else. Don't make comparisons.'

Diego Maradona, after a friendly game between Lazio and Seville,
November 1992.

'Because they [Glenn Hoddle and Kevin Keegan] enjoyed highly lucrative careers, because their talent carried them to the rich pastures of the European game, they can indulge their love of the game. They do not have to live with the grinding insecurity of having their livelihood hinge on the next result, however it is achieved.'

Republic of Ireland international, member of Don Revie's all-conquering Leeds and ex-manager of West Bromwich Albion,
John Giles.

It was the goal the whole nation had been waiting for. Not any old goal, but one bearing the mark of undoubted class. A little shimmy left the Turkish goalkeeper and a defender sitting on their backsides, allowing Paul Gascoigne to plant the ball anywhere he chose in the opposition's net to make the score 4–0 in England's favour. Of all the players available to Graham Taylor for that night's World Cup qualifying match at Wembley, only Gazza possessed the talent and the confidence to produce a finish like that. His performance had rejuvenated the England team. As Stuart Jones put it in *The Times*: 'Gascoigne has acted as a catalyst, transforming England from the negative to the positive. Without him last summer a confused bunch of moderate representatives finished seventh in the European Championships. With him at Wembley on Wednesday a compact and purposeful unit achieved their biggest win for three and a half years.'

Although the standard of the opposition in Sweden was in a different class to the one at Wembley, the importance of Gazza to England's cause was never more apparent than when, for whatever reason, he was not playing. After the debacle in Sweden the England team, and Graham Taylor, had fences to mend with the public. The first opportunity came in September 1992 with an away friendly against Spain in the northern port of Santander. But the outlook was bleak. There was little evidence that the manager had decided upon a specific tactical plan for his side. Gazza, meanwhile, although he travelled with the party, had still not recovered sufficiently from the horrific knee injury he sustained in the 1991 Cup final to have any chance of playing. And, for some unknown reason, England traditionally perform poorly during the month of September.

While the 1–0 defeat in Santander – courtesy of a splendid run by Martin Vasquez and a shot by Fonseca after Des Walker had given the ball away – represented only the third reverse in twenty-five games under Taylor, it was worrying for a number of reasons. It came straight after the appalling Swedish performances, was the second loss in a row, and England created few chances beyond a glaring miss during the opening exchanges by new cap David White. In addition, the team had scored only one goal in its last five games. Ironically, Spain, playing for the first time under a new coach, the highly respected Javier Clemente, beat England by using a game plan for which England were once famous, just as Taylor claimed Sweden had done three months before in Gothenburg. Then, the use of four forwards had bemused the English midfield and defence; now the Spanish midfield displayed a mobility and a willingness to get forward which continually stretched the England defence.

After the match, Taylor bridled at criticism of his team's performance. When Martin Tyler, commentating on the match for BSkyB, put it to the manager that the display had been 'dismal', Taylor disagreed vehemently: 'I don't agree that

Spain could have buried us. We had an early chance that we didn't take and we then presented them with a goal.' Taylor perhaps gave away his true feelings when he continued: 'My players have got to be encouraged and supported. Criticism like that won't help them.' Once again the manager seemed to have forgotten that it is not the job of the media to help him, but to report on events. Players and spectators alike know full well the difference between a good performance and a bad one. It does nobody any good to pretend one is the other, as if footballers inhabit some looking-glass world where the evidence of the eyes is disavowed.

Predictably, the press were less than charitable in their assessment of the defeat. The *Sun*, having started a new fashion with its 'Turnips' headline after the Swedish debacle, was now calling Graham Taylor a Spanish Onion and put him on notice of what would happen if things did not improve in time for the next England game, at Wembley against Norway in the first qualifier for the 1994 World Cup finals in the USA. Its editorial on the subject stated: 'The land of the Vikings does not have its own national vegetable, but it does grow some enormous carrots!' A competition was started for recipes to go in the Graham Taylor Cookbook. However, the momentum of the *Sun*'s vegetable attack would be rendered academic if Taylor took the advice of yet another comment headlined: SUNSPORT SPEAKS ITS MIND. FOR CRYING OUT LOUD, GO, it screamed. Not to be outdone, the *Daily Mirror* devoted the whole of its back page to a massive headline calling on Taylor to resign, summed up by the words, ADIOS TAYLOR.

There was no chance of that happening, but it was now all too clear that something dramatic was needed if the World Cup qualifying campaign was not to end in tears. Commenting on the call for him to quit, Taylor leaned on contractual, rather than footballing reasons for his decision to soldier on. 'I have a job to do and I will do that job until the end of my contract,' he said. 'It is not a question of whether I am the best man for the job or not because I was appointed and I have the job.' The facts were that England looked dull and boring. There was a noticeable deficiency in skill throughout the team and nothing seemed to have been learned from events in Sweden. Once again, the manager had made a rod for his own back with his pre-match predictions.

Taylor's crystal ball-gazing was fast turning him into the Gipsy Rose Lee of British football. Before the game, he had not only promised to win, he had also told fans that his team would entertain. When they failed on both counts, Taylor was left to explain why, if he wanted so much to put on an attractive display, he signally ignored players of skill such as Peter Beardsley and Chris Waddle, who were capable of delivering just that.

Of course, the perennial shambles that passes for the professional game in England did not help the cause of its national team in Spain. A dozen players were ruled out of the squad through injuries, a result of the almost unbelievable number of games in the Premier League at the beginning of the season. This had come about because four Saturdays had to be kept free to accommodate England's preparations for World Cup games in 1992–93. With the emergence of a number of new nation states in eastern and central Europe, there were far more European entrants for the World Cup but no increase in the number of qualifying places. This meant larger groups and more matches. None of this was taken into account by those who blithely forged ahead with the forty-two-game Premier League, despite the fact, as Colin Malam pointed out in the *Sunday Telegraph*, that 'the whole purpose of the Premier League, its *raison d'être*, was to improve the chances of the national team by lightening the domestic load on players.' The price for that lack of foresight was an increasing number of injuries and another failure by the England team. The whole sorry situation was summed up in an aside George Graham made to David Dein after a quarter of an hour of Arsenal's game against Wimbledon the Saturday before the match against Spain. 'The boys,' he declared, 'are knackered.'

As England, like a runaway train, careered towards the buffers of another World Cup fiasco, there were at least a couple of reasons for a certain amount of guarded optimism. First, Paul Gascoigne was at last beginning his comeback with Lazio, and had scored a goal in a friendly match against Tottenham. Second, Taylor had gone out of his way to publicly mend his relationships with Peter Beardsley and Chris Waddle following the misunderstandings concerning their supposed reluctance to play for England. On the minus side, having made such a big thing of the reconciliation,

Taylor proceeded to name neither player in his squad for the upcoming Norway game.

Taylor decided to recall Gazza to the squad and much of the country's attention focused on his comeback at Lazio, which the whole nation could follow as a consequence of the Italian league matches being screened by Channel 4. As far as England were concerned, no one was entirely sure whether Gazza would be in the starting line-up or what formation Taylor would employ. By the time of the match Gazza had played only three games for Lazio and had not stayed the course in any of them. Two of these were league matches and in both he showed enough to suggest that he might, in time, recover fully from his knee injury. Nonetheless, he was obviously well short of match fitness and his inclusion in the important game England were about to play could only ever be a gamble.

Aside from the Gazza question, Taylor had still not accepted that he should have an overall tactical plan and pick the players to implement it. 'I would like to introduce a long-term strategy,' he said, 'but in international football you have to design tactics around the players you have and the needs and circumstances of the fixture.' This was a philosophy to which hardly any successful international manager in living memory has subscribed. Alf Ramsey often said that the reason he didn't pick wingers in 1966 was because there weren't any of sufficient quality around the time. This led to a strategic decision to play in a 4–4–2 formation. Once this was decided upon, Ramsey implemented it with ruthless efficiency and, by and large, this was the formation used in every game no matter which players came and went or who the opposition were. Bryan Robson, having retired from international football, felt free to put the players' perspective: 'Where there's no pattern and players are out of touch a team becomes disjointed. It doesn't matter how good your players are, every team needs a system to fall back on.'

There was a simple objective as far as England were concerned and it applied not just to the game against Norway. England had three successive home World Cup matches to come and they needed to win them all. As for Norway, they were coming to Wembley with three straight World Cup wins (including a 3–2 defeat of Holland, the group favourites) and had a maximum six points. It was likely that they would view a draw as an excellent result. By defeating them, England could dent their confidence and self-belief as well as collect two points. In a group containing Holland and Poland, the early elimination of Norway was almost a prerequisite to qualifying for the finals.

In the event, Taylor decided to take the gamble and play his mercurial star from the start. Amazingly, Gazza lasted the full ninety minutes. He was assisted by Taylor's decision to use David Batty and Paul Ince to win the ball in midfield. However, having dominated most of the game, England failed to turn their superiority into goals and could not improve on David Platt's solitary effort, which left the Juventus player having scored England's last five. As is always a possibility when the score is 1–0, Norway grabbed a draw with a wonderful shot by Rekdal, a real screamer from the edge of the box which left Chris Woods clutching air. Norway had hardly threatened the England goal all game but one moment of opportunism had sent them home with the point they desired.

Apart from the result, the game was characterised by a superb performance by Gazza which caught the eye time and again. In the following days, the nation was once again submerged in Gazzamania with the press leading the way. It wasn't only the press, though. Gary Lineker was equally enthusiastic. 'His performance was incredible, absolutely outstanding,' he enthused. 'He never slowed down for ninety minutes and he can do things on the field you don't usually see from ordinary mortals.' Lineker was in danger of being carried away by his own hyperbole as he continued his panegyric: 'If anything, his lack of match fitness worked for him. He didn't go chasing the ball in suicidal situations as he normally does. It also meant he was more likely to pass the ball, as opposed to only giving it away when he knows he's going to get it back.' It was hard to suppress the image of Graham Taylor asking Lawrie McMenemy to wait outside the stadium with a baseball bat every time Gazza played to give him a good whack across the knees – just to ensure he didn't regain full match fitness.

It was left to less enthusiastic analysts to put the performance of Gazza and England into some sort of perspective. To them, this had been a home World Cup game against opponents who put on a mediocre display and had little ambition beyond securing a point. Yet England had failed to win. Hugh McIlvanney, writing in the *Observer*, posed the question: 'Have we been so institutionalised by the recent diet of workhouse gruel that we are prepared to burst into rapturous applause at the first taste of something more palatable?' While praising the contribution made by Gazza, McIlvanney went on: 'At the risk of reintroducing that old bugbear, perspective, it should be said that if Bobby Charlton in his prime had done precisely as well as Gascoigne did on Wednesday he would not have been praised to anything like the same extent.' Colin Malam, football correspondent of the *Sunday Telegraph*, saw both sides of the argument and came to the conclusion that, while England's display had not been out of the top drawer, 'the majority of us who had seen goalless draws with Denmark and France and the defeats by Sweden and Spain were simply glad to discern distinct signs of individual and collective improvement. For the first time in quite a while, England were recognisably a team in shape and attitude.' If such improvement could be maintained as Gazza regained full fitness, then there was some hope for the future, particularly since Norway were nowhere near as poor a side as the pessimists made out. Nonetheless, the fact of the matter was that England had lost a vital point at home, which might yet come back to haunt them later in the competition. Gazza, moreover, was one booking away from suspension, having picked up a yellow card in the Norway match for elbowing an opponent.

Graham Taylor seemed convinced that he had now got his selection right. 'I hope we can keep the majority of the squad together,' he said. 'We have to improve on the way we played but all we have to do is a bit of fine tuning.' This view of Taylor's thinking was confirmed when the party for the next World Cup game against Turkey at Wembley in November was announced. It contained virtually the same players as that for Norway. Even Ian Wright, (at last given his opportunity following the departure of Gary Lineker) who had let nerves get the better of him against the Norwegians and might have been expected to make way for another, was retained. Perhaps mindful of the furore that greeted his treatment of Gary Lineker, the inclusion of Wright, about whom Taylor had expressed doubts in the past, showed that the manager was prepared to give someone with undoubted prowess in the penalty area more than one chance. When the team took to the field, the only change was Carlton Palmer coming in for David Batty, who was injured. Also, for perhaps the first time in twenty-seven games under Taylor, the tactical approach was going to be the same for two consecutive matches. The midfield was built around Gazza, with Ince, Palmer and Platt there to ensure the Lazio man constantly received the ball.

While the draw against Norway was accepted because of what had gone before (2 wins in 10 games), against Turkey, nothing less than a win would do. Taylor thought as much himself. 'All hell will break loose if we don't win this one,' he said. The game did not begin particularly well and England could have gone behind when Unal crashed a shot against the bar with the unprotected goal at his mercy. Paul Gascoigne, however, was not to be denied. Running the midfield imperiously, he scored the first goal himself, provided a delicious flick to set in motion the move which led to the third, then produced that shimmy which left Turks spreadeagled on the deck while he calmly side-footed the fourth and final goal. It was the most emphatic win in Graham Taylor's tenure as England manager and provided the country's supporters with their first real cheer since Italia '90. If this was what a settled tactical plan could produce after two games, perhaps Taylor was at last on to something.

Afterwards, Taylor was quick to point to the performances of those who had done the fetching and carrying for Gazza. 'We're trying to create a squad togetherness,' the manager said. Psychologically, this was probably the right thing to say, but there could be no denying that England without Gazza were nothing more than a moderate side, whereas with him they could reach the heights. It is not simply the man's talent and ability, it is the way he plays the game, the infectious enthusiasm he brings to all he does. Unlike many gifted players, he also possesses a never-say-die attitude. As long as Gazza is on the pitch, team-mates and fans alike sense that there is a chance of a result no matter what the odds. Hearing the applause ring around Wembley brought back memories of long-ago England performances that many thought had gone forever. Taylor's real concerns emerged later, when he said:

'For two years, we've been trying to eke out results without Gascoigne. You find yourself saying, please God, don't let anything go wrong with him.'

At the risk of appearing to carp, it must be said that if Norway were thought to be mediocre, Turkey, although coached by that wily old fox Sepp Piontek, who had master-minded Denmark's rise from the football wilderness, were simply third rate. Would Gazza be allowed the same space to express his skills by the likes of Holland and Poland? Moreover, was it not dangerous to be so beholden to one indi-vidual, no matter how talented? Gascoigne is always liable to get booked or injured, and what happens to the side in his absence? In answer to these questions it can be said that the opposition, no matter how poor, has to be beaten and a team cannot do better than to win well and convincingly. And Turkey were not the first team to fail to man-mark Gascoigne out of a game. Throughout his career, many opposing coaches have believed that if they gave him enough rope, he would hang himself. In other words, they were deceived by Gazza's reputation for pressing the self-destruct button. In addition, if you attempt to restrict him, Gascoigne can beat even the best markers so easily and so often that detailing one player to shadow him is often deemed a waste of time.

The truth is that, like George Best (though many will find the comparison odious), when Gascoigne is on song it doesn't matter what you try to do, you simply will not stop him. Finally, although it is difficult to remember another side which relied so heavily on one player (Argentina and Maradona in 1990, perhaps), at least Graham Taylor had the courage to realise that the gamble was worth taking and he could now point to his England displaying a recognisable tactical formation from game to game, rather than the chop-ping and changing which characterised life without Gazza. Anyway, if England are going to fail, as they surely will without Gascoigne, they might as well fail gloriously, playing football which induces the public to put their hands in their pockets and feel they have not, for once, been short-changed.

This is not to disparage the contribution of the rest of the team, especially the midfield. Ince and Palmer played their parts perfectly, without any sign of envy for the luxurious role given to Gascoigne. And David Platt, who, let us not forget, cost Juventus £6.5 million, is to be particularly commended for carrying out his tasks as second fiddle so assiduously. For this, Graham Taylor must take most of the credit, although some of the plaudits go to Gazza himself, for his own modest attitude. For all the others' worthiness in diligently following orders, though, it was plain to see that Gazza was indispensable, and that Taylor, for all his wariness of stars (apart, that is, from John Barnes) knew he was. This made Gazza's omission for the Irish game the previous season all the more mystifying. This matter was cleared up somewhat when Taylor, not long after the Turkish game, offered a different version of events to the one he had given at the time. 'I can never actually say everything about that decision,' the manager revealed. 'I was concerned about his health. It was my first experience of seeing somebody who looked quite glazed at times. Everybody always wants a bit of the boy but I need him for England. That's the tightrope. The reasons to drop him were not tactical. There were certain incidents before the game. The boy was in a state and I was concerned about his health. I don't think he knew what was happening to him but it shook him when he knew he was not going to play.'

Like it or not, Gazza had assumed the mantle of irreplaceability that once belonged to Bobby Charlton. When the England team were in training for the 1970 World Cup there was some confusion around a complex tactical manoeuvre. Alan Mullery later recalled how the manager, Alf Ramsey, sorted it out in his usual brusque fashion. 'You,' he said, pointing at Mullery, 'give the ball to him,' pointing to Bobby Charlton.

For Charlton read Gazza, but of course the 1970 World Cup side had one or two other quality players. Gordon Banks was one, and who could forget the way Terry Cooper attacked from the back? Moreover, according to Mullery, 'Bobby Moore was the greatest reader of a game you've ever seen.' There was also Alan Ball and Martin Peters alongside Mullery in midfield, while in attack, Ramsey played Geoff Hurst and Francis Lee and had Colin Bell and Peter Osgood on the bench. The 1992 side could boast no one beyond Gazza to mention in the same breath as these. Anyone who saw the marvellous game between England and Brazil, won narrowly by the future champions, Brazil, with a single goal from Jairzinho, could ever forget it. A superhuman save by Banks from Pele is one of the most famous pieces of sporting film ever. Lee Dixon's continual forays down the touchline against Turkey in 1992 were certainly praiseworthy in terms of effort, but they bore little resemblance to the game of football produced by the England class of 1970.

This makes Taylor's decision to build a team round the talents of Paul Gascoigne even more praiseworthy. It was certainly more than Bobby Robson had been prepared to do, his quixotic passage to the semi-finals of Italia 90 notwithstanding. Robson could have done it prior to the arrival of Gazza but never did. Perhaps Gazza is extremely lucky to have found Graham Taylor as his manager with England, otherwise he might have gone the same way as Glenn Hoddle.

Compared to Gazza, Hoddle was an angel, even before he found equanimity in more spiritual matters. On the field he could play like one, off it he retained the respect of all his peers. But neither Ron Greenwood, the manager who first picked him for England, nor Bobby Robson ever had the confidence to build a team round him in the way Taylor came to believe in Gascoigne.

Hoddle scored on his debut for England, a 20-yard volley with his instep against Bulgaria, but was immediately dropped by Ron Greenwood, who made the immortal remark: 'Glenn has to learn that the career of a footballer is built on disappointments.' In contrast to his approach at club level when he was manager of West Ham, on taking over the England job, Greenwood became afflicted by the all-consuming fear that seems to grip all occupants of the hot seat. Thereafter, Hoddle was used intermittently while Greenwood and his successor, Bobby Robson, preferred to put their faith in the more prosaic talents of Bryan Robson, who was always seen as a more 'reliable' player than Hoddle. These managers paid lip-service to Hoddle's ability. Greenwood called it 'prodigious' while Robson said: 'Hoddle is a fantastic player.' Neither, however, was prepared to let him lord it over England's midfield as he did for Tottenham.

Hoddle does not fit entirely into the pattern set when creative players from a previous generation, such as Frank Worthington, Rodney Marsh, Stan Bowles, Alan Hudson,

Charlie George and Tony Currie, to name but six, were ignored by England managers. However, he was rarely able to get a decent run in the team to establish himself and was often made the scapegoat when things went wrong. Hoddle had his detractors, one of whom was Alf Ramsey, who criticised his commitment in a newspaper column. It is probably true that it was possible to put Hoddle out of the game by excessive physical challenges. Nevertheless, as one H. Davidson, writing in the *Spur* fanzine, put it: 'Just like Tottenham Hotspur FC, Glenn Hoddle was unpredictable, glamorous, erratic, frustrating and glorious – with the ability to take you from ecstasy to despair (and sometimes back again).' Unlike Gascoigne against Norway and Turkey, Hoddle had no minders to do his tackling or his fetching and carrying. As Hoddle himself recalls: 'I played one game [out of fifty-three] off the front in a free role like I did for Tottenham. I was never given the freedom to play in their [the opposition's] half.'

Others believed that the misuse of Hoddle was criminal. George Best, speaking in 1992, said, 'If you are honest, when he was at the peak of his career he should have been the first player on the team sheet. The guy had so much talent. He was such a great player.' Danny Blanchflower, the captain of the Tottenham double team in 1961, neatly turned the argument that Hoddle was a luxury player on its head when he declared: 'It is bad players who are the luxuries.' The central point about Hoddle, which also applies to the other players of flair who rarely played for England, was that while he was sitting on the sidelines there was hardly a plethora of skilful alternatives occupying his place, and England's record during Hoddle's time was characterised in the main by disappointment and, the World Cup quarter-final place in 1986 apart, abject failure.

After he had moved to France to play for Monaco, Hoddle gained a new perspective on his playing style. 'I had my admirers in England, especially at Tottenham,' he said, 'but I was always being criticised for a lack of defensive work. When I look back to the days when I first went to Spurs at fourteen, I remember some of the players then and I feel they had their natural game knocked out of them. I'm doing more defensive work here than I ever did at Tottenham, but I'm doing it in the opposition's half of the field.' This was one of the precepts Hoddle put into practice when he went into management with Swindon.

As he moved from player to player-manager, taking up the role of sweeper en route, there was never any danger of him not utilising players of talent and flair. A club like Swindon cannot compete when it comes to buying power but Hoddle nevertheless produced a side which, because it played attractive, passing football, people wanted to watch. Hoddle was adamant that this system is the one that should be employed throughout the English game. 'If you give them [the players] the platform, if you give them the system, if you create the chances that we can at Swindon in a minor way. At the very top level the sky's the limit.' Hoddle's way of management is naturally based on a passing game. 'At times,' he said, 'it would be five at the back, at times, three at the back. I believe in nice, wide full backs stretching teams to the limit but there are times when you have to push them in. You play with a very good player on the ball at the back. He has to be possibly the best passer in the team. You definitely need that for the system to work offensively, going forward.'

This, in Hoddle's view, is the crucial area where the national side comes unstuck. 'I think,' he continued, 'the midfield and the attacking players are as good as anyone in the world.' The problems, he feels, are at the back. 'Technically, at the back we would need to develop from a younger age. The back players need a lot of work with their touch to be comfortable with the ball. If the system I believe [in were to be] played, it would give the back players a little more time on the ball. Whether, at the moment, they are ready to use it as well as the French and Germans, I'm not so sure.' Whatever the imperfections, perhaps there is really no choice as the natural English inclination to stuff the defence with big centre backs seems out of time with the realities of modern international football. As Hoddle says, 'I've always thought, why put two six-foot centre halves there waiting for a ball to be knocked into the channel? It never happens in international football. You've got to have a bit of security [a sweeper] behind you because of the pace, touch and ability they've got to go by you.' Putting his theories into practice, Hoddle made sure that all teams at Swindon, down to the youth side, played in the same manner. 'I'm not doing it to make an impression,' he said. 'I'm doing it because I believe it is the right way to play. I believe it is the right way to be successful in the long run. It's the way I wanted to play the game so why make other people play a different way?'

The key, Hoddle says, is in training. He refutes the notion that because we play so many games there is no time to work on technique. 'Within the [training] session,' he revealed, 'we will always have a fifteen- to twenty-minute spell to work on our techniques – hitting a person's chest, dropping it on his thigh. Then you might do a [group of] threes where you work half-volleys, which all clubs do pre-season, but when the season starts [they] don't do that sort of thing. Come February we will still be doing it and players get better and better. I've seen it with my own eyes [at Swindon]. Big Sean Taylor from Exeter and Colin Calderwood – they're doing things now on the pitch they never dreamed they'd do. They've been given the confidence, they've worked hard at it. It starts to come in training and then it's happening on the pitch. Bingo!'

Another Swindon player who benefited from the Hoddle style is Martin Ling, who has been a revelation since his move from Southend. 'I'm twenty-six,' Ling remarked to the *Observer*'s Patrick Barclay in 1992, 'and wish Glenn had got hold of me at sixteen. I'm sure I'd have had a different career. He's brought me on unbelievably. But all the players feel the same. We're constantly encouraged to play to feet and the more it comes to feet, the more comfortable you get. Glenn brings out ability by giving you the confidence to express yourself. Most players are at clubs, I've been at them, where you're told to hoof the ball. When you are chained, you have no choice. You do it or get dropped. I believe that if every manager were like ours, English football would improve out of all recognition.'

Hoddle's success at Swindon pleasantly surprised his former chairman at Spurs, Irving Scholar, who reflected the prevailing view of those who knew Hoddle well that while he would make a good coach, he was not tough enough to be a manager. It goes to show that genius makes its own rules. Having succeeded as a player at the highest level there is a well of respect and admiration for Hoddle to draw on to facilitate the difficult task of man-management. Of course the continentals have always known this, so Cruyff, Beckenbauer and Platini were able to make the transition from great player to successful manager. Like them, Hoddle surely deserves the biggest possible stage to display his wares.

After guiding Swindon to the Premier League via the play-offs, Hoddle probably felt he had taken a club of limited resources as far as he could. Speculation mounted in the summer of 1993 that he would take over the reins at Spurs following the dismissal of Terry Venables, but it was Ken Bates who tempted him back to London, and Hoddle became player-manager of Chelsea. It remains to be seen whether he will go the way of his predecessors at Stamford Bridge. Chelsea have gone through five managers in eight years, some not coming up to Ken Bates' expectations, others proving unable to withstand the force of the chairman's personality. Having laboured long and successfully to secure Chelsea's future at Stamford Bridge, perhaps Bates now realised that the best chance for the club, which in the words of one observer, 'hasn't won an egg cup in years' (the ZDS trophy is presumably less than an egg cup), is to give Hoddle the space and time to develop his ideas. Paradoxically, if Hoddle does succeed, Ken Bates will probably have rendered his greatest service to English football, not only by rejuvenating his club but perhaps also by grooming the future manager of the national team.

Hoddle is one of three outstanding examples of former star players who, in 1992–93, were shaking up the old managerial order. One of the others was Osvaldo Ardiles, the Argentinian who preceded Hoddle at Swindon, gained the club promotion to the First Division for the first time in its history, only to have the achievement snatched away because of financial irregularities during the reign of a previous manager, Lou Macari. FA regulations excluded Ardiles from holding an English coaching badge because he is a foreigner. This strange state of affairs meant, according to the FA's director of coaching, Charles Hughes, that he should not be allowed to manage a league club. Fortunately for Swindon and Ardiles' subsequent clubs, Newcastle, West Brom and Tottenham, the game's rules have no such stipulation. Hughes was not necessarily being xenophobic: he simply believed that all managers should have earned the right to manage via the FA coaching system. Indeed, Hughes was taken aback when he learned that Hoddle would be replacing Ardiles at Swindon. 'I'm sure he's a nice enough chap,' Hughes said, 'but what does he know of management? Where's his [FA] qualification?' Hughes would be hard pushed to find anyone in Wiltshire or west London to agree with him.

Even during his spell at Newcastle, when a young team slipped perilously towards relegation, Ardiles did not have to suffer the sort of humiliating treatment at the hands of the fans that signalled the impending demise of many of his predecessors. A drop to the lower levels for the first time in the club's history would have proved catastrophic to Newcastle, and Ardiles was fired, to be replaced by one of English football's most charismatic figures, Kevin Keegan, who had been allowed to lounge on a Spanish beach in the eight years since his retirement from playing, his experience and knowledge denied to the English game.

Keegan, while not as naturally gifted a player as either Hoddle or Ardiles, nevertheless achieved a greatness comparable to both and was twice elected European Footballer of the Year. In Keegan's case it was done with hard work and a tremendous appetite for the game. Keegan's game as a player was built on work-rate, willpower and intelligence. He was not a naturally creative player like Hoddle, but through his determination to succeed allied to boundless energy he brought out the best in those around him. A leader by example on the field, Keegan was instrumental in Liverpool's first European Cup win in 1977, after which he moved to SV Hamburg in Germany, where he propelled the team to a Bundesliga triumph – the club's first in twenty years – and a European Cup final. Yet after a career characterised as much by his shrewdness in business dealings as by his achievements on the pitch, Keegan was forgotten by the English game until Newcastle's chairman, Sir John Hall, needed a messiah to lead his battered army away from the deep waters of relegation to the high ground which every Newcastle fan believes is the club's rightful place.

Keegan knew all about Newcastle. As a player he had seen out his career at St James's Park with an amazing promotion season under Arthur Cox. When Keegan bowed out, he left behind a team containing Chris Waddle and Peter Beardsley, with a young lad named Paul Gascoigne in the youth side. Still, Keegan believed that Newcastle needed more quality players to survive in the top flight. Not only were they not forthcoming, but one by one Beardsley, Waddle and Gascoigne were sold for huge sums in a vain attempt to balance the books. Not surprisingly, Keegan was proved right and after a constant battle for survival Newcastle were relegated in 1989. When he came back as manager, Keegan made it clear that he would not stay if this attitude persisted.

There were many who believed Keegan had been out of the game for too long to be able to save United from Division 3. Keegan showed, however, that you do not lose your football touch, just as you do not forget how to ride a bike. By putting together a mixture of youth and experience (something Ardiles was not allowed to do), relegation was duly avoided amid great celebrations with a win away at Leicester in the final game of the season. Having occupied one of the relegation places for most of the season, it was a stupendous achievement. Keegan began the following campaign with an astonishing eleven straight wins and Newcastle won promotion to the Premier League as champions of the new Football League. It was an astonishing turn-around, accomplished in the course of one season. In the final match of the season at St James's Park, again against Leicester City, Keegan's team thrashed the visitors 7–1, encapsulating in ninety minutes the evidence of how the manager had revitalised the club. Keegan described the performance as 'a shot across the bows of the Premier league – but it will take a lot of living up to'.

Like Hoddle, Keegan chose to eschew the long-ball game, although Keegan's team is more pragmatic than Hoddle's. 'We haven't changed anything massive in the way we play,' he said by way of explanation of his side's upturn in form. 'There is no way you can go so quickly from the bottom to the top. We have . . . tried to play more in the opponents' half. But you can't make a system and say play that way. You have to suit the players you have got.'

Keegan always believed he had the ability to become a successful manager but was only ever going to do it on his terms. There were, he said, only two managerial jobs he would consider. One was Newcastle, where he was an idol following his exploits in Arthur Cox's 1984 promotion team. Keegan also understood the unique craving for success that is both the blessing and the curse of Tyneside. His return as manager was a truly emotional experience as United saw off

Bristol City in front of a full house. Not long afterwards, Keegan threatened to resign as he felt that promises made to him by the board concerning the money available to him for transfers were not being kept. Under intense pressure, Sir John Hall and the board publicly declared that Keegan would get the finance he needed. The threat of resignation receded, and Keegan had shown both courage, in standing up to the board, and realism, in his assessment of what the club need-ed to prosper. His talent for man-management could also be seen in his relationships with his players, more than one of whom turned down offers to play Premier League football with other clubs to be with Keegan on his great Geordie adventure. As Dean Christopher, writing in the Newcastle fanzine, *The Mag*, put it, 'I know we shouldn't build our hopes up too high, especially on the evidence of seasons past, but you've got to have your dreams. And in Kevin Keegan, we do have someone who has a habit of making them come true.'

The other job which Keegan would have no hesitation in taking is that of England manager. Unlike on the continent, where Beckenbauer, Vogts and Platini stepped into international management after illustrious playing careers, the credentials of Hoddle or Keegan have never been seriously contemplated by the FA. It is still felt, despite all the evidence to the contrary that has stacked up over the years, that a safe bet, a successful club manager, is the answer. Perhaps it isn't. Certainly Paul Gascoigne is now benefiting from Graham Taylor's late conversion, but it was a situation forced on the manager by the threadbare nature of the alternatives to giving Gazza his head. Moreover, Taylor has reaped the benefit of Gascoigne's move to Italy, where many thought he would be out of his depth, emotionally as much as in his playing ability.

Apart from the usual England muddle, a new dimension to the country's footballing problems was about to rear its head. If the England national team has consistently got it wrong, then at least the country could always point to the success of its clubs in Europe as a unique strength in the English game. The advent of the Premier League was supposed to help reinforce this position by providing a showcase for the best. As events were about to show, however, that was just one more illusion waiting to be shattered.

7

Little England

**How Leeds fight a lone battle in Europe and the English system
finally helps bring Liverpool down to everyone else's level**

> *'It frightens me, the way our game is going.'*
>
> John Mortimore, assistant manager of Southampton and former
> Portuguese championship-winning coach with Benfica.

> *'Mind, I've been here during the bad times too. One
> year we came second.'*
>
> Bob Paisley, former Liverpool manager.

By Christmas 1992, no English club had survived in any of the
season's three European competitions. Even worse to English
eyes was the unpleasant fact that the Scottish champions,
Glasgow Rangers, were left to carry the flag as Britain's sole
representative. In the UEFA Cup, Sheffield Wednesday and
Manchester United suffered ignominious exits. Wednesday
went out at the hands of the German team Kaiserslautern,
losing the services of David Hirst for most of the two legs after
he was sent off in Germany, while United failed to get past
Torpedo Moscow. Liverpool, after Bruce Grobbelaar had
surpassed his own capacity for eccentricity in the opening
leg, were dumped out of the Cup-winners' Cup in unceremo-
nious fashion by another Muscovite side, Spartak. David
Lacey, writing in the *Guardian*, summed up football's 'Black
Wednesday', when he proclaimed that the English game had
been 'wiped off the map of Europe'. Not only that, according
to Lacey, England's representatives had been revealed as 'a
handful of hapless homespun hopalongs playing second

fiddle to Turkey and Greece'. The most disappointing performance of all, however, came from Leeds United in the Champions' Cup. Moreover, Leeds' tormentors were not one of the continental giants, but Glasgow Rangers.

In truth, Leeds should not have reached the second round. Their first-round tie against the German champions, Stuttgart, was lost over the two legs but a deciding match was played after it was discovered that the Germans had fielded an ineligible player for part of the second leg. In their most outstanding display of the season, Leeds won the sudden-death play-off in Barcelona 2–1, with Carl Shutt coming on as a substitute to score a superb winner. By the time of the match in Barcelona, the momentum was with the English club. Stuttgart by then were a spent force who had seen defeat snatched from the jaws of victory, both on the pitch, where they started the second leg leading by three goals, and in the committee rooms of UEFA, where Leeds' presence in the competition was saved, not by the eloquence of the FA or a commitment to justice on the part of UEFA, but by the intervention of an executive of a British television company.

Poor defending, compounded by their naïve chasing of the game after they conceded a goal an hour into the first leg in Germany, saw Leeds virtually written off. They eventually went down by 3–0. The English system, as much as Leeds' failings, was largely culpable as the English champions looked doomed for the second year running. Not only was it Leeds' tenth game in thirty-two days, but their fixture the previous Saturday had been moved back a day to Sunday by BSkyB, allowing them even less time to prepare. In an heroic effort in the return leg at Elland Road two weeks later, Leeds almost turned the tie round but conceded an all-important away goal, rendering the 4–1 win insufficient. The club and its supporters resigned themselves to elimination. The following day it emerged that the normally ultra-efficient Germans had made an inexplicable mistake. UEFA had established new rules restricting the number of foreign players allowed to appear in European competitions to three per club. The definition of 'foreign' was peculiar to UEFA in that it did not necessarily refer to citizens of other nation states or political entities, but to those who hailed from countries which had separate membership of UEFA. This meant that for English clubs, Scottish, Welsh and Irish players were deemed 'foreign'.

Many saw the UEFA directive as a direct assault on traditional British privileges. Graham Kelly stoutly denied it, saying that UEFA were in favour of the retention of separate identities for the four home associations as they bolstered the European power base inside FIFA, the world governing body. It was also argued by more cynical minds that UEFA's policy was deliberately designed by the Latin lobby to work against British clubs by weakening their playing strength. The rule change had little real effect outside the UK as most clubs fielded, in the main, their own nationals. Indeed, it could be said that Manchester United's success in winning the Cup-winners' Cup hastened the rule change. The regulation was brought in the following season and from then on, if English teams were to do well in Europe, it would be under the greatest of handicaps. 'It's no coincidence,' said Alex Ferguson, Manchester United's manager, 'that we won the Cup-winners' Cup in the last season when we could play who we wanted.' Whatever the case, Jacques Georges, the UEFA president in 1988 when restrictions on foreign players were first discussed, pointed out the consistency of UEFA's argument when he said: 'The British FAs want four votes on the international bodies and want to enter four national teams in the European Championships and the World Cup so they must be regarded as four separate federations.' After protests, mainly from the British, the rule was eventually refined to include a further category. If a player had been in a 'foreign' country long enough, he could become 'assimilated', and two 'assimilated' players could play in addition to three 'foreigners'. The quota system was part of an attempt, by UEFA, along with the various national associations, to prevent the free movement of players within the European Community. It therefore represented a clear breach of the Treaty of Rome. Although discussions within the European Commission have so far stopped the issue reaching the courts, it seems it will be only a matter of time before UEFA are forced by an unhappy player to answer a restraint of trade charge. When that happens the whole quota system should be blown apart.

Although the rules concerning what constitutes a foreign or

assimilated player are confusing (indeed, Manchester United excluded Ryan Giggs from the first leg of their tie against Torpedo Moscow because they misinterpreted the regulation), there is no reason beyond simple incompetence to explain why Stuttgart should flout them. In the squad for the second leg at Elland Road, the Stuttgart coach, Christoph Daum, named four foreigners, an infringement which no one noticed until after the game. Simply including the fourth foreign player among the substitutes was enough to constitute an offence, but late in the second half Daum compounded the transgression when he introduced the Croat Jova Simanic for the last seven minutes. Having already played three foreigners, Stuttgart found themselves the winners on the pitch but the subject of turmoil off it as speculation mounted over what UEFA would do about the situation.

Europe's governing body had three courses of action open to it. It might view Stuttgart's action as a minor offence and fine the club; it could order a replay; or it could throw Stuttgart out and reinstate Leeds. The Germans were quick to realise the implications and threw everything behind a campaign to lobby UEFA into imposing a fine. In their efforts, Stuttgart drew support from the television company RTL Plus, which had paid UEFA the colossal sum of 30 million marks (£12 million) for the exclusive German rights to the later phase of the European Cup, now grandly renamed the Champions' League, which began at the old quarter-final stage. If their team were removed, the Germans would lose their representation in the Champions' League, the television audience would be decimated and consequently advertising income would nose-dive. Millions of marks were at stake.

ITV, like RTL Plus, had paid a large sum of money for rights to the Champions' League, in the British company's case, a reputed £3 million. Trevor East, ITV's head of football, was more than a little concerned that if Leeds were out, his viewing figures would suffer. Not only that, since he had lost the Premier League to BSkyB and possessed rights only to the Coca-Cola Cup and regional coverage of the Football League, Europe was one of the few areas left with which he could bring top-class football back on to ITV. With no Leeds, it would be difficult for him to get matches from the Champions' League on to the network. While in Geneva for the draw for the second round of the European competitions, East telephoned Howard Wilkinson and was dismayed to learn that the Leeds delegation, which had been convened to plead the club's case at the UEFA hearing, did not include any legal representative. East strongly advocated that the Leeds vice-president, Peter McCormick, a well-known sports lawyer, should attend. His words were heeded and after meeting the Leeds contingent the following day, East briefed McCormick on the train from Geneva to Zurich, where the hearing was to take place.

It was now that the German Federation, the DFB, rallied to Stuttgart's cause with a vengeance – 'the German mafia', they were called by the Italian press. By contrast, the English FA were conspicuous by their absence. According to Trevor East, UEFA had no statutory scale of punishments for this partic-ular offence and the Germans were pressing hard for leniency. Leeds' managing director, Bill Fotherby, was certainly worried by the DFB's policy of support. 'It was clear from the start,' he said afterwards, 'just how powerful the German influence was within UEFA. I realised we had a major challenge to get rein-stated.' Stuttgart also attempted to muddy the waters by questioning the eligibility of Leeds' Welsh midfield player, Gary Speed, who was, in fact, 'assimilated'.

At the time of the hearing, Graham Kelly was, of course, abroad. Kelly's absence from these shores could have actually helped Leeds since this time he was scheduled to be just down the road from Zurich, in Geneva, attending the draw for the second round of the European competitions and UEFA committee meetings. FA Chairman Sir Bert Millichip was also due to be in Geneva but neither man saw fit to make the short journey to Zurich to assist 'their' club in the way the DFB were helping Stuttgart. If he had gone to Zurich, Kelly could have told the tribunal that if such a transgression of the rules had occurred in the oldest competition of all, the FA Cup, the offending team would have been summarily thrown out of the tournament. Not unnaturally, Leeds felt somewhat let down. 'I never saw the FA party in Geneva,' Bill Fotherby complained. 'I was chasing around looking for them. In the circumstances you would have thought they would be looking for me. I was even told by a UEFA official when I arrived in Geneva that Stuttgart were in the draw and Leeds were out.'

After four hours of deliberation, UEFA held back from the ultimate sanction, which was to throw Stuttgart out. If the German lobby had failed in its first objective of getting their team off with a fine, then it had a fall-back position, which was to press for a replay. After all, the Germans argued, it was a genuine mistake rather than a deliberate offence against the rules. It was this argument that swayed UEFA and it was decided that the Elland Road second leg would be awarded to Leeds by the notional score of 3–0. This left the scores level so the extra game in Barcelona was ordered. The decision was subject to much criticism in England. Leeds' manager, Howard Wilkinson, said: 'Stuttgart have committed a red card offence and have been shown the yellow. They [UEFA] have decided that the result of the second leg was 3–0 to us, so logically we should now have to play thirty minutes' extra time on our ground. Instead, we're having to play ninety minutes on a neutral ground.' It has to be said, however, that Leeds hardly deserved to go through by default. A replay, however much it smacked of compromise to Anglo-Saxon sensibilities, at least meant that a messy business would be settled where it ought to be – on the field of play.

The decider was played before a crowd of 11,000 in the huge Nou Camp stadium in Barcelona (capacity 115,000) on October 9. A fine game, it deserved a bigger crowd and was the closest of the three contests between the clubs. Stuttgart equalised Gordon Strachan's opener before going out to Carl Shutt's winner. It was, according to the general manager of Stuttgart, the ex-international Dieter Hoeness, 'a sporting solution on the pitch'.

The amazing affair of Leeds' progress past Stuttgart pointed to a prevailing ineptitude in the game which was not just confined to England. Quite how no one on Stuttgart's staff had noticed that they had four foreigners in their squad will never be known, but the real villain of the piece was UEFA, which not only introduced a rule of dubious legality but was unsure of how to punish a club which had broken it. It would be fair to say that Leeds' victory owed much to that strike of Carl Shutt's with an assist from Trevor East, who saw 'his' team live to fight another day and achieved the biggest football audience of the season in the UK when over 9 million watched the live transmission of the Barcelona replay. It had worked out all right in the end for Leeds, and there was now the mouthwatering prospect of the so-called 'Battle of Britain' – a second-round encounter between the English and Scottish champions.

In previews of the game, the English media chauvinistically wrote off Rangers and the bookmakers installed Leeds as firm favourites. Hadn't Rangers' recent record in Europe been dismal? And surely the gods had favoured Leeds with that dramatic resolution of the tie against Stuttgart? Yet somehow, the mind could not help but go back to another time, when the English and Scottish champions had last met in the European Cup. Leeds were involved then, too, in 1970, at the semi-final stage against Celtic. It was Don Revie against Jock Stein. The hot favourites were beaten twice and it was Celtic who went on to contest the final against the Dutch side Feyenoord. Now it seemed, just as in 1970, that Leeds, in common with the English public and media, were in serious danger of underestimating the Scots.

To English eyes, the achievement of Rangers in winning four successive Scottish League titles was downgraded because of the paucity of competition north of the border. What went largely unnoticed was that since the departure of Graeme Souness for Liverpool, Rangers, under his successor, Walter Smith, had moved up a gear. Smith not only guided the club to a League title, he won the Cup as well, the first time Rangers had achieved the double since Jock Wallace's side of 1977–78. Rangers had also, since the arrival of Souness, pioneered the idea of bringing in players from England and further afield. From the Ukraine came Mikhailichenko and Kusnetsov; from Holland, Huistra; and there was the English contingent consisting of Hateley, Steven, Gordon and Stevens. Apart from these, Rangers possessed home-grown talents such as Richard Gough, Ally McCoist (holder of Europe's Golden Boot award) and Ian Durrant, one of the the most creative playmakers in the British game.

Apart from the opening twenty minutes of the first leg in Glasgow, when Leeds went a goal up through Gary McAllister, Rangers dominated both games and won each 2–1 to run out more than worthy victors. In the return at Elland Road,

Hateley similarly opened the scoring for the away club early on but Rangers were far more adept at holding on to the advantage than Leeds had been at Ibrox. The result brought much delight to the Scottish press as their English counterparts were forced to eat humble pie. It must have been particularly galling for John Sadler of the *Sun*, who had been dismissive of the way Rangers had come back to win the first match after losing the early goal. The result, according to Sadler, 'didn't disguise the truth'. He went on to describe just what the truth was in unequivocal terms. It was that 'Rangers are no great side at all . . . If a British League is to develop on a distant horizon, the Scottish champions might just be good enough to earn a place in the top half.' In the end, Rangers fully deserved to win and although the Leeds goalkeeper, John Lukic, gave an undistinguished performance at Ibrox, Rangers had one asset Leeds lacked, namely the character to come back from conceding a goal in the opening minutes. Like Arsenal twelve months before, Leeds had found out the hard way that success in the English League no longer struck fear into the hearts of other Europeans.

It was Rangers then, rather than Leeds, who looked forward to the riches and high profile that would come from participation in the Champions' League. Leeds were left to reflect that, as Shakespeare observed, the gods play with the human race much as little boys play with flies. The fact that Leeds had been smiled upon against Stuttgart was no guarantee that they had any divine right to progress further. Rangers, meanwhile, were on the threshold of greatness on the pitch and commercial prosperity off it. Just for reaching the last eight the club earned almost £1 million. From then on every point gained from the six matches they would play in the Champions' League would bring a further £225,000. In addition, they would take a share of the biggest television, advertising and sponsorship deal ever concluded in world club football. They would keep home gate receipts and hospitality income from their three ties at Ibrox. All told, Rangers could expect to make in excess of £5 million. They could truly call themselves Britain's biggest club. A magnificent stadium with large crowds and a well-organised and lucrative commercial operation had already put them among Europe's top twenty clubs. Now the current team propelled

them into the European élite, into a league competition
against the likes of Marseille and Milan (although there was
no Barcelona, since Cruyff's team had been knocked out by
the Russian side CSKA after throwing away a two-goal lead).
The result against Leeds was, said Rangers captain Richard
Gough, 'a vindication of Scottish football'. So although teams
from Greece and Turkey (not to mention Russia, which had
survivors in all three competitions) were left to compete in
Europe, all the English clubs had gone and, it must be said,
deservedly so.

Was this just a hiccup, a blip in the learning process that
had had to begin again following the long years when English
clubs were banned from Europe? Manchester United, after all,
had won the the Cup-winners' Cup in 1990, in the English
clubs' first season back after the ban. Those who advanced
this line of thinking displayed ostrich-like qualities of the
highest order. It was more likely that Manchester United's
success was the blip. Any examination of the facts behind the
English failure revealed a multitude of reasons why the
performance of English clubs, once the envy of Europe, had
slipped so far. Everton manager Howard Kendall, who won
the Cup-winners' Cup in 1985, suggested that 'we don't seem
to be producing many outstanding players'. In fact, England
can still produce quality players, but the best are now more
likely to be tempted to play abroad.

Traditionally, the English style of play troubled the
continentals. However, the Milan of Arrigo Sacchi had
started a trend of adding English-style athleticism to
continental skills, producing in the process the pressing
game. European teams now had resilience and aggression to
go with tactics and technique. Rangers' manager, Walter
Smith, put it best when he remarked that 'British teams have
always played with a zonal back four without a sweeper. A lot
of top European teams are taking up that system, learned from
the British. But within it the passing and control have been
kept.' Arsenal's George Graham had noticed as much when
his side were dumped out of the European Cup by Benfica in
1991. 'We were prepared for them to be more skilful but not
for their strength and determination,' he said. 'Once they
established equality in those departments, fighting hard for
every ball, we were in trouble.' If European teams had added

English qualities, the English, it seemed, learned little from the continentals.

The then manager of Glasgow Celtic, Liam Brady, whose views were based on first-hand experience gained while winning trophies with Arsenal and Juventus, was adamant. 'It is harder to be successful in Europe,' he said. 'Because our game is now so fast and physical we are even more divorced from the continentals than we were in years gone by.' Skill, according to the theory espoused by Brady and others, is at a premium as the sheer grind of domestic competitions, coupled with the fear of failure, has produced a levelling down of standards. In England in 1993 it was a rarity for any team to play football of a consistently high standard over the course of a marathon season, the like of which no other European country (except Scotland) is prepared to impose on its top clubs. Tony Waddington, manager of Stoke City in the days when English clubs commanded respect for their unique approach, said: 'The game in England today is about three things: pace, pace and more pace. We are creating athletes, not footballers.'

Too many games, particularly in the early part of the season, were leading to injuries and jaded players by the time the European matches came around. Two games a week allow little time for improving technique. In Italy and Germany, there are only thirty-four league games, with thirty-eight in France and Spain, so players suffer less wear and tear and can train, not just to eliminate mistakes or to practise set pieces, but to work on technical skills. Trevor Francis, who scored the winning goal for Nottingham Forest in the European Cup final of 1979 and was now manager of Sheffield Wednesday, remarked before his team were knocked out of the UEFA Cup by Kaiserslautern: 'Because of injuries I've already used twenty-one players this season and not once have I been able to prepare in the way I wanted. It's a question of patching players up and getting them out there.' John Jensen, Arsenal's Danish acquisition, said that in the time he had played twelve games in England, he would have only played six in Denmark.

English players and coaches had also, since the ban from Europe, forgotten the way to deal with the special demands of the two-legged tie of which Liverpool used to be the arch-exponents; how to kill the away leg or, at worst, exercise damage limitation, and above all to win the home leg without conceding the precious away goal.

Lastly, the three foreigners rule had undoubtedly hit English clubs the hardest, although Stuttgart might disagree with that sentiment. And as the Wales manager, Terry Yorath, pointed out, if Swansea won the Welsh Cup and entered the Cup-winners' Cup, they would only have two Welsh players on their books. All successful English teams have traditionally been liberally peppered with Scots, Welsh and Irish. Indeed, the Liverpool double-winning side of 1985–86 sometimes had no Englishmen in it at all. Apart from illustrating the debt English clubs owed to their Celtic and Gaelic imports, the new rules now meant that squads had to be juggled around, with the team representing the club in the Premier League (where Scots, Irish and Welsh are not deemed to be foreigners) not able to be on duty for European games. In the long run, there will be further repercussions as players with dual qualifications are encouraged to opt for English status, thereby limiting the international prospects of the other home countries. Republic of Ireland manager Jack Charlton won't find it so easy in future to build a team on the back of Irish grandparents if it endangers the livelihoods of English-based players. UEFA have ensured that in the UK, at least, club will come before country even more than it does at present.

If the general outlook was bleak for English football, nowhere could the decline be better illustrated than at the most successful British club of all time: Liverpool. Until the latter days of Kenny Dalglish's time as manager, Liverpool, in the thirty or so years since the start of the club's renaissance under Bill Shankly, had taken the world of football by storm. It wasn't just the trophies and the unparalleled playing record, impressive though both were. A special relationship, created by Shankly but carried on by his successors, had been forged with the club's supporters which tied club and fans together in a way never matched before or since by other English clubs, except perhaps during the Matt Busby era at Manchester United.

Liverpool's dizzy climb to the footballing peaks had begun just as the city also began to exert a profound influence on world culture through the Beatles and the rest of the

Merseybeat generation. The effect on Liverpool was reminiscent of its nineteenth-century heyday as the main European port for goods and cargo travelling to and from North America. In fact, the 1960s was a time when Liverpool's morale had never been higher and the football club provided an almost mystical focus for the self-esteem.

Rising from Second Division obscurity, Shankly and Liverpool were about to bestride the English game like a colossus. The other Liverpool team, Everton, was the old establishment club, and had been in the First Division for all but four seasons of its 114-year history. Under manager Harry Catterick, in the 1960s Everton was known as the 'School of Science' winning the Championship in 1963 and 1970 and the FA Cup in 1966. That team, however, did not fulfil its potential, certainly in European terms, largely because the board, dominated by the Littlewoods Pools family, were reluctant to build on success. Players were sold while still in their prime in order to keep the club out of debt. Alan Ball, a 1966 World Cup-winner who was transferred to Arsenal a year after Everton won the Championship, provides the best example of the Goodison club's lack of vision.

So it was that Anfield became the spiritual home of Liverpudlians. Liverpool drew the 1960s working class who, for the first time, had spare cash to spend. To be a Scouser, to support Liverpool, was to identify with the new, to experience every Saturday the kind of streetwise self-confidence that can only be born of hardship and struggle. Bill Shankly once admonished a policeman for kicking a Liverpool scarf, telling the errant officer, 'Don't do that, that's someone's life.' Like his oft-quoted remark about football being more important than life and death, he didn't mean the aphorism to be taken literally. Shankly was a master of hyperbole. He was demonstrating in his idiosyncratic way that he was on the same wavelength as the supporters. He instinctively understood how important a club can be in the life of a fan. He was the custodian of their dreams and to hear the Kop belting out 'Shan-kly, Shan-kly' to the tune of 'Amazing Grace' was to experience the unique bond between the club and its supporters. In the process of building the football club, the personification of Liverpool's affection, Bill Shankly, founded a dynasty and a culture of success so secure that it would outlast his own time on the planet.

Twenty times champions or runners-up in twenty-six years, not to mention four European Cups and innumerable other trophies, both domestic and European, is a record that tells its own story. Shankly intuitively knew exactly when a player was approaching his sell-by date. Preparations would begin at least a year before, when a replacement would be signed and put into the reserves to learn the Liverpool way. Then, when Shankly deemed the time was right, the new boy would become a regular with the older player stepping down either to become a squad member or to be sent on his way to pastures new. Shankly constructed a well-oiled machine which, with a little tinkering here and there, had the ability to renew itself constantly. It was a machine which those who inherited Shankly's mantle, his erstwhile assistants Bob Paisley and Joe Fagan, and the player he brought to Liverpool to replace Kevin Keegan, the incomparable Kenny Dalglish, simply had to service occasionally to keep on the track of success.

Kenny Dalglish took over in 1985 after the horrendous tragedy at the European Cup final in Brussels, at which thirty-nine people, mainly Juventus supporters, were killed when a wall collapsed following widespread hooliganism by a section of the crowd. The next season, Dalglish's first as manager, Liverpool achieved the double of League and FA Cup for the only time in their history. After that, the team, if anything, got even better. Many believe that the side which won the Championship in 1987–88, and in the same season lost the Cup final to Wimbledon by a single goal, was the best in Liverpool's history. Tom Finney thought their display that season in beating Nottingham Forest 5–0 was the best club performance he had ever seen. That team was never allowed to test itself against the best in Europe since at the time English clubs were banned from European competition.

The terrible events at Hillsborough in April 1989, when ninety-six Liverpool fans lost their lives in a crush, affected the city and the club deeply. The progress on the field was hardly halted, however. That season the team finished runners-up in the League and won the FA Cup. The following year the Championship was regained. But as the 1990s approached, the machine was in need of an overhaul and one or two wheels were in danger of coming off. Dalglish had seemingly lost his touch. As the ever-present pressure to succeed began to overwhelm the manager, Liverpool, for the first time in almost thirty years, appeared to fear the opposition. The creaking machinery was exposed to the nation in a televised top-of-the-table game against Arsenal in December 1990, when an ultra-defensive Liverpool formation crashed 3–0. Dalglish then began to depart from the club's long-standing transfer policy in a way that went from the bizarre (Jimmy Carter), to the absurd (David Speedie). For Dalglish, Hillsborough had taken a heavy toll. He, like the players, had been expected to pick up the pieces and carry on doing his job normally during those dark months following the tragedy. In the end it proved too heavy a burden and Dalglish resigned quite suddenly. He was only a few months into a three-year contract. Fortunately, after a six-month break, he felt rejuvenated enough to return to the game, but by then Liverpool had moved on and Dalglish was tempted by Jack Walker's millions to take over the reins at Second Division Blackburn Rovers.

Meanwhile, Liverpool had broken with tradition by appointing a man from outside to get the team back into shape. For the first time since Shankly's arrival, the succession was not conferred on someone from within. There was, though, one element of continuity. Graeme Souness had been one of Liverpool's greatest players, his period at the club coinciding with its greatest success. When he left to play for Sampdoria in Italy, Souness's reputation on Merseyside seemed secure forever. Then, out of the blue, he was offered the job of player-manager at Glasgow Rangers. A turbulent though successful period followed, and he ended up owning 7 per cent of the club when his friend David Murray bought Rangers in 1988. He pledged his future to Rangers and gave the impression that his commitment to their cause was total. 'Owning part of the club excites me,' he wrote in his 1989 book, *Graeme Souness: A Manager's Diary*. 'And if my own money is in then it should stop the knockers telling people that I am only at Ibrox until something bigger turns up. How could you get any bigger club? It beats me, but they still persist in believing that I am only along for a joyride.'

There was, however, a darker side to his time in Scotland.

There were continual bust-ups with the authorities involving sendings-off as a player and touchline bans as a manager. While he can be credited with bringing Scottish football into the twentieth century by enticing the best English players to Ibrox and signing the club's first major Catholic player in Maurice Johnston, Souness was dogged by failure in the European Cup. His stated ambition was to turn Rangers into a major European force but the team failed to progress beyond the second round of any European competition while he was there. When Dalglish left Liverpool and the board approached Souness, he accepted, saying enigmatically that he felt he had 'gone as far as I will be allowed in trying to achieve success at Rangers'.

Souness arrived back on Merseyside hailed as a saviour. But if the board or the fans thought that, as a former player, Souness would keep to the club's traditional way of doing things, they were sadly mistaken. The new manager saw much that was wrong and he opted for revolutionary change. 'The club needed major surgery when I came,' Souness claimed. 'Players were in disarray after Kenny Dalglish left. A lot of people had lost their desire . . . Every manager since Bill Shankly inherited a stronger squad. I didn't. For the first time since the 1950s the Liverpool manager has a job on his hands.' Souness proceeded to rip apart Dalglish's team as Peter Beardsley, Steve Staunton, Ray Houghton, Gary Ablett and Barry Venison were sold. 'I was confronted by a Catch 22 situation,' Souness later explained. 'There were several players who had either reached or were close to thirty. They were looking for new, big-money contracts. I knew I could get another season or possibly two out of them at the most. My dilemma was whether to cash in on their market value and hopefully bring in younger players or sit still and do nothing.' With the looming costs of implementing the Taylor Report lurking in the background (the £8 million Centenary Stand was opened in 1992 and the famous Kop was redeveloped in 1993), the manager chose the former course, even if it meant ousting players who were likely to perform well when they went to other clubs.

As the team embarked on a series of indifferent results, stories appeared to the effect that Souness was interfering with time-honoured training and preparation practices, and although the manager denied it the dismissal of a former colleague, the youth team coach, Phil Thomson, did nothing to reduce the criticism. What was incontrovertible was that the Liverpool style of play, utilising good passers of the ball allied to intelligent movement, was changing. Now there was a more direct approach and the best passer at the club, Jan Molby, could not get into the team when fit unless there was a severe number of injuries.

Should this have come as any surprise? Such was the euphoria over the appointment of someone who was seen as a member of the family, and one with such a surfeit of charisma, that Souness's record as a manager could not have been fully scrutinised. When he went to Rangers, a number of leading sides, including Aberdeen, Hearts and Dundee United, all of whom had risen to prominence over the previous decade, were finding it increasingly difficult to keep pace and were in a state of transition. But more important, the one club that could always challenge, and often surpass, Rangers, was itself about to enter a deep decline characterised by catastrophic performances on and off the field. Glasgow Celtic, after one last fling when they won the double in their centenary year the season after Souness took over at Ibrox, were in serious trouble, with a poor squad, a dilapidated stadium and a growing debt. Into this weakened Scottish League Souness threw unprecedented amounts of cash. He spent it on players, but they were an erratic assortment of ill-tempered, high-cost stars rather than a coherent team. Of course they could dominate the rest of the impoverished Scottish clubs and could be guaranteed to win the League or a cup north of the border, but whenever the real test was applied, which was in Europe, Souness's sides were horribly exposed.

Players came and went at Rangers in a flurry of transfer activity, yet Souness never gave the impression that he was building to a preconceived plan. It was the very antithesis of what Liverpool required, yet the Anfield directors chose to ignore it. Dalglish's resignation had caught them unawares and left them no time to plan ahead.

At Liverpool, Souness's transfer dealing was prodigious but none of the new arrivals lived up to expectations (apart, that is, from Rob Jones, who exceeded them). Some had flair, such as Mark Wright, Michael Thomas, Mark Walters and Dean

Saunders: others – Paul Stewart, Torben Piechnik and Stig Bjornebye – were more prosaic. It didn't seem to matter which category they came into, they all suffered a dip in form. Anfield had never had such an effect on players – they used to get better when they went to Liverpool, not worse. A classic example was the goalkeeper, David James, signed for over £1 million from Watford and widely tipped as a future England keeper. It was not clear where he stood in the pecking order once he got to Anfield because Souness already had Bruce Grobbelaar and his more than able deputy, Mike Hooper. As Grobbelaar's performances became stranger and more incomprehensible than usual, Hooper came in for a while, then Souness turned to James. At a time when the Liverpool defence was the worst anyone could remember, James underwent his baptism of fire. Still not assured of his place in the scheme of things, it wasn't long before the young keeper lost confidence and form. Despite their individual setbacks, Souness now possessed three classy but unconfident and out-of-form goalkeepers, none of whom knew who was first, second or third choice.

Having posted a net loss of £4 million on transfers by 1993, Souness was forced to admit that he had made mistakes. 'I have not had the return I was looking for from some of the players I have brought in. I have been disappointed,' the manager conceded. Meanwhile, Dean Saunders, who had been bought by Souness then sold to Aston Villa at a loss of £600,000, rediscovered the goalscoring touch which had gone missing while he was at Anfield.

Many, including Souness himself, pointed to a long injury list as the cause of the turmoil and it was certainly true that Liverpool had sustained an unprecedented wave of casualties. John Barnes, Ronnie Whelan and Jan Molby were all sidelined for months on end. 'I have never been able to pick my strongest team,' Souness reflected. 'Not since I came back as manager have I been able to write eleven names on the sheet and say, that's the side I've been waiting to put out.' As players dropped like ninepins, some questioned the manager's training methods, but the truth was that in the crazy world of English football, more and more players were getting injured. Virtually every Premier League team suffered debilitating injuries from the first month of the League's inception.

The worst moment for Souness came after a great personal crisis. Early in 1992 the manager was discovered to have a serious heart problem and had to undergo bypass surgery. As he was recovering in hospital he gave an exclusive interview to the *Sun*, which on April 15 printed his story alongside a large picture spread of Souness with his girlfriend under the front-page banner LOVERPOOL. The *Sun* had run an article in the days following the Hillsborough disaster accusing the Liverpool supporters of unspeakable acts of hooliganism and drunkenness on the day of the tragedy, followed by further depravities at the scene of the disaster itself. This caused outrage in Liverpool, where the newspaper's allegations were dismissed as malicious lies. The *Sun* was subjected to a mass boycott and its sales on Merseyside took a pounding. Three years later the incident still festered and the fact that Souness had struck his deal with that particular newspaper was taken by many Liverpudlians as an insult to them, the city, and the relatives of the dead, particularly as publication came on the third anniversary of that terrible day in 1989. It was certainly a crass and insensitive thing to do, and Souness apologised when the full impact was brought home to him. But the damage was done. It was the crucial incident which broke the club's deep relationship with its fans.

When the directors did nothing more than admonish Souness, serious disaffection reared its head at Anfield for the first time in thirty years. The fanzine *Through the Wind and Rain* said Souness should go. One contributor, Gary White, spoke for a large number when he wrote: 'For myself and many other fans who were drawn to the club by Bill Shankly, the ability or inability of Souness to win games has long since ceased to be the key issue. On April 15 1992, Souness forfeited the right to manage Liverpool Football Club. The sooner he leaves, the better.' Souness's response to this was to play down the criticism. 'We're having a crisis with injuries,' he said. 'That's the only crisis we're having.'

Liverpool-watchers in the media saw it somewhat differently. John Keith of the *Daily Express* felt that 'there are barriers in and around Anfield that never existed only a short time ago'. Colin Wood of the *Daily Mail* was sure that the changes at Liverpool were not for the better. 'I feel that the family spirit has gone,' he opined. 'The family used to include the fans and it doesn't any more.'

Suddenly all kinds of stories were coming out of the Liverpool camp and a battle appeared to be taking place behind the scenes. Souness apologists fed stories to the media in defence of the manager, but a number of former players weighed in with some fierce criticism. Among the most vocal was a former captain, Tommy Smith. 'Nobody is ever going to be bigger than Liverpool,' Smith declared. 'Unfortunately, it looks as though Graeme Souness is trying. People at the club are afraid and that's true of what happens on the pitch.'

As far as playing performances were concerned, Liverpool's League form dipped in 1992 although they saved their season by getting to the Cup final. Reappearing before the fans for the first time since his heart operation, Souness was given a rousing reception as his team beat Second Division Sunderland 2–0. The Cup win was, however, merely the prelude to more trials and tribulations. Opening the 1992–93 season in the Charity Shield match at Wembley, they were beaten by Leeds and their Premier League form thereafter was a model of un-Liverpool-like inconsistency. The defeat by Spartak Moscow in the Cup-winners' Cup was galling enough but worse was to follow as they suffered one of their most embarrassing defeats. In their first defence of the FA Cup in 1993 they were beaten at home in a third-round replay by Bolton Wanderers, who were all of two divisions below them. They also went out of the League Cup at Anfield to Crystal Palace. Their league form had slipped to such an alarming extent that at the time of the defeat by Bolton, they had dropped to twelfth place.

Souness now blamed his players. 'Too many of ours,' he fumed, 'have no real interest or love of the football club. This club's history is based on and steeped in passion. The vast majority of my players . . . played as if they had never been told that passion is what Liverpool FC is all about.' Since most of them had either been bought by the manager or promoted by him from within, it was an astonishing outburst. Emlyn Hughes, another ex-captain and the first man in Liverpool colours to hold aloft the European Cup, was not optimistic. 'Liverpool have never hit long balls,' he wrote in the *Daily Mirror*, castigating the style of play that had developed under Souness's management. 'They always played it to feet, ran with it, passed it, went through teams, past them, round them and if that didn't work they started it all over again. But this present side can't do that. They are the worst defensively I have ever seen. Ordinary teams expose them and they have not had a class back four player since Alan Hansen called it a day.'

Graeme Souness put up a stout defence whenever criticisms of his stewardship were raised. He believed the machine had broken down before his arrival. Money was being diverted to ground improvements, he was forced to sell aging players and the injuries meant he had to blood youngsters before they were ready. The lack of motivation, or passion as Souness calls it, however, was surely something only the manager and his coaching staff could address. All Souness could offer was a lament to changing times: 'A successful football career used to be about winning things. Now it is about how much money you end up with at the end of the day.'

Few tears were shed by fans outside Merseyside as Liverpool slid down the table and failed to make any impression on the Cup competitions at home or abroad. Supporters of other clubs had long since taken a dislike to Liverpool. Criticisms centred on the supposed bias of referees and fawning coverage in all sections of the media. The reality was, however, that envy had overtaken judgement, for the great years of Liverpool will always be remembered for the supreme performances of the team and the unending commitment of the fans. If the cost of throwing open the Premier League – competitive parity as it is called in the USA – was to be achieved by destroying the standard-bearers of English football, then perhaps the price was too high, despite the view of Ken Bates that the situation has improved now that the smaller clubs can afford to hang on to players. It would be fair enough if Liverpool's decline were the result of genuine challenges of high quality like those they saw off in the 1960s, 70s and 80s from such outstanding teams as Leeds, the two Manchester clubs, Chelsea, Arsenal, Derby County and Nottingham Forest, but, their own errors notwithstanding, it was the Premier League philosophy of equality (without designing the support structure of the game to facilitate it, as happens in the college draft system in the USA) which had resulted in stronger opposition from teams which possess nowhere near the level of skill that would have been required in a previous generation. It was now a case of common denominator football with the emphasis on survival. Failing the introduction of a Premier League of reduced size, Liverpool are just going to have to slog it out with the rest of them. In their heyday they were simply more talented and thus ultimately more successful. For Liverpool, and by extension other English clubs, it will be the end of an era, unless the new Manchester United team or some other contender can rise to the occasion. Could it be that a Liverpool in decline without another great club side taking their place represents a national game in decline? This view though, would be writing off the most exciting Manchester United side since the 1960's.

Although the team rallied to finish sixth in the Premier League, there were no other trophies by way of consolation. Moreover, it was the first time in over thirty years that Liverpool had failed to qualify for Europe. With an unpopular manager, a seemingly divided coaching and playing staff, and dirty linen being washed in public, morale had taken a battering. So when Souness asked for a vote of confidence in the last weeks of the season it was not surprising that the board got it all wrong. They dithered for a week, holding a secret meeting from which clearly orchestrated leaks convinced all and sundry, including Souness himself, that he would be leaving at the end of the season. Notwithstanding the costs involved – £1 million to pay off the remainder of Souness's contract – they decided to go for it, but in a most un-Liverpool-like scenario had left themselves no fall-back position. They knew who they were going to fire but didn't have a clue who they would hire in his place. Thus, when the manager had all but run out of time, his staunchest ally on the board, the chairman, David Moores, was able to persuade a majority of his co-directors that Souness should stay. This was too much for one board member, Tony Ensor, who resigned 'because of genuine differences, [and my] strongly held views were not compatible with continuing [as a director]'. By moving from a general consensus that Souness should go to a reaffirmation of his position for the remaining three years of his contract,

the Liverpool board underwent a U-turn of amazing proportions.

Of course nothing like this would have been allowed to
happen under the previous regime. Then, Liverpool always
presented a united front to the world. On occasion this was
seen by outsiders as a superiority complex or an 'us and them'
mentality. But at least their incomparable record of success
could be pointed to in mitigation. Now, in the course of three
seasons under Dalglish and Souness, Liverpool had declined
to the status of just another club.

Despite the costly building renovations and massive
transfer deficit, the board felt compelled to back the manager
with even more cash to improve playing resources. Whether
Souness will modify his abrasive style as a result of the events
of 1992–93 or see them as a vindication of his methods, only
time will tell.

While Souness's problems at Liverpool intensified, his old
club, Glasgow Rangers, had serenely gone from strength to
strength. When Souness left, with Rangers top of the table, he
was replaced by his assistant, Walter Smith. Smith duly won
the title but more important, with the victory over Leeds he
had done something Souness had been signally unable to do.
He had pushed Rangers into the higher reaches of European
football, which was where they desperately wanted to be. At
home, Celtic were a spent force and Rangers lorded it
over everyone. The one achievement Rangers envied their
neighbours was the winning of the European Cup in 1967.
With a British competition closed to them because of the
parochial concerns of the home associations, they looked
more and more towards Europe. In the few short years since
Souness had gone to Glasgow, the Scottish scene had been
completely transformed. Where it would lead, however, was
anyone's guess. But the Scots, having managed their affairs
with creditable aplomb during the decade of warfare within
the English game, had finally succumbed to the English
disease and the granite façade of stability was beginning to
show signs of terminal decay.

8

Lone Rangers

**How Celtic and the rest attempt to come to terms with Rangers'
domination of Scottish Football**

> *'Celtic looked greatness in the face and ran away
> screaming.'*
>
> Patrick Reilly, Celtic fan and lecturer at Glasgow University.

> *'Rangers are the biggest club in Britain and we have to
> stand alongside the European giants.'*
>
> Graeme Souness, Rangers manager 1988.

> *'Having chosen to adopt "screw every bastard for a few
> pennies more" as their central ideology, it was
> inevitable that the only solution they would offer would
> be its [Scottish football's] systematic destruction.'*
>
> Archie MacGregor, on the launch of the Scottish Superleague in
> The Absolute Game.

Graeme Souness's career in Scotland spanned less than five
seasons but its effect was seismic. When he departed
for Liverpool in April 1991, Scottish football had been
transformed as Souness swept through the game north of the
border like a whirlwind. While others had begun the process
and it has continued since Souness left, Scotland's destiny as
a football nation is now inextricably bound up with the
progress of the club which Souness revitalised after a period
in the doldrums: Glasgow Rangers, now the country's most
famous and successful team.

The genesis of Scotland's predicament can be traced to

1971, ironically as a consequence of a visionary decision taken by those in charge of Rangers to redevelop the club's Ibrox stadium in order to turn it into one of the finest football grounds in Europe. The move followed an horrendous tragedy that took place at Ibrox on January 2 that year, when sixty-six people were killed after a stairway collapsed near the end of a game between Rangers and Celtic. The Sheriff's report at the time laid most of the blame on the Rangers administration, pointing out that it was not the first time that accidents had occurred at Ibrox, yet little had been done to improve safety. In response, Rangers cleaned up their act and plans for a new stadium were drawn up. As he surveyed the magnificence of Ibrox many years later, the Rangers chairman, David Murray, acknowledged the fact when he said: 'The stadium we see today is a fitting memorial to those who gave their lives, because there's no doubt the stadium wouldn't exist today unless that had happened.'

Murray had bought the club for £6 million in 1988 from Lawrence Marlborough, whose family connection with Rangers went back to the early fifties when his grandfather, John Lawrence, the founder of a construction empire, joined the board of directors. Marlborough, an absentee landlord ensconced in Nevada, USA, had appointed a long-standing family employee, David Holmes, as chairman. It was Holmes and another newcomer, commercial director Freddie Fletcher, who started the revolution in Scottish football. Holmes lured Graeme Souness from Sampdoria as player-manager in April 1986, while Fletcher, in the two years following Souness's appointment, was responsible for a complete turn-around in Rangers' fortunes by increasing commercial income from under £250,000 in 1986 to £2.25 million by the time of the sale of the club to David Murray. When Murray, who was a friend of Souness, took over, the manager also became a director. Describing his new position as 'one of the most important steps I have ever taken in my life', Souness bought a 7 per cent stake in the club for £600,000. This meant that he had a larger shareholding than his nominal bosses, Holmes and Fletcher, which was hardly conducive to boardroom harmony. Sure enough, within six months, Holmes and Fletcher had departed, emphasising that although ownership might have passed into new hands, it was business as usual in the Rangers boardroom, where in-fighting had been the usual state of affairs since the club's foundation in the nineteenth century.

Before he assumed control at Ibrox, David Murray had tried and failed to take over his home-town club, Ayr United. After the triumphant acquisition of Rangers he was prompted to remark that 'perhaps Ayr United will now realise what I could have done for them'. For Murray, commercial prosperity came early in life, from a company involved in steel stockholding, which remains his core business today. In 1976, when he was only twenty-four he suffered a terrible accident while driving his Lotus sports car home from a rugby match and both his legs had to be amputated. Such a catastrophe would have blighted the lives of most men, but Murray said 'it makes you more determined' and thereafter he concentrated on building up his industrial operation until it was a leading player on the UK business scene, with over fifty companies producing a turnover in excess of £200 million a year. In business, most of what Murray touched became an immediate success, with one notable exception. In 1990, he launched a new tabloid newspaper, the *Sunday Scot*. The paper folded quickly (having become known as the Sunday Scud), costing its proprietor some £5 million during its brief existence.

Although he at first rejected the prospect, when Holmes and Fletcher left and Murray assumed the chairmanship, Rangers were about to take over his life. The importance of football to Scottish society and culture, and the paramount role played by Rangers, soon convinced Murray that the club was not merely another piece in his jigsaw of companies but the jewel in his crown, much as Silvio Berlusconi had discovered when he took over AC Milan. As in Milan, city rivalry was of all-consuming importance, but in Rangers' case the battle with Celtic transcended both the sporting and the cultural. Both clubs owed their existence to and drew support from Glasgow's (and, to a lesser extent, Scotland's) two main religious communities. Rangers, as the embodiment of the Protestant ruling majority, demanded and expected success as a divine right. Success, however, had to be achieved on the club's terms. Under the regime of John Lawrence, religious discrimination, particularly the refusal to sign Roman Catholic players, was actively practised, both as an ideology and to protect Rangers' supremacist status. Success by any other means was not worth having.

The identity of Glasgow Celtic is bound up with the Catholic minority, which consists mostly of working-class descendants of Irish immigrants. Although there is a growing element of middle-class support, the club began as a charitable institution to aid the Irish poor of Glasgow's east end. As their tradition would indicate, Celtic have been the underdogs for most of their existence, a position they seem determined to preserve for all time. Opposition and antagonism from the Scottish establishment facilitated the rise of an élite group of three families which have controlled Celtic for most of this century, the Grants, the Whites and the Kellys. These families survived and flourished as owners of the club until the 1990s, when, in the wake of the Taylor Report and Rangers' continual success, the Celtic directors were forced to face up to what had become the biggest crisis in the club's history.

To Celtic, success brought community pride and remuneration for the directors, who have always had a reputation for putting money in their pockets rather than spending it on the team, and indeed voted themselves a dividend almost as soon as the club was incorporated as a limited company in 1897. So important were these twin objectives that at Parkhead pragmatism took precedence over dogma. This is why Celtic have never had any problem justifying the widespread employment of Protestants. Thus it was that Robert Kelly, who presided over the club for a quarter of a century, could appoint the Protestant Jock Stein as manager. Unlike in England, where the honours were distributed rather more evenly until Liverpool's ascendancy, the pinnacles of success in Scotland were reached alternately by Rangers and Celtic, with one or more of a handful of smaller clubs providing the odd relief from the monotony of what was, in effect, an almost permanent duopoly.

In the forty-six years following the end of the Second World War, clubs other than Rangers or Celtic won the Scottish League Championship on twelve occasions. However, only twice in the same period – in 1951–52, when the great Hibernian team was at its peak, and again in 1954–55 – did both clubs fail to win any of the three domestic trophies. There were times when one or the other established supremacy for a number of years, most notably in the 1960s and early 1970s, when Jock Stein produced at Celtic what was arguably the best ever Scottish club side: the Lisbon Lions who won the European Cup in 1967. Stein's team won nine straight Championships from 1966, five Cup finals, five League Cups and a clean sweep of all three trophies in 1967 and 1969. The ramifications of Stein's success, in particular the victory over Internazionale in Lisbon, which brought national as well as community pride, were far-reaching. It was now acceptable for any Scottish youngster to support the club, especially if football rather than religion was the greater passion. Moreover, abroad Celtic were accorded the status that only the winning of Europe's premier trophy can bring. As a small (in European terms) club from a small country, they epitomised the dream factor and demonstrated to fans and clubs everywhere that *catennacio*, the ultra-defensive system created and perfected by Italian teams in the 1960s, could be defeated. And when Celtic destroyed Inter's tactics, they did it with brio and gained a reputation for flair that still survives to this day, to the abiding resentment of Rangers and their followers.

At Ibrox, both David Holmes and David Murray came with a burning ambition to win the European Cup, first, because Celtic had won the trophy while Rangers had not, and second because both men realised that in a League with the disparities between clubs that existed in Scotland, a club as big as Rangers had to possess European credentials if it were to have a voice in the changing shape of European competitions. When Graeme Souness arrived, he brought with him the same obsession, in his case fuelled by his years of incredible success as a player. Rangers under Souness, however, while dominating at home, which was the manager's first target after a number of years of relative decline, failed to get very far in the European Cup.

To Souness, defeat, even at the hands of some big names like Bayorn Munich and Red Star Belgrade, who won the European Cup the season they knocked out Rangers, hurt. Until his appointment, neither Rangers nor Celtic had felt the need to splash out large sums of money on transfers. Every talented Scottish boy wanted to play for one or the other and recruiting players from England or further afield was not considered necessary. The Rangers manager changed that insular approach for good, bringing big-name English and European players to the Scottish League, a trend subsequently continued by most Premier Division clubs. He also signed a Catholic in Maurice Johnston. This was akin to heresy for some of Rangers' ultra-Protestant fans. One revealed how he telephoned a relative in the USA to tell him the news: 'It was 5.00 am over there. He asked me if someone in the family had died. I said, no, it's worse than that, Rangers have signed Maurice Johnston.' David Murray, the chairman who sanctioned the purchase of Johnston, showed how he was no longer concerned with parochial issues like sectarianism and wanted to take Rangers into a new era. 'We mustn't be narrow-minded,' he said. 'We have got to rise above that as something from the past and leave it behind.'

By breaking down the religious barrier, Rangers were opening the door to the European stage, which could have remained off-limits had the bigotry persisted. However, in so doing, the club found themselves resented in Scotland as an institution on the make, prepared to do anything, even to abandon century-old principles, to achieve their goals. In Scottish terms, Rangers are rich, powerful and successful, therefore they are unpopular. They had set themselves up as Scotland's heroes and Scotland was not altogether impressed. In true British fashion, support for the underdog saw Celtic bestowed with a wealth of goodwill. They, not Rangers, were, after all, the 'true' representatives of Scottish football. Scottish fans have, in recent years, lowered their at times unrealistically high expectations of the national team, but these have been transferred to the clubs. Celtic, although they were not winning as much as in previous decades, still tried to play entertaining football, and anyway, life and the big battalions were constantly ranged against them. As for Rangers, they provided the only viable route to international success and received grudging support from all except those committed to Celtic, but a knowing smile could always be expected to appear on those same faces when the team once again failed to become victors on the European scene.

When David Murray took over at Rangers, he stated: 'This is a challenge for us all and I see no shortage of confidence or determination around me. My colleagues and I believe that only success at the highest level will do for Rangers.' One of the English players recruited to the cause, Nigel Spackman, pointed out on his transfer back to Chelsea how difficult that would be: 'Winning the championship doesn't stretch them as it should, and playing in Europe is very different from playing in Scotland . . . they come under less pressure in the Scottish League where they are by far the best side. Rangers have a fantastic stadium, their pitch is perfect and the organisation behind the scenes could not be bettered. I have no doubt that they are the biggest club in Britain. Unfortunately, they need a stronger League to bring the best out of them.'

Murray added some hard evidence to back up what everyone knew to be the case. 'We have spent £35 million on the club in four years, £26 million on the stadium and £9 million net on players,' he said in 1992. When I came the overdraft was £7 million and now it's £10 million. But we can afford debt. I would rather be in debt and win something than have no debt and win nothing. I bought 76 per cent of the club for £6 million and the club is now valued, excluding players, at £34.5 million. Not a bad wee return, eh? It's not for sale, by the way.' The confident statements apart, it is difficult to verify the actual financial health of the club. Murray promised shareholders, for instance, that he would take action to reduce the overdraft but so far this has not happened. Rangers' status as the biggest club in Britain was, however, something Murray was keen to push. His view was that the whole world should recognise what they had achieved. 'You could take other clubs where individual areas are better,' he said. 'Liverpool in pure footballing terms, Manchester United for their history, but overall Rangers are the biggest club in the country.'

The larger Scottish clubs, in common with their English counterparts, had begun to feel that their smaller brethren were only continuing to exist because of tradition and the hand-outs that came their way from their association with the big clubs, through pools pay-outs and a share of television and sponsorship money. With a turnover in excess of £15 million it was becoming increasingly apparent that it was an absurdity for Rangers to be playing in the same League as the likes of Airdrie. While Rangers could boast crowd attendances of 40,000 (and could draw 5,000 to a reserve match), Airdrie were lucky to attract more than 3,000 to home League games. Clubs from the bottom part of the Premier Division and the top section of the First Division had been forced to live beyond their means in order to ensure survival in, or promotion to, the top flight. For most, the gamble of going full-time would fail since only the Premier Division produce enough revenue to justify anything more than semi-professionalism. Add to this an inherently unstable structure, where the rules for promotion and relegation and the number of clubs in the Premier Division have been in a constant state of flux, and you have a recipe for at best uncertainty, at worst chaos.

In many ways the situation was an historical accident. In the far-off days of the nineteenth century it was simply not feasible for English and Scottish clubs to overcome the travelling difficulties that would arise in an integrated British league. Because of this, and a natural tendency towards asserting Englishness and Scottishness (and, for that matter, Welshness and Irishness) on the part of the population, the game developed separately in the different nations of the United Kingdom, despite it being one political entity. As long as football could survive on a shoestring, this was no problem domestically, although there were always rumblings in football's international arenas because the UK had four representatives in the World Cup and European Champion-ships. When the harsh commercial winds began to blow, however, the reality was brought home. For the Scots, quite simply, the country and its population were too small to support a fully fledged League unless it were operated and controlled along strictly commercial lines.

When commercialism first became a major issue in the 1970s, the Scottish League responded by agreeing to form a smaller First Division. This became the Premier Division, which has alternated between ten and twelve members ever since. In such a small division, it was necessary for each team to play all the others four times a season. At the time this was seen as a bonus for the lesser clubs, which would play two home games a season against Rangers and Celtic, thus ensuring at least four big pay-days. It was always an artificial device, though, which, while it worked for a time because of its novelty, eventually began to destroy the scarcity value of Old Firm games, bore the fans and depreciate still further the value of fixtures against teams other than the big two. Not only that, when the Premier Division was in twelve-team mode, the number of League fixtures became, at forty-four, the highest in Europe.

The situation at home began, after Aberdeen's triumph in the Cup-winners' Cup in 1985, to be reflected in Scottish clubs' performances in Europe. Despite Dundee United's exceptional displays when they were runners-up to Gothenburg in the 1987 UEFA Cup, the truth was that Scottish clubs looked less likely than ever to win a European trophy.

Celtic, meanwhile, were caught napping by the arrival of Souness at Ibrox. It seemed that they believed Souness would not succeed with his bold policies and they failed to respond to what was happening. Tom Grant, a Celtic board member, said at the time: 'Celtic will not splash out outrageous sums of cash, just because people see Rangers doing it,' which entirely missed the point that Rangers had lifted their eyes to new horizons while Celtic still saw everything in terms of Old Firm rivalry. Souness, meanwhile, went on to win the Championship in his first season. This success prompted Celtic to sack their manager, David Hay, who had pleaded in vain with the directors for cash to strengthen the team. Hay's departure paved the way for the return of Billy McNeil, who at first managed to recapture some glory in the club's centenary year, after the board performed an about-turn and spent heavily in the transfer market. Even this spending was offset to some extent by sales. Maurice Johnston, Brian McClair and Murdo McLeod, among others, left for large sums. Their success was, however, short-lived, and McNeil himself was sacked in 1991. This led to the installation of Liam Brady as manager, in a belated attempt to emulate Rangers by hiring a man who had been a playing legend (though like Souness with Rangers, Brady had never played for Celtic). More money, some £6 million, was made available for players than any previous Celtic manager had been given but once again it was counterbalanced by the sale of important players such as Paul, Elliot and Derek Whyte. It was still nothing like the amount that Souness could throw at the transfer market. Some of the buys Brady made, such as Tony Cascarino and Gary Gillespie, were catastrophic. They failed to lift Celtic back towards parity with Rangers and after a dismal start to the 1993/4 season, Brady resigned following two trophy-less years.

By the 1990s, the choices for Celtic were stark, and not just on the field. Finances and the dreadful state of the ground were the pressing problems. If they stayed at Parkhead they would either have to refurbish it completely at astronomical cost or see its capacity reduced to 6,500 in compliance with the Taylor Report. Amid protests from fans, and attempts to wrest control of the club by disaffected former board members and outside shareholders, the Celtic directors came up with a plan totally out of character with their staid image. A proposal for a new stadium complex at Cambuslang, ten minutes' drive from Celtic Park, was unveiled, comprising a hotel, offices and other leisure facilities. The board claimed that the £100 million development would require an investment of £2 million on the part of Celtic to purchase the site, the cost of the stadium being funded by land sales for the other elements such as the hotel and long-term sponsorship contracts. The project said the board, would solve their financial problems.

One of the main proponents of the plan was Terry Cassidy, whose two-year reign as Celtic's chief executive was, according to the fanzine *Once a Tim*, 'yet another shambles which Celtic have failed to sever without the entire football world watching with laughter and disbelief'. Eventually, after alienating the players, the Lisbon Lions, the manager, fans and sponsors, as well as making potential business investors feel unwelcome and contradicting statements emanating from the board, Cassidy was paid off. He left behind the unfinished debate over Cambuslang, which assumed sinister proportions when the site was described by environmental experts as 'a timebomb', due to its previous existence as a waste disposal dump. Now, when a Celtic forward misses an open goal and hopes the ground will open up and swallow him, his wish will be in danger of being fulfilled. Under the circumstances, it is not surprising that planning permission was held up and August 1994 is now looming on the horizon. In pinning their hopes on Cambuslang the board have left themselves with no alternative to patching up Parkhead in the interim, and major redevelopment is out of the question. The only place where seating can be bolted on to existing terracing is in the famous 'Jungle' (the West Terrace), to the detriment of atmosphere, capacity and revenue.

The Cambuslang venture was planned when the club had made a pre-tax trading loss of over £3 million in 1991–92 and had secured its overdraft with the Bank of Scotland by a charge on the Parkhead stadium. The overall debt, meanwhile, had risen alarmingly to £7 million. It was a debt that Celtic, unlike Rangers, would have difficulty in managing. David Low, a financial consultant and disgruntled shareholder who sought a change in the club's management, was scathing in his assessment of the board's performance. 'The club have reported a loss in six out of the last seven years,' he said. 'One reason for this state of affairs is that the club is trying to keep up with the Rangers revolution . . . but the current board do not seem to have the ability to bring the club around. The board may have been unlucky with current events such as the Taylor Report and the recession but they lack the skill required to return the club to its former glory.'

The board refused to contemplate a public share issue to raise money and remained reluctant to admit others to the inner sanctum. One person who was taken on, builder Brian Dempsey, probably so shocked the board with his ambitious plans for the club that his directorship was not ratified by the AGM after the existing board lobbied against his appointment. In fact an agreement had been made between five board members who owned 60 per cent of the club whereby if anyone wanted to sell his shares, they would be offered to the other four directors first. This was called a suicide pact by wishful-thinking fans and a non-aggression treaty by other observers. Either way, it was certainly sharp practice as it deliberately excluded the views of minority shareholders who are supposed to be protected by law. The agreement was presented as a means of achieving stability following threatened boardroom coups, but as a former Celtic player Davie Provan pointed out, 'The reason for the pact is self-preservation'. Brian Dempsey agreed and described the board's attitude as 'we are not getting it right but so long as we stick together we can stay where we are'. It was not an acceptable situation for most fans.

The board appeared complacent in the face of the crisis. Dr Michael Kelly, the latest family member to become a director and the head of a public relations company which looks after the Celtic account, dismissed all talk of disasters. 'Crisis is not a word I would use,' he said. 'The debts are not rising and we can return to a trading profit soon . . . the situation is not deteriorating. I'm confident that with the present board we can turn the whole thing around.' The board were pinning their hopes on a combination of the new stadium and some sort of change in the Scottish League. In fact, the reluctance to allow a share issue, was, as Davie Provan had remarked, designed to ensure that the three families retained their traditional control.

While success on the pitch could keep the fans in check, when the situation got out of hand it became increasingly clear that the gravy train on which the three families had ridden for so many years had all but disappeared over the precipice, leaving behind huge debts that in the short term could only be serviced by the sale of star players like Paul McStay and John Collins. Considering the miserable state of affairs, the loyalty of the Celtic fans has been astonishing (the average gate of 26,000 in 1993 was among the top half-dozen in Britain). Perhaps it is time for the unthinkable, for the fans to vote with their feet, as they did at West Ham. For change to occur at Celtic, a similar fans' revolt will have to take place. The desperate need for revenue might yet force the board to open the door to cash-rich benefactors like Fergus McCann or Gerald Weisfeld, whose blandishments they have so far been able to resist. The more likely scenario, though, is that if the fans don't take matters into their own hands, there is little hope of change.

Throughout the period of Rangers' success and Celtic's decline, two other clubs, Aberdeen and Hearts, had been expressing worries of their own. They could see clearly that if there were no Celtic to challenge Rangers, then the Ibrox club might easily look elsewhere and make plans to leave the Scottish League altogether. Locking Rangers, and to a lesser extent, Celtic, into a Scottish dimension was imperative for the smaller clubs. Their alarm proved justified as in 1990

Rangers took a leading role in moves to create a European League, and when that failed to materialise they were instrumental in achieving changes to the format of the European Cup in 1992, under which the knock-out format was replaced from the quarter-final stage by a pool system which became the Champions' League.

Rangers had long since realised that the Scottish League was a marketing man's nightmare. Increasing the number of clubs from ten to twelve simply strained the fitness and technique of players and the loyalty of fans. In January 1992, a Rangers-Aberdeen proposal to cut the number of league matches to thirty-six a season was put forward. After each club had played each other twice, the division would regroup into two mini-divisions, the top six to fight for the Championship and a UEFA place while the bottom six would take part in a promotion-relegation play off with the top clubs of the First Division. When the plan was scuppered by the smaller clubs, who feared the loss of home fixtures against the Old Firm, David Murray intimated that maybe the vote would prove to be a watershed. 'What we have,' he said, 'is a classic case of the tail wagging the dog. We shall have to wait and see if the dog does not shed its tail.'

The wait was not a long one. On June 26, Rangers, Celtic, Aberdeen, Dundee United and Hearts gave the statutory two years' notice of their intention to leave the Scottish League. They formed themselves into a limited company called the Scottish Superleague (SSL) under the chairmanship of Hearts supremo Wallace Mercer, and announced that they were prepared to consider applications from other prospective members. It was a move, according to Gary Oliver, writing in *When Saturday Comes*, akin to 'appointing Herod to the board of Mothercare'. A Murray-sponsored company, the Carnegie Partnership, produced a marketing plan for the SSL which they described as 'radical and far-reaching'. It would, they said, 'take the game in Scotland into the twenty-first century and onto a basis where it can compete in Europe'. In truth, though, it was a rag-bag of proposals that included the introduction of a British Cup and a Superleague Cup, and as its cornerstone envisaged a League of ten invited clubs based on a franchise system, with relegation suspended for two seasons.

The mainstream media reaction was generally favourable, as any change was seen as a positive move forward. *The Sunday Times* editorial in the Scottish edition, for instance, carried the headline, A RED CARD FOR HASBEENS, a reference to the 'backward-looking' Scottish football establishment. When the dust cleared, however, the SSL looked like an exercise to retain and expand the commercial base of the five big clubs unencumbered by the necessity of worrying any longer about the Brechins and the Clydebanks of their world. It also appeared to be an attempt to avoid the pitfalls of the twenty-two-club English Premier League, where the all-for-one mentality was holding back the élite. Naturally, nobody asked the punters what they wanted. It was just assumed they would take whatever they were given, even if they had to pay more at the turnstiles. The supporters of teams which would not be invited to join the SSL after they had won promotion because they did not live up to certain criteria would be hardest hit of all. Of course, the criteria would not be applied too stringently to the big five themselves, otherwise Celtic and Hearts would be financial non-starters. Speaking for the small clubs (and on this occasion for most of the fans as well), Jack Steedman, a former Scottish League president and chairman of Clydebank, described the plan as 'the best piece of Scottish fiction I've seen since Compton Mackenzie'.

Initially, the Scottish FA refused to acknowledge the SSL but after much drum-beating on both sides some concessions were made. By this time, five more clubs had joined the SSL, which magnanimously conceded the principle of promotion and relegation for one team via a play-off. They even said they might be prepared to stay in the fold if they could have commercial autonomy. The Scottish League then came up with an alternative plan, comprising a fourteen-club Premier Division, which harked back to the Rangers-Aberdeen proposal but contained the ludicrous suggestion that points gained in the first half of the season should be discounted. So the bizarre situation could transpire whereby a team winning the twenty-six-game League could lose out to a sixth-placed team winning the ten-game championship decider.

Even stranger was Celtic's decision to switch sides at the last minute and back the Scottish League's plan, rather than the SSL, of which they were members. Chairman Kevin Kelly felt he had done 'the honourable thing' because 'the other clubs in the Superleague would prefer to stay in the Scottish League and if they're honest they'd admit it'. Perhaps Celtic's action shouldn't have come as such a surprise as the Carnegie Partnership was widely regarded as a tool of Rangers. It now appeared that Celtic had only gone along with the SSL scheme as a negotiating ploy. It was all to no avail, however, as at an extraordinary general meeting of the Scottish League on January 14 1993, the SSL clubs, even without Celtic, comfortably prevented the necessary two-thirds majority for constitutional change within the Scottish League being reached.

Eventually, the SSL disappeared (along with Wallace Mercer, who emigrated to the south of France) in a compromise formula consisting of four divisions of ten clubs, with two new clubs recruited from the Highland and/or other minor leagues. For their agreement to the plan, the SSL clubs were granted more commercial autonomy as well as having fewer meaningless fixtures in a thirty-six-game League. However, it was touch and go and change was only effected by the vote of the newest member of the Premier Division, Raith Rovers, which increased the club's chances of relegation by so doing. The new structure, due to come into being in 1994–95, is probably the best system as long as four games between the big clubs is regarded as a prerequisite for survival.

The real problems afflicting Scottish football appeared no nearer a solution, despite the readjustment. Attendances were down, prices were up and Rangers' unchallenged dominance looked set to continue. Because of its tradition, Scotland had been too democratic for its own good. To keep both Rangers and Stenhousemuir in the same league, a complete reorganisation to reflect their differing needs is required. At the top, Rangers must be given the chance to play their way through a season rather than having to slog through too many matches. Lower down, where the game is part-time, parochialism can come to the fore, which would lead to regional football and an increase in the number of clubs through the addition of more Highland League and Northern Premier League teams. To allow full integration, the big clubs' reserve teams could also be included. A pyramid structure maintaining promotion and relegation, with perhaps the addition of play-offs, would enable clubs to find their true level. Unfortunately, the biggest compromise will have to be made in the Premier Division. Because of a lack of depth, a sixteen-team League would see a number of rugby scores but, as other smaller countries such as Holland and Belgium have shown, this can be part of the entertainment and is a small price to pay for enabling the likes of Ajax and Anderlecht to discharge their responsibilities at home while making successful assaults on Europe. By making sure that clubs play each other only twice in the top league in Scotland, the scarcity value of the big encounters will be restored. Since there will always be a league within a league, the competition among the élite will be enhanced, while matches against the smaller clubs will become more important as the season inevitably throws up a number of surprising results. While Rangers will still be favourites in any circumstances, they will have to face a greater challenge under this system than they would under any of the artificial leagues that have hitherto been proposed, all of which are dependent on Rangers and Celtic playing each other four times a season.

The situation north of the border has been totally turned upside down since the day Graeme Souness walked into Ibrox for the first time. The old certainties have been shaken. For years, there was little real expectation on the part of Scottish fans that their clubs could match the best in Europe. In Rangers' case, that has now changed, and in 1993 they came within a whisker of reaching the European Cup final. On the other hand, the Scots had for many years held completely unrealistic ideas about the quality of their national team.

In 1974, Scotland at last managed to make it to the World Cup finals, their first appearance since 1958, where they were eliminated although they didn't lose any of their three games in the first round. In 1978, Ally MacLeod's team and its supporters had gone to Argentina actually believing they could win the tournament. The debacle the team suffered, with a draw against Iran and an embarrassing defeat by Peru, failed to diminish expectations by the time the next World Cup came around, and the Scots still believed they possessed a team that could live with the world's best. However, as the emphasis shifted towards the clubs, the Scots began to take a more realistic view. Simply reaching the finals of major international tournaments was an achievement for such a small nation. In Sweden in 1992, the Scots played in the final stages of the European Championships for the first time, and although they were eliminated, like England, in the first round, unlike in England, satisfaction was derived from their performances, particularly a victory over the CIS. The team's campaign to qualify for the USA in 1994 was always going to be difficult in a group containing Italy and Portugal. A measure of the Scots' changing attitudes could be seen in the reaction to some disappointing results early on in the qualifying tournament, which included a defeat in Switzerland and goalless draws at home against Portugal and Italy. Instead of having to endure the abuse heaped on Graham Taylor, the Scottish coach, Andy Roxborough, was hardly criticised at all. If anything showed how the Scots were becoming club-orientated, this was it.

It was Rangers' defeat of Leeds which became a symbolic victory for the whole of Scottish football. The clubs were now the standard-bearers. However, the pots of gold the Scots have seen piling up in the English game, and the lucrative European dimension which beckon any successful club, could have damaging consequences across the whole game. For instance, the media exhorted the fans to get behind Rangers, which belittled the satisfactory performances of Hibs, Hearts and Celtic in Europe and ignored not only centuries of traditional rivalry but the obvious resentment among fans of what they felt was Rangers' selfish opportunism. How long will it be before the Scots' ambitions force their game to succumb completely to the baser temptations that so afflict their neighbours?

9

Money Talks

Scotland shows it won't be pushed around by Europe's big powers, while bribery, corruption or incompetence surround European TV deals and the FA's dealings with Wembley Stadium

> *'Football remains my passion. It's that that keeps me going and not the money that people say I do it for.'*
>
> Jean-Claude Darmon, television adviser to the French Football Federation.

> *'You're a joke. You've got to fall in line with the rest of them or you'll disappear.'*
>
> British television executive to Alex Fynn.

There has always been a weight around the neck of football in Scotland which has influenced the development of the game north of the border. It is, quite simply, the proximity of the English. Seen through Scottish eyes, the English have lorded it over the UK scene as if they were the only ones who mattered. Fear of being overwhelmed by their neighbour has resulted in the Scottish football authorities jealously guarding their independence, so relations with their counterparts at Lancaster Gate in London have inevitably come under strain.

The Scots have every reason to be wary about English interference in their affairs. The meddling has never been direct but has rather taken the form of an arrogant approach to decision-making that takes little or no account of the consequences for the Scottish game. The classic example is the English FA's high-handed and unilateral decision to end the annual match between England and

Scotland – the oldest international fixture in football – using the cloak of hooliganism as justification. It is revealing that the FA never imposed the suspension of games as a solution to the problems caused by English troublemakers at home.

Two possible scenarios have worried Scotland most. First, any integration of the two Leagues or the institution of a British Cup might give fresh impetus to a long-simmering campaign to end the anomaly of the UK having four teams entering international tournaments and four votes in FIFA and UEFA councils. If that ever came to pass it would be Lancaster Gate that would inevitably become the head-quarters of the British game and the Scottish FA would be reduced to a parochial body along the lines of county FAs in England. Second, and perhaps of more immediate concern, is the issue of televising English and Scottish League games on a regular basis. The Scots have for many years adhered to a policy of severely rationing the transmission of live matches from home while above all keeping English games off Scottish screens entirely. They have done this in the belief that practically any exposure to such games would reduce crowds at Scottish matches, which would sound the death knell for the Scottish game by hastening the demise of a large wedge of Scottish clubs. The English FA never had to bother with addressing the reverse possibility because English television companies have always believed that no one in England is interested in Scottish club football and has therefore never even tried to screen it. Even the Scottish Cup final is limited to goal highlights in England.

The old ITV-BBC system was tailor-made for Scottish football. Regionalised companies, in the case of ITV, and regional divisions in the case of the BBC meant that programmes originating in one region could easily be barred from transmission in another. In this the Scots were assisted by a UEFA regulation, article 14, which states that the FA of any country can refuse permission for a game being played in a foreign land to be screened in their territory. When the authorities in England did a complete volte face on their longstanding policy towards live televised football in the 1980s, it was taken as read that none of the live games would be shown in Scotland. For their part, the Scots continued to resist any extension of live coverage of their own domestic football beyond a few League matches and the two Cup finals.

All this changed with the advent of satellite television and the increasing challenges being made concerning the compatibility of article 14 with the provisions of the Treaty of Rome. Although not tested in the courts until BSkyB won a judgement against the FA in October 1992, it was widely believed that article 14 was an artificial hindrance to the free movement of goods and services and as such was a restraint of trade, anti-competitive and unlawful. When the English FA sold television rights to the FA Cup and England internationals to BSB in 1988, director of external affairs Glen Kirton conceded that the FA had adopted an 'open-door policy' towards international television transmissions. This was because, whether the Scots liked it or not, satellite technology allowed neither BSB nor Sky to black out one particular region or country, and thus English games would now be seen in Scotland for the first time. In retaliation, the Scots also struck a deal with BSB in 1988 but in their case never accepted that their fixtures being shown in England on BSB established a precedent. Jim Farry, chief executive of the Scottish FA, claimed the agreement was 'reached with BSB because at the time the service was seen by only a tiny minority of the population', and that 'as the numbers [of viewers] increased so the policy might have to be reassessed'.

A residual problem for the Scots was that the small population of their country ensured that they could never achieve the amounts of money television was prepared to pay in England. Yet they believed they had a far more coherent strategy towards television than the English, who appeared to agree to almost any demand of the television companies as long as the price was right. Money seemed to fall into the hands of the English while the Scots had to work hard for every penny. Scandinavia, for instance, showed live English games on television during their midwinter break, bringing extra rights fees and huge amounts of revenue from perimeter advertising. In the community of unrestrained competition that Europe had become by the 1980s, however, it was the harsh reality that television markets were strictly defined as major or minor, and Scottish football would always occupy the latter category.

It is the right of the home association or club to sell television rights to a game to a broadcasting company in their own territory and in return receive (in addition to the fee) a 'free' signal which the association or club can then sell to an overseas television company, if a demand exists. Thus the one possibility for a small nation like Scotland to cash in on huge television fees is in European or World Cup competitions, when either a Scottish club or the national team is pitted against a major market opponent, from England, Italy, France, Germany or Spain. This is because it is irrelevant to a potential television audience where a game of special interest is taking place. For instance, if Scotland are playing Italy, the Italian viewer does not care whether the game is played in Glasgow or Rome, it is still a big event which the Italian television networks will want to screen during peak viewing time.

In the days before satellites and deregulation, European television companies operated a restrictive practice which kept the price down. If a team from Scotland were drawn against a team from Italy, either the BBC or ITV bid for the rights. Neither company would bid against the other but operated on the Buggins' turn principle. A small amount of money would be offered for exclusive world rights, take it or leave it. Invariably the offer was accepted as some money was better than no money and extra revenue could be generated from advertising boards if there were guaranteed television exposure. The British company which screened the game would then give the pictures free to an Italian television service like the state broadcaster, RAI. When the return match was played in Italy, RAI would make the same deal in reverse, giving their pictures free to a television network in Britain. This was known as the principle of reciprocity.

When deregulation began in Europe in the mid-1980s, the picture changed rapidly. The new stations upset the cosy relationship that had hitherto existed between cosseted television channels. Football, like movies, became a prize to be battled over and as the traditional television networks fought back, the money being offered to the game skyrocketed. At the same time, clubs, agents and national associations realised that they no longer had to accept take-it-or-leave-it deals. In France, football's television negotiator, Jean-Claude Darmon, who is known as 'Monsieur Pub' (Mr Publicity), along with Claude Bez, the president of Bordeaux, which at the time was the country's leading club, developed the concept of selling rights case by case rather than wholesale. This meant that a television company could buy only the right to screen a match in its own territory and possessed no authority to sell or give the picture to any third party such as a foreign television service.

Some of football's administrators understood the implications of this change quicker than others. In Scotland, where little money was on offer from television for the domestic game, the possibilities opened up by competition in the major markets of Europe were spotted immediately. The rest of Europe failed to understand the depth of the Scots' tenacity, believing them to be ignorant and unsophisticated Picts, but the Scots had lived under the shadow of the English for too long to give up on their one opportunity for a big pay-day. In the battle that ensued, an incredible game of brinkmanship took place which involved no less a personage than François Mitterand, the president of the French Republic.

Jean-Claude Darmon is the head of a company called Mediafoot, which represents the French Football Federation in matters to do with television, sponsorship and advertising. He is perhaps the most important man in French sport, being known as *un brasseur d'affaires* – a wheeler-dealer or Mr Fixit. In addition to the football federation, Darmon acts for the French Rugby Union and more than a dozen First Division football clubs. He also runs the Parc des Princes stadium in Paris. He has a reputation as something of a megalomaniac in his native country, born, no doubt, of his role in generating a staggering income for both the French Football Federation and the clubs. In less than ten years, France went from relative football obscurity to become a major force in the world game, both on and off the field. It was Darmon who masterminded the off-field successes. So omnipotent did he become that when in 1990 he was tainted by a scandal that rocked French football, which resulted in the imprisonment of club officials and the demotion of two clubs, Bordeaux and Brest, for financial irregularities, Darmon continued to work freely for his clients despite the fact that he had been arrested and released only on bail.

The thrust of Darmon's plan was to establish a partnership between football and television, so that there could be an equitable distribution of matches by channel and revenue by club. The arrival in 1984 of a new subscription television service called Canal Plus gave Darmon the opportunity to achieve his objectives. Canal Plus's strategy to win subscribers was based on being able to provide them with something extra special in two product fields, movies and sport. As far as movies were concerned, this meant Canal Plus had to be the first television station to show them. As for sport, the station screened more unusual (for French audiences) offerings such as NBA basketball and American Football (both of which were successful) and Australian Rules (which wasn't). Canal Plus, through its head of sport, Charles Bietry, a former France Presse journalist and friend of Darmon, also determined to show mainstream sports, but in a different way. Live football matches from the French League became the centrepiece of Bietry's new approach. Production techniques were revolutionised as Bietry aimed to 'search for truth'. His idea was 'to try to show the emotions . . . of a dynamic, modern, beautiful drama in which nobody knows what's going to happen next'. More important for French football, perhaps, than Bietry's 'search for truth' was the fact that Canal Plus were willing to pay large amounts of money to the game. In return they wanted a level of access the English media could only dream about. This was freely given because, as Bietry says, 'We [at Canal Plus] are all supporters and when you film a match you do it as if you're filming someone you love.'

The success of Canal Plus was instant and it immediately set a standard for others to follow, using more cameras, tight close-ups and a succession of replays that would become a model for other European television networks, including the British. As the company went from strength to strength, its relationship with the game underwent a metamorphosis. In 1991, Canal Plus bought the ailing Paris St Germain club. According to Bietry, this was almost an altruistic move. 'It would be bad for football and therefore bad for television,' he said, 'if there wasn't a flourishing team in Paris.' Others might be a touch less charitable in discerning the company's motives. A voice and thus a vote in the councils of the game certainly does nothing to harm Canal Plus's long-term prospects of retaining its football rights. There is also a larger principle at stake. All over Europe, television, by offering large sums of money, has become football's most important paymaster. The timing of matches in many countries, for instance, is no longer set for the convenience of the paying supporter but for the maximisation of television companies' revenue. Often television companies themselves form a part of a wider media empire. It is only a short step from there before influence, as in the case of Paris SG, becomes ownership. However, there is no resentment in France over Canal Plus's purchase of one of the nation's great sporting institutions, because in Bietry's view, Canal Plus goes out of its way to respect football rather than exploit it. Similarly, there is little adverse comment over the way Jean-Claude Darmon has organised television matters. In a country where the average First Division gate is only 10,000, Darmon's revenue-generating capabilities have been a godsend. What would happen, however, if, in a few years' time, television stations owned a number of clubs? And suppose there grew a feeling that live football on television was a bad thing. How would the television-owned clubs vote when the issue came up for discussion? With the argument in England over the vote of Alan Sugar's Tottenham Hotspur in the television debate, the issue is perhaps not as far away as it at might, at first sight, seem.

The success of Canal Plus – its subscription renewal rate, at 96 per cent, is the highest in the world – forced the other channels to respond. Today, Jean-Claude Darmon dishes out games to all like some grand old Santa Claus, only this Santa receives rich rewards himself. The League, Cup and internationals are divided between TF1, France 2 and Canal Plus. European games come under Darmon's 'pool' system. Under this scheme, it matters nothing whether the opponent is Milan or Wrexham, or whether the game is broadcast live on TF1 at peak time or in the afternoon on Canal Plus, there is a sliding scale of earnings to which all clubs and channels stick. Having carved up the domestic scene, Darmon turned his attention to internationals. This was a different game, the nature of which was to do the best deal. If that meant bending the rules – well, it was in the name of France.

In March 1990, Scotland were due to play France at Hampden Park in a match to decide which one of them would qualify for Italia 90. Darmon knew the game was eagerly anticipated in his homeland and he saw the opportunity to pull off a coup. He believed the Scots did not know the value of the match and approached them with an offer which was nothing less than derisory. He already possessed, he told the Scottish FA, the right to sell the game to French television through his contract with the federation (technically the federation could refuse permission for the game to be screened if Darmon were bypassed, but it is inconceivable that they would have deprived their public in order to placate one man, however powerful), and he offered £40,000 as a facility fee.

The Scots knew perfectly well that the game was worth more, considerably more, than Darmon was offering. Moreover, they knew that they could sell the game to whomever they chose. Annoyed by Darmon's attitude, the Scottish FA told the Frenchman that he could indeed buy the French television rights, but they would cost him, not £40,000, but ten times that amount, a massive £400,000. Darmon couldn't believe his ears. He thought the Scots were 'utterly mad'. Unfortunately, he underestimated his adversaries and initially refused to increase his offer. As the day of the match approached Darmon did offer more money but the Scots were adamant. They wanted the full £400,000, otherwise the game would not be televised in France.

Darmon played one last card to get his way. It was quite a ploy, too. Having put his faith in the magnetic power of his own personality, which had failed in this case, probably due to the utter inscrutability of the strange Celtic race with which he was dealing, Darmon reasoned that the only course left open to him was to bring in someone who possessed even more clout than himself. Darmon asked the head of the French Federation, Jean Fournet-Fayard, to persuade the president of France, François Mitterand, to intervene. Mitterand duly telephoned Jim Farry and told him that the game was so important it would be a tragedy if it were not to be shown in France. Mitterand hoped some accommodation could be reached. Farry listened politely but refused to alter his conditions.

The Scottish obduracy, probably exacerbated by Darmon's high-handed tactics, was based on the simple philosophy that they had always managed to exist without overseas television money, and anyway it was not a source of income that could be relied upon. However, when circumstances were right, as they were in this case, then they should hold out for as much as they could get, thereby gaining a reputation for a willingness to stop a match being televised to an overseas audience if their asking price were not met. In fact, the £400,000 was not a precise valuation on the part of the Scots but had more to do with Darmon's initial offer of a miserly £40,000. Asking ten times what was offered was nothing if not audacious and belied the dour image of the Scots that exists in most English minds.

Faced with the wrath of an expectant public, the French caved in at the last minute and paid the Scots every last penny. In the event, it was good value even at that price, as the game was among the top ten most-watched programmes in France during 1990 and as such produced significant advertising and broadcast sponsorship revenues for the station that screened it, TF1.

But the Scottish victory had painful repercussions for Darmon. 'When I go abroad to buy rights,' he ruefully reflected later, 'I am bled dry . . . because unfortunately we paid too much for the [Scotland] game. We shall be suffering the consequences for ages.' Sure enough, when the Dutch team, Feyenoord, played Monaco in the semi-final of the Cup-winners' Cup in 1992, the Feyenoord president, believing he could better the Scots, asked for £1 million. TF1 eventually offered £350,000, the most they had ever bid for a club game, while the Dutch came down to £800,000 on the day of the match. Again, a head of state became involved. Prince Rainier and his son Prince Albert were both patrons and fans of AS Monaco. While in Rotterdam for the away leg, Darmon was afraid that the two royals would accede to Dutch pressure so that the game could be seen on French television. The Princes, however, along with TF1 and the French Federation, kept to the hard line Darmon had now established. Feyenoord's demands were rejected and the match was not televised in France and according to Jean-Claude Dassier, head of sport at TF1, the final decision was made only five minutes before the kick-off. The seemingly inexorable rise in rights fees was checked for the moment. (Monaco duly qualified for the final but their big day was overshadowed when, before their match in the semi-final of the French Cup, a temporary stand in Bastia, Corsica, collapsed and over fifty people were killed after which a number of football administrators resigned while others faced criminal charges. No such fate was suffered by any of their English counterparts following Hillsborough.)

Emboldened by their success over the French, the Scots tried their luck again two years later when they were drawn to play Italy in the qualifying stages for the 1994 World Cup. Italy had sparked off the television revolution in the first place, albeit in a totally disorganised fashion, which led to an amazing inflationary spiral in the cost of football to the small screen. Media magnate and president of Milan Silvio Berlusconi found a loophole in the law which allowed him to operate a national television network under the guise of a number of local stations. So popular and powerful did his network become that the Italian government was forced to legitimise it as Canale 5. Once established, it did not take Berlusconi long to realise that if he had football, he could mount a serious challenge to the hegemony of the state broadcaster, RAI. RAI reacted to the threat posed by Berlusconi by offering amounts of money unheard of outside the USA. For the 1987–88 season, RAI offered the Italian League £40 million for rights to show matches, not live, but recorded. At the time, English football was receiving less than £5 million a year for all its matches, League, FA Cup and internationals. Later, RAI paid Napoli a guaranteed £2 million for exclusive coverage of their European Cup campaign alone. Unfortunately, Napoli were knocked out early on and RAI were left having to justify their outlay. It was a type of deal which would become popular, despite RAI's experience, and has been followed in a number of countries, not least England. It is one way television companies can avoid having to bid in auction conditions after each round of European competitions, although as RAI discovered, it is a policy that has its risks.

The Scotland-Italy encounter took place in October 1992. This was the chance the Scots had been waiting for ever since the French game and they demanded £600,000 from the

Italians for rights to cover the game at Ibrox. In a move worthy of the Jeffrey Archer novel from whence the phrase gained its currency, the Italians, according to the commercial director of the Scottish FA, Bill Wilson, were informed that the price was non-negotiable – £600,000; 'not a penny more, not a penny less'.

At first RAI, like Darmon before them, dismissed the Scots out of hand. Once again, as showtime approached and the Scots presented an unflinching resolve, the opposition began to get jittery. RAI told Bill Wilson that they would make a maximum and final offer of £280,000. The Scots would either have to accept it or they would get nothing. Then, out of the blue, competition arrived on the scene. A new, twenty-four-hour sports subscription channel called Tele Piu had recently been started by Silvio Berlusconi, but he had been forced to divest himself of his controlling interest in it by the Italian courts under laws governing ownership of the media, which many believed to have been enacted to curb Berlusconi's domination of the mass media. Although he disposed of his newspaper interests it was no secret that Berlusconi retained a significant influence in Tele Piu after he was no longer officially the proprietor. In an audacious attempt to upstage its bigger rivals and make a name for itself in the process, Tele Piu agreed to meet Scotland's asking price. Moreover, it further agreed to pay the whole £600,000 in advance into the Scottish FA account at the Bank of Scotland. The involvement of Berlusconi is significant because his network had refused to bid for the game (as had the other privately owned national station, Tele Monte Carlo) in what looked suspiciously like a cartel arrangement with RAI. The two already had an 'arrangement' concerning UEFA Cup matches. Could it be that Berlusconi or his cohorts gave RAI a false sense of security, tacitly encouraging them to bid low, before launching a bid from another quarter which would catch RAI off-guard and humble it in the public eye?

When news of Tele Piu's coup reached Italy all hell broke loose. How, the football-mad Italians wanted to know, could an upstart station with only 100,000 subscribers outbid the Italian state broadcaster for a match which was so important to the whole country? Under pressure from the president of the Italian Football Federation, Antonio Matarrese, Tele Piu agreed to split their rights with RAI, but only if RAI paid the lion's share of the fee. In the end RAI paid £400,000 of the cost, while Tele Piu retained the right to show the match for only £200,000. Tele Piu, of course, also gained valuable publicity. Berlusconi then moved to buy the ground advertising rights through his agency Publitalia, for which the Scottish FA received a further £90,000. Bill Wilson, not to put too fine a point on it, was staggered by the turn of events. The valuation of £600,000 had not been precisely worked out. 'We asked for £600,000,' said Wilson, 'because we got £400,000 [from France] in 1990.'

Italy, a country which has resisted live television for its own domestic league matches, now had the same game live on two channels. For the occasion, Tele Piu removed its encryption, which made RAI's embarrassment complete. Giberto Evangelisti, RAI's head of sport, put a brave face on it: 'It's the best solution but maybe in future we should avoid can-cans. We shall get our act together to respond better to the new forces in the market.' Evangelisti went on to assert that the time was rapidly approaching when an agreement of £15 million would be made for future internationals, although he did not elaborate on that particular matter. In one last fit of pique, an Italian commentator, Bruno Pizzul, had a pop at Scotland manager Andy Roxborough, remembering how in 1988, 'we met them [Roxborough and two Scottish players] in the middle of the night outside a nightclub in Perugia, outraged because they couldn't get any more to drink . . . [it was] two in the morning on the day of the match'. (Italy won 2–0.)

What all these events showed was that enormous sums of money were available around Europe for television and advertising deals. Since most federations had neither the understanding nor the nerve of the Scots, the way was left open for a plethora of middle-men, agents, television companies and sports marketing organisations to step into the breach. With so much money in the offing, it is not surprising that a number of individuals saw the opportunity to make a killing. The madness of the market that has resulted is epitomised by the draws for each round of European competitions, which take place at the Noga Hilton Hotel in Geneva. These intermediaries gather like vultures to pounce on clubs from small countries who are drawn to play a big-time opponent. Talk of huge fees and massive financial guarantees is bandied about as they seek to sign clubs up. It is a free-for-all in which some do well, while the naïveté of others is unmercifully exploited.

For clubs in Europe, and for that matter, national associations dealing on behalf of their international teams, the problem has become one of deciding which of these middle-men is really offering them the best deal. The task is made all the more difficult by the fact that the competing bids are not always made on the same basis. An international advertising agency, for instance, spends millions of pounds of its clients' money on television and thus has a very good idea of what any particular match is worth. This means it can predict the revenue any given television programme will generate. An agency will also know about revenue that can be obtained from other countries and can provide skilled negotiators. However, since advertising agencies work on a commission basis, they do not offer clubs guarantees, which sports marketing companies tend to do. If the draw is kind to a small country, then an advertising agency is probably the best bet to make the really big money, but if two small countries are drawn together then the revenues will be minimal and a guarantee from a sports marketing company will probably bring in more. It is an old dilemma. For football clubs and countries, the issue is whether a bird in the hand is worth more than two in the bush.

In the countries of Eastern Europe, domestic television is dominated by the public service sector. Unlike their Western counterparts, television networks in these countries cannot afford to pay rights fees for games. They will screen matches, of course, as a service, with basic facilities in terms of the numbers of cameras. Sometimes they will even demand a fee themselves for screening a particular game, in the knowledge that the club or association requires a signal for overseas sales. By the 1980's rights to important football matches had become a highly prized commodity for their ability to earn hard currency. Thus an environment has been created in the East which is ripe for exploitation. More often than not, clubs and associations are totally ignorant of the value of their product to Western television. At the same time they need the currency and are tempted to accept any amount of dollars as long as the payment is up-front. Sometimes, hard-nosed agents will pay cash under the table, then sell on the rights to a broadcaster for many times more than the amount paid. The football authorities were quick learners, though. Once they realised what was happening they countered in kind. They began to dish out 'exclusive rights' at a price to all and sundry and it became a case of the biter being bit. David Keir, the contracts manager for BBC Sport, confirms that it is not unusual for four or five different agents to be offering him the same game from Eastern Europe.

For the qualifying campaign for the the 1992 European Championships, the Polish FA hired Saatchi and Saatchi to act for them. The draw pitted the Poles against some major-market countries, including England. Poland did extremely well financially: gross revenues were over $1.5 million (£1.14 million), much more than they had ever earned before, and Saatchis were given the rights for the qualifying games for the 1994 World Cup. What happened subsequently became the subject of a bitter dispute.

Initial negotiations took place in London between Saatchis and a Polish go-between, Roman Manuszewski, of a company called Sport UK. After protracted talks an agreement was reached before the draw for the World Cup qualifying groups took place in New York. For the Poles, the agreement was signed by the president of the Polish FA, the general secretary and a vice-president. Under the agreement, Saatchis were given exclusive television and advertisng rights for all Poland's home World Cup and European Championship matches until 1996. Negotiations were finalised over a dinner at the RAC Club in London in late November 1991. The actual amount received by the Poles would depend on who they were drawn against, since Saatchis would not provide guarantees, preferring to operate on a commission basis. Revenues were to be split, 75 per cent to the Poles, 25 per cent to Saatchi's and Sport UK. As legal documents submitted later make clear, all parties agreed that a binding arrangement had been entered into.

The World Cup draw took place amid much fanfare in New York on December 4 1991. Poland once again got lucky and were drawn in the same group as England, Holland, Norway and Turkey, all games for which there would be high demand from television. Saatchis were not represented at the jamboree in New York but it was reported back to them that a member of the Polish delegation had used the occasion to seek offers from other parties, despite the fact that everyone was aware of the existence of a signed agreement with Saatchis.

Events moved on to Amsterdam in February 1992, where a meeting between the group's representatives was held to schedule the matches within the qualifying group. Saatchis were informed via Roman Manuszewski that if they wanted to activate their agreement, a sum of US$75,000 (£51,000) would have to be paid to members of the Polish FA in what can only be described as a bribe. Saatchis refused, and the whole matter went into an uneasy abeyance. A month later, Saatchis sent on request an estimate of potential revenues to Poland which indicated that the sum of US$2.9 million (£1.96 million) could be raised from the qualifying games from television and advertising. The Poles responded by saying they would consider the sum along with other offers they had received. Saatchis informed them that they 'were not in a position to do this due to our agreement'.

Eventually, a meeting was convened in Warsaw for March 10 to thrash out the problems. At the gathering, Saatchis were told that a Polish company, Profus Management, which had no experience in the field of sports marketing, had offered US$1 million (£676,000) in cash to purchase the rights. Saatchis responded by saying that although guarantees were against company policy they were, in this case, prepared to offer an advance against receipts of US$500,000 (£338,000) provided that their commission was increased by 5 per cent. The Poles asked for a US$1 million advance with no increase in commission. Saatchis refused to budge.

During a recess, Alex Fynn, who was negotiating on behalf of Saatchis, was asked by one of the Polish delegation to accompany him to a private area. The Pole's motive soon became clear. He wanted to know if Fynn had brought the US$75,000 (£51,000) which had been discussed in Amsterdam. Fynn feigned ignorance of the whole matter, whereupon he was informed that in that case, Saatchis would not get the contract.

Nothing was resolved at the meeting as the Poles put off making any decision. Then in April the Polish FA informed Saatchis that the contract was going to be put out to tender.

Saatchis retaliated by threatening legal action for breach of the November agreement. On April 13, at a meeting of a Polish FA committee in Warsaw, it was decided to award the television and advertising contract to yet another company, Sport Management BV, a Belgian organisation run by a former Polish international, Wlodek Lubanski (the same Lubanski who virtually killed English hopes of qualifying for the 1974 World Cup with both goals in a 2–0 victory).

Saatchis took a hard line over this development and warned television companies that it would seek an injunction to stop them screening any Polish games unless their agreement was honoured. The company also complained to UEFA, in the person of its general secretary, Gerhard Aigner, who, after speaking to the Poles, declined to intervene.

In the event, Sport Management BV failed to come up with the guarantee they had promised, which left the Polish FA in the embarrassing position of having no alternative but to deal with Saatchis. A firm contract was eventually signed and within a month, agreements had been made with television and advertisers worth over US$1 million (£676,000). The Poles received an advance payment of US$250,000 (£169,000). Although no guarantee had been given, by the middle of 1993, gross rights sales had exceeded US$2 million (£1.35 million). The Poles, who perhaps should have been happy with the way things had worked out, nevertheless continued to look for opportunities to break the contract with Saatchis and planted anti-Saatchi stories in the Polish press. Moreover, Marek Pietruska, the general secretary of the Polish FA and a respected UEFA representative, was fired because he was the man who had initially introduced Saatchis to the Poles.

It is difficult to understand the attitude of the Polish FA in the saga. After all, they almost sold for US$1 million (£676,000) what eventually would earn them double that figure. The problem arose because the Poles, as an East European nation in need of foreign currency, had heard about the great riches television could bring but had no idea what their own product was worth or how best to maximise their income from it. And they were desperately short of cash. In addition, certain individuals saw a chance to line their own pockets. Into the confusion stepped a number of companies offering unrealistic guarantees which they would find impossible to meet. If Poland had not been so lucky in the draw, Saatchis may not have been able to get them much at all but as it was, the Poles had to contend with a number of people telling them that they should ditch Saatchis because they would end up with next to nothing when they could receive US$1 million straight away. When a million dollars is at stake, the niceties of a contractual relationship can slip far down the list of priorities. The incident clearly showed how the money coming into football was a magnet that attracted those with baser instincts and it was difficult, if not impossible, to say who was on the straight and narrow and who was prepared to use any unscrupulous means to get his hands on the massive amounts of cash swilling around.

The experience of Saatchis could be considered a purely foreign fiasco of greed and corruption which could not happen at home. This, however, would be a mistake. Speaking from the standpoint of many years experience of negotiating rights, Volker Kosters, of CWL Telesport AG, one of the biggest operators in the field, thinks there has been a decline in the standards of English behaviour. 'You can shake hands three times with a chairman of an English club and it means nothing,' he said. 'You can shake hands once with a Romanian and it's a deal.' It's not just the clubs who can be criticised in this regard. Charles Hughes, in a discussion with Alex Fynn following Fynn's application for the post of FA commercial director, remarked that in addition to the basic salary, the commercial director would naturally expect to receive a commission on the revenue he brought in. Such commissions, according to Hughes, were not unknown at Lancaster Gate. He himself earned royalties from the FA book he had written, *The Winning Formula*. While this can be justified on the basis that a writer deserves to earn a royalty on his work, others might argue that as the head of the FA coaching department, it was part of Hughes' job description to disseminate his views and FA policy on the subject. That example, Hughes maintained, was nothing compared to some of the other things that were going on at Lancaster Gate. Hughes claimed commissions were earned by senior FA staff and cited one example where an item of leisurewear was introduced to the England players for the 1990 World Cup.

Although the total sum to the players' pool was only £25,000, it is alleged that a personal commission was taken by a senior FA employee on the basis that he had introduced extra money and was therefore entitled to a small part of it. When sponsorship was sought for the FA Cup, Bass, before turning its attention to the Premier League, was very keen but the deal fell through when, to its credit, Bass refused to pay a commission to a third party.

Other deals were conducted in a piecemeal manner, with no overall strategy. Many of these smacked more of incompetence than graft but were nonetheless symptomatic of a lack of control on the part of those whose job it is to run the game in England. A good illustration of this was the sponsorship of the FA National School by Vauxhall. The then FA secretary, Ted Croker, told Charles Hughes that he believed sponsorship would not be forthcoming from Vauxhall and cast doubt on the viability of the school. 'All you'll get is cars,' Croker said. 'Anyway, you drive a Rolls-Royce, you wouldn't be seen dead in a Vauxhall.' Despite Croker's view, Hughes went to see Vauxhall with the England manager at the time, Bobby Robson, and the two men came back with a deal in cash and kind which would finance the school, much to the chagrin of Croker. To make his point, Hughes, not long afterwards, traded in his Rolls for a company-supplied Vauxhall.

The lack of an overall marketing plan notwithstanding, sometimes, as in the case of the National School, matters worked out in the FA's favour. When the balance sheet of deals is examined, however, the lack of acumen on the part of the FA has cost far more than it has ever realised. The worst example of FA profligacy concerns the controversial contract with Wembley Stadium.

Wembley occupies a mythical place in football folklore. It is an ambition of just about every player in the world to play there. The place has an image that goes far beyond a mere football stadium: it is *the* stadium, a football shrine. This status was attained through more than fifty years of historic matches, beginning with the famous 'white horse' Cup final between West Ham and Bolton in 1923, when the estimated 200,000 people who crammed into a ground with a capacity of 126,000 were controlled by police, the most striking being an officer on the most beautiful grey anyone could imagine. The dramatic pictures were reproduced in newspapers and magazines across the world and Wembley's reputation was secured.

The Wembley pitch occupies the site of what was once known as Watkin's Folly, which was the base of a tower intended by the architect, Sir Edward Watkin, to emulate the Eiffel Tower in Paris. The structure was only part-completed when the money for the project ran out and it was abandoned. At the time, Wembley was typical of the suburban fringes of north-west London. It was a rural delight that was in the process of transformation into metroland, being linked to central London by the Metropolitan railway which encouraged much quasi-urban development. The turning-point for the area came in 1920, when it was chosen as the site of the proposed British Empire Exhibition. Watkin's folly was dismantled and replaced by the centrepiece of the exhibition, a national stadium. Built in a little under a year for less than £1 million, the Empire Stadium was completed four days before the historic Cup final of 1923.

After the close of the exhibition in 1925, there was a danger that Wembley would become a white elephant. It was saved by Sir Arthur Elvin, who bought from the official receiver the whole Wembley site and a twenty-one-year contract with the FA to stage Cup finals at the stadium. Elvin introduced greyhound racing (the income from regular meetings proved to be Wembley's salvation), Rugby League Cup finals and speedway. In 1934 he added the Empire Pool (now known as the Arena) and the stage was set for the 1948 Olympics, when Wembley was used for the athletics and swimming. By 1951 Elvin had secured exclusive rights to stage England football internationals. On his death in 1957 the complex was bought by the British Electric Traction Company, which made some significant improvements to the stadium, including the updating of the floodlights and a roof for the whole ground, finally completed in 1963.

By the late 1970s, however, Wembley faced another financial crisis. Improvements were again needed but there was not enough money in the kitty and the whole future of the stadium was in doubt. It was then that the FA, in the shape of Ted Croker and Bert Millichip, negotiated an astonishing twenty-year contract, executed in 1982, which once again delivered Wembley from the hands of the receiver. The terms of the contract seem quite unbelievable today. It was agreed at the outset that payment by the FA for its use of the stadium would include a contribution towards the costs of improvement works. In addition, Wembley would retain a proportion of the admission receipts and television fees. This was set at 32 per cent for FA Cup finals and Charity Shield matches, 25 per cent for other games. In addition, Wembley kept all income from ground advertising, programme sales, car-parking and catering, effectively preventing a shared sponsorship programme being put together for the FA Cup. The FA also agreed to stage all Cup finals and replays, plus all England internationals and the Vase and Trophy finals, at Wembley until 2002. The one-sidedness of the agreement hardly needs emphasising but the laxity of the FA is shown by the one comparable arrangement in European football, between the French Federation and the Parc des Princes in Paris. There, the stadium takes less than 20 per cent of receipts from all sources.

In defence of the FA, it can only be said that at the time, the revenue from Wembley, even when the Wembley share was taken into account, was greater than it would have been if games were played at any other ground. However, Wembley needed the FA as much as the FA needed Wembley, and the financial position of Wembley at the time meant that the FA was negotiating from a position of strength. Quite why it so undersold itself remains a mystery.

The contract placed no restrictions on the ability of Wembley to assign its rights to another party and the company that owned the stadium duly changed hands twice, ending up in 1986 under the control of a consortium headed by Brian Wolfson of the Anglo-Nordic Engineering Group, a former head of Granada. By the time the new regime was installed, Wembley, largely thanks to the FA, which had provided funds for improvements and guaranteed the stadium's income for the next twenty years, had begun to make a profit. Wolfson was determined to extend utilisation of the site as a whole. The Wembley complex now includes a conference centre and hotel, a leisure centre, exhibition halls and the Arena, in addition to the stadium itself, which is now all-seat with a capacity of 80,000, the result of another refurbishment programme, this time costing £50 million. Moreover, usage of the stadium has expanded and it now puts on many more football matches than in the past (fifteen in 1990–91), as well as pop concerts, American Football and Rugby Union.

In 1990, the Wembley company turned in a profit of £13.2 million. Since the FA's income comes from football fans, it is the fans who have forked out in order that Wolfson's company could make large profits. It was good business for Wolfson, but a betrayal of loyal fans on the part of the FA who have the last say on admission charges for their matches. When England played San Marino in 1993, ticket prices were as high as £40 for a decent seat. There was little alternative to high prices, however, as Wolfson's ambitious acquisition policy, including greyhound tracks, catering and hospitality companies, bingo halls, nightclubs, ticketing systems and shopfitters, began to founder on the rocks of the recession. The profits of 1990 turned into a loss of £8.3 million in 1991, forcing Wembley plc to concentrate on its core business, the stadium.

Despite all the money spent on improvements, Wembley has continued to attract criticism. The Football Licensing Authority claimed that many seats, which were planted upon the existing terracing, were ill-conceived and gave customers an appalling view. The authority's chief executive, John de Quidt, was scathing. 'Anybody who puts seats on old terracing like this is liable to have problems,' he declared. 'Our message is, if you are going to do the job, do it properly.' Equally condemnatory was Simon Inglis, who said: 'At Wembley, the rake [the angle of elevation of the rows of seats or terracing] is terrible. It is well below the minimum standards set by geometric calculation to determine viewing. But it is not a question of putting a bit of concrete down to realign the rake. There is no solution except at vast expenditure to take out the greyhound track, lower the pitch and rebuild the whole of the lower tier. But this would affect sightlines on the top tier and TV angles and mean remodelling the stadium.' Graham Kelly, when he was planning an application to host the 1998 World Cup, also expressed his reservations about the famous old venue. 'I doubt,' said Kelly, 'if it will ever be a comfortable 80,000 all-seater stadium. It just wasn't purpose-built.' Kelly, though, might have had other motives for his statement, since he was at the time of his comment in 1991 pushing his plan for national stadia as part of his Blueprint.

Wolfson, as would be expected, put up a spirited defence of his enterprise. Pointing to the £8 million Wembley was spending to refurbish the Wembley Park tube station, he claimed: 'When the customer arrives at the station, he will feel he is already in the complex. There will be no traffic, touts or pirate merchandising. We can control it as a civilised aesthetic environment. Those who have looked behind the scenes appreciate what we have done in taking a place they called a white elephant into the twenty-first century.' None of this cuts any ice with Simon Inglis, who laments the lost opportunity to create a world-class stadium. 'They should have done to it what they did to Barcelona [the Estadio Olimpico Montjuic],' he said. 'Gutted it. The outside walls, the exterior and the twin towers are the only things worth preserving, and [they should have] rebuilt it as a modern, new stadium with cantilevered roofing all round, proper sightlines and a running track.' Inglis forecasts increasing customer dissatisfaction at Wembley as conditions at other grounds rapidly improve. 'People went to it, it was Wembley, a day out and all that. Now supporters are going to go from their new stands at their own grounds to Wembley, where they will be paying much more, and they are going to get even angrier than they are now.' It is possible, according to Inglis, 'that Wembley will be the least comfortable [of England's 1996 European Championship venues], but it won't stop people wanting to go there because it is very much an event-orientated place. It's a great place to be, and even as much as I hate it, during the big games I think, wow, Wembley.' Despite this, the bottom line for Inglis is that 'compared to virtually every other major stadium in the world it's a dog's dinner'. He doesn't blame Wembley plc, though. Inglis lays the blame squarely on the government and the FA.

The result of the Wembley contract can be seen in the share of receipts for any match held there. From the 1991 Cup final between Nottingham Forest and Tottenham, the FA earned £2 million. Wembley, with revenues from advertising, programmes, catering and car-parking, in addition to its 32 per cent share of gate and television receipts, earned more.

Perhaps even worse, Wembley has used the FA contract to impose similar conditions on other users of the stadium. The English Schools Football Association, for instance, has to operate under the same financial constraints for schoolboy internationals, which deprives schools football of much-needed revenue. Wembley imposes the same stringent conditions precisely because it gets away with it with its biggest customer.

By 1991 it was clear, even to the FA, that something was seriously amiss in the relationship with Wembley. With talk of a new national stadium in the Blueprint, some within the FA believed they could renegotiate the terms of the contract with Wolfson as there was a clause which permitted renegotiation if either party could demonstrate a material financial disadvantage. The FA only had to show that Wembley made more than they, the FA, did out of the Cup final, and they surely could demand a review, particularly if they raised the example of the Parc des Princes and the capital sums they had provided for the improvements. Moreover, in the case of the parties failing to agree acceptable financial terms, then the agreement automatically terminates four years later. If Graham Kelly knew by 1991, a full two years into his job, that the Wembley contract was hindering the FA's ability to earn a reasonable share of income, he could have given notice of renegotiation. If agreement were not reached, the FA could be completely out of it by 1995, with a full four years to organise a replacement for Wembley, if one were deemed necessary (neither Italy, Germany nor Spain have national stadia). But apart from Charles Hughes, there was not much stomach for a fight within the FA and when plans for a new stadium were consigned to oblivion, the moment had passed. So today, the FA is stuck with its Wembley contract for another eight years unless the arrival of Trevor Phillips as the FA's first commercial director encourages a rethink. For its part, the stadium is once again in need of improvements. It has twenty-five pillars in an era of cantilevered roofs, its toilet and catering facilities are not up to scratch and it charges exhorbitant prices for tickets (apparently with no reductions for obstructed views), food and the car-park. Wembley really only has its name and the charisma of seventy years, which still exert an emotional pull on footballers and supporters alike. And it is surely the case that in a stadium as old as Wembley, improvements will constantly have to be made for the forseeable future.

If Croker and Millichip were misguided in their actions towards Wembley, the fact that the new regime at Lancaster Gate, which understands the commercial consequences only too well, has failed to exercise its rights to renegotiate is perhaps an even worse example of maladministration. The FA has always pulled a veil of secrecy over the contracts it enters into. Nothing of substance is ever made public. Sometimes, something might be leaked, and the veil is partially lifted, but rarely is the whole story as much as glimpsed. Ted Croker once said he believed the public had no right to know how much the FA received from television. It is a culture of secrecy that permeates so much of English life and its result is that it cloaks the incompetent and the corrupt and works against the very thing it purports to serve, in this case the promotion and success of the game of football at all levels.

Some might take the view that the FA's monumental ineptitude in its dealings with Wembley ought to disbar the organisation from being in control of the finances of football. Instead, the body has rushed headlong into further questionable deals, which include Wembley being made the centrepiece of the 1996 European Championships, which Glen Kirton will manage. While all this was going on, the FA could hardly sit in judgement on the financial affairs of others in the game. In fact, the money at stake was creating another huge mountain of cash which was attracting the predators.

10

All in the Game

How managers, players, clubs, and even the authorities now rely on those scorned creatures, agents

> *'Screen stars work with people who have slept with him or her, in television it's who knows him or her, in football there are always stories of money and drugs.'*

> Bernard Tapie, president, Olympique de Marseille FC.

> *'Lots of times managers have to be cheats and conmen. We are the biggest hypocrites. We cheat. The only way to survive is by cheating.'*

> Tommy Docherty, ex-player and Scottish international; manager of more clubs than Eric Morley, talking loosely in 1979.

Inside football, people like to talk about 'our profession', as if there were some universally accepted academic qualifications, code of conduct and standards of behaviour. Of course, there are rules and regulations but they are flouted more than they are observed, particularly in the matter of players' contracts and transfers between clubs. The causes of the infringements are generally accepted to be those reviled interlopers who now perform complex dramas on a once straightforward stage, agents.

Until the early 1960s, players were constrained by the maximum wage (£20 per week during the playing season, £17 per week in summer), and the retain-and-transfer system, which left them little more than chattels. Huge crowds flocked to games in the post-war period but little of the cash generated made its way into players' pockets. This meant that players, even at the biggest clubs, lived in the same areas and in much the same way as the fans of the clubs they played for. It also meant that players had no bargaining position when it came to securing a future for themselves and their families. Such a system could not survive indefinitely and as the country basked in the 'you've never had it so good' era of the late 1950s, a movement began to end the maximum wage, which succeeded in 1961 after a campaign led by Jimmy Hill and Cliff Lloyd, then respectively the chairman and secretary of the players' union, the PFA. Immediately, Tommy Trinder, a famous comedian of the time and chairman of Fulham (there are those who say you have to be the one to be the other), announced that to keep his star player, Johnny Haynes, he was prepared to pay the then unheard of wage of £100 per week.

However, despite the abolition of the maximum wage, footballers were still the property of their clubs, who could keep them against their will even when out of contract. This system was challenged by an England international, George Eastham, who took Newcastle United to the High Court, and in 1963, won his case. The inevitable consequence was complete freedom of contract, which was finally achieved in the 1980s. By then the pendulum had swung the other way and it was players, at least those for whom there was a demand, who became the aristocratic élite of the football world. At the same time there were also dramatic changes in boardrooms. Club chairmen, until quite recently, were invariably local businessmen made good who attained the same status as that enjoyed by the local mayor. When, in the early 1980s, the football authorities allowed directors to be paid by their clubs, they opened the door to a new breed of director. Although many chairmen remain genuine fans, boardrooms up and down the country became inhabited with what could be termed Thatcherite entrepreneurs anxious to make yet more money.

These developments meant that football would never be the same again. The new generation of stars turned the game into a branch of showbusiness. Along with the rich rewards came increased media attention, hangers-on and agents. Top footballers no longer lived in club houses, nor did they drink any more in the same pubs as the supporters. The First Division footballer was soon to become upwardly mobile, aspiring to a large house on the leafy fringe of the city and an expensive car and lifestyle to match. All this needed ever-increasing amounts of money and since most professional athletes spend so much of their time and effort becoming great performers, their competence in getting themselves the best possible financial deal did not match their ability on the pitch. It wasn't long before agents were whispering to them of how they were being ripped off and how they could, and should, be making their fortunes.

FA and League rules are quite specific when it comes to agents. A player is allowed to be represented by a third party in negotiations but an agent cannot hold a player's registration. That can only be held by a club. For their part, clubs are barred from employing agents to act on their behalf, either in contract or transfer negotiations. When agents first appeared, they were generally shunned by clubs and hated by managers. Many a manager has gone into print to denounce agents, usually claiming that a hitherto contented player has been incited by an agent to seek a transfer. There were also stories of players who trusted agents with all their earnings and lived to regret it. With terrible public relations like this it is not surprising that agents gained an image somewhere between that of a used-car salesman and a corrupt politician. On the other hand, players who were represented by a good agent had never been so well off. Why should a footballer also be expected to be a skilled negotiator on his own behalf? Some are, of course, but most are not, and managers themselves have not always been known for their scrupulous behaviour when it comes to negotiating with players. Thus the agent who can get the maximum amount possible for his client is worth every penny of his commission and then some.

As agents made inroads into the traditional relationship between managers and players, clubs began to realise that what was sauce for the goose was sauce for the gander. By the 1980s clubs were using agents themselves, either to find new players needed to fill problem positions or to renegotiate contracts with a player they desired to keep. This practice is, of course, against the rules, but it has become widespread in recent years. Everybody knows it goes on but nobody does anything about it unless a story appears somewhere in the media. The FA, for instance, which should impartially investigate such matters, has itself developed relationships with agents, who were allowed into the FA to organise the money-making activities of international teams. Jon Smith, for example, of the First Artists agency, is responsible for the England players' pool, in addition to handling the affairs of individual players within the pool. First Artists is retained by the FA on a consultancy basis for an annual fee of £150,000. Prior to this arrangement the agency worked on commission, with no money going to the FA. In order to put together a more comprehensive sponsorship package for the England team, the FA bought out First Artists' rights for £2 million in addition to the yearly fee. Thus there is now the ironic situation where governing bodies are creating opportunities for agents to prosper.

The most successful of the modern agents is Dennis Roach, whose company, PRO, has been involved in a veritable host of transfers worth many millions of pounds. Roach is not universally liked among his fellow agents, probably because of his capacity to smell a potential deal at forty paces. Roach was a semi-pro player for Hendon, Barnet and Bedford Town, at the same time as building himself up in the furniture import and export business. While on a family holiday in Spain, his young son made friends with another child, who turned out to be the daughter of Johan Cruyff. Roach and Cruyff became friends and it wasn't long before Roach was representing Cruyff's UK interests. From such beginnings, Roach became the most powerful of all in his line of work. He is probably the one agent who can walk into the boardroom of any big European club, a position he has achieved by a continuing run of successful deals. These include Mark Hateley to Milan, Glenn Hoddle to Monaco, Mark Hughes to Barcelona, Trevor Steven to Marseille, Des Walker to Sampdoria and John Toshack as coach to Real Madrid.

Certain clubs tend to favour particular agents and over the years Roach developed an ongoing relationship with Brian Clough, the manager of Nottingham Forest – so much so that he was made welcome in Forest's inner sanctum. Clough invited Roach into the dressing room at Highbury in 1990 when Forest were the visitors. It was fifteen minutes before kick-off and Clough wanted Roach to join him for a glass of scotch. Clough then shouted across the room to Franz Carr,

'I'm going to get Roachy to sell you, do you fancy a French club?' 'Whatever you say, boss,' was Carr's intimidated reply. Subsequently, Clough wrote in the Forest programme that he had good news and bad news. The good news was that Franz Carr had come back from his loan period at Sheffield Wednesday. The bad news was that he still couldn't cross a ball. Clough went on to ask whether the player's agent, whom he dubbed 'the cockroach', might fix him up with a transfer.

The low price of Des Walker's move to Sampdoria, £1.5 million, raised a few eyebrows. With the limits in Italy of three foreigners and with Milan paying £8 million for Papin (who is not guaranteed a place), the premium placed on first-team choices such as Walker is generally much higher than the fee paid by Sampdoria, even though, as a defender, Walker is a rarity as far as foreign imports go. Roach justifies the low fee by pointing out that the player could have moved abroad three years previously but didn't, so Clough 'got those three extra years out of him'. After the 1990 World Cup, Juventus offered £5 million for the England defender but their approach was rejected by Forest. Roach then made a deal with Forest along the lines of one he had made previously with Manchester United for Mark Hughes. A fixed time limit was added to Walker's contract. When the time was up it was Roach, not Forest, who would be making the deal. The transfer fee was low by Italian standards so Walker's signing-on fee and wages were correspondingly high. Despite rumours of undisclosed payments, Roach claimed there was nothing improper about the arrangement. It was, he said 'the cleanest deal in sixty years', and he insisted that he was paid nothing by Forest and took a commission only from the player's share.

Because of Roach's standing in Europe, it behoves even a national team manager to change his principles. During his time as manager of Watford, the England boss, Graham Taylor, refused to have any dealings with agents. In order to effect the transfer of Maurice Johnston to Celtic, a lawyer, Mel Goldberg, was called in because Taylor barred Johnston's agent at the time, Frank Boyd, from the club. The same fate might have befallen Goldberg but for the intervention of a Watford director, the former Arsenal manager Bertie Mee, who vouched for Goldberg's credentials. During Walker's season in

Italy, Taylor had no compunction about using Dennis Roach as a conduit to Sampdoria, bombarding him with contacts and asking Roach to represent him in discussions with the Italians, particularly to facilitate the smooth release of Walker for England international duty.

One morning in August 1989, the day, in fact, when Gary Lineker's transfer to Tottenham from Barcelona was announced at a press conference, the Tottenham chairman, Irving Scholar, received a telephone call from a Yugoslav agent, Lubjo Barin. According to Barin, Marseille wanted to buy Chris Waddle and were prepared to offer £2.5 million. Initially, Scholar dismissed the offer (one of the reasons Lineker had agreed to move to White Hart Lane was the prospect of playing with Waddle and Gascoigne), but by the end of the conversation Barin had increased it to £3 million. Although he remained non-committal, Scholar agreed to meet Marseille's president, Bernard Tapie, the next day in London.

At the meeting, which was also attended by Terry Venables, Tapie raised his offer to £4 million. This was far in excess of the valuation Tottenham had put on the player. Nevertheless, Scholar was reluctant to sell because he felt that the partnership of Gazza, Lineker and Waddle would give Tottenham an attacking force capable of reviving the club's fortunes and perhaps emulating the double team of 1961. Scholar did, however, feel that he owed it to Waddle to allow the player to consider what was, as he put it, 'a once-in-a-lifetime opportunity'.

Dennis Roach is particularly close to Glenn Hoddle, his number one client. Hoddle and Waddle are good friends (they even made a hit record together) and Hoddle had persuaded Waddle to let Roach negotiate his contract with Tottenham. Scholar felt that if Roach got to hear about Marseille's interest he would influence Waddle to go 'in about five seconds'. To counter that possibility, Scholar agreed with Mel Stein, Waddle's lawyer, that Waddle should be given sufficient time to think the offer over.

The personal terms offered to Waddle were higher than he could have imagined at that stage of his career so it should not have come as a shock to any of those involved that he said he wanted to go (although Scholar professed surprise).

The deal was put in hand and Stein represented the player's interest. When Dennis Roach found out about it from Bernard Tapie he went bananas. He felt Scholar and Stein had ganged up on him and in the words of one of Roach's colleagues, who overheard him on the the phone to Scholar, Roach gave the Tottenham chairman 'a terrible rucking'. Roach ended by accusing Scholar of being 'just like the rest of them', that is, a vainglorious chairman seeking a selfish, short-term return. This was too much for Scholar to take and was the source of a rift between the two which was only mended some time later when Roach apologised and Scholar realised that they both needed each other. In fact, although Stein maintains he did the deal – and he certainly handled the player's terms – it was Roach who was involved on a club-to-club basis. 'I sat on the phone in Paris with Tapie,' Roach recalled, 'Irving wanted £5 million, Tapie wanted to pay four and they settled at four and a half.' Tottenham subsequently appointed Roach to represent them in the Gascoigne transfer.

There was no such rapprochement between Roach and Mel Stein, and as a result of the affair they became adversaries. Although both Stein (as Gazza's lawyer) and Roach (as Tottenham's representative) were involved in the Gascoigne transfer to Lazio, Stein insists that he 'won't be in the same room as him [Roach]'.

Bernard Tapie's massive transfer payment for Chris Waddle was later to come under the scrutiny of the Fraud Squad. However, the British police only became involved at the request of the French judiciary which was probing into the affairs of a number of French clubs. In France, there is a much more rigorous examination of financial accounts than is the case in England. At the end of the 1992–93 season, for instance, Toulon, who were relegated from the First Division, were forced by the French Federation to drop into the Third Division, which is regional, because they were all but bankrupt. In the Waddle case, questions were asked about financial irregularities in the Marseille accounts. There have been a number of financial scandals over the years in France but, unlike in England, they tend to be thoroughly investigated, not just by the football authorities but often by the police or other civil authorities.

Until 1990, French football clubs had to operate under a

law of 1901 which took no account of sport as a business. Therefore, to be successful, clubs had to circumnavigate the law in order to get star players. Slush funds were established, dubious loans organised and false documentation was commonplace. The St Etienne club, for instance, was riddled with such practices in the great years of the late 1970s. Players, including Michel Platini, were paid non-accountable sums from the *caisse noir* (black box). When this was revealed, players were fined and the president, Roger Rocher, was sent to prison.

A further series of scandals hit French football in 1990. The manager of Toulon, Roland Courbis, was arrested after it was discovered that money had been siphoned off from transfers into a Monaco bank account. The cash was used by Courbis to top up players' wages and even settle some of his own gambling debts. Then Claude Bez, the president of Bordeaux (at the time the leading French club) and one of the most influential figures in French football – he had been instrumental in getting Michel Platini the national team manager's job in 1988 – was arrested for a fraud relating to favoured construction contracts at the club. On investigation it transpired that Bez had made prostitutes available to referees in European matches and Bordeaux were £25 million in the red. Disgraced and insolvent, the club was immediately relegated to Division 2. Less than two years later, Courbis was back – as manager of Bordeaux, who have regained their First Division place and are pushing to regain their old status.

There is a widespread view in France that everyone in politics and business is on the take so no long-term stigma attaches to those involved. The scope of the investigation was such that even Bernard Tapie was tainted. Three Marseille players who had been at Toulon (one of whom, Bernard Pardo, subsequently spent some time in jail on a drugs charge) were hauled from a training session by the police. It turned out that Tapie had made a loan to Toulon along the same lines as the Robert Maxwell loan to Tottenham. (In 1990, while chairman of Derby County, Robert Maxwell secretly loaned Tottenham Hotspur £1.1 million so that his friend, Irving Scholar, Tottenham's chairman, could pay the final instalment on Gary Lineker's transfer from Barcelona.)

But accompanying the Tapie loan to Toulon were fictitious invoices and non-returnable loans to players. One such loan, made to Jean-Pierre Papin, was explained away by Tapie, who said, in all seriousness, 'He didn't have any money to pay his taxes after buying a Ferrari.'

It is important to note that while the offences in France would not have been necessary in England, the transgressions were investigated by the authorities and punishments meted out to those found guilty, no matter what their position. The French Federation, moreover, did not have to be cajoled into action by the media but took the responsibility on themselves. The system was changed in 1991 on the recommendation of a government enquiry into the commercialisation of the game. Henceforth, each club could opt for one of three systems: a private company controlled by an individual entrepreneur or commercial operation; a semi-public company subsidised in part by the local authority; or an amended version of a '1901' company with stringent controls on directors' powers and obligations. This was a recognition that someone like Tapie, for all his faults, had, through football, provided a community service to the Marseilles public, a fact they recognised when Tapie retained his deputy's seat in the 1993 parliamentary elections, against the national trend. The matter does not rest there, however. It has emerged that Marseille had been running up an enormous deficit which is now being scrutinised. The French police's interest in the Chris Waddle transfer also brought to light that in addition to Waddle's FF150,000 (£17,000) monthly salary, he received part of almost FF17 million (£2 million) paid to two British companies, Happy Promotion and Consensus Ltd. This was a way of avoiding French taxes. This type of deal – *contracts d'image* – has been common in France. A colleague of Waddle's, the French international Manuel Amoros, received FF2.5 million (£300,000), which was paid into the account of an Irish company upon his arrival from Monaco. Waddle's return to England should have been accompanied by a procedural revision of his affairs as he was no longer an expatriate. Perhaps it was this that concerned the French police, or perhaps they recalled the words of the Marseille general manager, Jean-Pierre Bernes, who, when under examination by a local magistrate in 1990, revealed that 'this player [Waddle] collected, as did other players, hidden sums as a result of the production of false invoices.'

It may well be that the transfer of Des Walker was above board and there was certainly no suggestion of any impropriety in the Waddle deal before the Marseille investigation began to trawl through all the records. In other transactions, it is more difficult to discern exactly for whom the agent is working. Dennis Roach, for instance, has good relations with a number of clubs, among them Glasgow Rangers and Marseille. He sold Kingston Basketball Club to Rangers and provided them with a number of star players, Mark Hateley and Trevor Steven among them. When Marseille sold the midfielder Bruno Germain to Paris SG, Roach convinced Bernard Tapie to buy Trevor Steven from Rangers for £5 million as a replacement. Tapie, according to Roach, 'makes snap decisions and it's important that when he makes those snap decisions you are on the spot. The reason I get the deals from him is that I am prepared to get up off my backside and go to France to see him [and talk to him] in the language he understands. He likes to negotiate in French.'

Roach had previously been the link man in Steven's transfer from Everton to Rangers in 1989 for £1 million. Following Marseille's failure to beat Benfica in the semi-final of the European Cup in 1990 – they were knocked out by 'the hand of Vata' when the Benfica substitute punched the winning goal, à la Maradona against England in the 1986 World Cup – they reached the final in 1991, only to produce a dreadful performance against Red Star Belgrade. The loss on penalties was even more galling considering the fine display they had conjured in the quarter-final to put out Milan. Matters got worse in 1992 when Marseille failed to reach the last eight of the European Cup after being knocked out by Sparta Prague. This was too much to bear for Tapie, who broke up the team in disappointment. At Tapie's instigation, Roach now sold Trevor Steven once again – back to Glasgow Rangers, this time for £2 million. In fact the fee was somewhat higher (or the £5 million Marseille had agreed to pay was lowered), since the French club never paid the last instalment of the transfer fee to Rangers. So Steven had shuttled between three clubs for a total of over £8 million, and each time Roach collected his not inconsiderable percentage.

When Steven left Marseille, he was only eighteen months into a lucrative contract and had expressed no desire to leave. The move could only have taken place if Tapie had both initiated and sanctioned it. Roach got Rangers the same player after an eighteen-month hiatus plus £3 million. It could be said that on each occasion Roach was acting for the player but it cannot be denied that there were at least spin-off benefits for the clubs concerned. In fact, it was jolly good business for all parties (although there were one or two bouncing cheques along the way), and Roach continues to have dealings with both clubs.

An agent who has been around for many years, John Mac, was asked by a BBC radio programme, *File on Four*, in 1990 whether his operations were within football's rules. 'That's a nice question, it's a difficult answer,' Mac replied. 'It's almost impossible in this country for an agent to operate within the Football League rules we have at the moment . . . The answer is no, we're probably not, no.' Mac went on to say that he often worked on behalf of chairmen and managers, and thus clubs, as well as players. Besides being against the rules, this presents an obvious possibility for a conflict of interests. If the agent represents more than one party in a deal, just whose interests are paramount? For instance, take the situation where a player's contract is coming to an end. The club wants to keep him or alternatively sell him for the highest price they can get. If the player doesn't sign a new contract before the old one expires, he has the right under freedom of contract to go and sign up with any club he likes, with the transfer fee likely to be set by a tribunal. In this scenario it may well be that the club hires an agent to convince the player that it is in his interest to re-sign. Of course, it may not be in the player's interest to re-sign at all. This was why the Football League banned agents from setting up transfer deals or renegotiating existing contracts.

In 1986, John Mac was hired by Norwich City to renegotiate the contract of Steve Bruce. After first denying any wrongdoing, Mac was shown an invoice from his company to Norwich City which read: 'To professional charges relative to negotiations on your behalf with Steven Bruce resulting in him signing a further contract with you for three years.' When it was put to him that this was renegotiating a contract on behalf of a club, Mac agreed, but still denied that he had worked for Norwich City. 'As far as I was concerned . . . I was able to put [the] parties together and they came to a deal.'

The most remarkable aspect of the Steve Bruce affair was a so-called investigation by the Football League. No one from the League spoke to Mac and they seemed to have been reassured by the blandishments of Robert Chase, the Norwich chairman. Chase, at the time, was a member of the Football League's Management Committee. Chase claimed he knew of 'no regulation which prohibits the use of an agent in assisting with negotiating the terms of a new contract of a player when the transfer of his registration is not involved'. However, Football League regulations clearly state that 'all . . . contracts of service shall be arranged directly between the clubs concerned and the player and not through or by an agent.' Chase's attention was drawn to this regulation in a memo of October 20 1987 from the then club secretary, Nigel Pleasance. Chase claimed that all transactions at Norwich were conducted between club and player. One month before this statement, the minutes of a Norwich board meeting show Chase saying that payments totalling £275,000 had been paid to Mac's company under a contract called a 'promotional agreement'. Despite a number of questions being asked, not least by local councillors, the Football League took no action. The fact that Mac had a contractual relationship with both parties was underlined in 1992, when Steve Bruce, then playing for Manchester United, sued Mac for dereliction of duty in regard to his pension arrangements.

The football authorities in England have shown themselves to be more than a little lax in enforcing their rules in this area. This may be because, as John Mac believes, the rules are unenforcible. In fact the only time anything seems to happen is when one of these cases is exposed by the media. Then a great fuss is made, but little, if anything is done. There is certainly a discrepancy in attitude between the wholesale breaking of rules in clubs' dealings with agents and other rule-breaking which produces safer targets for the authorities. For making illegal payments to players, Swindon were denied promotion to the First Division in 1991 and, if the Football League had had its way, the club would have been relegated to Division 3 (the Football League's punishment was reduced on appeal by the FA). The complacency of the authorities over the role of agents, however, ensured that, sooner or later, the press would have a field day. Thus the whole issue came to a head again in 1993, when allegations appeared concerning the transfers of three Australian players to English clubs.

This time the charges surfaced in the *Daily Mail*, which claimed that an agent, Graham Smith, had received payments of up to £300,000 from two clubs, Aston Villa and Notts County, for arranging the transfers of Mark Bosnich, Bob Catlin and Shaun Murphy through his company, First Wave Sport Management, which he runs in conjunction with the captain of the Arsenal double team of 1971, Frank McLintock. If the *Mail*'s article is correct, there was a clear infringement of FIFA article 17 which states: 'The use of agents or other intermediaries in the transfer of players is prohibited.' A FIFA representative explained that agents could advise clubs or players but not be directly involved in a transfer.

Bob Catlin claimed he knew nothing of the £72,500 First Wave had received from Notts County for his 'transfer'. 'I would never have signed the contract with County if I had known the size of the fee,' he said. 'I asked to see the chairman as I had read the articles in which it was claimed I had cost £72,500. I asked the chairman if this was right. He got out the files and confirmed this was the case.' The County chairman, Derek Pavis, admitted publicly what he had told Catlin. 'I can state,' he said, 'we thought the money was paid as a transfer fee.' In addition to payments for the transfers, First Wave were also entitled to extra sums linked to the number of games played and a percentage of any future transfer fee. Graham Smith arranged for a copy of the letter of agreement with Aston Villa chairman Doug Ellis, on the matter of Mark Bosnich, to be given to Pavis, who merely copied the details on to Notts County notepaper (Pavis subsequently showed the Ellis letter to the *Daily Mail*, escalating the affair). Pavis could not have appreciated what he signed as the letter makes it clear that Smith was not technically breaking FIFA rules because he was employed as a consultant to the club. However, the fact that the consultancy fee was directly related to appearances and future transfers highlights another side of the agreement.

The most successful of the trio of players, Villa goalkeeper

Mark Bosnich, is unconcerned over the arrangements made between Smith and his club. He regards Smith as a friend and adviser – as a former goalkeeper himself with West Bromwich Albion and Colchester, Smith is well positioned to help Bosnich both on and off the field – and he was eternally grateful to be given the opportunity to join a Premier League club. Moreover, he was delighted with the contract that Villa offered him. Villa must have been equally pleased, as Bosnich succeeded in establishing himself as the first-choice keeper, replacing the long-serving Nigel Spink for the Championship run-in in 1993.

Graham Smith denied that he had done anything wrong, stating that 'Notts County, the chief executive at Notts County, the manager at Notts County and all the officials at Aston Villa knew these boys were free agents and they [the clubs] were paying me for my services and not a transfer fee.' Bosnich, he said, had bought himself out of his contract, Catlin had done the same before Smith had even heard of him, while Murphy's contract allowed him to move for AUS$3,000 (£1,400). The *Daily Mail* claimed documents in its possession showed that First Wave had reimbursed the buy-out fees paid by Bosnich and Catlin and had encouraged them to become free agents. Murphy's club had tried to get the amount up to AUS$40,000 (£18,000) but eventually settled for AUS$10,000 (£4,500). Nobody else, according to Smith, was in the market for the players and it was his involvement alone which secured their careers in England. Moreover, he insisted that 'not a penny' was taken by him or his company from the players' shares of the deals. Smith also claimed that 'the payments that were made to me had no bearing whatsoever on the monies those boys received. They all received excellent contracts and probably Catlin and Murphy were paid too much because they've been flops'. Smith went on to say that the Australian clubs concerned had not been exploited. He backed this up with the claim that Murphy's old club, Perth Italia, have asked him to find clubs for two more of their players, both Australian youth internationals.

The FIFA rule governing agents' involvement in transfers seems clear enough, but the apparent loophole that allows advisers seems to be merely a way of avoiding bringing anyone to book for transgressing article 17. Smith certainly denies making a fortune, claiming that his Australian contact took 48 per cent of the money he received for Bosnich. Even if there was nothing in the deals which harmed the players, the fact remains that an agent involved directly in a transfer is against the rules. FIFA's spokesman in the matter, Guido Tognoni, said that the rules needed clarifying. 'Not every agent is a bad guy,' he opined, 'but we have to weed out the ones who are. Twenty years ago, each country had one agent. Now they are all over the place. We have to control the market.' Tognoni was confident that a new set of rules would soon be passed by FIFA which would rectify the matter by granting to national associations the power to license agents. 'We have to live with the fact that agents exist,' concluded Tognoni. 'The basic principle of our recommendations is that they must hold a licence. They must respect the statutes of the national association and work in the correct way. It's up to national federations to take away licences if the agents do not act correctly.' Surprisingly, Dennis Roach agrees. 'I'm totally committed to football and always have been,' he said, pointing out that his involvement with tours and tournaments has 'brought a lot of money into the game'. Contrary to the perceived stigma attached to agents, Roach is proud of the fact that he is licensed as such by FIFA and feels it is the agents who have notgrown up with football who do the game a disservice.

Meanwhile, the FA summoned both Notts County and Aston Villa for a breach of transfer regulations but then promptly adjourned the case (perhaps because of their difficulty in arriving at an objective judgement when one of their own council members – Doug Ellis, the Villa chairman – was involved). Graham Smith believes the exposure of his case is linked to what he sees as the PFA's hypocritical attitude regarding pension and investment schemes. The PFA, claims Smith, tries to tempt players into joining its own schemes while decrying those of agents. Smith's view is supported by at least one Premier League chairman who cites instances in which the PFA actually works, to all intents and purposes, as an agent, particularly in negotiating players' contracts. In addition, there is a long-running feud between the PFA and First Wave over the import of foreign players, which Smith thinks is behind the press exposé. The PFA reluctantly accepts that the Treaty of Rome gives freedom of movement for all EC citizens, including footballers. UEFA does not agree. Still there is no uniform classification system. In the UK, although there is a limit of three foreigners (which was originally proposed by Irving Scholar because 'we should be there or thereabouts with Europe'), Irish, Welsh, Scots and English are all treated as nationals of the UK and cannot be restricted. UEFA, however, regards them as foreigners in each other's countries. Elsewhere, national associations have their own rules. Only three foreigners are allowed in Italy while France imposes a maximum of two non-EC players per club.

Although the UEFA restriction is being investigated by the European Commission in Brussels, the real problem for the PFA is the influx of relatively cheap imports from Scandinavia and Eastern Europe. According to the PFA chairman, Gordon Taylor, 'millions of pounds are going out of the English game, money which will not return'. The PFA believes that its own members' jobs are at risk if the process continues, particularly in the lower divisions. There is also the matter of the 5 per cent levy paid to the PFA on all transfers within the UK, which is not paid on international transfers. This has fuelled the campaign against agents who, according to Taylor, are little better than slave traders. 'If agents are trailing the world telling players to buy out their contracts and then the agent keeps the registration and trails it around the world, you're almost back to trading in people . . . to the highest bidder.' As a result of Taylor's agitation the Home Office has been persuaded to tighten requirements for non-EC footballers, so that in future only established internationals will receive a work permit, which will be reviewed annually. Taylor thinks this will force clubs to develop their own players and call a halt to the agents' manoeuvrings. Judging by the way agents and clubs get around existing rules, it may be a forlorn hope. Indeed, an examination of how clubs acquire young players opens up another can of worms. Arsenal, who can justifiably persuade youngsters to join them on the basis of their track record in giving opportunities to the products of their youth policy (eight of Arsenal's 1991 Championship-winning squad were home-grown), believe they have lost out on potential stars like Nicky Barmby because they won't play the game of paying gratuitous 'attention' to the families of sought-after youngsters.

As the commercialisation of football gathered pace in the 1980s, the number of agents increased, which often led to some unseemly squabbles between them as they vied for a slice of a finite market. This has been intensified by the introduction of a new type of operator, one who isn't strictly an agent at all. Many players, for instance, now use the services of a solicitor or accountant. A solicitor might carry out exactly the same function as an agent but is he really an agent? And how can a player be denied legal advice at any stage in his negotiations with a club? Mel Stein, Paul Gascoigne's adviser, falls into this category.

Stein became a Newcastle United fan after seeing them beat Arsenal in the 1951 Cup final. Stein's religious obligations do not allow him to go to football on Saturdays so he does not attend matches unless he is prepared to walk the ten-mile round trip to watch his local team, Barnet. He has always taken the opportunity to watch Newcastle in midweek, however. Through his association with Newcastle, he eventually, in 1981, became Chris Waddle's solicitor.

Along with his work for Waddle, Stein came to represent some of Newcastle's younger players, including Paul Gascoigne. 'Gascoigne is family,' Stein said. 'Someone I trust implicitly, someone who trusts me implicitly . . . I would do anything for him and he would do anything for me.' At the time of the original transfer discussions between Tottenham and Lazio, when Tottenham were in dire financial trouble, Dennis Roach had been appointed by the British club to see if he could sell any players to help alleviate the club's massive debt. Stein says, however, that the first approach concerning Gazza came from Lazio, rather than through a sales effort by Roach. 'Roach,' said an emphatic Stein, 'did not do the deal,' and Gascoigne, barring injury, 'will be in Italy for the next five years'. There is, though, a different version of events. According to Roach, 'I was appointed by Spurs to go into the market and examine the possibilities of selling Paul Gascoigne and Gary Lineker because they knew I had the contacts to go into Italy and find out. I came back with two offers, one from Lazio and the other from Milan. The one from Lazio was superior by a long way. We then contacted Lazio and we had a secret meeting in London with their president and secretary, Irving [Scholar] and myself, at an hotel in

London, which has never been mentioned or recorded, and that was the first time there was ever any interest shown in Gascoigne. From that it developed. Their first offer wasn't enough and negotiations started and I continued in those negotiations. There were probably five or six further meetings in London and Mr Stein was not involved until it became time to negotiate Gascoigne's terms.'

By 1993, Mel Stein was recognised as one of the country's foremost agents, although he doesn't see himself in that category. On his work for Alan Shearer, Stein remarked, 'There were other people making propositions to him but he didn't want to deal with agents in any circumstances.' Under Stein's regime, the relationship between himself and his partner, the accountant Len Lazarus, on the one hand and the player on the other is one of a solicitor and an accountant and their client. 'We don't take commissions,' he said. 'We're not in partnership with our clients, we just charge them [by an hourly rate]. Because we have no agreements, we stand or fall by what we do. I don't think that anybody who is on commission could possibly act in the client's best interests, because how can you advise your client to say no if you know you are going to lose your commission? It also affects the way you arrange the contract if you are on a commission that is only geared to signing-on fees. Then you're going to push for as much as a signing-on fee as you can, which is not always right for the player.'

Stein has a jaundiced view of agents and is quick to distance himself from their activities. 'The classic story,' he said, 'is a player being told "I will charge you nothing." It's a lie. All it means is that if there is £100,000 on the table they will tell the player there is £80,000 and "I'm not going to charge you anything." Then they will take the £20,000 directly from the club. Even worse, they will say there's £80,000 on the table and they'll charge their commission and they'll cream off at both ends. Football League regulations are absolutely clear on this point. They say they [the clubs] are not allowed to pay any commissions or payments to third parties on behalf of the player. The payments can only be made to the player. I heard a story last week . . . where the player was told that he was going to get a car and the club didn't put it in the contract. The player was then told that [the value of] the car was being given to him in a payment to his agent. The agent then said to the player, "Well I've got your money for the car but my commission is x and I'm going to take my commission out of this, but there is some change for you, so will you give me an invoice in relation to moving expenses?" The player innocently gave him the invoice and then gave him the money back. So the club had effectively laundered that money through his agent, and the agent has obviously nobbled the money for himself. Now whether or not the agent then in turn gave money back to the manager who contrived this deal (because this particular agent works very closely with this particular manager), who knows? It's well known that in the field of football many managers are on the take and only allow their players to deal with certain agents because they know that that agent will make a charge to the player or will receive a payment directly from the club and will then give it back to the manager. That is theft . . . because the manager is in a fiduciary position vis à vis the club.' Stein repeated the allegations to a Sunday newspaper but his case was somewhat weakened by his refusal to name names. The chairman of the Managers Association, Frank Clarke, then the managing director of Leyton Orient, was so incensed by the general slur on managers as a body that he took the criticism as personal slander and called upon Stein to put up or shut up. Stein, though, soon became embroiled in more serious troubles when he was indicted by a Federal Grand Jury in Louisiana on charges of mail fraud and money-laundering in connection with the Anglo-American Insurance company.

Certain clubs, according to Stein, will deal only with particular agents. Under the Venables regime at Tottenham, Stein was persona non grata, the 'accredited' agents being Frank McLintock and Eric Hall. So when Venables wanted to buy Teddy Sheringham from Nottingham Forest, he asked one of them, McLintock, to set up the deal. McLintock was the natural choice since he had worked with Sheringham while assistant manager at Millwall. McLintock had subsequently effected the transfer of Sheringham to Nottingham Forest.

Teddy Sheringham was transferred from Forest to Tottenham in August 1992. Some months later he had become the linchpin of a Spurs revival and finished the season as the

Premier League's top goalscorer. He was also called up to
play for England and received his first cap in a World Cup
qualifier against Poland. However, Frank McLintock and First
Wave had not been paid their commission. Eventually,
McLintock extracted a promise from Terry Venables and went
to the ground to collect his money. Expecting a banker's draft
or cheque, McLintock was surprised to be paid £58,500 in
cash. When he informed his partner, Graham Smith, an
invoice was quickly raised to cover the transaction. The
wording reflected work carried out by First Wave in other
areas of the club's operation, including overseas scouting. The
ruse was effected in order to avoid infringing the regulation
which stipulated that a club cannot pay an agent a
commission on a transfer fee. When he received the invoice,
Venables contacted McLintock and told him. 'You've topped
me up, Frank.' The reason for Venables' chagrin was that First
Wave added VAT to its invoice. In Venables' mind the
payment of £50,000 was an all-in figure, so McLintock was
obliged to return the VAT element (17.5 per cent) along with
a credit note to keep the books straight. The money was
returned, as it was paid, in cash, McLintock handing over
£8,500, which was put in the club safe by secretary Peter
Barnes and not banked.

Graham Smith denies that he or his partner took the cash
and gave it to Brian Clough, as was alleged in court during the
battle between Venables and Alan Sugar for control of
Tottenham. 'Neither myself nor Frank McLintock,' said
Smith, 'have seen Brian Clough since the day the deal was
agreed.' Perhaps part of the problem was that at the
last minute, the transfer fee was upped by £100,000 to £2.1
million so that Forest could discharge their final responsibilities on Sheringham's contract. 'Let Tottenham pay, he's their
player now,' was Brian Clough's opinion as communicated to
Spurs, much to Venables' annoyance since it caused him to
scramble around for even more money.

The fact remains that First Wave's payment was made in
cash. Without wishing to appear holier than thou, an insider
at Highbury was horrified at the situation. 'You'd have to wait
outside Ken Friar's [the managing director] office for three
weeks to get five pounds in petty cash,' he said. To him and
many others, there was no smoke without fire. In the modern

world, payment by cash is often associated with underhand dealing but the truth is that cash is still legal tender and it would be an injustice if the mere fact of payment in cash were viewed, in itself, as a dubious activity. More interestingly, £50,000 is a relatively small sum for an agent's work in putting together an expensive deal. A six-figure payment is not unusual for million-pound plus transfers.

Despite the denials, it is well known in football circles that some managers take a percentage of transfer sales and it is widely believed that over the years Brian Clough was permitted, within the terms of his contract, a share of income from such activity by Forest. When Graham Smith was an Adidas rep he always ensured he got a receipt from the club secretary for the money he paid over as part of the supplier's arrangement with the club. He was told in no uncertain terms by Clough's assistant, the late Peter Taylor, that when he came to Forest he was to bring money for him as well.

The situation seems to be completely out of hand. Regulations are routinely broken, there are no proper guidelines to govern the way transfers and contracts are negotiated and, at the end of the day, it is the law of the jungle. Many blame this laissez-faire system for the spiralling wages and transfer fees, and thus the ever-upward march of prices that supporters have to pay to watch their teams. Mel Stein puts it another way. 'There's all sorts of ideas that I think we've brought to contracts,' he said. 'I don't think many agents even bother to read the standard Football League contract. I've not only read it, I've gone through it with a fine-tooth comb. I've amended it. There are certain clauses in it which are simply not acceptable. For example, the one about the club being able to terminate the player's contract on six months' notice if he gets injured. I wonder how many agents even know that.'

Stein thinks you cannot overstate the importance of professional representation. 'Now, if you think about it,' he said, 'most managers were only footballers themselves but they've got much more experience than a young seventeen- or eighteen-year-old player. It's all very well them saying to the player, "you come in and let's talk man to man." But if the manager's got a problem who does he talk to? He talks to the board of directors. And who's on the board of directors?

Almost inevitably businessmen, an accountant and a lawyer.
So he's got all this bank of experience behind him. Therefore
a manager negotiating with a footballer on a one-to-one basis
is very unequal. It's not fair.'

Stein stressed that he has always tried to operate on
incentives, so that the more successful the club becomes, the
more the player earns. 'I seek for a player to try to get an
interest in his own contract. He should do so because the only
reason he has become more valuable is because of his own
abilities,' he said. Paul Gascoigne, for instance, when he was
transferred to Tottenham from Newcastle, had a clause in his
contract negotiated by Stein to the effect that when the
player was sold, any amount received over the £2.2 million
Tottenham paid Newcastle would be split equally between
club and player. Thus Gazza's £5.5 million sale to Lazio
netted a profit of £3.3 million, which was shared between
Gazza and Tottenham.

There can be no doubt that the system is a mess. The
football authorities have shown a marked reluctance to do
anything other than castigate agents for the fact of their
existence. The only way forward is surely either to enforce
the regulations or to change them. A fairer system would
actually permit payments to agents by clubs, and at least then
everything could be above board. Certainly, agents acting as
consultants could be paid a facility fee for helping to hire or
off-load staff, which could be based on a percentage of the
player's salary, transfer fee or signing-on payment. As one
agent put it, 'This has all been put into the pot by the FA
trying to enforce something which no other authority across
Europe enforces.' He admits that 'technically it's against FIFA
rules, but FIFA knows the world goes round'. Another
remembers that it was all so much fairer when the FA turned
a blind eye to clubs paying agents directly. 'It has caused all
this hypocrisy, where trumped-up invoices are put into clubs
when in fact most of it relates to perfectly good work done
on the clubs' behalf. They [the clubs] pay solicitors and
accountants but they can't openly pay an agent for bringing
them top players on terms and conditions acceptable to the
clubs. It's not right.' Paradoxically, it is this legitimate area of
agents' business that is the most open to abuse because
'players don't like paying [agents] money. If you can say to

them, "I'm not taking anything off you, I'm getting mine from the club," they're delighted and the club is happy because they are getting the player they want and they include it [the agent's commission] in the package. It's much cleaner.'

In addition, the relationship between agent and player could be regularised by allowing the contractual arrangement to be approved by the authorities. At present some managers allow agents to negotiate, others do not. At Arsenal, for instance, George Graham always conducts negotiations direct with players, even to the extent of excluding his friend Frank McLintock from the room when McLintock's client, Jimmy Carter, was transferred to Arsenal from Liverpool. It should be a relatively simple matter to ensure that players have the right to be represented when negotiating with clubs. The point made by Mel Stein about the back-up that managers can call on is not without merit. As Stein himself put it: 'Why are they scared? The only reason they're scared is that they think we might get a fair deal for the player.' As in so many other matters, however, it appears that the football authorities would prefer not to get involved unless they absolutely have to.

Once again, it may well be that the English will have to be bailed out of the situation by FIFA, if FIFA's move to license all agents comes to anything. The number of international transfers has shot up in recent years and this is bringing extra pressure to bear on what is, essentially, an unregulated marketplace, or at least a marketplace where any regulation is widely disregarded. And while the influence of agents can be used by the unscrupulous to explain away some of the more outrageous incidents, clubs and national associations must take the lion's share of the blame for the way matters have turned out. Clubs, of course, have their own ways and means of achieving their ends, and not all of them stand up to close scrutiny. It is then left to agents such as the flamboyant Eric Hall to claim credit for bringing players out of the feudal system that once pertained and to some extent, still does. 'I make the poor player rich and the rich player richer,' said Hall. 'I'm not a one-man band, I'm a one-man orchestra.'

11

Business 1 Football 0

Terry Venables and Alan Sugar: the irresistible force meets the immovable object

> *'In this business you've got to be a dictator or you haven't got a chance.'*
>
> Brian Clough.

> *'To treat sport like sport is to fail to understand the seriousness of your business.'*
>
> Roy Hofheinz, owner of Houston Astros, after building Houston Astrodome.

> *'Anyone who invests in sport has an ego problem to start with.'*
>
> Herman Sarkowsky, owner of Portland Trailblazers basketball team.

Eric Hall, an expansive character to say the least, reached his position as orchestra leader over a long and well-publicised career as an agent. From a background in showbusiness, Hall became involved in football in the 1980s and has never looked back. He is known for the propensity with which he uses the telephone, an instrument which is never far from his lips, and his overuse of the word 'monster' to describe everything he does. Hall loves a deal, especially a monster deal, and always makes sure he gets his cut. Even when the money for Glynn Hodges' transfer from Wimbledon to Sheffield United was paid for by the United fans raising the necessary cash, Hall, Hodges' agent, and indeed the player, made sure he got his percentage. One of Hall's most lucrative connections came from his friendship with Terry Venables, forged way back when Venables was a Chelsea player under Tommy Docherty.

When Venables became chief executive of Tottenham Hotspur Football Club in June 1991, it was Hall who became the most influential agent at the club and handled the affairs of a number of Tottenham players. During this period he could often be heard extolling his love of the club. He even paid over £2,000 a season for the privilege of becoming a life president. When Venables and Alan Sugar went to court, Hall's players were the most outspoken in their criticism of Sugar and virtually all of them, according to Hall, expressed a desire to leave if Venables' dismissal was upheld. In the event, the only immediate departure was that of Neil Ruddock, the defender who had started with Tottenham but was sold as a youngster and eventually brought back to White Hart Lane from Southampton. In the fall-out from the Tottenham affair, Ruddock was sold to Liverpool for £2.5 million, but not before Hall had demanded the payment of a £150,000 'loyalty bonus' for the three seasons remaining on Ruddock's contract. The new Tottenham manager, Osvaldo Ardiles, commented: 'He asked for a transfer, then wants to be paid for three years. That's unbelievable.' Unbelievable or not, Tottenham paid Ruddock £50,000 in settlement, after which Eric Hall suddenly became a Liverpool fan, to the extent of wearing a red jacket and telling the world that Graeme Souness was the best manager in existence.

Souness may or may not be the best manager in the world but at the end of the 1992–93 season the whole of English football was fully expecting him to be dismissed from his position at Liverpool. It was only at the eleventh hour that chairman David Moores, who had taken over from Noel White, was able to persuade a majority of the board to keep Souness, using the argument that there was no viable alternative and the club would incur heavy financial penalties through having to pay up the remainder of Souness's contract. If Souness's staying caused a surprise, there was general stupefaction when, on May 13 1993, ITV's *News At Ten* announced that Terry Venables was expected to be sacked the following day. A punter could have cleaned up on a win double of Souness staying and Venables going.

Tottenham's 1992–93 season had begun poorly but had turned around after Venables had been persuaded to dust off his tracksuit and become more involved in team matters. The problem was that Venables' job was as chief executive of a subsidiary to a company – Tottenham Hotspur plc – which was quoted on the stock exchange. According to the chairman of the plc, Alan Sugar, Venables was not doing a good enough job on the business side and should be sticking to football. To add weight to his concerns, Sugar, already at the head of the plc, installed himself as chairman of the football club in place of Tony Berry, the former head of Blue Arrow. The truth of Venables' capabilities as a chief executive was soon lost amid acrimonious exchanges in the High Court as the two men engaged in a war for control of the club.

The first public inkling that something was wrong with the relationship, described as a 'dream ticket' when they wrested control of Tottenham from the clutches of Robert Maxwell and Irving Scholar in 1991, came when Venables told the media at the Football Writers' annual dinner on May 13 that he expected to be ousted at the following day's board meeting (hence the story on *News At Ten*). In fact, the writing had been on the wall for some time. Sugar had come to the opinion that he wanted Venables to run the football side but Venables insisted on being in control of all aspects of the club. Matters came to a head on May 6, when Sugar proposed at a board meeting that the Spurs computer base be moved to Amstrad's headquarters in Brentwood, Essex. Venables, supported by another director, Jonathan Crystal, an associate of his for many years, opposed the measure. Sugar, used to getting his own way, lost his temper and stormed out of the meeting. Afterwards, Sugar wrote to Venables offering to buy his shares. The offer was rejected.

Before the fateful board meeting of May 14 which got rid of Venables, the chief executive was taken aside by the two other directors who had been retained after the take-over, Tony Berry and Douglas Alexiou. The latter was Tottenham's great survivor, who had managed to keep his directorship through three different administrations. The two men told Venables to accept the inevitable and go quietly in the interests of the club. Alexiou said that Venables could always 'get a job in Spain'.

'I don't want to go to fucking Spain,' Venables replied. 'Why don't you take your practice [Alexiou is a lawyer] to Yorkshire?' He then reminded the two that when the club was in dire trouble they had not put in their own money but instead had left it to him to mortgage himself up to the eyeballs.

The axe was not long in falling. At 11.40 am, Terry Venables was sacked by the board as chief executive. Later that day Venables went to the High Court to lodge an application under section 459 of the Companies Act. The court would have to decide whether his removal was sufficiently prejudicial to a significant number of shareholders for Sugar to be forced to sell his shares to Venables or his nominee. Since the court case would not be heard for months, Venables' lawyers further argued that he should be granted an injunction which would return him to his post. His case was that if he were not present at the club, it could suffer. An interim injunction was granted pending a full court hearing on the narrow issue of whether or not Venables should be allowed to stay until the section 459 action was heard in its entirety.

The full hearing on Venables' injunction application took place in that new football venue, the law courts in the Strand, in mid-June. Venables had won the support of the Tottenham fans during his battle with Scholar and Maxwell and the supporters rallied to his cause now. A hard core of about 300 kept up a barrage of noise outside the court throughout the hearing. It slowed traffic around the Aldwych to a snail's pace and the chanting and singing could be heard inside the hallowed halls themselves. Banners had been prepared asking motorists to 'toot for Terry' and Alan Sugar was reviled in the chants of the crowd.

While the media made much of the allegations of both parties, particularly 'the bung' (which Sugar claimed was how Venables had described the kick-backs paid out when some transfers took place), the judge, Sir Donald Nicholls, head of the chancery division of the High Court, was concerned only with the injunction issue. Whatever the rights and wrongs of the situation, Sir Donald ruled that while Venables had the support of most players and fans, this did not outweigh the fact that Sugar and Venables could no longer work together, and if the court ordered them to do so, chaos would ensue. Keeping Venables in position would, according to the judge, 'merely postpone the date at which all concerned must face up to the fact that his appointment, for better or worse, has been terminated'. The judge also made some pointed remarks about the behaviour of the fans outside the court, saying it was disgraceful, particularly when Sugar arrived and had to run the gauntlet of abuse. Sir Donald used the fans' behaviour as a pretext for dropping a contempt of court charge against Sugar for threatening one of Venables' witnesses, the Tottenham director, Jonathan Crystal. To add to Venables' woes, the judge ruled that Sugar's legal costs, estimated to be over £100,000, would have to be paid by the now unemployed chief executive. In addition, Sugar's lawyers went back to court with an 'application for security of costs', which was granted. This meant that Venables had to pay into court £300,000 to cover some of Sugar's costs if Venables lost the full section 459 case. Any second thoughts Venables might have had about continuing the fight were set aside as Sugar put the boot in. 'We don't want him at the club,' Sugar said, 'and if I have anything to do with it, he's not coming back at all.' Sugar went on to savage Venables' business expertise and Venables felt he now had to fight on to salvage his reputation. Dragging out the agony even more, the date for the new hearing was set for October, later put back until November, which ensured that the uncertainty at Spurs would continue well into the new season.

When Venables and Sugar won control in their battle at Tottenham, Irving Scholar had remarked that the honeymoon would last a year. The divorce, he declared, was bound to happen in year two. It proved to be a prophetic announcement. For many, the more interesting aspect of the union was the reason why Sugar got involved in the first place. He was not a football fan, nor, it seemed, did he possess anything in the way of knowledge about the game – not that ignorance has ever been a bar to becoming a football director.

At the time of the take-over, Sugar was experiencing troubles within the company that made (and carried) his name, Amstrad (Alan Michael Sugar Trading), makers of electronic consumer goods. Sugar had turned Amstrad into a public company, but as the recession wiped out millions off its value on the stock exchange, Sugar became unhappy about the level of control he was having to relinquish to City institutions. He tried to buy back the company's shares but was thwarted by an angry reaction from shareholders, who felt they were being conned, although Sugar was always adamant that his offer was in the best interests of all shareholders. Sugar, who was one of the great entrepreneurs of the 1980s, was experiencing the first serious challenge to his reputation as an innovative whizz-kid.

One area of growth for Amstrad was the conclusion of a deal with Rupert Murdoch's BSkyB and the Astra satellite company to manufacture and distribute domestic satellite dishes. However, at the time, Sky was losing vast amounts of money and the future of satellite television in the UK was uncertain. Meanwhile, Sugar had become interested in the way the Americans marketed sport in order to maximise its income and its appeal to television viewers. There was also the example of Silvio Berlusconi, who had risen from relative obscurity to worldwide fame once he had taken over AC Milan and integrated it with the rest of his media empire. Perhaps even more important than these considerations was the opportunity to influence the performance of his core business. As Sharp and JVC had shown through their respective sponsorships of Manchester United and Arsenal, football is a vehicle for communication with customers. Every serious fan has a video recorder and research has shown that fans are predisposed to those companies which are associated with their club. Before long, these elements would combine to provide Sugar with compelling reasons for getting involved with a top-class football club. The result, as we have seen, was Sugar's pivotal role in securing the Premier League television contract for BSkyB, which put £7 million on Amstrad's share price at a stroke. Beyond this, Sugar understood that the value of Tottenham property assets, plus the market value of players like Paul Gascoigne, meant that the club's chronic financial problems could be turned around. In fact, if the Midland, Tottenham's bankers, hadn't put undue pressure on the company to repay a loan taken out primarily to finance the building of the East Stand,

Alan Sugar and Terry Venables would have had to pay far more for their purchase of the club. The quick sale of Paul Gascoigne for £5.5 million, along with advance income from season tickets and executive boxes, which between them brought in almost the same amount, meant that the elimination of most of the punitive interest charges arising out of the Midland loan and a rights issue of shares in December 1991 could be accomplished fairly painlessly. For his stake of £5 million Alan Sugar possessed a controlling interest in a company that was probably worth three times as much. It was a good business decision. Alan Sugar is no sugar daddy and he was determined that the subject of his investment would be profitable.

At the start, Sugar and Venables believed they could work together but that rose-tinted view was based on misconceptions. Venables thought Sugar had his hands full looking after Amstrad and would be happy to act as a silent backer, leaving him to get on with what he had always wanted to do, run a football club from top to bottom. This flew in the face of a comment Sugar made at the time: 'I will take care of the £11 million at the bank [a reference to Tottenham's debt] and he'll take care of the eleven men on the field.' For his part, Sugar believed that Venables would make a good figurehead, providing the key footballing knowledge that the club required, but would allow Sugar to keep his hands on the tiller of the public company. At root was a common belief that, as two east-end boys made good, they were, despite their very different personalities, soul-mates in business if not their social milieu. Sugar had in fact employed Venables in the past, in an advertisement for an Amstrad product, an audio system Venables described as 'the best player I ever bought'.

When the financial situation at White Hart Lane began to improve significantly, most of the public credit went to Venables, a state of affairs which Sugar found irksome, believing he was not getting his full share of the plaudits. On Venables' side, one insider remembers that the chief executive went from hardly mentioning Sugar at all to being all but obsessed by him, decrying his lack of understanding of football. One area of conflict concerned the jungle which was the transfer market. In his own business Sugar was street-smart: Amstrad usually managed to get extended credit and tried to leave payment until the last moment. Although he was continually moving the goalposts, at least his customers knew what game he was playing. In the football transfer business there were rules, but they were widely disregarded. There were cash payments (the famous 'bungs'), commissions often hidden as 'payments for promotional work', and all manner of devices, especially financial, which made a mockery of normal contractual relationships. Sugar must have been amazed at the inefficiency of it all. To Venables, of course, this was the way all football business took place, and it was only through long experience of it that anyone could understand its nuances.

Although the two men had originally gone into Tottenham as equal partners, a rights issue of shares in December 1991 meant that Sugar increased his holding significantly, which relegated Venables – who had borrowed heavily through his company, Edennote, to finance his involvement – to the status of minority shareholder with only 23 per cent. One of Venables' chief allegations in his evidence to support his section 459 action was that he had been misled by Sugar concerning the effects of the rights issue. Venables said he agreed to it because he knew the company was under-capitalised and Sugar assured him that it would not alter their respective voting powers (indeed, a director has one vote in board meetings no matter what the size of his shareholding. A majority shareholder, however, can always call a meeting of shareholders to overturn any board decision). Perhaps it was naïve of Venables to believe that Sugar, having achieved majority control, would behave any differently with Tottenham than he did with Amstrad. Sugar had never worked on a consensus basis and he wasn't going to start now. As the largest shareholder with the most money at risk, Sugar, who with his family and friends now held over 50 per cent of the shares, was determined to exercise control, if need be as an autocrat.

In fact, Sugar controlled the business well before the rights issue through the appointment of his own men to key positions. Out went managing director Ian Gray and financial advisers Brown Shipley, while Colin Sandys, a long-serving Sugar associate, came in as financial director. It was not surprising, in such an environment, that there would be a confrontation sooner rather than later.

The first point of the attack on Venables was felt not by the chief executive himself but by his advisers. If Venables had an Achilles' heel, Sugar had found it. Venables is known for the loyalty he inspires among those around him. It is virtually impossible, for instance, to find a footballer who has played under him who will say a bad word about him. Even Clive Allen, whom Venables sold three times when he was manager at different clubs, will only sing his praises. When the new board was constituted in 1991, one of Venables' appointees was a long-time colleague, Jonathan Crystal, while another, Eddy Ashby, was made a consultant to the club. Crystal was later accused by Sugar of being at the root of all the problems. 'He has been loading up bullets in a gun which regrettably Terry has been constantly firing,' Sugar said. Ashby, unfortunately for Venables, was an undischarged bankrupt and Sugar was able to question Venables' judgement in appointing someone with such a track record to such an important position at a major football club.

Fingers were also pointed at Venables' over-reliance on Eric Hall, who would certainly win no popularity contest among the public or the football authorities. Hall, who was also Venables' agent, handled the players' pool for the 1991 Cup final and barred the media from the training ground unless they made a contribution, necessitating a personal intervention from Venables to rescind the order. After the final, the players had to wait an inordinate length of time before they received their share. When the trouble between Venables and Sugar surfaced, Hall backed Venables and claimed the players for whom he acted wanted to leave. One by one, however, all settled their differences with Sugar – except Neil Ruddock, the most vociferous Venables supporter among the players. However, the Tottenham supporters felt let down by Ruddock's failure to come to terms with the new club structure, as many of them reluctantly had, and by the fact that his eventual departure to Liverpool appeared to be merely a question of money.

Hall organised demonstrations in support of his sacked client even after he was asked to desist by Venables himself. The conflict led to Hall being barred from the training ground,

just as he had barred journalists two years before. This led to
the ludicrous spectacle of Hall attempting to conduct his
business from the pavement outside, always with the ever-
present mobile telephone at his lips. For months afterwards,
Hall continued to agitate on behalf of his friend, although he
was probably more of a hindrance than a help to the cause. In
fact, some of Venables' closest friends told him to get rid of
Hall, which he steadfastly refused to do. Although Venables'
loyalty spoke eloquently of his qualities as an honourable
man, it did little for his image as an objective businessman.

Sugar followed up by making a foray into Venables' own
territory. Tottenham's results on the pitch, he declared, did
not justify the £3.5 million outlay Venables had expended on
three players, Gordon Durie, Andy Gray and Jason Cundy.
At the same time he felt Gary Lineker had been sold too
cheaply. In one particularly bizarre move, when Venables
couldn't get Paul Parker, who went to Manchester United and
a Championship-winners' medal, he bought Durie. Durie is an
exciting but erratic attacker in the Tottenham tradition but
was hardly what was required at the time since it was their
defence which needed reinforcement. Sugar argued that his
money was being squandered. In this sense, Sugar's outlook
owed more to the philosophy of small clubs like Wimbledon
than big ones like Manchester United. The small fry were to
be commended, he felt, for the way they did business. They
achieved stability with low overheads and by being sellers of
players rather than buyers. This was not what the fans
wanted. As Steve Davies, of the Tottenham Independent
Supporters Association (TISA) put it: 'I don't think Sugar has
got any great commitment to winning the League or winning
European Cups. His aims are more modest than that. Provided
things are ticking over he will probably be happy, which isn't
really good enough.'

Since becoming chief executive, Venables had, according to
his previous boss, ex-chairman Irving Scholar, 'abdicated his
responsibility as team manager'. To support his line, Scholar
could point to the coaching staff Venables put in place. Peter
Shreeve, who had previously managed Tottenham between
1984 and 1986 and had been fired by Irving Scholar, was
brought back but was in an invidious position. If the team
were successful, Venables would get the credit; if not, it

would be Shreeves' fault. When results did not go too well in 1992, it was Shreeves, not Venables, who was fired. It was incidents such as this which brought it home to Scholar that Venables would always be ready with an excuse. After six years in charge, he was still describing the team as being in a state of transition.

After Venables was sacked, he was probably lucky to get the temporary injunction to return to his post. The judge perhaps recognised the special circumstances surrounding the case. Buoyed by the false sense of security the injunction, along with the support of the football media and the Tottenham fans, gave him, perhaps Venables became too confident and overplayed his hand. In a television interview with the BBC's Des Lynham, he revealed that Tottenham's finances had been turned around and the club was on course to make a trading profit of £5 million. This was against stock exchange regulations, which state that shareholders must be informed of the year's accounts before the information is made public, and an investigation was ordered after the Tottenham shares went up by 14p to 103p in the days after Venables' revelation. Moreover, Sugar was able to counter by saying that the sale of Paul Gascoigne to Lazio, agreed before Venables became chief executive, accounted for most of the trading profit. The offer Sugar had made to buy Venables' shares had, by this time, been made public. The offer was that Sugar would buy the shares at the price Venables paid for them. This would mean Venables losing money because it took no account of the interest which attached to the loan he took out in order to buy the shares. In the same television interview with Lynham, Venables dismissed Sugar's offer as 'derisory'. Immediately prior to the court case, Sugar apparently made what he called another 'generous offer', which 'would have been enough to have paid off his borrowings and leave him with an amount of money', but Venables again turned it down. According to Sugar, his words were, 'I have a death wish. I will fight you to the bitter end.'

Terry Venables, in his quest to own a football club, had broken a cardinal rule. He had borrowed money to make his investment. Sooner or later, that situation was bound to cause problems, since football, in the main, is not a profit-making business. Venables thought that the emergence of a good, young team, based on more than a few home-grown talents, would, through its success, eventually see him get his money back. After he was sacked, there were few potential buyers for his shares – except Alan Sugar, who didn't need them. Venables was now between a rock and a hard place. Even if he were to win the court case and to be granted the right to buy Sugar's shares, where would the money come from? And if the upheaval caused by his departure led to a period of uncertainty on the pitch, then he would find it increasingly difficult either to service the debt or to find an alternative buyer.

As for Alan Sugar, he felt he had not been accorded due recognition for saving Tottenham. He was particularly upset at the Charity Shield game against Arsenal at Wembley in 1991 when he thought he was cold-shouldered by the football establishment while Venables basked in the glory of being at the centre of everyone's attention. Moreover, Sugar resented the way Venables could play to the crowd and win. A Tottenham employee was quoted as saying: 'Sugar was jealous of Terry and how the fans chanted "Terry Venables' blue and white army". He would say, "What about me?"'

It was not enough for Sugar to claim that Venables had merely lost the support of the board. When the court case to decide the validity of Venables' sacking took place, it was Sugar's intention to show that Venables was unfit to hold the job of chief executive of a public company. The main area of attack came with allegations of cash pay-outs on transfer dealings, including an alleged 'bung' to the then Nottingham Forest manager, Brian Clough, when Teddy Sheringham was transferred to Tottenham. The previous chairman, Irving Scholar, had always been very much involved with transfers and contracts. Scholar may not have been the easiest person in the world to work with but he always sought to get the best deal for the club in a 'clean' way, although even he was not averse to infringing the unrealistic Football League regulations when it suited him, as when the club employed Dennis Roach to try to force the sale of Paul Gascoigne and Gary Lineker. Certainly, Scholar felt that he couldn't rely on Venables' business acumen. Apparently, Alan Sugar concurred with this view.

In his book about his time at White Hart Lane, entitled

Behind Closed Doors, Irving Scholar quotes Alan Sugar as being unequivocal in his assessment of Venables' capabilities as a businessman. 'Terry Venables thinks he's an entrepreneur, but I don't,' Sugar told Scholar. Scholar also outlined previous opportunities to become involved in executive decisions at Tottenham which had not, according to Scholar, been taken up by Venables. 'He was off after one o'clock to do his thing,' Scholar said. At Queens Park Rangers Venables had flirted with the idea of leasing the ground from chairman Jim Gregory and buying the club. Perhaps he was spreading himself too thinly with too many fingers in too many pies. The QPR type of scheme was again investigated when Venables attempted to take over Tottenham from Scholar, but the idea was rejected by Sugar.

To his credit, Venables always recognised the support he gained from TISA in the battle with Irving Scholar and Robert Maxwell. Once victory was secured he carried on the dialogue, one of the few executives at a football club who bothered with such an independent organisation. Recognising the effect the sacking of Venables might have on the fans, Alan Sugar, on the morning of the crucial board meeting of May 14, phoned Steve Davies of TISA and asked him not to support Venables. 'Until we have good reasons not to we shall continue to [support him],' was Davies's response. TISA quickly mounted effective action, organising affidavits and petitioning the Department of Trade and Industry to hold an enquiry. They also raised £5,000 towards a fighting fund. Apart from the natural feelings of support for a football man against a businessman, Davies outlined another reason why they felt so strongly.

'At Tottenham there was the most amazing feeling from January [1993],' he said. 'The people who said this were not just young supporters but people who have been going for forty years. They've never known such a good atmosphere. You really had this fantastic feeling and the club and the fans were all in it together. You knew Venables was in it for the football – to make money out of it as well – but basically for the football. You had this very open relationship with people like Chris Belt [the ticket office manager], who would explain club policy, and you had a collection of young players like Austin, Edinburgh and Barmby who really looked like they just wanted to play for Tottenham and didn't want to go anywhere else. In recent years Gascoigne and Lineker were good. Lineker couldn't have done more for Tottenham, but you didn't feel he was really doing it for Tottenham, he was really doing it for Lineker. Now it's almost like we're going back to the bad old days and the close relationship between the club, supporters and players just won't be there. It will just be Tottenham, a big team, and people will come along and watch or won't as the case may be.'

Whether or not they are on fantasy island, the fact is that Tottenham fans, brought up on the tradition of the great sides of the fifties and sixties and a plethora of gifted individuals stretching from Greaves to Gascoigne, regard themselves as a breed apart. The editor of the fanzine the *Spur*, Stuart Mutler, probably spoke for many when he wrote: 'Yeah, Sugar may be a hard-headed "winner" with a lot of dosh and some "good ideas", but that interests me about as much as winning the title every season playing dull football.'

Early on in his tussles with Irving Scholar, Venables told his chairman that he was 'getting quite fond of Tottenham'. To Scholar, who had only blue and white blood running through his veins, the club was and always would be an affair of the heart. To Venables it was perhaps more than just a business opportunity, but more than anything else it was a vehicle to realise his long-cherished ambition to own a football club. He was finding out, however, that passion and commitment weren't enough. The sound of money talking was drowning them out. To all intents and purposes, the businessman had seen off the football man.

For Sugar, the appointment of a new manager now became crucial. It had to be someone who could gain the respect of the players and placate the fans, the vast majority of whom continued to support Venables. Season ticket sales proved sluggish and talk of boycotts filled the air. It was then that Sugar pulled off what many saw as a master-stroke by bringing Osvaldo Ardiles back to the stage he had graced so successfully as a player, this time as manager. Ardiles, the Argentinian World Cup-winner who had formed part of the exciting Tottenham midfield of the late 1970s and early 1980s with Glenn Hoddle, was much beloved by the fans and if anybody could pull them round, it was him. Sugar leaned very heavily on the advice of Tony Berry, his vice-chairman, and Douglas Alexiou. Irving Scholar told them Ardiles was the only choice as 'you can't be a player-manager in the Premier League', which effectively, ruled out the other Tottenham icon, Glenn Hoddle. In any case, Hoddle had accepted the overtures of Ken Bates and left Swindon to manage Chelsea.

The appointment of Ardiles could prove a double-edged sword, however. If Sugar had kept the existing coaching team of Doug Livermore and Ray Clemence and the side were successful, he could reasonably say: who needs Terry Venables? If the team did not perform he could then be seen to act decisively by bringing in Ardiles (assuming he were still available). If Ardiles fails, to whom will Sugar then turn?

Even the appointment of Ardiles was not without its trials. Ardiles' former club, West Bromwich Albion, threatened to take him and Tottenham to court. The club's chairman, Trevor Summers, went off at the deep end 'If Alan Sugar thinks he can just walk in and take West Brom's manager, I'll be down the motorway like an exocet and I'll blow up his bloody computers', he raged. Later, Summers put his money where his mouth was and announced his intention to sue Tottenham and Ardiles for £1 million. 'Everything Spurs have done, he concluded, 'is totally unethical.'

With Ardiles as manager there was no doubt that Sugar had to change his priorities. 'I'm here,' Ardiles said succinctly, 'to take Tottenham to the top – not to act as peacemaker.' In the wake of Ardiles' arrival a sort of Stalinist purge took place as scout Ted Buxton, physiotherapist David Butler, and coach Ray Clemence were fired, while Doug Livermore was moved to scouting duties, as if to erase the last vestiges of the Venables regime. In their places came former Tottenham favourites Steve Perryman, Chris Hughton and Pat Jennings, all of whom, at any other time, would have been welcomed with open arms by the fans.

Interestingly, when Venables first arrived at Tottenham, his good friend Morris Keston suggested he consider employing Ardiles as coach. Keston's son-in-law, Paul Miller, a member of the first team when Ardiles was a player, sang his praises as a master tactician. 'He comes into the dressing room at half-time and it's unbelievable what he sees,' Miller said. 'It's funny you should say that,' Venables replied when Keston repeated Miller's observation to him, 'but I think he [Ardiles] resents me.' Keston did, nonetheless, persuade Venables to take the matter further. A week later Venables phoned and said: 'It's no-go, I can't get near him. When he sees me he goes the other way.'

At the beginning of the 1993–94 season, Ardiles gently rebuked Irving Scholar, telling him that he, not Venables, should have been appointed as David Pleat's successor in 1987. Scholar told him: 'It was too soon. You had to go away and do it elsewhere. Now you've done that, you're back where you belong.' Perhaps it was the feeling that Venables was in his job that rankled with Ardiles.

While wishing Ardiles well, Venables remained determined to continue his fight, even though his chances of success appeared slim. Although feeling morally bound to support his friend, Morris Keston illustrated how Venables was beginning to run out of time. Most fans, like Keston, supported Venables, but when push came to shove, even a personal friendship would not stop a fan supporting his club. 'Of course I'll carry on going [to watch games],' Keston said, 'Tottenham has been my life. I've seen off eleven chairmen and ten managers.' Sugar was counting on the rest of the supporters having similar feelings. He seemed to be proved right as Ardiles' arrival gave a tremendous boost to season ticket sales. By the start of the 1993–94 season, sales were running at approximately the same rate as the previous year, guaranteeing almost £3 million in advance revenue. Another Venables supporter ruefully summed up the situation: 'Give the players another ten pounds and it will be Terry who? It's the same with supporters. If Spurs win the first four matches [of the season] it will be the same reaction.'

Despite Venables' desire to fight his corner, his position was fast becoming untenable. One main pressure on him was the requirement to find the £300,000 security of costs. This move by Sugar's lawyers proved to be a decisive one. Venables asked for, and was granted, more time to find the cash but the realisation was dawning on him that he had an impossible task. As the new season got into full swing and Ossie Ardiles' team performed reasonably well, Venables made the decision to pull out of the section 459 application and pursue another, lesser action for unfair dismissal, which even if won would at most result only in financial compensation. There was now no way back to White Hart Lane for Terry Venables and on September 4 he announced that he had sold the majority of his shares. The amount he received was less than the offers from Sugar he had previously rejected.

Why Alan Sugar should want to remain in charge in the face of the vilification to which he has been subjected is open to question. It may be that he has been bitten by the football bug, but it is more likely that the successes of Silvio Berlusconi and David Murray, not to mention the big sports teams in the USA, have led Sugar to believe that if he were in overall control, as the aforementioned owners are, he could propel his business empire to new heights. Terry Venables, as the man who took all the publicity, was a considerable obstacle to such an objective.

As for Venables himself, the case for unfair dismissal remains the only way for him to clear his name of the allegations of impropriety made against him. He told a friend that he actually welcomed the prospect. 'I'm so lucky,' he claimed. 'What do you mean? You've just lost your job,' asked his friend. 'Because,' replied Venables, 'I've never taken a penny for myself.' While this may be true, allegations of improper business behaviour made against Venables by BBC's *Panorama* and Channel 4's *Despatches* were serious enough to merit legal investigations. The odour of bad publicity certainly curtailed discussions with the Japanese about the possibility of Venables coaching Grampus 8, Gary Lineker's club. The road back now was not going to be an easy one.

The one thing that all agree upon is that Venables is one of the best football coaches in the world. Perhaps if he had been put in charge of England in 1990, he would have found his true métier, with the time to indulge his extra-curricular activities. But like Brian Clough before him, the FA mistrusted his personality. Meanwhile, the place Venables should have occupied was in an even more parlous state than Tottenham, and matters in the England camp seemed to be going from bad to worse.

12

The Young Ones

Graham Taylor, Chris Waddle and England's further attempts to qualify for the World Cup finals. How we treat youngsters and the way they do it at Ajax and Auxerre

> *'I have been watching youth games lately and it's not a football match, it's a war. It's a battle. I've never seen such bad fouls, so much aggression. With the long-ball game that's what it is, a war.'*

> *Malcolm Allison, former coach at Manchester City, Sporting Lisbon etc.*

> *'It's between six and twelve that a player becomes either a footballer or an anti-kicker. It's then that one learns what you can't learn at eighteen or twenty.'*

> *Paul Breitner, former captain of West Germany.*

> *'AC Milan are the epitome of what I'm advocating.'*

> *Charles Hughes, director of education and training, FA.*

For England, reaching the USA World Cup finals in 1994 means far more than an affirmation of the nation's footballing prowess. It could give the England team its best chance of winning the trophy since 1966 – if it can qualify. This may seem fanciful, but there are a number of factors which could give the team a psychological boost and from that the players could gain a distinct advantage. The question is, will the English authorities remain true to form and throw away the opportunity by failing to grasp the nettle and insisting that in the pre-World Cup season, everything should be subordinated to the needs of Graham Taylor and the England team? The question of course, is now rhetorical.

English players are notoriously bad at enjoying other cultures. For most World Cups, the England squad has been holed up in some hotel for the duration of the tournament, rarely venturing out into the real world. This often happens as a backlash against a hostile local population and the excesses of the English tabloid press. In the USA, while English reporters will not be any less lurid than usual, at least the locals will be on England's side. Despite the war against us which attended the nation's birth, the USA sees Britain as its staunchest, most dependable ally and friend. Moreover, the USA is perhaps the one foreign country where British footballers can feel at home. It will be the first overseas tournament where the predominant language is English. Even the food will be as palatable to English stomachs as home produced fare. These things mean a lot to the average England international.

When Graham Taylor's team performed so poorly in Sweden in the 1992 European Championships, the manager stated that his number one target was the 1994 World Cup. Before England could take advantage of the most propitious venue since 1966, however, there was the small matter of the qualifying tournament to negotiate. After they took only a draw from the home game against the group's pace-setters, Norway, the pressure began to make itself felt. By February, 1993, the easiest of the group's ties, against San Marino, was due to be played at Wembley but the England camp was beset with problems, most of them yet again stemming from injuries to key players. The attack was hardest hit, with both first-choice strikers, Alan Shearer and Ian Wright, unable to play. In the event, Graham Taylor moved David Platt to partner Queens Park Rangers' Les Ferdinand up front and England won by 6–0 with Platt, who was making his first appearance as captain following an injury to Stuart Pearce, helping himself to four of the goals.

It may seem carping to find fault with a 6–0 victory, but the truth was that England's performance was stuttering and laboured. The final four goals only arrived in the last thirty minutes, by which time the opposition, which contained only two professionals, was tiring rapidly. There were some lamentable individual displays and John Barnes, looking overweight and a shadow of the player who could once mesmerise defences without any apparent effort, was struggling to put in a decent cross. The Wembley crowd didn't help since they booed Barnes every time he was in possession of the ball, a vendetta that had its origins in racism. Although unfair and cruel, it was fuelled by the disappointment the fans felt about Barnes's under-achievement at international level and by press reports about his reputed annual salary of £500,000. It was the first time anyone could remember an England player being barracked so much by the country's own fans.

Barnes wasn't the only one who looked below par. Most worrying was the performance (or non-performance) produced by Paul Gascoigne. Having proved his return to form in scintillating style against Turkey, Gazza seemed to have regressed. Graham Taylor now felt that the long fight to come back after the knee ligament injury Gazza sustained in the 1991 Cup final had given the player the motivation to get fit, but he was now going backwards. 'He is not in as good physical condition as he was when he had that target to prove,' Taylor said. 'I saw a slight deterioration prior to Turkey and I have seen a deterioration in his fitness. There is something there with the player at the moment that isn't right and that is affecting his fitness.' Yet again, Taylor was making allusions to Gazza's mental state without going the whole hog and saying what he really thought.

With both his play-makers lacking match-fitness (which begs the question, why pick them?), Taylor was indebted to the positive role played by David Platt, who provided just about the only crumb of comfort. Questions were again raised concerning the manager's selection and tactics. When England appeared to be running out of ideas, no substitutes were used to try to change the pattern. Rather than bringing on Andy Sinton, for instance, to give the side some width, England pushed Tony Adams forward while Lee Dixon pumped up the long balls looking for his club-mate's head. The performance revealed the truth about Taylor's England: if Gascoigne failed to perform, then the team was nothing more than a bunch of plodders. Taylor, of course, was watching a different match. 'We had 33 shots at goal, 21 of them on target,' enthused the manager. We put 62 crosses into the box (which if taken literally was one every 75 seconds), not counting corners and free kicks, of which admittedly too many were not of the highest quality. We had a penalty saved, Gazza hit the crossbar and David Batty had a couple cleared off the line. We got six, it could have been ten, and if we'd scored three or four more playing exactly the same way everyone would have been satisfied. After three home games I expected to have six points and we've got five. We shouldn't be too unhappy.'

Six weeks later, England had another chance to show how far Taylor had gone in producing a team fit to grace the World Cup with an away match against Turkey. For this tie, Taylor's perennial problem with full-backs once more came to the fore. Stuart Pearce's injury had been diagnosed as long-term, while the next two in line, Tony Dorigo and Nigel Winterburn, were themselves injured. Instead of bringing in another specialist left back, Taylor chose to play Andy Sinton on the grounds that there was no out-and-out winger on the Turkish side to mark and that anyway, Sinton would only be playing 'twenty-five yards deeper' than he normally did. Taylor also made the point that it was better to play an existing squad member than to bring in someone from the outside who would be inexperienced at international level. This line of thinking was a consequence of Taylor's wish to produce a squad which could achieve the same spirit and camaraderie as a club side – 'Club England', Taylor called it. This is all well and good, but Taylor contradicted himself by picking Sheffield Wednesday's defender-converted-to-striker, Paul Warhurst, for the Turkish game. Not only was Warhurst outside the squad and thus inexperienced, but he had only played a handful of club games as a striker (Warhurst had to pull out of the squad through injury, never to reappear).

The game itself was a poor encounter during which the Turkish players (and the crowd) tried to intimidate the England team. This was a disastrous ploy. The surest way of beating this England side is to play with skill and pace. Trying to overwhelm them physically and psychologically, as Turkey and their fans tried to do, merely played into England's hands. In the event, England ran out 2–0 winners. Platt again pushed up into the attack and scored his tenth goal in ten games. Ian Wright, back after injury, failed to score in his eighth international, a mystery for someone so prolific at club level.

The match was punctuated by incessant missile-throwing by the Turkish supporters which resulted in an England fan being blinded in one eye. Subsequently, FIFA fined the Turkish FA and banned Izmir, where the match was played, from holding international games for eight months. In such a hostile atmosphere, it was no surprise that Tony Adams played his best game yet for England. But again Gazza was peripheral to the main action, although he did score the vital second goal. The *Sun*, which could hardly knock Taylor after an away victory in the World Cup, did the next best thing by falling back on chauvinism and xenophobia. YOU PLUCKING MARVELS, screamed the headline. After belching and farting for the Italian media, and telling the Norwegians to 'fuck off', Gazza gave the *Sun* the picture it wanted, a V-sign, reproduced under the heading, GAZZA SALUTES THE TURKS. Graham Taylor for once recognised that far more would be needed against the stronger teams of the group. 'We had a good result but let's not kid ourselves,' he said. 'There are many, many things in our football which can be improved. On Wednesday we lost the ball in some bad areas and this could have hurt us but for some very good defensive play by Adams, in particular, and Walker.'

With Gascoigne stuttering and Barnes suffering, the media once again began to push the claims of Chris Waddle. Waddle, after an early-season injury following his return home from Marseille, had taken time to adjust to the different demands of the English game. By the new year, however he was beginning to turn in the kind of performances that had prompted Bernard Tapie to shell out over £4 million for him. No call-up came for the San Marino game, however, and many felt the reason harked back to the previous misunderstanding over Waddle's availability and to some criticisms the player, who has a reputation in some quarters as a barrack-room lawyer with strong views on the game, had publicly voiced concerning Taylor's methods. Moreover, Taylor seemed ill at ease with stars who had a mind of their own. After the San Marino game, Waddle's solicitor, Mel Stein, refused to talk about any rift with Taylor and a feeling emerged that Stein was trying to encourage a positive response from the manager. Stein certainly believed that a recall for Waddle was on the cards, possibly for Turkey or the next World Cup game against Holland at Wembley. In fact, despite a brilliant display in the FA Cup semi-final against Sheffield United, Waddle failed to make Taylor's squad for either match. Lee Chapman,

previewing the Coca-Cola Cup final between Arsenal and
Sheffield Wednesday in the *Observer*, wrote: 'I can't speak for
other clubs, but the omission of Chris Waddle from the England
squad came as a great surprise to me and many of my colleagues
at Leeds – a decision which has reduced Graham Taylor's
options . . . Waddle's continued exclusion in the middle of a
wonderful run of form – he is at the moment the most creative
English player in the Premier League – is a great shame.' Trevor
Brooking made much the same point, saying, 'It's all very well
to say that Waddle can't play in the same team as Gascoigne
and Barnes, but surely he should at least be on the bench to
come on to change things if the plans don't work out.' While
George Best thought Waddle was simply the best player in the
Premier League. 'I can't understand,' he said, 'why he is not in
the England team.'

Taylor claimed that he had nothing against Waddle
personally but his argument seemed extremely thin. 'I can't
convince myself,' he said, 'that we wouldn't lose something
on the pitch. We are looking for continuity and I'm not going
to treat the Dutch [game] as a one-off. We have a highly individual player who is causing us a few concerns [Gascoigne].
We've got another highly gifted individual player on whom
the public have turned their backs, and I can understand why
[Barnes]. The inclusion of a third highly gifted player starts to
put the whole thing in the melting-pot. We've got to have stability. We're looking to the future and I'm not too sure that we
are yet as stable as I would like us to be for us to bring another
one in. It may not be the time for Waddle to add something to
what we've got, but it may be that there comes a time when he
has to replace someone. But the time is not right.' Just as
perplexing was Taylor's assertion that if he picked Waddle for
the squad he 'would have to play him'. The manager followed
that up by insisting that if Waddle played 'I would have to
rearrange the team, one player would have to go and I don't
think that would be fair to those who have done so well over
the last four matches.' Neither did Taylor accept that by picking Barnes ahead of Waddle he was turning logic on its head.
'I don't think you can compare the two,' Taylor reasoned,
'Chris starts on the right and wanders, Barnes will give me
something down the left side.' It now appeared that Taylor had
completely dispensed with the main elements of Bobby

Robson's old guard (Robson, Beardsley, Waddle, Lineker) and was determined to create a team in his own image, functional and hard-working. Perhaps he had indulged Gazza against his better judgement, but Barnes was a different case. Taylor had introduced him to professional football at Watford, and anyway Barnes was not the type of personality to rock the boat. Waddle was simply one opinionated maverick too many. The campaign for Waddle was all to no avail, and by the time of the Holland game, he was as far from an England recall as ever.

Waddle's problems with Graham Taylor first came to public notice when the player dropped out of a European Championship qualifier against the Republic of Ireland in 1990 at the last minute. It happened again for the return match a few months later. These withdrawals were ostensibly through injury although Waddle's club, Marseille, were always reluctant to release him. Matters came to a head in another European Championship qualifier against Turkey in November 1991, when Taylor expressed annoyance that Waddle had stayed out wide and had not sought to exploit the roving role he had been given. For his part, Waddle retorted that he had been told to stay on the wing by Taylor. Waddle aggravated the situation by criticising England's style of play in a newspaper article, saying that the rigid system Taylor employed was failing to bring out the players' maximum potential. Realising he might have gone too far, Waddle seemed to accept that the chances of him playing for England again while Taylor was in charge were probably slim.

As Taylor's team began to take shape without Waddle, the player's Marseille colleagues, like those of Lee Chapman at Leeds and countless other players who had faced him, were astounded by his omission from the England set-up. Waddle had suffered early on in his career in France when he was asked to perform defensive duties under coach Tomaslav Ivic, but began to flower when given a freer role under Franz Beckenbauer and Raymond Goethals. This culminated in an attacking central midfield position behind Jean-Pierre Papin in his third season. During those three years Waddle spent by the Mediterranean the French Championship was won three times and the team reached both the semi-final and the final of the European Cup. Acknowledged as the team's playmaker and a scorer of spectacular and vital goals (including the winner against Milan in the European Cup quarter-final in 1991), Waddle was popular with his team-mates and adored by the Marseille fans – he was known as *Le Magicien*. In fact, Waddle only left Marseille because of Bernard Tapie's belief that his side needs a complete overhaul each year if it is to progress. Tapie was also extremely disappointed with Marseille's failure to win the European Cup. In the 1991–92 season, Marseille were dispatched by Sparta Prague before the new League system had started and Waddle was one of those who took the blame for the failure. Three key players were transferred at the end of the season. Apart from Waddle, who came back home to Sheffield Wednesday, Papin went to Milan and defender Carlos Moser was sold to Benfica.

By the beginning of 1993, Waddle was back to his best and propelled Wednesday to two Cup finals. Wednesday also finished seventh in the League, a position that could have been somewhat higher but for a slow start to the campaign. Wednesday were beaten in both Cup finals by Arsenal, however, and Waddle's performances in the games were not as influential as had been expected thereby perhaps vindicating Taylor's judgement in not picking him. He was, nonetheless, elected by football journalists as their Footballer of the Year.

Chris Waddle is a deep thinker about the game of football – a real fan. Irving Scholar, his chairman at Tottenham, was rarely known to listen to the views of others but Waddle was one of the few who could actually hold a conversation with him. Given the choice Waddle would prefer to spend his free time watching any game rather than joining in the group activities so beloved of England managers down the years. They are an essential part of Graham Taylor's Club England programme. Like Glenn Hoddle (53 caps but only once played in his Tottenham role), Waddle (62 caps, 6 goals) hardly ever played in a system for England which got the best out of him. Told to stay in his given zone and not wander he often became ineffectual in internationals. England's bosses always seemed terrified of the prospect of getting caught on the break if the team lost the ball. If Waddle drifted inside to find some space to play, the opposition full back could move into the vacated space and exploit Waddle's reluctance to carry out too many defensive duties. Again, like Hoddle, Waddle believed this was a task others should undertake. He was in the team to create chances. How could he be at his best if he was expected to make seventy-five-yard defensive runs? This fact was recognised by Waddle's club managers. At Marseille a system was constructed to ensure his optimum use. He was given freedom to roam because of the presence of a sweeper to provide cover, and although he was invariably man-marked, he countered with intelligent movement that took his marker into unfamiliar territory. By doing this he either made space for others or gave himself the best chance to outwit his marker. If Taylor was not going to play with a sweeper or spare man at the back, it is difficult to see how he could get an effective performance out of Waddle. Taylor feels he can rely on John Barnes more than Waddle to subdue his natural creative instincts in the interests of the team plan. However, logic suggests that at the very least Taylor ought to take Trevor Brooking's advice and have Waddle on the bench to change the approach should it prove necessary.

Although he turned in some outstanding individual performances for Spurs and his first club, Newcastle United, it was in France that Chris Waddle really blossomed, much as Eric Cantona has by travelling in the opposite direction. Whereas Cantona's problems in France stemmed from his contempt for the intellectual capacity of those in authority, Waddle's place in the English game and his potential as an England international were determined by the system under which youngsters progress to become professionals. That system would ultimately reject him. For all Cantona's brushes with those who administer the game in France, he is still very much a current international. With Waddle, the feeling persisted that he would stand a chance of getting back only if something disastrous happened.

When young children first begin to play football it matters not whether they are in Rio or Rochdale. They want to express themselves to the limit of their ability. The English child is blessed with no less natural skill than that of the children of any other nation. The country that produced Bobby Charlton, Stanley Matthews and Bobby Moore can't be all bad. But somewhere along the way, the competitive nature of English football at every level forced the game along a different path of pragmatism which was often devoid of any real talent or flair. As in so many other areas of the game, the rot sets in early, in the very traditions which made English football the best in the first place.

When a child reaches an age at which team play is possible, the game in England operates under a two-tier system which few other countries would tolerate. First there is the game as organised in schools, run by the English Schools Football Association (ESFA), an independent organisation affiliated to the FA. Then there is an entirely separate network organised around youth clubs, which comes loosely under the jurisdiction of the FA. The ESFA is the official body, having been established in 1904, and has tenaciously fought off challenges to its autonomy and influence over the years from the FA, the rise of the 'youth' game, and the professional clubs. The ESFA is staffed entirely by volunteers and all its coaches and team organisers are schoolteachers devoting their spare time free to promote the game they love. No one can question the good intentions of the ESFA. The organisation has, however, come under attack in recent times because of its pre-eminent role in the development of young players.

A number of circumstances coincided to make the 1980s a time of change in the youth game in England. First, FIFA's stated intention was to develop the international game by the introduction of 'mini World Cups' for Under-20, Under-18 and Under-16 (later to become Under-17) teams. The FA could enter teams in the Under-20 category, for which it held responsibility, but at Under-18 level its role was entwined with that of the ESFA. The ESFA has responsibility for boys who stay on at school until the age of eighteen and to this day runs an Under-18 international team entirely separate from the FA. The Under-15s were obviously under the control of the ESFA, since all boys were still at school. The FIFA competitions often came at a time of exams in England and since the ESFA is run by teachers, they take the view that academic work should take priority over sport. The ESFA is the custodian, not just of the gifted few who go on to become professionals, but also of the tens of thousands of good schoolboy players who will go no further than the amateur game, so will need all the qualifications they can get. These children will also form the bedrock of the next generation of fans and administrators.

Second was a growing nationwide feeling that saw competition as a bad thing among schoolchildren. English football at
all levels has historically been based on strong competition.
Thus schoolchildren play competitive games for their school
and if they are talented will turn out for any number of local
youth teams. The result is that a gifted young player plays four
or five games a week during the season. Support for the anti-
competition lobby came from the medical profession. New
techniques of diagnosis which emerged in the 1980s were used
on entrants to the FA's National School and an alarming
number of potential entrants – supposedly the best young
players in the country – were found to have serious injuries,
particularly stress fractures, the direct result of overplaying.

The third reason for the assault on the old ways was that
the debate over the decline in playing standards of English
professional football, which had long raged, began to be
focused on the young. Charles Hughes, the FA director of
national coaching, had developed his controversial theory of
'direct play' and believed that only by taking control of the
best young players out of the hands of the amateur coaches of
the ESFA could they be taught the method from an early age.
Hughes, with Bobby Robson's support, persuaded Vauxhall to
sponsor his National School, which would take the sixteen
best fourteen-year-olds and coach them in a boarding-school
environment, at the same time continuing their education.
The ESFA opposed the National School on the grounds that
it was élitist, too limited in its intake, and anyway it was
impossible to say which boys at fourteen years of age would
develop into future internationals as there were too many
imponderables. Perhaps more important, though, was the
criticism that it diverted funds away from other areas of the
youth game which could be used, for example, to provide
residential courses for hundreds of promising players, rather
than catering for a select few.

Finally, the professional clubs got in on the act and
demanded greater access to youngsters as an alternative to the
increasing dependence on the transfer market. Because of the
dominant position of the ESFA, clubs were only allowed to
coach boys for two hours a week. Many thought this was more
than enough since clubs had done little over the years to
convince people that they had the best interests of youngsters

at heart, often subjecting them to a sort of continuous trial rather than coaching them. For their part, the clubs felt that the restriction was a classic case of interference by amateurs who were putting the future of the professional game in jeopardy. Ron Noades, chairman of Crystal Palace, was convinced this was the case, saying, 'We must devise a system where the English schools do not have total control over the schoolboy's development. The clubs should have unrestricted access to boys who are looking to become professionals, just as they do on the continent.' To Noades, the problems of English football did not lie in the number of games played at the top level but rather in the way the game was taught at the bottom. 'If we don't put youth football right very soon,' he warned, 'we will not see any benefits for many years and we really will become a second- or third-rate football nation.'

The ESFA did not take the attacks on its position lying down. In fact it conducted an extremely effective fightback. From its headquarters in the quiet county town of Stafford it mobilised its power base to resist on every front. The main enemy in the ESFA's view was the FA, particularly Charles Hughes, who took every opportunity to press his case against the ESFA. During the course of the estrangement, the FA, then led by Ted Croker, tried to squeeze the ESFA financially. Croker supported Hughes because Hughes had delivered the Vauxhall sponsorship against all Croker's expectations, which had considerably strengthened Hughes' influence. Thus the national school went ahead despite fierce opposition from the ESFA.

In what proved to be a shrewd tactical move, the ESFA chose to fight its battle in the FA Council. As the governing body of the game all major decisions have to be ratified by the Council meeting in open session and voting on the issues. Charles Hughes' position began to be weakened as his theory of direct play was challenged on a number of fronts. The most damaging criticism came from John Cartwright, former technical director at the National School, who had resigned, publicly citing as his reason the disaffection he felt with the way the youth game was being organised and coached. 'Football here is an ugly fight, even in under-9 games,' he complained. 'We produce youngsters for the battlefield.' Cartwright particularly singled out his erstwhile boss, Charles Hughes, for criticism. His diatribes were also directed at the ESFA (mainly over the too-many-games issue), but it was Charles Hughes and his theories that bore the brunt of his attacks.

Behind the scenes, the ESFA, first under secretary Steve Allatt, then under chief executive Malcolm Berry, began to soften their position on a number of issues. The key to the eventual resolution of their differences with the FA was the appointment of Graham Kelly, who was more sympathetic to the ESFA's case than Ted Croker had been. The ESFA began to garner support from the professional clubs by agreeing in principle to increased access if an overall settlement could be achieved. The clubs threw in their lot with the ESFA because they disliked Charles Hughes' influence more than that of the ESFA. This was also a period, in the late 1980s, when the League was feeling powerful and was looking to advance itself on every front, particularly if it was at the expense of the FA. Eventually, an accommodation was reached between the Football League and the ESFA, which gave the ESFA the League's whole-hearted support. Part of this support, of course, would be exercised by League representatives on the FA Council.

The ESFA gave support to the idea of fewer games, although on closer inspection it was the youth clubs that would lose matches rather than the schools. It gained further support by agreeing that more attention should be paid to the teaching of skills. To show its commitment it embraced the Coerver Method, named after the Dutch coach, Weil Coerver, who invented it. In essence, Coerver analysed the special skills of the world's great players (the Cruyff turn, for example), broke their moves down into simple steps by watching video footage, then devised a way of teaching the skills to youngsters of virtually any age. There was no competitive element; indeed, Coerver display teams are reminiscent of formation dancers or synchronised swimmers. The kids were expected to use what they had learned when they played a game. Coerver also realised that by utilising the names of the children's heroes and teaching their unique abilities, he could demonstrate the pleasure that can be derived through mastering techniques which continually help youngsters control the ball. Since the method had been endorsed by FIFA the FA could do nothing but support the ESFA's initiative. The final master-stroke was to engage the whole of football in an open debate about an issue that had received scant publicity but was morally and politically correct and showed the ESFA as the most forward-thinking organisation in the British game. That issue was the participation of girls. The FA had long discouraged girls from playing with boys. The ESFA began a campaign for integration up to eleven years old, which the FA was eventually persuaded to vote through.

Surprisingly, the FA provides no regular funding for the youth game. It has occasionally helped the ESFA, most notably when it contributed to the costs of bringing over the Brazilian youth team in 1987, the first time it had played in Europe, but in the main, there was little financial help. When the FA began to seek control, all funds to the ESFA, however meagre, were cut off. The financial squeeze, while providing some cause for alarm, did not have the desired effect of putting the ESFA under pressure because it had long ceased to rely on the FA for its funding and had two lucrative Under-15 internationals at Wembley each year which brought in television and sponsorship income. By effective husbandry and an impressive list of sponsors, which includes British Gas, McDonalds, Smiths Crisps (a division of Pepsi-Cola) and Adidas, it saw off the FA's fiscal attack.

Eventually, a compromise was reached and hostilities ceased. Hughes was allowed more influence through centres of excellence which would now be regional and more often than not attached to professional clubs. The ESFA would support the centres of excellence through which the clubs would get increased access but the independence of the ESFA and all its activities was assured. The FA would take responsibility for youth teams in international competitions, but in return the ESFA was allowed to run an Under-16 team if it wished.

But where did this internecine battle leave the state of English youth football and its ability to produce the standard of player required? Today there are over 150 regional centres of excellence which take boys aged nine to sixteen with no time restrictions. Since most centres are at professional clubs this alone dramatically increases the time young players can spend at clubs. However, this may not necessarily be a good thing, since most English clubs do not possess a reputation for looking after young players. In addition, many youngsters are fine until they go to professional clubs, where all but the most determined have the natural skill coached out of them in the interests of team tactics.

The National School continues to attract criticism but its continuing existence seems certain for the foreseeable future at least. Costing in excess of £4 million since its inception in 1984, the National School had produced by 1993 twelve Under-21 internationals. In defence of this seemingly poor record the FA point out that graduates of the school are valued by their respective clubs for insurance purposes at more than £20 million.

The one thing that all parties have now agreed upon is that there is just too much competitive football played at too early an age. The issue is not quite that simple, though. There is too much competitive football for the really talented, but those who will never be professional footballers also have to be catered for and they enjoy the competition and look back on it in later years with fondness. It is to be hoped that increased time at clubs can resolve this inherent conflict of interests at youth level. Despite this, there is an understandable desire on the part of the whole country to produce world-class players at the professional level. The shift is certainly towards more emphasis being placed on the development of skills, and while this may result in a natural wastage of some competition, no one should underestimate the lure of the competitive instinct. The vast majority of ESFA sponsorship, for instance, is competition-based. Sponsors in the main prefer competition as they believe it gives them their best chance of exposure. The FA, which licenses the centres of excellence, intends to keep a watching brief to ensure that the onus is on the teaching of skills. Whether this fills anyone with confidence is another matter.

During the battles of the 1980s nobody, of course, thought the unthinkable: that perhaps we should look at the way other countries do it to see whether we could learn something from them. A gaze around Europe would reveal that the number of gifted players turned out in the last twenty years is nowhere greater, on a per capita basis, than Holland. One place the FA could have instructively looked at is the club that epitomises the Dutch way, Ajax Amsterdam.

There is no schools football to speak of in the Netherlands but to compensate most Dutch football clubs run teams and coaching schemes for every age group. A youngster can progress from nine years old to the first team at Ajax. Annual trials take place to select the best applicants and those who are successful attend coaching sessions three days a week. The emphasis is on skill and flexibility. In developing this programme, Ajax have their own interests at heart because the club cannot afford to hold on to its greatest stars – its ancient and small Van Meer stadium cannot generate sufficient income – and it must continually roll new candidates off its conveyor belt if it is to remain one of Europe's leading clubs.

There is a clear objective the Ajax coaches set for their players, Johan Cruyff has said. Players are taught to be 'alert' to all the possibilities when in possession of the ball. This awareness, according to Jan Wouters, the former Ajax midfielder now with Bayern Munich, lets 'everyone make the most of his position'. The Ajax style of player was perfected by the coach who set the club on its road to three consecutive European Cup triumphs between 1971 and 1974, Rinus Michels, and the man who was the embodiment of that success, Johan Cruyff. The supreme ability of the European Cup-winning sides was the versatility they displayed in what became known as total football. Wim Surbier and Ruud Krol were attacking full backs (Krol was later converted to sweeper); Arie Haan and particularly Johan Neeskens were world-class midfielders; Piet Keizer was a cultured left winger while Johnny Rep was a more than effective striker. But the most formidable of all was Johan Cruyff, who, with astonishing clairvoyance, could anticipate the movement around him, decide what was required and carry it out. The Ajax side also formed the nucleus of the Dutch national team which reached the World Cup finals of 1974 (when complacency cost the players football's greatest prize) and 1978, and the era of Michels and Cruyff left a legacy of, to use Michels' term, 'creative football', which has been maintained ever since through the likes of Ronald Koeman, Frank Rijkaard, Marco Van Basten and the latest sensation, Denis Bergkamp. Bergkamp symbolises the continuing process. He was at Ajax as a young child and was then picked out by the coach, none other than Johan Cruyff himself, from a group of eighteen-year-olds and promoted to the first team. His first appearance was as substitute for Arnold Muhren. Such was

Bergkamp's impact that he soon forced his way into the Dutch team alongside his predecessor at Ajax, Van Basten. It was inevitable that Bergkamp would go to Italy. Ajax simply cannot match the salaries that are on offer in the Italian League to the world's best players. Together with midfielder Wim Jonk, he was transferred to Inter in 1993 for a combined fee of £12 million. Through this acquisition Inter hope to recreate the Ajax attacking style and challenge their all-conquering neighbours, AC Milan. Indeed, Serie A could now stand for Serie Ajax as so many of the club's former players are now plying their trade south of the Alps.

The Ajax president, Michael Van Praag, who is the son of Jaap Van Praag, the Ajax president in the glory days of the 1970s, tried to explain the success of the Ajax youth policy: 'Our goal has always been the same: to produce 70 per cent of our squad from our youth scheme and ensure the kids coming through play the only type of football we know – attacking football. If richer clubs want to buy our players we find it difficult to refuse since we don't get a cent [of subsidy] from the Amsterdam council and we refuse to become the property of a company.' (A reference, perhaps to Ajax's arch-rival, PSV Eindhoven, which is owned by the multi-national electronics giant, Philips).

Amazingly, the first coach at Ajax who put emphasis on attacking play and the development of the junior structure was an Englishman, Jack Reynolds, in the late 1940s. The baton was then taken up by his successors and the dynasty founded. In 1993, the new stars off the production line were creating as much excitement as previous generations. Twenty-year-old Marc Overmars is the latest to be capped by Holland, while sixteen-year-old Clarence Seedorf is being hailed as the next midfield genius. Denis Bergkamp, who these players hope to emulate, told how the system develops the mental strength to succeed as well as the physical attributes needed at the highest level. 'At Ajax,' he said, 'we are young, we hold our heads high and we go on to the pitch with the belief that we are the best . . . I began here aged eleven thinking only one thing, attack. I also learned of the perpetual competitive environment. Right from the youngest, when a player doesn't make the grade, he is asked to leave. So when you stay at Ajax year after year you get the feeling you are the best. And the day you play for the first team you have all this past history supporting you. You know that you are the only one to have succeeded when a hundred others have failed. The Ajax players will always have this pride, the drive to always be the best.'

So Ajax in particular and the Dutch in general have not eschewed the competitive spirit. In fact, it is part of the reason for the club's success but, unlike in the English game, the competition is not altogether match-based. The emphasis is on the development of skills rather than the ability to win kick-and-rush junior games. There seems to be a consensus that this is the right way forward, whereas the English continually indulge in petty squabbles over who is in control, which has completely overshadowed the requirement for fresh thinking in the interests of future development. The Dutch rarely win at youth level but that is not their concern. The end product for them is not a successful Under-15 team but young players who enjoy themselves and the production of gifted professionals.

Another club that could have something to teach the English is Auxerre in France, a small club which nonetheless has produced its own conveyor belt of talent through a youth scheme based on a centre of excellence. Each year, sixteen youngsters, including a maximum of four foreigners, are chosen to enter its academy (in recent years these have included two graduates from the FA National School, Jamie Forrester and Kevin Sharp). There are twenty-eight teams at Auxerre from the French First Division side all the way to regional leagues and youth teams. In recent times, French international goalkeepers Joel Bats and Bruno Martini, as well as Eric Cantona and Basile Boli, have emerged from the Auxerre system. The club employs five full-time coaches and two part-time, including two women who look after the younger children between six and nine years old.

At Auxerre, everything is under the control of Guy Roux, who became coach in 1963, aged twenty-three, when Auxerre were in the *Division D'honneur*, the French equivalent of the Beazer Homes League. From there, Roux has taken them through the divisions, Wimbledon-like, to the point where they are now an established First Division club. After narrowly losing to Liverpool in the UEFA Cup in 1991, they almost went all the way in 1993, eventually losing on penalties in the semi-final to Borussia Dortmund, having beaten Ajax in the previous round. Roux puts the success of Auxerre down to the system – the children, the teams, the coaches and the continual search to improve methods.

While the continentals were developing these articles of faith, the English carried on as if nothing had changed. In fact, the argument in England became bogged down in a futile debate over Charles Hughes' theories of direct play. Keen to discover 'what were the common denominators of the best teams', Hughes looked at the most successful teams in World Cup finals, starting with England in 1966. He then added Liverpool and the England Under-21 and Under-16 teams as being representative of success at club and junior levels respectively. From his analysis, Hughes came to the conclusion that over 80 per cent of goals came from moves of five passes or fewer. From this he determined that elaborate passing moves rarely ended in goals and that the best way to play – the winning formula – was to move the ball forward as soon as possible. Hughes maintains that when possession is gained, the ball should immediately be played into the opposition's danger area, as they will be at their most vulnerable when they have just lost the ball.

As the FA's director of coaching, Hughes lays down the strategy for coaching across the whole range of the English game. While professional clubs and, for that matter, the England team, go their own way in coaching matters, Hughes' position still carries weight. At the youth level his policy is carried out at the centres of excellence and the National School. His ideas, however, have come under constant attack, Malcolm Allison and George Best, for instance, have both recently accused him of being a malign influence on English football. Hughes' reply is that his theories are deliberately misunderstood. 'The media have chosen not to look at the facts and not to portray them accurately,' he said. It is somewhat ironic that Hughes cites great players like Cruyff, Beckenbauer and Best as exemplifying direct play. 'I could persuade George Best that I'm nearer to his concept of football than he thinks,' Hughes declared. 'He would do a lot of things in direct play that prove my point. For example, the ability to run with the ball, dribble and shoot – that's the embodiment of direct play.' George Best, however, saw the game as a canvas upon which he could paint an infinite variety of differing and complex images. He did indeed employ his talents to the effect Hughes described – but he also often deliberately kept the ball away from the opposition's danger area until he was ready to exploit a momentary lapse in concentration with a piece of impudent skill.

Bobby Charlton tells a story of how, during a league game, Best received the ball out wide, beat the full back, waited for him to recover, then beat him again. He moved inside, turned and went back out to the wing. Charlton, believing himself in a good position, was exasperated. 'Pass it, pass it!' he shouted. Best took no notice as he juggled the ball from foot to foot. 'Pass it, for Christ's sake, pass it!' Still no response. Charlton was now angry and started to berate his team-mate. 'Jesus, Besty, why don't you pass the bloody . . . What a goal!' True to form, Best had suddenly, with the minimum of backlift, unleashed an unstoppable shot just as the goal-keeper was lulled into believing there was no danger.

Charles Hughes is irritated that the teams which are often cited as examples of direct play are Wimbledon and Sheffield United. 'If they possessed the skills of direct play then they wouldn't play their way,' he says, 'because there are better and more effective alternatives. To play directly, you need high levels of technical efficacy and if you don't have the technique there will be many occasions when you can't play directly'. However, in *The Winning Formula*, Hughes states categorically that direct play is achieved by getting the ball forward as quickly as possible. Dave Bassett has merely taken him at his word, but Hughes insists that it is limited teams which will resort to the long ball, perceived by his critics to be the be-all and end-all of direct play. If there is a preponderance of ordinary players over gifted ones then the most obvious form of direct play will be the long, high ball and because limited teams outnumber gifted teams, direct play is damned by its ubiquity.

More heinous in Hughes' eyes than the long-ball merchants are gifted teams which he thinks fail to make the most of the players' abilities. They will jockey for an opening, playing the ball backwards and sideways, when in Hughes' view it should be played forward at every opportunity.

One of Hughes' main problems lies in the differing interpretations of statistics. For instance, Hughes breaks down goals into categories. These include set plays. From his analysis Holland have not scored any goals in World Cup finals from more than five passes. This, of course, obscures the real story and perhaps the real lesson. The first goal the Dutch scored in the 1974 final came from a penalty and thus goes down in Hughes' analysis as a goal from a set play. What his analysis fails to reflect, however, is what went on before in the move which led to the foul that resulted in the penalty. From the kick-off, Holland strung seventeen passes together, including a number going sideways or backwards. The Germans did not touch the ball during this period. Eventually, a foul was committed out of frustration at not being able to gain possession. The goal certainly came from a penalty but the penalty was won through an intricate series of passes – though Hughes would say the penalty was won only after Cruyff launched a direct run on goal. This is why so many people question the validity of statistics. They do not (and can never) tell the whole story. Brazil's second goal in a 1990 friendly against France at Parc des Princes came after a move of more than a dozen passes. The Hughes idea of direct play was apparent only at the culmination of the move which was designed to find an opening. Once the gap was found, direct play could increase the tempo and catch the defence unawares.

Hughes believes that the whole world could learn from his ideas. He is reported to have said on a coaching trip to the USA in 1989: 'Brazil have got it wrong in their method of playing.' Having come under severe criticism for such a statement, he clarified his position, saying, 'Strategically they [the Brazilians] haven't got it right. I think technically they are marvellous, and I wish we were as good as they are technically. They can control the ball, their first touch is good, they play the ball with accuracy. When they play the ball forward they can play it through small gaps and they can play it over people's heads with the right weight. They can turn with the ball and they can run with the ball. They can shoot and they can dribble. All these are techniques I think are marvellous. I can't understand why they pass the ball square and back so often and therefore negate those attacking qualities. So whilst I would be very critical of Brazil it is a strategic criticism not a technical criticism. Their technique is very good, their strategies not so good. If they do get their strategy right they will be a tremendous force to be reckoned with.' Once again, though, there is an alternative view. It can be stated quite simply. Brazil have won the World Cup three times, are the only country to have won a World Cup outside their own continent and, even when their standards fall below those set between 1958 and 1970, they remain a tremendous force to be reckoned with.

Perhaps the debate is a case of 'to thine own self be true'. Paul Breitner, a former captain of West Germany, eloquently summed up why football is such a fascinating game, particularly at international level, where the clash is as much between cultural approaches which dictate the way national teams play as it is a battle of tactics. Speaking about the success of West Germany, he said: 'It goes back to 1974 in football, as in other areas like economic life. Everyone wanted to change things to the German way. It's not possible. Nobody can implant the German mentality, whether it's a question of play or training. In the mid-1970s the Brazilians . . . changed their approach. They didn't go to the beach but to the training ground instead. It was a fiasco because, in trying to remodel their flair, it stripped Brazil of their skills, their intuition and their ball sense.' Breitner is surely right. The Brazilians excel when they are able to combine a naturally languid style with the injection of explosive and sustained pace at crucial moments. The Brazilian sees a sideways or backward pass as a means of probing for an opponent's weakness. When they tried to play a more direct, German type of game, they were simply unable to cope. Likewise, it is difficult to see any other country making some of the comebacks the Germans have managed: Leon in 1970, during the Mexico World Cup, for instance, turning a 2–0 deficit against England into a 3–2 win; sixteen years later, again in Mexico, when they fought back against Maradona's Argentina, again from 2–0 down, only to lose at the last gasp by 3–2. More recently, in the US Cup in 1993, they staged a remarkable comeback against Brazil. Losing 3–0 inside half an hour to some scintillating Brazilian football which had reporters favourably comparing the South Americans with the

1970 side, the Germans seized their chance in the second half
when the Brazilians eased off slightly and the game ended in
a 3–3 draw. Each nation gives to football its own special
variation on the theme.

Arguments have continued in England about the best way
to play. It is as if confidence has been lost in any uniquely
English style. That style has not always been as it is now
perceived. In the past, the technique and flair of Stanley
Matthews, Tom Finney, Duncan Edwards, Johnny Haynes,
Jimmy Greaves and Bobby Charlton, to name but a few, were
stamped indelibly on England's way of playing. In 1993,
England qualified for the Under-20 World Cup finals in
Australia. Charles Hughes stayed in London and the side was
coached by David Burnside, a former West Bromwich Albion
forward, who as a youngster used to entertain the crowd at the
Hawthorns with his ball-juggling skills during the half-time
break. Burnside's team finished third in the championship,
the highest position England have ever achieved, but in the
process the team drew some stinging criticism for a complete
lack of imagination in their play. The England formation was
based on safety first, not to lose seemed the main idea and the
tactical plan looked to be based on not conceding a goal by
stifling the game. Playing with only one forward baffled the
Australian public. It baffled a few people back home, too,
particularly since Nicky Barmby, Tottenham's young prodigy,
was asked to plough a lone furrow up front for most of the
time. Trevor Brooking observed in his column in the *Sunday
Express* that 'creative midfield play is virtually impossible
when there is only one forward target available and so most
of the threatening goalscoring chances have to come from set
pieces such as corners or long throws.'

It baffled Charles Hughes, too. He had seen the team play in
the warm-up games before they left England and told David
Burnside bluntly: 'You won't win it that way.' (A view shared
by George Best, who said: 'If you're only playing with one
guy up front you're not going to win anything.') Hughes'
criticism was that he thought Burnside's 4-5-1 formation did
not make the best use of the players' abilities. 'I know the
skills Barmby has,' he said, 'I knew what he could bring to the
party. If we could have played with two up front – it wouldn't
have required a great rearrangement of the players – that

would have taken not just the pressure off Barmby but it would have allowed him to display some of his attacking skills. There's no point in turning with the ball with no one up front. So we've taken out Barmby's particular skills and I know that is a 20 per cent factor as an element in scoring goals. That can't be good strategic thinking. That's got to be wrong. Therefore, we come back to the basic concept of management, which is this: it's getting the best out of the players as individuals and the best out of them as a team. So if we start by saying this skill [turning with the ball] is very difficult to apply but Barmby happens to be able to do it and we take it out, we won't get the best out of Barmby. And as Barmby happens to be a key player . . . we won't get the best out of the players in the team. We have therefore negated the first principle of management and I don't see how you are going to succeed on that basis. It really is as simple as that, and a succession of England team managers have fallen at that point.'

Ken Bates didn't think Barmby should have gone to Australia at all. Before the tournament Tottenham had tried to argue that the player was needed at home. Bates agreed, claiming that he would learn more playing for Spurs than he would in an international tournament on the other side of the world.

Despite the fact that Hughes is director of national coaching, David Burnside was able to insist that since he was specifically employed to coach the team going to Australia, he must be able to decide how that team played. Once the criticism began to mount in the Australian media, Burnside became somewhat defensive and at one stage he was reported to have alluded to tactics being decided in London, which the media took to mean devised by Charles Hughes. Hughes stood accused not only of instituting the tactical plan but of not even going to Australia to see it applied. At least he gained some of the credit for the Under-18 team, which won the European Championship, and the Under-21 side, which was victorious in the Toulon tournament (both in the summer of 1993). In both competitions, the 4-5-1 formation used by Burnside was eschewed in favour of playing two up front.

In Australia, when Nicky Barmby was injured, Leicester's boy wonder, Julian Joachim, played the lone role. In fact it was mainly through Joachim's brilliance rather than Burnside's tactics that England got so far in the tournament. While Barmby is a player who is at his best when bringing others into the game, Joachim is more individualistic. The injury to Barmby thus paradoxically helped England, since Joachim was better able to handle the isolation up front and scored the goal that gave England third place. By sticking to his guns so vehemently, Burnside displayed the lack of insight so common in the English game. When asked why he refused to play Barmby and Joachim in the same side, he replied, 'Why should we? We've been playing this way for two years and have only lost one competitive match – excluding penalty shoot-outs – in that time.' The enlightening part of this explanation is that Burnside chose to emphasise matches not lost rather than matches won. David Lacey provided the most telling comment on this attitude. Writing in the *Guardian*, he argued that: 'Too many of the performances were designed to win a useful point at Stoke rather than glory in Sydney.' Furthermore, at youth level, surely the task is to give young players a taste of international competition so that they can later make the transition to full internationals more easily. The requirement is surely to express skills rather than win. And anyway, England didn't win, they finished third. That nation with the bad strategies, Brazil, won the tournament, playing a skilful, exciting game of attacking football with lots of passes.

Whatever the rights and wrongs in Australia, what happened showed once again that when it comes to strategies and tactics, England simply do not have any which are consistently applied. It is all very well debating the best methods of playing but what the young player really needs is the opportunity to develop both mental and physical skills. While the arguments over who is right rage it is hardly surprising that the players themselves are beset by confusion. This is why the systems at Ajax, Auxerre and any number of other places are so important. They provide the environment and the basic philosophy – to succeed through the development of skill. Tactics can come later.

The confusion was evident once again in the senior ranks as England played a vital World Cup qualifying tie against a depleted Dutch side at Wembley in April 1993. England's start to the match was stunning: they were two goals up before the Dutch had settled, including a splendid free kick from John Barnes (inevitably, David Platt scored the other). By the end of the game, however, the euphoria had worn off as Holland came back to force a 2–2 draw. The first Dutch goal, a delicate volley from Bergkamp after a delicious chip from Wouters had opened up the English defence, was bad enough, but worse was to come as Des Walker gave away a penalty with only five minutes to go when, ominously, he was beaten for pace by the young Overmars. Although the England performance was satisfactory in many respects and poor defensive play by both sides contributed to an open, exciting match, the plain fact was that England had dropped another home point to one of their main rivals. With away games in Poland and Norway coming up, the outlook for England was not good. Tactically, the team became more exposed the longer the game went on. When Ruud Gullit was substituted, for instance, England were left with three centre backs (Adams, Walker and Keown), none of whom seemed to know who he was supposed to mark.

In the end, although there were certainly some things to admire, England's inflexibility, compounded by tactical naïveté, let the Dutch back into a game that should have been well and truly beyond them. Where the team would go from here was anyone's guess. Two differing views come from Glenn Hoddle and Johan Cruyff. Hoddle thinks England have the players but do not have a system to get the best out of them, while Cruyff believes that the country no longer produces enough world-class performers. Either way, it was a sad reflection of the complete absence, at all levels of the game, of any consistent policy whatsoever.

While confusion reigned at home, Europe was gathering itself together for another radical rethink. The English game still believes it is respected around the world but the credit balance is sliding alarmingly towards the red. If Europe comes up with another change in structure, the English will be once again in severe danger of being left far behind, this time with even direr consequences than in the past. Unlike on previous occasions, when the English stayed aloof, this time they will be excluded on merit.

13

The Italian Job

Silvio Berlusconi, with the help of Marco Van Basten, conquers Milan and Italy. Next comes Europe and the world

> *'The objective was to entertain people because from entertainment, from spectacle, comes results.'*
>
> Franco Baresi (Milan and Italy).

> *'He may be successful with the newspapers and television channels but no one would know of Berlusconi without football. He is simply using Milan to gain fame. He is not interested in the human aspect, only the economics.'*
>
> Jurgen Klinsmann (ex-Internazionale and Germany).

Italian football has always been rich. In the late fifties and early sixties, the Italian game raided Britain and took away some of the most revered names in the country, including John Charles, Joe Baker, Denis Law and Jimmy Greaves. Once overseas players got to Italy, the bonuses offered by clubs to win important games always astonished the rest of Europe, especially England, where up until relatively recently pay structures had been set in stone and the award of an England cap was considered incentive enough, thus obviating the need to offer anything so sordid as large sums of money.

In Italy, football is a classless pursuit whose patrons consist of all sections of the population. The strongly regionalised bias of Italian society ensures that aspiring businessmen and politicians like to be seen at games and if possible become involved with their local clubs. Because of football's importance to

Italian life and culture, to be associated with the game is good for both an individual's business fortunes and his social progress. Ernesto Pellegrini was unknown outside his own industry – catering – until he became president of Internazionale. Now he is a household name, prompting a remark when Inter lifted the League title in 1989, which has been attributed to Gianni Agnelli, owner of Fiat and Juventus. 'Look!' Agnelli is reported to have said, 'our chef has won the Championship.' The president of a Serie A or even a Serie B club is as important as any politician. Often, they are one and the same. Achille Lauro, for example, was a shipping owner who owed the political status he gained to a large number of grateful Neapolitans. They voted for him as a reward for turning Napoli into a front-rank club. At the other end of the scale, the mass of the populace is also passionately involved, often committing body and soul to the local team. Indeed, everybody is expected to have a view from the prime minister to Sophia Loren.

The attitude of the Italian government to the game has been shaped by the country's history. Benito Mussolini helped create a national consciousness in a young nation but, because of fascism and war, national values were discredited. Sport filled the void, with football and Ferrari becoming the most important symbols of national pride. All sport in Italy is supervised by the Italian Olympic Committee (Coni), which is itself financed through the state-run football pools (Toto Calcio). The Italian Football Federation is responsible to Coni, which has become an important political force through its access to the purse-strings controlled by politicians. Thus politics and sport are inextricably linked and are seen to be so. The president of the Italian Federation, Antonio Matarrese, is an MP, a man of status and power derived from a family background of privilege. Even someone as advantaged as he is can find it easier to fulfil his ambitions through football.

A further reason for the success of the finances of Italian football is one that does not seem to be understood in the UK. Each game possesses a scarcity value and is an event in its own right. Until recently, the Italian Serie A comprised only sixteen teams and would probably have reverted back to that from the current eighteen-team, thirty-four-game structure if the national side had been drawn in a seven-nation qualifying group for the 1994 World Cup, instead of the six-team

Group 1. With every game important, the revenue each gen-
erates far exceeds that of clubs in England and Scotland
where games proliferate (over £1 million accrues from gate
receipts alone in the Milan and Turin derbies). With the
Italian Cup considered a secondary competition despite being
a route into Europe, a fan has a mere seventeen home League
games to attend.

These considerable benefits have been boosted in recent
times by the advent of huge television fees being paid for
football matches. It was in Italy that rights fees first became
inflated in the mid-1980s following the establishment of Silvio
Berlusconi's Canale 5 network, which made its name with
some audacious bids for football rights. This led the state
television service, RAI, to offer enormous sums to screen the
same football matches it had previously secured for a minimal
amount. No matter what television was prepared to pay,
however, two controls were exerted by the football authorities
which were conceded in England the moment the money on
offer began to multiply. First, there would be no live league
matches on television, although a host of highlights in
recorded form were allowed. For £60 million per season, RAI
alone transmitted four football programmes on its three
channels on Sundays. There are also review, discussion and
preview programmes on most other days of the week. Although
RAI continues to dominate, goals in league matches are
deemed to contain news value, facilitating the transmission of
hours of football on a weekly basis by Berlusconi and other
independent stations. This helps fulfil, along with the three
daily sports papers, a seemingly insatiable public appetite for
news of the game and those who play it, coach it or run it.

The second proviso the Italian authorities insisted upon
was that the traditional football day, Sunday, was preserved
intact. Television was not allowed to make changes to the
scheduling of games. The protection of a weekly day of
focus may seem trivial, yet it has a profound effect on the
perception of the game. Spreading the league programme
across a number of days dissipates interest since few
supporters can devote three days a week to watching live
games on television. When football is totally or in large part
concentrated on one day, the whole nation tends to give the
game its attention and it becomes a cherished ritual. When it

is diffused, only the hard-core fan with little else to do can keep up with all the events as they unfold. The home of commercialisation, the USA, recognised this important truth. There, professional American Football is played on Sundays (Saturday is reserved for the college game), with one game only moved to Monday night.

There are signs that Italy may be moving in this direction. When teams have brought forward their league matches to aid their European Cup preparations, RAI has been given the rights to broadcast them live. This has set a precedent. With the domestic television contract up for renewal in 1993, RAI pressed for one game to be taken out of the Sunday afternoon schedules for live transmission on Sunday evening. For this concession RAI were prepared to pay more than double their previous outlay and offered almost £130 million in rights fees for one season. Little resistance to the proposal came from the clubs, or the pools, in contrast to their previous position. If that is the only change, it may be, as in the American model, that the position of the game is actually enhanced as television viewers the world over are now more interested in live action. The problems will come if the Italians follow the English model, which started with one game being moved but has now demolished what for decades had been English football's day of focus, Saturday.

RAI's offer was, in the event, resisted by the federation but they did agree to sell one Serie B and one Serie A game a week (except for the last six weeks of the season) to be transmitted live on Saturday night and Sunday night respectively to the subscription channel, Tele Piu 2, which paid almost £20 million for the privilege. It is the first time league football has been allowed on national television on a regular basis but the restricted penetration of Tele Piu 2 will ensure that the live event is not endangered. RAI kept its rights for the recorded matches but had to increase its payment to over £66 million. The important point is that the Italians were prepared to accept less money (£86 million, as opposed to £130 million) in order to get the contract they wanted and restrict the amount of football on television.

Before television ruled the roost in England, the Saturday day of focus was sacrosanct. The readiness with which the football authorities were prepared to abandon it at the first hint of a pot of gold, however, brings home the realisation that most good things in the administration of the English game are there by accident or through the foresight of an earlier generation. By placing restrictions on television output, the Italians have forced the television companies to innovate and to offer the public a better product. The Italians began to use more cameras, they have perfected the use of slow motion – *la moviola* –also known as 'the eye of truth' in a way the BBC can only dream about.

After the Italian national team's disastrous performance in the World Cup in 1966, when the players returned home at the end of the first round having been knocked out by North Korea and encountered a hostile crowd which pelted them with rotten fruit, the Italians decided to continue a ban on foreign imports which had been introduced the previous year to help the national team in its preparations. As memories of the débâcle in England receded, however, and Italian club sides' performances in European competitions suffered, so the clamour started to ease the rules on overseas stars. Those who argued for a return to tradition were vindicated, first by the incredible success of Michel Platini and his all-conquering Juventus, then by the way Diego Maradona single-handedly galvanised a moribund Napoli, a club which had never before won the Championship, to two League titles. During this period, a number of Italian clubs again put their faith in British players. Trevor Francis, Mark Hateley, Graeme Souness, Paul Elliot and Ray Wilkins all did well, but none apart from Liam Brady matched the two outstanding successes of a previous era, Gerry Hitchens and John Charles. Both of these, like the more successful of their successors, found the key to be their ability to integrate into the Italian way of life. Others, like Luther Blisset and Ian Rush, struggled. Brady in particular is remembered with enduring affection by Italian fans. He won the Championship with Juventus in 1981 and finished that season as their top goalscorer with eight from midfield. That feat was repeated the following season and Brady even took a vital penalty against Catanzaro in the last game of the season when a win was required to secure the title. Most of his colleagues didn't want to know, and although Brady knew at the time he was to be discarded in favour of Platini, he took responsibility, scored the goal in a 1–0 win and is remembered for his courage as well as his skill. Subsequently, he played with distinction for Sampdoria and Inter and finished a seven-season career in Serie A with Ascoli.

None of the three England internationals playing in Italy in 1993 was an unqualified success. Injury and fitness problems, as well as coming to terms with the Roman way of life, hampered Paul Gascoigne but sporadically there have been brilliant cameos and some important goals (a last-gasp equaliser in the Rome derby, for instance). David Platt, following his transfer from relegated Bari to Juventus, found it hard to command a regular place and when he did get into the team he was asked to play a holding role in midfield which nullified one of his most impressive attributes, the ability to time runs into the penalty box and score goals. By the end of the 1992–93 season, Platt was hardly called upon at all, although he, like Gascoigne, could recall some important goals for his new club. At the end of the season, England's leading goalscorer was deemed surplus to requirements and he was sold to Sampdoria for £5 million. It was his third Italian club in three seasons and he had been involved in transfers worth £17 million. The most disappointing of all the English players, though, was Des Walker. After Italia '90 he was recognised as one of the world's best defenders. He joined Sampdoria to play in central defence with Pietro Vierchowod but they duplicated each other's roles and Walker was unsuccessfully tried at left back before being relegated to the substitutes' bench. Sven Goran Eriksson, the Sampdoria coach, admitted that Walker was the casualty of his poor planning but in Italy there is rarely an opportunity for a second chance. At the end of the 1992–93 season Walker was on his way back to England, where Sheffield Wednesday paid £2.5 million for his services.

By 1993, the Italians had bought up a large percentage of the world's greatest footballers. This elevated the already impressive Serie A to the undisputed status of the best League in the world, with the best players, the biggest audience (both on television and live) and the highest revenue from sponsors and the gate. (Channel 4 trailed its coverage of the 1993–94 season with the slogan, 'Watch the World's Premier League'.) Since the early eighties, television coverage of the Italian League has been sold abroad, at first to South America to follow the Brazilian stars, Falcao and Zico. Despite already possessing some of the world's best players, the Italian game was never as popular abroad as the English game with its thrills and spills, goalmouth incident and committed play. By 1992, however, even England was showing Italian League football and Serie A had left the Premier League far behind in the quality entertainment stakes. Channel 4's *Football Italia* has not just concentrated on English exiles but has capitalised on the lack of network coverage of domestic league football to gain an average audience of just under 2 million. Delighted with this success, Channel 4 increased its commitment from twenty-four to thirty live games in the first season of transmission. With the League now shown in sixty-five countries, it is no exaggeration to say that the Italian game is awash with money.

Alongside the income, Italian football has always lived with the taint of scandal. The most famous examples came in European matches during the 1970s when a simple method – nobbling the ref – was employed in an attempt to give Italian clubs a winning hand in a game of increasingly high stakes. The list of offenders, which included Inter, Juventus and Roma, and the feeble response from UEFA, has been chronicled by Brian Glanville in his excellent book, *Champions of Europe*, and in his numerous articles for *The Sunday Times*. However, as in France, at least domestic transgressions are investigated vigorously and, more often than not, punished. In 1980, Felice Colombo, president of Milan, was found guilty of attempting to bribe Lazio players and the club was relegated from Serie A. Colombo's successor, Giussy Farina, was forced to flee the country, leaving behind a legacy of a corrupt regime, a mountain of debt and a record of illegal payments to players. The Colombo and Farina scandals lifted the lid off a dustbin of widespread chicanery which reached the very top. Paolo Rossi, one of the greats of Italian football, whose goals brought victory in the 1982 World Cup and who, according to *Gazzetta dello Sport*, was 'synonymous with Italy at least as much as pizza and Pope John-Paul II' (who is, in fact, Polish), was banned from the game for a year when in his prime for his role in a betting scandal. More recently, Roma were under investigation for financial irregularities and were given a strict deadline by which they had to comply with the demands of the League or face the consequences.

At the same time the stability of Italian society generally

has been shaken by a series of political and commercial scandals (high-ranking politicians, including ex-prime ministers, and Fiat executives have been charged with corruption and bribery) and as a natural consequence, given the link between football, business and politics, Italian football has also come under investigation. Corrado Ferlaino of Napoli, the longest-serving president in Serie A, has been arrested and charged with bribing local politicians to the tune of £300,000 for favours to his construction company in the distribution of contracts intended to help the victims of the 1980 earthquake. Roma's president, Giuseppe Ciarrapico, as well as having to contend with the problems over his club's finances, was also charged with improper use of funds belonging to a group of health clinics, while a precautionary warrant was issued to Lazio's president, Sergio Cragnotti.

Following the Milan scandals of the early 1980s, the return to Serie A was immediate, and the club did fairly well in the next three seasons, finishing eighth, fifth and seventh. Enter Silvio Berlusconi. Born the son of a bank manager in Milan in 1936, Berlusconi studied law at the city's university before working as a tour guide, then a photographer and sometimes a singer in the coastal resorts of the Adriatic. He first came to the attention of the Italian public in the 1960s, when he developed a number of housing projects. In 1978 he moved into television when he created the Canale 5 network, which was at the time illegal. The law protected RAI's monopoly position and the establishment of another national channel was banned. Berlusconi cunningly circumnavigated the legislation by putting together a network of local stations under the collective title of Canale 5. He provided them with tapes of popular American soaps like Dallas which all the stations broadcast simultaneously. After a long battle, Canale 5 was eventually legitimised and Berlusconi's business was set to take off. Since then, he has established two further channels (Rete 4 and Italia 7), a publishing empire of newspapers, magazines and books, an advertising agency, film and video production, distribution companies, a chain of cinemas and a film library containing thousands of Hollywood titles. When these are added to his non-media interests, such as insurance, financial services and retailing, the astronomical income produced makes Berlusconi one of Europe's wealthiest men. His family-controlled Fininvest group, with a turnover of $9 billion and profits of over $150 million, is Italy's third-largest private company. But perhaps his most prized possession is a comparatively small, bankrupt company he acquired in 1986; Athletico Calcio Milan, the football club he had supported since he was a boy.

'At that time', Berlusconi said, 'Milan was a forgotten squad, a team that no longer made the headlines. Somebody had to come along and make sure that everyone said Milan is back.' It did not take Berlusconi long to realise how the status his control of Milan brought could be used to boost all sections of his empire. A period of what he called 'symbiosis' followed, whereby the Milan name and the club's players were used as publicity vehicles for other parts of Berlusconi's business empire. It is perhaps no coincidence that Berlusconi's operations, already large by Italian standards, took a quantum leap towards the real giants of global communications like Time Warner and Sony-CBS only after he had purchased the Milan football club. Although it accounts for only a half of 1 per cent of his turnover, its contribution in terms of attracting other business spin-offs is incalculable. And the profile a successful Milan brought could not be acquired by any amount of advertising or PR campaigns. With Milan, Berlusconi could really challenge RAI, but to succeed the team had to become champions because that brought with it live television rights to the most important club competition of them all, the European Cup. Already Berlusconi recognised that to become a successful television station in Italy, some exclusive football is a prerequisite.

Berlusconi's commitment to commercial television was laid bare when he said it was 'a gift we have given to improve the lives of tens of millions of viewers throughout Europe'. Thus his plan for Milan fitted exactly into his wider strategy for the rest of his empire. He announced himself to the Milanese faithful in dramatic fashion, arriving with the players in his helicopter in a show of personal wealth and power. To achieve the breakthrough he wanted, Berlusconi did two things. He made money available to bring Europe's best players to Milan and he hired a coach whom he believed could produce a style of play that would excite, first Milan, then Italy and the world, creating a winning team in the process. He certainly recognised the value of producing entertaining football, not just in the abstract, aesthetic sense, but because it was good for business. With an attractive team, more people will pay to watch live and even more will want to watch on television. 'A quality game is very important,' Berlusconi stated. 'The game is a spectacle. It fills stadia, it gathers masses of viewers around the television and gets readers for newspapers.'

The man Berlusconi employed to take charge of team matters was Arrigo Sacchi, now the coach of the Italian national team, then a respected Serie B coach, but hardly a well-known figure. Sacchi had impressed Berlusconi when his Parma team, using tactics which attempted to marry British athleticism to Italian technique, had given Milan a tough contest in the Italian Cup. It is to Berlusconi's credit that he saw in this obscure, unpretentious man the tactical genius to head the *rossoneri* (red and blacks) challenge and question the attritional attitude of the traditional Italian method. Most owners want a winning team. They believe that fans will soon forget any poverty in the playing style. Berlusconi wanted more. He wanted a winning team that pleased, not just the Milan faithful, but the whole world.

In Sacchi's first season at the helm in Milan the team finished fifth, but it was already clear that something special was happening in Lombardy. With good players at his disposal he refined the pressing game, which was based on a highly mobile attack-minded side pressurising opponents. This was accomplished by compressing the play in the opposition's half. To succeed, the attacking style had to be complemented by a commitment to high work-rate and physical presence. Through these means, Sacchi began to destroy the old defence-first attitude that had stifled Italian football for so long. Under Sacchi's system, defenders, midfield players and forwards challenged opponents as soon as the team lost possession of the ball, rather than dropping back until the other side reached a danger area. This owed something to the British approach but required a higher level of technical ability to make it work against the best defences in the world. This was supplied by what became the most potent attacking force in world football, the Dutch trio of Ruud Gullit, Marco Van Basten and Frank Rijkaard.

Van Basten and Gullit arrived in Milan in 1987 but the team did not have sufficient quality in midfield to bring out the best in the Dutchmen. Berlusconi was determined that Milan should assume its rightful place at the very top of world club football and to achieve that he was prepared to pay whatever was necessary. So when Sacchi said that with the addition of Rijkaard he would have a Championship-winning team, Berlusconi was happy to sanction the outlay of another £1.8 million. The money was well spent. The performances turned in by the Milan team of 1987–88, when they stormed to a first *scudetto* (title) in nine years, recalled the days of Silvio Berlusconi's youth, when a similar attack-minded Milan won the Championship in 1951 with a side based on three Swedish imports, Gren, Nordhall and Liedholm. Berlusconi was an instant hero and his companies saw a huge increase in business as everyone wanted to be associated with the man who had not only restored the pride of the Milanese, but had transformed the negative image of Italian club football. Not only was it the best, technically, it was about to become the most exciting. 'I think,' mused Berlusconi, 'our games are the most popular with television companies around the world who show football. That's a direct result of the quality of our game; that's why the standard of our game is extremely important.'

Conquering Europe was Berlusconi's next ambition, both in his business empire and with Milan. In fact, the success of Milan in the European Cup became an integral part of Berlusconi's overall plans for the expansion of his media interests. Milan duly won the European Cup, setting the competition alight with the kind of performances fans had not seen for a generation. The semi-final matches against Real Madrid, who Milan dismissed 5–0 at San Siro, will long be remembered. The final, against Steaua Bucharest in Barcelona, was no exception, as Milan crushed the Romanians 4–0. It was Berlusconi's promise fulfilled. He had said there would be a 'big show' in Barcelona and he was absolutely right. 'Eighty thousand Milanese have come to Barcelona and that's a real victory,' was how Berlusconi summed it up, adding, 'This is not just a European Cup but it is a cup of love for the club.'

The same season, Milan's great city rivals, Internazionale, with a German contingent of Mathaus, Brehme and, later, Klinsmann, won the League as Milan, perhaps with their eyes on the European Cup, were runners-up. In a sense, it was the perfect outcome. It set things up for a season in which two clubs from the same city were in the European Cup – the first time that had happened since 1969, when the two Manchester clubs were in the competition – and thus heralded a money-spinning year and even more publicity for Berlusconi. But it also had a deeper significance. Sacchi had banished the old ideas in Italian football. This precursed a national self-examination by Italians in all spheres of social and political life. In the process a resurgent regionalism gained widespread support. Nowhere was it more successful than in Lombardy, where the Lombard League, one of the old northern political leagues that based its right-wing, anti-corruption philosophy on the exploits of the medieval Lombard knights who fought against the Holy Roman Empire and had, in the twentieth century, given the country Mussolini, became a serious political force for the first time since the 1930s. In 1993 a coalition of the various leagues under the general banner of the Northern League swept to power in local elections, smashing the Socialists and Christian Democrats who had dominated Italian politics at all levels since 1945. In Milan, the capital of Lombardy, the Northern League won more votes than any party since Mussolini's Fascists. There can be no doubt that the success of Milanese football expressed a certain superiority the Lombards traditionally felt over the rest of Italy and helped fuel the political momentum of the Lombard and Northern Leagues. Suppressed in most walks of life for many years, anti-southern sentiment always found an outlet at football grounds. When Napoli play away in Milan or Turin you can see banners saying 'Welcome to Italy'. The irony of the success of the new movement for Berlusconi was that politically, he had always aligned himself with the Socialists, yet his very success was accelerating their decline.

Milan retained the European Cup in 1990, although again they failed to win the Italian League as Maradona had one last fling with Napoli. In the following year, however, the first cracks began to appear in the varnished image when the Milan team disgraced itself before a worldwide audience in the quarter-final of the European Cup against Marseille. Right at the end of the second leg in France, with Milan a beaten side, the floodlights failed. The Milan team refused to carry on with the match when the referee decided that the lights were sufficient for the game to proceed to a finish. It was a blatant attempt to force the match to be abandoned and replayed. For their pains they were banned from European competitions for a year by UEFA. In the League, Sampdoria triumphed. It was an ignominious turn of events, and one Berlusconi could not have found pleasing.

It also marked the end of Sacchi's reign. When most had expected a big name, Berlusconi plumped for the brightest coach. Sacchi, for his part, had arrived with a plan of his own – the pressing game – which he employed to devastating effect. Eventually he took it too far and Marco Van Basten objected to being used as a lone striker. In the row that followed, Berlusconi backed Van Basten and Sacchi was on his way. It was not the first spat between president and coach. Initially, Berlusconi had not been too impressed with Rijkaard but thankfully for club and player, Sacchi's view prevailed. Berlusconi wanted to sign the Argentinian, Borghi, but when Sacchi objected, Berlusconi gave way. It was obvious, though, that the pugnacious Sacchi was treading a fine line. Berlusconi put it another way. 'This is a constitutional monarchy,' he said. 'The coach has final responsibility for the team but it has happened that at certain times there have been disagreements. But happily' – this part was accompanied by an enigmatic smile – 'the coach was right.' Presumably, when it came to Van Basten, Berlusconi judged that this time the coach was wrong.

For Sacchi's successor, Berlusconi once again made an unusual choice. While many yet again expected a high-profile, experienced manager who would be able to handle the array of stars, particularly the outspoken Dutch, Berlusconi appointed Fabio Capello, a former Juventus player and Italian international who had been on the coaching staff at Milan for some time. Many felt the president had taken the soft option and that Capello would be more susceptible to Berlusconi's wishes than Sacchi had been, but Capello surprised everyone (and perhaps even Berlusconi) with his quiet determination to succeed. In his first season, Capello's team surpassed all expectations. Not only did they win the League by a mile, eight points clear of Juventus, they went through the whole season without losing a league game, their only reverse coming in the semi-final of the Cup, when they were beaten by Juventus. Their eventual record in Serie A that season, played 34, won 22, drawn 12, was the best ever. Capello didn't change much, but he had a settled team (eleven players were used in twenty-four matches) and he had Marco Van Basten at his absolute best. Van Basten scored 25 goals in 31 appearances, which beat a record which had stood for over thirty years. The season was characterised by Rijkaard and the rest producing stunning demonstrations of total football, while Baresi shackled the most gifted of opposition forwards. If anything, Capello was even more attack-minded than Sacchi and committed his players to going forward at every opportunity. In a welter of goals, Milan once again showed the world how football should be played. Their approach was epitomised in the last match of the season, which evoked memories of the game from an earlier era. Away to Foggia, and with the Championship safely in the bag, Milan found themselves 2–1 down at half-time. In the second half they scored seven goals to finish 8–2 winners. Seldom can a half-time talk have been more productive.

Having served the ban from Europe, Berlusconi became even more determined to recapture the European Cup and at the same time win another Italian Championship. To this end he agreed to the spending of millions of pounds to buy a plethora of expensive stars, many of whom could not expect an automatic place in the team. One such was Jean-Pierre Papin, one of world's top goalscorers, who was recruited from Marseille at a cost of £5.5 million but who had to compete for his place with Marco Van Basten. Other foreigners who came to Milan as a result of Berlusconi's spending spree were Savicevic from Red Star Belgrade, for £4.5 million, and the Croat, Zvonimir Boban, who was recalled from a loan period with Bari. The outlay didn't stop there. Milan broke the world record for a transfer fee when they bought Lentini from Torino for £13 million. Another £8 million was splashed out on Eranio and De Napoli.

As the season kicked off, Milan had six foreigners competing for the three places the Italian League allows each club to allocate to imports. There were also five Italian internationals competing for the three midfield positions, including Donadoni and Evani. With a quality squad of twenty-four, Capello was quite clear on what he had to do. 'Here, foreigners have to adapt to the style of Milan according to my strategy,' he said. 'If the team had two stars we could build our game around them. But Milan has six foreigners, different nationalities, all super players, so it is better to establish our game, a system to which foreigners can adapt. It's more efficient.' Although not guaranteed a place, Boban, for one, concurred, saying, 'I do not believe that Milan should change its game. Milan wins all the time. Its game remains the same and as a result it is us foreigners who have to adapt to it and not the other way round.'

Berlusconi was immediately accused of buying to prevent other clubs getting the players, rather than on the basis of need. For Berlusconi and Capello, however, a club that aspires to world dominance needs a squad of top-class players, not merely a team. Commenting on the adverse reaction, Berlusconi said: 'No one can fix limits. The market itself defines the limits. If a football team is in a position to attract more spectators and especially more television viewers – and that's the football of the future – then the amount of money paid to the company for television rights as well as the players' salaries will have to be higher. The market is the lord and master which sets its own parameters and I personally think that is good.'

Although much of the criticism came from other presidents, they soon saw which way the wind was blowing and began to respond by throwing their own money around in large quantities. In the pre-season scramble over £200 million changed hands in transfer fees (compared to £30 million in the UK, which nevertheless drew critical comment). Juventus, for instance, bought Vialli and Platt, while Internazionale acquired Schillaci, Pancev and Shalimov and Lazio lined up with four foreigners, Gascoigne, Riedle, Winter and Doll, competing for three places. Berlusconi had forced a response which would raise the standard of the whole Italian game. As Liam Brady remarked when comparing 1992–93 with previous seasons, 'You would get teams going away from home and just camping in their own half but I don't see that happening too much this season. Sacchi, and Capello after him, have started a trend that other people are not frightened to follow. The winning teams have always been fashion-makers.'

The emphasis of Italian spending showed just how far Sacchi and Berlusconi, and now Capello, had changed the nature of the Italian game. Of the top twenty transfers in money terms, only Roberto Policano, who moved from Torino to Napoli, was an out-and-out defender. The rest were forwards or attacking midfield players. Every team now possessed a formidable squad. In a country with no reserve-team football many stars, both foreigners and Italians, found themselves hardly playing at all. If a player were injured, there was no guarantee his place would still be available when he recovered fitness, as Ruud Gullit found out at Milan. Gullit was unable to command a regular place once he began to recover from the knee injuries which blighted his career from 1989 and was sold to Sampdoria at the end of the 1992–93 season. Capello was in no doubt about the debt Italian football now owed to Berlusconi: 'Berlusconi has passed on his philosophy to Milan and in turn to the whole of Italian football.' According to Berlusconi, you have to play with more commitment to score goals. 'People pay a lot of money for their tickets,' he said. 'They don't want to look at a team that plays defensively by keeping the ball out of the penalty area.'

The result of the spending on attacking personnel was that the Italian League suddenly found itself in the midst of a feast of goals. The change in the back-pass rule also contributed as the *libero* (sweeper) could not work in tandem with his goalkeeper any longer. Average goals per game, which had stood at around 2.1 for many years, suddenly exploded. After the first fifty games of the 1992–93 season the average had shot up to over three. October 4 1992, will be long remembered as Golden Sunday: 48 goals were scored in 9 League games, including a 7–3 away win by Milan at Fiorentina (a symbolic scoreline for all football fans with a sense of history, especially those of Real Madrid) and a 4–4 draw between Genoa and Ancona. *Gazzetta dello Sport* carried the headline, ITALY, KINGDOM OF THE GOAL. It was a revolution in the land that had produced the most defensive-minded system in Europe in a previous era. The *catenaccio* (literally, padlocked) defence had brought Italian clubs European success. Under Helenio Herrera, Inter reached three European finals (winning two) between 1964 and 1967 using the system. It reached its apotheosis when Fiorentina won the title in 1969 scoring only 38 goals in 30 games. Then, Italy was the kingdom of the 1–0 win and the 0–0 draw.

Such was the measure of Milan's revolution that their success transcended both local and international allegiances, a position not seen in European football since the Real Madrid side of Puskas, Di Stefano and Gento in the 1950s, which won the first five European Cup finals and achieved worldwide fame and support. Like the Brazil side of 1970 and the Hungarians of the early 1950s, through the expression of their skills they belong to us all as football fans, whatever our parochial loyalties. Jimmy Greaves, who spent a short and unhappy (though not unsuccessful) period at Milan in 1961 (9 goals in 10 Serie A games), was moved to say of the new Milan: 'I have watched Capello's dream machine in action . . . and it is like watching football from another planet.' David Miller, chief sports correspondent of *The Times*, whose experience goes back even further, wrote: 'In all my years following the game I cannot recall a team that was more of a unit. We expect extravagance from Italian sides but not players who are simultaneously workaholics.' Commenting on Milan's 2–1 away win against PSV Eindhoven in the Champions' League in 1992–93, Miller was even more enthusiastic: 'Milan are playing a class of football that not only made PSV look second-rate on their own ground, but would, I believe, have subdued any of the great teams of the past. Honved, Real, Manchester United, Benfica, Ajax, Bayern, Liverpool.'

Capello and Berlusconi were proved absolutely correct in their pre-season analysis as Milan lost a number of players, including Van Basten and Papin, to injuries. A club without its resources would undoubtedly have struggled but Milan again led the Italian League by a huge margin entering the home straight, and cruised through the Champions' League with a 100 per cent record to reach their third European Cup final in five years. But after starting the final against Marseille with a string of misses, Milan conceded a goal shortly before half-time and began to lose their self-belief. The longer the game went on, the more Marseille looked the likely winners, and it was the French club that became European champions. Marseille had been the last team to beat Milan in the European Cup, in the quarter-final in 1991, when the Milan team disgraced itself. They had done it again, though this time Milan, taking their cue from their president, accepted defeat gracefully and it went some way to assuage what had happened two years before. Some compensation was derived four days later when a 1–1 draw at home to relegation-threatened Brescia in their penultimate league game gave Milan their thirteenth *scudetto*. Commenting on the match for Channel 4, Liam Brady suggested a 'stewards' enquiry' might not be out of place when Brescia equalised. Later, he explained that he was certain that the result wasn't fixed in advance, but 'there was probably an appreciation that both teams needed at least a point and played accordingly'.

It was, however, a stuttering end to a season that had been filled with such promise. In their final 11 games of that campaign, Milan drew 8 and lost 2. The title had effectively been wrapped up by Christmas, the points in hand enabling them to see off late runs by Inter and Juventus.

It was no coincidence that Milan's dip in form occurred when Marco Van Basten was unavailable. Yet, despite suffering an ankle injury which kept him out of the side for over half the season, Van Basten responded magnificently to the challenge posed by the arrival of Papin and was the eminence grise of a star-studded side. Van Basten, a true child of Dutch football, began his career at Utrecht but soon moved to the leading team of the time, Ajax Amsterdam, where he came under the wing of Johan Cruyff, one of the best players the world has ever seen. At the time Cruyff was winding down his playing career, and indeed Van Basten's debut for Ajax came when he went on as substitute for Cruyff. Later, Van Basten played under Cruyff's management and the team won the European Cup-winners' Cup in 1987, after which Van Basten departed for Milan. He left behind a record of 128 goals in 133 matches, a strike rate unrivalled in the modern game.

Van Basten has always acknowledged the debt he owes to Cruyff, for his example, advice and friendship. He will not hear of himself being called Cruyff's equal. 'Cruyff,' according to Van Basten, 'was more gifted, stronger and more versatile. I shall never reach his level of perfection.' As Cruyff helped Van Basten, so Van Basten in his turn has helped the new star of Dutch football, Denis Bergkamp, whom he recognises as 'the future'. Following Bergkamp's transfer to Inter, Van Basten dismissed any possibility of club rivalry disturbing the progress of the national team. 'It is,' he said, 'the Dutch way.'

For much of his first season in Italy, 1987–88, Van Basten was on the sidelines through injury. He recovered in time to become the player of the tournament in Holland's 1988 European Championship triumph in Germany and followed that up with a blistering season for Milan, which ended with the European Cup victory. In the League, he scored 20 goals in 33 games and weighed in with 9 European Cup goals in as many matches. Milan retained the Cup in 1990 and finished second in the League, with Van Basten contributing 19 goals in 26 League appearances. These feats won him the European Footballer of the Year award for two years running. The campaign in 1991–92, when Milan won the title without losing a game under Capello, was Van Basten's best. Despite having a poor European Championship in Sweden (he missed the vital penalty as Holland were eliminated by Denmark in the semi-finals) he won the European Footballer of the Year title once again, having announced his return to form with a virtuoso display in the Champions' League against Gothenburg, a match in which he scored four goals. Having put the disappointment of Sweden behind him, Van Basten and Milan continued on their winning way. In the early part of the 1992–93 season he scored 12 goals in 12 games – and Milan headed the table before he had to undergo an ankle operation. While he was out, Milan rarely showed the same fluency, although the undefeated run was maintained until, on March 21 1993, after fifty-eight undefeated Serie A matches, Milan lost 1–0 to Parma. For that game Milan had lost the services of four of their foreign contingent (including all three Dutchmen) as well as Albertini, Donadoni and Tassotti, all missing through injury. It was bound to happen some time, and it left Milan a mere nine points clear at the top of the table. Although Inter tried hard to close the gap, there was little they could do to prevent Milan taking another title.

Van Basten thinks the current Milan side is superior to the 1989 team which took the European Cup to the San Siro. The '89 team was a revelation to non-Italians because it gave a different and more pleasing image to Italian football but it did not, says Van Basten, possess the consistency of the '92 side. A scorer of great goals like Bobby Charlton and a great goalscorer like Gerd Muller, Van Basten is, according to Jacques Thibert, the editor of *France Football*, the magazine responsible for the European Footballer of the Year award, 'at the height of his art . . . in his miraculous performances are repeated a part of childhood and innocence that was apparent in Pele, Bobby Charlton, Platini and a few others. A true artist, at the same time a free spirit and, with total authority, he is able to change black and white into techni-colour painting, able to make his dreams a superb reality.'

Van Basten takes pains to point to Berlusconi's influence on Milan and thus himself as a positive force in his career. Berlusconi 'knows how to relate to players . . . he respects the man and the player but will nevertheless take decisions as he sees it.' Van Basten also sees no problem in Milan having six foreigners on their books, realising that it is part of Berlusconi's ambitious policy, which has 'created an exceptional and unique quality in the team. 'In training,' says Van Basten, 'you must go flat out. If you are not at your best someone will take your place.'

At the start of the 1992–93 season, Milan had announced a target of four trophies. After beating Parma in the Italian Super Cup, they lost to Roma and Marseille in the Italian and European Cups respectively. The title was won despite the faltering climax, proving that even a squad with Milan's depth of talent could not win everything on offer. The influx of so many foreigners, however, showed how the big Italian clubs were becoming as important as the national team.

During the period when Berlusconi was leading the move-ment which sought to put Italian clubs in general and his club in particular at the pinnacle of the world game, the national team went into something of a decline. Having completed a third World Cup win against the odds in 1982, the Italians did not have to qualify in 1986 (as the holders) or in 1990 (as the hosts). The team's greatest chance to lift an unprecedented fourth trophy came in Italia '90, when the whole nation expected, even demanded, victory. There was no surprise when Italy beat Austria, the USA, Uruguay and the Republic of Ireland, but they failed the big test in the semi-final against a lacklustre Argentina. The team's eventual third place might look reasonable enough on paper, but in truth it was a shattering disappointment to millions of Italians. From there, they did not qualify for the 1992 European Championship finals, failing to beat Norway and the CIS at home. The coach, Azeglio Vincini, resigned and the Federation turned to the man who had restored pride to Milan, Arrigo Sacchi.

Most coaches or managers who make the transition from club to national team experience something of a culture shock in the early days. Sacchi began his tenure by building his side around the players and tactics that had served him so well in Milan. Seven of the Milan team played in Sacchi's opening game in his bid to qualify for USA '94, a 2–2 draw with Switzerland. Franco Baresi briefly retired from international football and his absence coincided with some ordinary performances in the World Cup against Scotland and Malta. Like Frank Sinatra (whatever team he plays for), however, Baresi just could not stay away and he made a triumphant comeback as Italy trounced Portugal 3–1 in Lisbon, which set up the team for home wins against Malta (6–1) and Estonia (2–0). These victories, however, were offset by an unlucky 1–0 away defeat in Switzerland after Dino Baggio was sent off in the first half.

While Italy, together with Switzerland, remained firm favourites to qualify for the USA, dangers lurk as the Italian League guards its new ascendancy, dangers which have produced such a lopsided balance in England. Although the Italians would never allow the number of competitive games that take place in the UK, the fact is that presidents are putting club before country and, aided by the break-up of the old political structure, are in danger of succeeding too well. A spin-off problem for Sacchi of Berlusconi's ambition is that his selection for the national team is circumscribed by the number of quality players unable to make it into the first teams of the big clubs. He would like to use Eranio and De Napoli, but their irregular appearances for Milan make it impossible to take the gamble. Sacchi's one advantage is that since most of the imports are forwards or attacking midfield players, his defenders are used to playing against the very best forwards week in, week out.

In attack, the emergence of Giuseppe Signori as a goalscoring force with Lazio has put Roberto Baggio and Gianluca Vialli on notice that they have to perform. In 1993, Sacchi used Signori out of position by playing him wide on the left. When Signori fulfils the central role with Baggio, Italy might once again have a team. However, it will only be a temporary reprieve if the likes of Berlusconi get their way. The irony of it is that the man who fashioned Berlusconi's plans and made them reality – Arrigo Sacchi – could be the man who presides over the further demise of the national team because of his and his previous employer's polices.

Silvio Berlusconi's immediate aim is the creation of a

European club superleague. In the long term, he envisages a World Leage, which will enable Milan to play the leading clubs in South America before a global television audience that will be measured in billions. When asked about the vast amounts of money that would accrue to such a league from television companies, Berlusconi replied: 'Yes, that's our goal, but I think this takes us outside current organisation, outside UEFA. It's very dangerous to even speak about these projects. I think that is what will happen in the future but I don't think lt will be tomorrow or even the day after tomorrow.' To be the powerbroker of the approaching European league, Berlusconi has to be in a position of dominance in Italian football. At the same time as pushing for a European future he recognises the importance of games against traditional Italian opponents such as Inter and Juventus. So a European league could never entirely displace the domestic club competition. In order to reconcile this with the attainment of his European objectives, Berlusconi believes it necessary to diminish the importance of national teams in favour of a club-orientated structure throughout Europe and, in the future, across the world. It is a revolutionary notion but it should be taken seriously all the same. Berlusconi has shown in the past that he can take on the most powerful vested interests and come out on top. Given his track record, the football authorities should be a doddle if he is of a mind to tackle them head-on.

In the USA and the UK, brand leaders in advertising take less than a 20 per cent share of the market. The Italian media market is dominated by Fininvest, which accounts for 55 per cent of the total advertising spend on Italian television. Of this, football, game shows and US soaps form the the central core of programming. Berlusconi owns the team, the networks, the shows and most of the airtime on RAI and the other main channels. However, recent legislation has forced him to divest himself of some of his interests, including the subscription channel Tele Piu. The only way to continued expansion is to become an ever larger player on the international stage. In other words, the prospects for the Milan football club, Italian football and the very future of the game in Europe, including the relationship between clubs and national teams, is intimately bound up with business decisions taken in the world's new muitinational power centres, the communications and media conglomerates of which Fininvest is a major player. As we head towards the millennium, never has the adage 'knowledge is power' held more force. Pressed on whether football's fate was now in the hands of these multinational companies, Berlusconi said: 'Yes, that could be, but everything will have to change or there will be a league formed outside UEFA with a team from each country sponsored by that country's biggest company. It will be able to attract the very best players. Then we shall have a super-professional football league like American Football, which will attract millions of viewers, really spectacular soccer.'

There can be no doubt that Italy now possesses the best league in the world. To prove the point, Italian clubs won all three European trophies in 1990, the first time a country had achieved the feat, and almost repeated it again three years later, winning two out of the three. As the British experience showed, however, such dominance is not always the prelude to unmitigated good times. In order for clubs to scale the heights, something has got to give. Unless specific steps are taken to preclude such an outcome, it is the national team that will have to pay the price for the continuing success of the clubs. It is difficult to see how FIFA can prevent this turn of events, and therefore the ambitions of Berlusconi will ensure that European football is in for a decade of upheavals and change. However, if England and Scotland are not to be left behind, a revolution is required because, as we have seen, outmoded infrastructures will debar them from the top table.

14

The Berlusconi Effect

The Champions' League, the Marseille scandal and the European Superleague

> *'Berlusconi tries to take the water to his own well but he knows there are limits beyond which even he cannot go.'*
>
> Antonio Matarrese, President, Italian League.

> *'The only way to play better football is to play against the best in Europe, and we should be aiming for a real European League.'*
>
> Bernard Tapie, president, Olympique de Marseille.

It was the most remarkable of scenes. The 1993 European Cup final was nearing its conclusion with Marseille leading the red-hot favourites, Milan, 1–0. The television pictures beamed around the world cut away from the action to show two faces in the crowd. As the final whistle blew, the television director's first instinct was not to show the joy and despair of the players, nor the emotions of the coaches, but those two faces again. They belonged to the presidents of the competing clubs, Silvio Berlusconi of Milan and Bernard Tapie of Marseille. Tapie, of course, was deliriously happy. Berlusconi looked sullen, depressed and angry. However, he immediately embraced Tapie, and, full of smiles, offered his congratulations. Berlusconi revealed then that Milan was more than capable of showing dignity in defeat. This game, despite the presence on the field (and on the substitutes benches) of some of the world's greatest players, despite the competition between the coaches, the old fox Raymond Goethals and the new boy Fabio Capello, had been billed essentially as a contest between the two presidents, both magnates of the business world and, in Tapie's case, a leading politician as well. It was a reminder, if any were needed, that football now embraced big business and politics as much as it did pure sporting endeavour.

The attention paid to Tapie and Berlusconi revealed how the European Cup has become a commercial as well as a sporting event. When the competition was founded, no one could have foreseen that financial considerations would eventually be just as important as the football. The inspiration for the European Cup came from Gabriel Hanot, a former French international who became a respected journalist with *L'Equipe*, the French sports newspaper. Hanot was the first to try to answer the question 'which is the best team in Europe?' Until then, matches between clubs from different countries had been a rarity, although the advent of floodlights in the 1950s enabled a number of friendly games to take place. In the absence of a competitive framework, these friendly games became big events. Here, credit must be given to one English club, Wolverhampton Wanderers, which was in the vanguard of the movement. Wolves' games against Honved of Budapest and Moscow Dinamo gave a significant boost to the credibility of international club competition. Subsequently eighteen of Europe's top clubs met in Paris to organise a competition to find the true answer to Hanot's conundrum. The result was the European Cup.

The format of the competition was the outcome of a compromise hammered out at the Paris meeting. Hanot himself, along with a number of presidents, including Santiago Bernabeu of Real Madrid, favoured a European league on the grounds that the only test of league champions is a league, not a knock-out tournament. They lost the argument, however, and the knock-out format was adopted, with the innovation of home and away legs rather than the FA Cup formula of a draw deciding the home team in a one-match contest. While the two-legged tie was probably the only practical way of organising a Europe-wide competition, the beauty of the FA Cup is that in a one-off situation, the chances of a shock result on the day are heightened.

The governing body of European football, UEFA, under pressure from individual associations which feared a loss of power and influence, refused outright to sanction a league but was prepared to give its blessing to the knock-out format, provided that clubs entering the competition had the approval of their home federation. Shortly after another competition, the Inter-Cities Fairs Cup, which had grown out of earlier, quasi-official tournaments, was instituted for teams made up of players from different clubs in the same city. This was always a secondary competition and for several years entry was by invitation from UEFA. The first Fairs Cup final took place in 1958, when a London composite team reached the (two-legged) final. Including some illustrious names, such as Danny Blanchflower, Jimmy Greaves and Johnny Haynes, London drew the first leg, played at Stamford Bridge against Barcelona, 2–2. The second leg was a disaster for London as they went down 6-0 to the Catalans.

The European Cup was an immediate success. The first final was, fittingly, played in Paris in 1956, when, before a crowd of 38,000, Real Madrid beat the French champions Stade de Reims 4–3. The status of the European Cup was secured but it was achieved without the English. The secretary of the Football League, the xenophobic Alan Hardaker, failed to see that the new competition actually enhanced the prestige of national leagues by giving clubs an extra incentive – a chance to test themselves against the very best in Europe – to win their domestic leagues. Instead of realising that if the English champions performed well it would improve the reputation of the Football League, Hardaker saw the European Cup as the thin end of a wedge which could eventually destroy his domain. Hardaker convinced the secretary of the FA, Sir Stanley Rous, to deny the English champions, Chelsea, permission to take part. Hibernian of Edinburgh, however, did enter the competition, although Aberdeen were the champions, showing again how the Scots possessed a more open outlook than their neighbours. *Plus ça change* . . .

What turned the English attitude around was the determination of one man, Matt Busby, the manager of Manchester United. He instinctively recognised the importance of the European Cup and refused to take no for an answer. The young United team – the Busby Babes – having won the

League in 1955–56 made it to the semi-final before going out to the holders, Real, who were fast becoming one of the great teams of all time. It was the second final, played in Madrid on May 30 1957, that cemented the European Cup as the continent's premier club competition when, in front of over 124,000 of their own delirious fans, Real retained the trophy, beating Fiorentina 2–0. Three years later, Real won their fifth European Cup in a row in what was undoubtedly one of the best games of football ever played anywhere. The biggest crowd yet for a final, at 135,000 one that is unlikely to be bettered, turned up at Hampden Park, Glasgow, to see the Real side of Puskas, Di Stefano and Gento slaughter Eintracht Frankfurt 7–3.

As the European competitions (the Cup-winners' Cup was added in 1960–61, while the Inter-Cities Fairs Cup became the European Fairs Cup in 1966–67 and the UEFA Cup in 1971–72. By then, composite teams had given way to entry being decided on League position) grew both in stature and the number of entrants, so changes were made in the format. The number of drawn ties, originally replayed, was reduced by the introduction of the away goals rule, then eliminated completely by the penalty shoot-out. Over the years there were always the odd rumblings about the desirability of a European league but by the 1980s the UEFA competitions were well entrenched and a Europe-wide league seemed about as likely as the collapse of the Berlin Wall. Then came television deregulation, resulting in competition between networks and increased rights fees. In 1987, Real Madrid beat Napoli in the first round of the European Cup. RAI, the Italian state broadcaster, lost heavily as it had gambled before the draw by buying Napoli's rights in the competition for £2 million, irrespective of how long they lasted in the tournament. After RAI's huge loss, television became more wary. This led to a clamour by television and the big clubs for the introduction of seeding, as the knock-out format meant that if the vagaries of chance drew two big clubs together in the first round, one of them would miss out on the riches that the later stages of the European Cup delivered. With television providing an increasing share of the income, loss of rights fees through early elimination hit a club hard. The reality was that the big clubs began to feel that the two-legged tie was, according to Silvio Berlusconi, 'not modern thinking', and back on to the agenda came the European League.

In 1988 Berlusconi commissioned his advertising agency, Saatchi and Saatchi, to prepare a plan for such a league. The proposals were rightly dismissed out of hand by UEFA since they were based on a franchise system. The Saatchi plan did, however, serve as a catalyst for the big clubs and once again ensured that the idea of a league was debated around Europe. In 1989, a group of clubs, led by Real Madrid with support from Glasgow Rangers, Bayern Munich and PSV Eindhoven, formulated yet another compromise plan. This time it was argued that the later stages of the European Cup be changed from a knock-out to a round-robin format. With seeding, the big clubs could more easily reach the later stages where in the new plan they would be guaranteed a minimum number of home games. At first, UEFA stalled but this time the clubs were in no mood to be put off and the threat of a break-away European superleague was floated to force a change of heart in the governing body.

Up until that moment, UEFA had never really examined the full implications of what a European league would entail. UEFA's power accrued from the strength of the national associations and federations affiliated to it and the money brought in by the European competitions and the European Championships. If there were a European league, national associations and thus national teams would be be diminished in importance and UEFA feared that this would eventually lead to a weakening of its influence within the world governing body, FIFA, and consequently a downgrading of its stature as the clubs became all-powerful. And anyway, why tamper with a competition that had proved itself over the years to be a success? When it became obvious that the clubs were intent on change, UEFA agreed to the compromise plan, more as a way of staving off the threatened league than because of any real enthusiasm for the idea.

As the details for the new format were being worked out, UEFA received some good news from its marketing consultants, a company called ISL, who held the sponsorship rights for the World Cup and the Olympics. Far from diminishing UEFA's power and control, ISL said, the change in format could be used by UEFA as a way of bringing all sponsorship, advertising and television rights under its central authority. By doing this, it could create a World Cup-type package of advertising and television rights which UEFA itself would devise and sell, receiving all income before making distributions to the clubs. With this idea on the back-burner, UEFA embraced the new system, which began in the 1991–92 season. At the quarter-final stage of the European Cup the eight teams were split into two groups of four, each playing the three other teams home and away. The winners of each group contested the final. Under this system, clubs reaching the quarter-finals were guaranteed three home games instead of the one or two under the old system.

In the first season, as it was something of an experiment, UEFA allowed the clubs to retain television rights to their home games, a convention which had been established by default over a number of years. At the same time, however, UEFA made it clear that central control would be introduced if the new format proved successful. Although a number of clubs opposed the idea, UEFA was adamant that this was the price of its support. The force behind the concept of central control was the general secretary, Gerhard Aigner, who, cognisant of the increasing scope of UEFA's responsibilities in the new Europe, wished to consolidate the organisation's financial base.

Moreover, UEFA was convinced that in the end, the clubs would make more money and it would be better distributed between clubs from both major and minor television markets. For the 1992–93 season, UEFA renamed the round-robin part of the competition the Champions' League. It came complete with centralised marketing organised by TEAM, a company formed by break-away personnel from ISL, which outbid UEFA's previous marketing partners by guaranteeing an astonishing minimum income of £30 million. The centralised strategy delivered to sponsors an exclusive package in the stadia at all Champions' League games and on television, where agreements were made with virtually every European country which guaranteed transmissions, for the most part live, throughout the continent. Four official sponsors were signed up – Nike, Snickers (Mars), Ford and Philips, with Olivetti providing computer services. A condition of sale to television companies was that they must promote the identity of the

Champions' League and its sponsors, each transmission using the same thematic links, which included a logo and music. In addition, the official sponsors had to have exclusivity in their product categories and were also guaranteed at least four advertising spots during a transmission, which precluded sale to public broadcasters like the BBC, even if they could afford the price of entry. Competing clubs, therefore, had to provide clean stadia (free from advertising boards) and remove sponsors' names from their shirts. Thus companies which had paid a high premium to sponsor front-line clubs were denied access to the ultimate platform, which they needed to exploit fully their association. The only 'advertising' permitted on shirts in Champions' League matches is the League's own logo. The strategy was successful for everyone else, however. UEFA called it a 'resounding success' as rights sales met the original guarantee. While most of the income went to the competing clubs, payments were also made to all national associations affiliated to UEFA, so even Iceland received £180,000 in the first season of central marketing.

For football purists, though, the new system is a hybrid. The dramatic quality of the later stages has in many ways been destroyed and a league instituted within what remains essentially a knock-out competition. It also went against the grain because in other tournaments, especially the World Cup and the European Championships, the league element comes in the early stages, with a knock-out system thereafter (which is the same system used by the NFL in the USA). However, UEFA got away with it because, for all its faults, the Champions' League revenue was distributed not only to the clubs taking part but also to the clubs in the other UEFA competitions and the national associations. With the guarantees from TEAM, UEFA could give an incentive by offering each participating club, in addition to the right to keep its home gate receipts, over £900,000 plus £225,000 per point gained in the Champions' League.

Although the 1992–93 Champions' League had some great games which produced real television spectaculars (TF1 in France devoted almost four hours of peak Wednesday night airtime to every round and was rewarded with audiences of over 10 million), its inherent limitations were exposed when teams from three of the major television markets, England

(Leeds), Germany (Stuttgart) and Spain (Barcelona) failed to reach the quarter-finals. The German television company, RTL Plus, which had struck a deal in the belief that Stuttgart would make it, had to renegotiate its contract hurriedly when the German champions were eliminated by Leeds. Nevertheless, Gerhard Aigner was able to write in the UEFA newsletter: 'With the Champions' League, European football has managed to create a mouthwatering shop window for itself, a symbol of its unity and of its openness to new ideas.'

It was certainly true that UEFA was willing to listen. When Lynton Guest was researching an article for the *Sunday Telegraph* on the Champions' League he happened to mention to UEFA that the one innovation the English game had tried which had worked extremely well was three points for a win. UEFA executives were more than interested, although they appeared not to have realised what an impact it had made on the attitude of away teams in England, who now looked to win games rather than hold out for a draw. UEFA passed on the information to FIFA, which is now debating whether to use the system for the World Cup finals. If FIFA does embrace three points for a win, it will undoubtedly help to get rid of the safety-first mentality which is evident in so many group games in the World Cup finals and would banish such non-spectacles and 'arranged' matches as the 1–0 result between West Germany and Austria in the 1982 finals (which enabled both to qualify for the second phase at the expense of Algeria) forever. As for UEFA, it would have its convictions tested as the mega-clubs who failed to qualify for the Champions' League looked on enviously and impatiently from the outside.

The incredible success of Silvio Berlusconi in Milan provided a role model for other aspiring owners. Berlusconi had shown that the big clubs of the future would be those which not only won, but played attractive football that appealed to an international television audience. Berlusconi, of course, is a media owner as well as a football president, which enabled him to maximise his football team's earning potential. Others, such as David Murray at Glasgow Rangers, learned the lesson. Murray's own abortive foray into the media world with *The Sunday Scot* newspaper can hardly be called a success, but it showed how much Murray now believed that he should add media ventures to his empire. There was even talk of Rangers applying for a Scottish television franchise, though nothing came of that idea. Perhaps the most interesting Berlusconi emulator, though, is Bernard Tapie, president of Olympique Marseille.

Tapie was born in Le Bourget, a suburb of Paris, in 1943. He came from a working-class background and showed no great talent for scholastic achievement. He was, however, an enthusiastic footballer. Like Berlusconi, Tapie had an undistinguished career as a singer before finding his true ability lay in business. After he acquired a bankrupt printing company, his fortunes began to rise. Wheeling and dealing his way through over forty companies in the 1970s, Tapie was, by the beginning of the 1980s, a well-established, flamboyant figure on the French business scene. Tapie's first association with sport as a businessman came in 1983 when one of his companies, La Vie Claire, sponsored a team in the Tour de France cycle race. It was a successful move as the team's two leading riders, Bernard Hinault and Greg Lemond, won the Tour two years running.

In 1985, the Socialist mayor of Marseille, Gaston Deferre, asked Tapie to take over the ailing football club which had been the main rival to the St Etienne team in the 1970s but which had fallen on hard times and had been relegated to Division 2 in 1980, returning to the top flight only in 1984. On taking control, Tapie stated that his ambition was to win the European Cup within five years, which might have seemed fanciful at the time, given Marseille's debt of £1.4 million. Tapie's solution was to throw money at the problem. He splashed out £2.5 million on the Uruguayan Enzo Francescoli, then another £4.5 million on Chris Waddle. Every season was announced with new stars, on both the playing and the coaching staff. He rejected any suggestion that changing the set-up so often was disruptive: 'We remember the great players who were here,' he said. He lets them go because 'it creates motivation and expectation if you change the team'. In pursuit of his goal, Tapie employed seven coaches in seven years: Gerard Banide, Gerard Gili, Franz Beckenbauer, Raymond Goethals, Tomislav Ivic, Jean Fernandez, then Goethals again. Goethals brushed aside any criticisms about continuity by saying that Marseille have had the same coach all along!

In 1988, Tapie was asked by President Mitterand to bring

his business skills to the aid of the Socialist party. Throwing himself into the task with his customary zeal, Tapie took on Jean Marie Le Pen, the populist right-wing politician, in a television debate and won it convincingly. In January 1989 he was elected to the French parliament as a Socialist deputy representing Bouches-du-Rhône, a constituency right next door to Le Pen's stronghold in Marseille. Nothing, it seemed, could now stop Tapie, and in 1992 his political career received a boost when he was given the job of Minister for Urban Affairs in the government of Pierre Beregovoy, who committed suicide after losing the 1993 General Election. In the hour of his triumph, however, Tapie was brought down to earth with a bump. A former business associate accused him of fraud and he was temporarily forced to resign his ministerial post.

The allegations came as no surprise to those involved in French football. According to one leading coach, Tapie 'has a tendency to use the methods [in football] he accuses his principal political opponent of'. This supposedly included bringing pressure to bear on referees, the media and his own players, the latter of whom would often complain about Tapie's pre-match lectures. Four disciplinary cases were brought against the Marseille president in 1990 concerning allegations that opposition players had been asked to 'take it easy' in league matches during the 1989–90 season. As a result of these and other investigations Tapie was suspended from all official duties at Marseille and banned from the bench and the dressing room for twelve months. His response was to resign from the presidency, but when a poll revealed that over 70 per cent of the French people and over 80 per cent of Marseillais wanted him to stay he returned like a triumphant General MacArthur, vindicated in his own mind, which led him to believe he could continue with the same policies as before.

By 1993, Marseille had become the dominant force in French football, winning five straight Championships. However, they did not win the European Cup in the five-year time frame Tapie had set himself. They came as close as possible, though, as semi-finalists in 1990 and beaten finalists the following year in a poor match against Red Star Belgrade, which went to penalties after a sterile 0–0 draw. Perhaps

Tapie had not taken into account the French hoodoo in Europe. It was the greatest irony that, until 1993, the French, the most international-minded of football nations and the inspiration behind European competitions in the first place, had failed to win any European club tournament, losing seven finals across the three competitions. Speaking before the triumph against Milan in 1993, Tapie took some of the blame for the defeat against Red Star when he admitted putting undue pressure on his players before the game. He recognised afterwards that it had been counter-productive, and he would not make the same mistake before the Milan match, when he would do all he could to take the pressure off by 'demystifying' the match. 'My work,' he now claimed, 'is to minimise the event.'

Milan were hot favourites to win the European Cup for the fifth time in 1993. They did, after all, possess the most formidable squad in world club football. And Van Basten was back after a long lay-off. There were, however, some factors in Marseille's favour. Of these, the most important was Milan's dismal current form. Eight draws and two defeats in their last eleven games must have given even this expensive collection of stars more than a moment of self-doubt. Moreover, of all the teams Milan had faced in Europe since the Berlusconi renaissance, none had caused them more problems than Marseille. During that period, Milan lost only one European tie, and that was to Marseille in the 1990–91 quarter-final.

Perhaps, after all the years of ill-luck that had dogged French teams' pursuit of a European prize, the tide had at last turned. In the opening half-hour of the 1993 final, played in Munich's Olympic stadium, Milan could, and should, have been several goals ahead and out of sight. Amazingly, Jean-Pierre Papin was left out of the Milan side in favour of Massaro partnering Van Basten up front. It was Massaro who missed crucial chances and, just before half-time, Marseille, not for the first time, broke away to create a scoring chance. From the subsequent corner, Basile Boli put away a glancing header and Marseille went in at half-time with a precious 1–0 lead. In the second half the Marseille defence, previously all over the place, now looked capable of containing the Italians. The introduction of Papin after half-time didn't seem to worry his former colleagues, and with Van Basten lacking match fitness, the longer the game went on, the less convincing Milan looked. In the end, Marseille were worthy winners.

Back home, Marseille's triumph was hailed as a victory for France, LE JOUR DE GLOIRE, according to the front-page headline in *L'Equipe*. In Marseille itself there was an almighty party which lasted well into the next day. The reaction was more than understandable. Marseille had broken the thirty-eight-year-old jinx and the country that pioneered European competition had finally won its greatest prize. Three days later, amid more euphoria, Marseille claimed their fifth Championship in a row, eclipsing the record of St Etienne in the 1970s, by beating their nearest rivals, Paris St Germain, 3–1 in the Stade Velodrome. Boli was again instrumental in the victory, scoring another stunning headed goal which won France's Goal of the Season competition.

In their moment of celebration, Marseille were suddenly embroiled in a bribery scandal. Days before the Milan game, they beat Valenciennes 1–0. It was a vital match for both teams. Marseille required both points in their quest for the Championship, while Valenciennes needed to win to avoid automatic relegation. Before the second half started the referee informed the Marseille captain, Didier Deschamps, that he would be including in his match report a complaint from Valenciennes that their performance had been adversely affected by being offered a bribe to throw the match. Afterwards, defender Jacques Glassmann confirmed the allegation. A month previously, Jean-Pierre Bernes, the Marseille general manager and Bernard Tapie's lieutenant, had said: 'The . . . success of Marseille in reaching the European Cup final has not made everybody happy and there is an attempt by any means to destabilise the club.' In their own minds, then, Marseille were able to brush the allegation aside as being a crude ploy to upset their preparations for Munich.

After the euphoria of Marseille's historic win began to die down, more details of the Valenciennes affair started to emerge. Three Valenciennes players, Christophe Robert, Jorge Burruchaga (a member of Argentina's World Cup-winning team of 1986) and Glassmann were phoned in their hotel rooms on the day before the crucial game by Jean-Jacques Eydelie, the Marseille midfielder and a former colleague of Robert and Burruchaga at Nantes. A person purporting to be

Jean Pierre Bernes also took part in the conversation. The three Valenciennes players were each offered FF250,000 (£30,000) in cash to take it easy. Robert and Burruchaga later admitted that all three had agreed to go along with the bribe but then had second thoughts and decided to play the game normally, though Robert went off injured after thirty minutes. Glassmann, on the other hand, vehemently denied ever being tempted. The football authorities turned the case over to the judiciary in Valenciennes. The public prosecutor, Eric de Montgolfier, and the investigating judge, Bernard Beffy, tackled the affair with gusto, seemingly happy to wash every piece of dirty linen in public, as a result of which it became a cause célèbre and led the nightly French television news bulletins for weeks.

Everyone now wanted to get in on the act and give Marseille a good kicking while they were down. CSKA Moscow, who Marseille beat 6–0 in the Champions' League, accused the French champions of trying to bribe them as well. The Russians also said their half-time drinks had been spiked. Although the accusations were later retracted (in fact, as soon as UEFA announced an investigation), the damage had been done. The ever-opportunistic Silvio Berlusconi suggested that if the Russian allegations were proved, the European Cup final should be replayed between Milan and Glasgow Rangers (who finished second in Marseille's group). Berlusconi did not ask for the title to be awarded to Milan by default but called for another match, another big pay-day. Nice one, Silvio!

Christophe Robert was arrested and admitted under interrogation to taking the money, which had been collected by his wife from Eydelie. The cash was subsequently retrieved from Robert's aunt's garden. At the same time the offices of Marseille were searched. Envelopes and staples found during the search were reported to match those found with Robert's money. Eydelie presented himself voluntarily to the public prosecutor in Valenciennes and, along with Burruchaga, was promptly arrested. All three players were banned from the League and told that the ban would be a lifetime one if they were found guilty by the court. Only Glassmann was allowed to resume training for the new season, which began on July 23.

The president of the League, Noel Le Graet, was forced

to take a pragmatic view of the coming season. 'The Championship will recommence with Marseille,' he said. 'We shall sanction the guilty party but protect the institution.' This statement did not prevent the entire Marseille squad being hauled off their training camp at Fort Romeu for interrogation. However, when it was Bernes's turn, he went missing. Eventually, he was tracked down to the psychiatric ward of a Marseille hospital where he had been admitted for 'depression and nervous exhaustion'.

With Tapie's right-hand man *hors de combat*, attention shifted to the president himself. In a bizarre twist, the former Valenciennes coach, Boro Primorac, who was fired when the club was finally relegated, claimed he was taken to Tapie's Paris headquarters and asked to carry the blame for the affair. Tapie, protected by parliamentary immunity, denied that the meeting ever took place, but a secretary who corroborated Tapie's story was hauled off to prison. Tapie was subsequently questioned by judge Beffy and stated that he could not have met Primorac at the time the ex-Valenciennes coach claimed the meeting took place and cited as a witness a fellow deputy and former minister, Jacques Mellick. On examination, it was discovered that in order for Mellick to have been at Tapie's office and been back in his constituency, where he attended a public meeting later the same day, he would have had to have driven like a bat out of hell.

The whole affair had now become a political scandal and the Marseille vice-president, Jean-Louis Levereau, described the attempt to implicate his boss as 'starting to look like a bad episode of Dallas'. Nevertheless, the Conservative prime minister, Edouard Balladur, talked about the country's top footballers setting a 'deplorable example' to the young. Tapie reacted furiously, denouncing the criticism as a personal vendetta aimed at him. The president of the Republic, François Mitterand, felt bound to defend his former minister. He called Marseille 'a great club' and questioned what they would have to gain from the 'unsavoury business'. Furthermore, the president said Tapie had been harshly treated. 'Why mix him in with this affair?' he asked, 'when to my knowledge his name has not been brought in by the judicial process?' Emboldened by such support from his main man, Tapie got carried away, claiming that the judiciary's tactics were 'worthy of the Gestapo'. For his pains, he was quickly served with a libel writ from the ministry of justice.

Meanwhile, Eydelie, unlike Robert and Burruchaga, who had confessed and were at liberty, denied any involvement whatsoever and languished in jail for ten days. Then Eydelie's wife, who had gone missing, turned up to confirm the version of events put forward by the Valenciennes players. At this, Eydelie cracked in front of the prosecutor and admitted acting as the go-between after being promised a place in the starting line-up against Milan and a new contract.

Bernes was now out on a limb and on his own. He left hospital and was taken to Valenciennes, charged with corruption and imprisoned. He steadfastly rejected the testimony against him, even when confronted with records of the telephone calls he made from his hotel room, which showed that a twenty-minute conversation had taken place with someone at the Valenciennes hotel. When brought face to face with his accusers in a specially convened tribunal, Bernes continued to maintain his innocence.

The case had now reached something of an impasse. Short of a confession by Bernes, the investigation would have to enter a new phase. Bernes, the last remaining protagonist in jail, was finally released and the judicial investigation wound down for the summer holidays. The case will eventually come to court but that might not happen for months or years. In the meantime, under pressure from fans, clubs and the media the French football authorities decided to hold its own hearing into the case before the matter receded into the background.

In Marseille, the news of Bernes's release was greeted as a battle won, if not the war. Marseille were at least free to play. Whether they were in the right frame of mind to do so was another matter. Their start to the season was the worst they had experienced for some years. Moreover, the knock-on effect on the national team, for which Marseille supplies a number of players, could have been disastrous, as the final qualifying matches for USA '94 were just around the corner.

In an attempt to shift the attention back to sporting matters, both the fans and the authorities seemed to be saying, enough is enough, why pick on football when corruption is believed to be rife throughout public life? As the manager of the national team, Gerard Houlier, put it, 'There is a lack of intelligence, a lack of honesty by involving all of football in this affair.' The respected football correspondent of the television station TF1, Thierry Roland, went even further, emphasising that there had been business malpractice which had not been as harshly treated as Marseille had been. 'After all,' he said, 'Marseille have not killed anyone . . . the majority of the team is innocent . . . One should think of them and how they exhilarated all France by winning the European Cup.' It remains to be seen whether the wheels of justice move slowly enough to give Marseille a chance to retain their titles.

While Marseille's French League title and the European Cup remained safe in the short term, the team's participation in the 1993–94 European Cup was under a more immediate threat. Unfortunately for the club, French television can be picked up in Switzerland and as the Marseille affair dominated the airwaves, both UEFA and FIFA officials could follow the intricacies of the case from their headquarters in Berne and Zurich respectively.

One who heard the news broadcasts and became increasingly concerned was the FIFA president, Joao Havelange. As the story unfolded, Havelange started to lose patience with what he saw as a tardy response to the scandal on the part of the French football authorities, which, if allowed to continue, would tarnish football's image in the run-up to the USA World Cup. Havelange, with support from UEFA, wrote to the French federation on August 31 urging them to take action and insisting that some decision be made before September 23. If the French did not comply, the FIFA president warned that the federation might be suspended from the world governing body, which if implemented would mean a ban on all other countries from having contacts with French football.

The problem faced by the French football authorities was that they had ceded control over the case to the civil investigators, thus their hands were tied until the criminal process was completed. This was too much for UEFA. With the first round of the European Cup less than a fortnight away, Marseille's presence would soon be irreversible and as such, an acute embarrassment if they were subsequently found guilty. The president of the federation, Jean Fournet-Fayard, and the head of the League, Noel Le Graet, were summoned to an extraordinary session of UEFA's executive committee.

Despite French protestations, the committee threw Marseille out of the European Cup and gave the French forty-eight hours to nominate a replacement.

The decision caused consternation and anger back in Marseille. Before the hearing, Bernard Tapie had warned that the club would explode if it was banned. Moreover, the loss of income, he pointed out, could be over £14 million. The city, hit harder than most by the recession and suffering from a decline in its status as a major port, had been given a massive boost of confidence by the European Cup win but now the euphoria had given way to despair. The emotion at large in Marseille at the turn of events was not confined to regular supporters. Everyone was convinced that the club and Tapie were the victims of a huge conspiracy. It was widely recognised that the football club had a significant role to play in the life of the city. 'It was more than a symbol, it was a unifying force,' said one fan. Once again, the importance of the game was being demonstrated for all to see. 'Football', Julian Nundy wrote in an article on the affair in the *Independent on Sunday*, 'has formed a social cement between (disparate) peoples and classes.' Over a picture of a shattered European Cup, *L'Equipe* simply displayed the headline, BROKEN DREAM.

As Marseille mourned, Fournet-Fayard and Le Graet were trying to comply with UEFA instructions by finding a team to take Marseille's place in the European Cup. It was not as easy as might be imagined. Paris St Germain, who finished the League in second place, flatly refused the offer. There is fierce rivalry between Paris SG and Marseille and the Paris club was unwilling to endure the taunts that were sure to come its way if it slipped into the European Cup through the back door. Eventually, Monaco, the third-placed club, was ordered to be the French representative, while Monaco's position in the UEFA Cup was awarded to Auxerre.

Fuelled by the support of the Marseillais, Tapie, who had earlier threatened to resign if Marseille were ejected from the European Cup, decided instead to go on the attack. He instructed lawyers to challenge UEFA's decision in the Swiss courts. The court which heard the case, in UEFA's home town of Berne, awarded Tapie an injunction which effectively restored Marseille to the competition because UEFA had acted unlawfully in banning a club on the basis of unproven allegations of corruption. Meanwhile, Tapie negotiated financial support from the mayor of Marseille and appeared before a delirious crowd of thousands which had gathered outside the Stade Velodrome. Tapie, like the consummate politician he had become, decided to make a speech. 'I had the feeling,' he told the assembled masses, 'that I could no longer serve my club because I was on the receiving end of permanent criticism, but any departure now would be considered a desertion and it is clear that we shall be together for some time to come. The only expression of joy I would like to make is not to crow in triumph but that we should be together next Wednesday to greet Athens' (Marseille's opponents in the first round of the European Cup).

While Marseille rejoiced, FIFA was seething. Fournet-Fayard was again summoned to Zurich and Sepp Blatter, FIFA's general secretary, issued a solemn warning to the French football authorities. 'This is the last chance for France,' he said. 'Nobody is forced to become a member of the great family of football but once he has, he has to accept with sporting spirit the decisions of sport's justice.' The problem with this argument was that it was not sport's justice but rough justice. The fact of the matter was, FIFA had become worried about the increasing use of litigation in football and had decreed that all those concerned in the game should not go to court over decisions made by governing bodies. While FIFA's stance certainly encouraged the quick investigation and resolution of problems that could only be achieved at the expense of certain legal rights, Blatter was being somewhat disingenuous. If a country or club wants to be involved in football it has to join FIFA, the alternative is ostracism from the world game. There is nothing voluntary about joining 'the great family of football'. Because those sitting in judgement would sometimes have a vested interest in the outcome (FIFA was concerned about damage to the image of the game and the effect the scandal might have on its biggest money-spinning event, the World Cup), there is always the possibility of other considerations influencing decisions and punishments. The natural safeguard for possible abuse is a civil court but FIFA's overriding concern is that if every decision is challenged, the game will degenerate into chaos. To achieve its aim, FIFA (and to a lesser extent,

UEFA) has become a state within the family of nations, with
its own legal process.

One thing was certain, Joao Havelange was not going to be
put off by the little matter of a court decision. Havelange is a
man who is used to being courted by the great and the
powerful and is treated almost like a head of state wherever
he goes. Now he decided to raise the stakes. Jean Fournet-
Fayard was left in no doubt that if Marseille's court action was
not withdrawn, all five French clubs which had qualified for
Europe would be removed from the three competitions and
the French national team would be expelled from the World
Cup. (This was a telling point as the previous day the national side, keeping its nerve admirably in the face of the pressures caused by the affair, had secured an excellent away win
in Finland, leaving it with only one point to get from two
home matches to be certain of qualifying for the USA.) If the
domesday scenario came to pass, Fournet-Fayard's nightmare
was the effect it might have on the 1998 World Cup, which is
due to be held in France. After all, what FIFA gives with one
hand, it can take away with the other.

Even Bernard Tapie saw that this latest threat could not
be resisted. He could call FIFA's bluff and perhaps win in
the courts but it was far less certain that he could bring
a successful action to force FIFA to allow France back into
the World Cup if the country were banned. To be seen as
the man who lost France its World Cup place in 1994 and
perhaps its position as host in 1998 would severely damage
his future as a politician. Moreover, since the bout of confessions, there was little doubt that a bribery attempt had been
made, whoever was involved. If Tapie sacrificed French
football in defence of what in the end would be proved
indefensible, it could mean the end of his political ambitions.
On September 11, Tapie faxed UEFA withdrawing his
court action and released the organisation from the injunction. By way of explanation, Tapie presented himself as
a wronged martyr who was laying down the success of
himself, his club and the city of Marseille in order to save
the French game from the ire of a greater power. 'I don't think
it is reasonable,' Tapie insisted, 'to expose French football
to sanctions which I would have exposed it to even though
my conscience is clear. I continue to believe I was in the

right. (I was) defending the rights of Marseille, no more no less.'

Although FIFA and UEFA won the day, a number of matters remained unresolved. For instance, by conceding on the central issue, would Marseille be allowed to contest the European Supercup (between the holders of the European Cup and the Cup-winners' Cup) and the Intercontinental Cup (against the South American Champions)? In addition, although the European episode was at an end, there were still the French internal enquiries (which could result in the League title being taken away) and FIFA's diktat that the football authorities resolve the situation by the end of September was still in place.

What lessons can be drawn from the Marseille affair? The main one surely is that proper procedures have to be put in place by FIFA. It is not enough merely to prohibit court actions. If people and organisations are to be asked to give up their legal rights then there must be clear rules by which the governing body has to abide. A traditional English concept might be of use to achieve this aim. Justice must not only be done, it must be seen to be done. Similarly clear procedures must be put in place to take account of cases where criminal activity is suspected.

Despite the chaotic nature of the Marseille case, it was at least properly investigated. The French football authorities were no slower than their English counterparts have been when confronted with wrongdoing, and were additionally hampered by their responsible attitude in turning the case over to the judiciary, which must take precedence if a breach of the criminal code is alleged. UEFA and FIFA, for all their hamfistedness, were prepared to intervene, an attitude singularly lacking in years gone by. However, no matter how accurate the allegations against Marseille eventually prove to be, the fact is that UEFA and FIFA abused the concept of natural justice. It was nothing less than trial by media. No properly constituted body had fully evaluated the evidence and the confessions. Furthermore, whether Marseille are guilty or not they deserve their day in court before a verdict is proclaimed. Even in the most punitive legal systems the punishment comes after the trial not before. What the case shows is that UEFA and FIFA are far more prepared to exert their control than hitherto. The international bodies have indicated by their actions in the Marseille affair that they are redrawing the map. The areas of the game they directly control will grow inexorably, particularly if they can continue to impose limitations on the right to legal redress. How far and how fast will depend on the response from the component parts of the great family.

Although Marseille hogged all the headlines, the club's troubles were only the tip of the iceberg in a summer of scandals which went from arranged matches in Italy, bungs in England to third-party bonuses in Spain which stimulated Tenerife to play above themselves in the last match of the season to deprive Real Madrid of the title for the second year in succession. Football everywhere seemed to be caught in a web of corruption. Because the responses to alleged wrongdoing depended on the vigour with which the various national associations tackled the problems, there was no uniformity either in the way cases were investigated or in the end result in terms of punishment or other sanction. In England, the FA, at their annual meeting in Bournemouth in the summer of 1993, decided to appoint Graham Kelly to investigate possible corrupt activity in the wake of the alleged transfer irregularities. Taking time off from his duties as roving ambassador, the chief executive's new incarnation as Kelly of the Yard hardly inspired confidence that the investigation would really get to the heart of the matter. For its part, UEFA could only investigate cases that occurred in European competitions, so if one particular national association was not inclined to look too closely, it would be difficult for UEFA to prevent contamination of its own competitions by teams which were tainted with corruption. One of the worst scandals, but perhaps the most typical of the way UEFA can only react to events outside its direct control, occurred, surprise, surprise, in Poland.

As the race for the Polish League title reached its climax in 1993 there were already widespread rumours of match-fixing. Then, on the last day of the season, Legia Warsaw and LKS Lodz were level on points at the top of the table. In order to claim the Championship, LKS had to win by three goals more than Legia. Legia were away to Wisla Krakow and LKS at home to Olimpia Poznan. Following the games on radio it appeared that every time Legia scored, LKS also got a goal and the matches finished with huge victory margins for both teams, Legia winning 6–0 and LKS 7–1. LKS's win was not enough to make up the goal difference and Legia, it appeared, would take the title. To the astonishment of the fans and the outrage of the media, which dubbed the games 'a cabaret of football', the Polish FA allowed the results to stand, merely fining all four clubs 500 million zlotys (£20,000). Eventually, bowing to pressure, the Polish FA had a rethink and decided to deduct the points Legia and LKS had gained in the two games. Without the points, both clubs were overtaken. The title was awarded to Lech Poznan, who had finished third. UEFA accepted the entry of Poznan into the European Cup but refused to allow either Legia or LKS to enter the UEFA Cup. In 1993–94, there were therefore no Polish participants in the competition.

Such was the response to the transgressions by the Polish FA that one correspondent asked whether 'the Polish mafia [was] controlling Polish football'. Despite the furore over television rights and the crass manipulation of the League title race, the Polish FA remains intact. For how long that state of affairs is allowed to continue will depend on UEFA's ultimate intentions. With the Champions' League providing UEFA with the financial clout to influence member associations, its central control should be strengthened. Despite its actions over the two Polish teams, UEFA's overall record does not inspire confidence. When CSKA withdrew its allegations against Marseille, UEFA was happy to call off its investigation. Yet the two Polish clubs were summarily ejected from the UEFA Cup, against the wishes of the Polish FA and without any allegation of match-fixing actually proven. Both FIFA and UEFA have turned a blind eye to more than circumstantial evidence when dealing with more powerful federations, such as the referee-bribing scandal in European matches involving Italian clubs in the 1970s. How ironic it would be if Marseille, after ending the French hoodoo in Europe after thirty-eight-years, were now to have the glory snatched away from them because of a messy business at home when the Italian clubs which perpetrated some of the worst excesses over the years never had to suffer such punishment. Such an outcome would, however, surely inflate the jinx on the French into Loch Ness Monster proportions.

Even when a French team wins the Cup on the field, it is likely to be somehow snatched away, this time by impropriety in its own backyard.

As for the the Champions' League, despite its anomalies it was certainly a success in its first season. It did not, however, kill the idea of a European league. But the old-style knock-out European event – a popular success with the fans – was well and truly dead, by UEFA's own hand, in order to keep the big clubs happy.

In 1992 a new plan for a European Superleague was produced by Alex Fynn after he talked to a number of clubs in the UK and abroad. There are two dynamic forces in football, he argued, the knock-out cup and the weekly league. If we can't have the former, what about the latter? The Fynn format for the European Superleague (ESL), published in *The Sunday Times* in December, called for a pyramid structure of forty clubs spread evenly between a Premier Division on top and three regional divisions below, to run concurrently with domestic leagues. The UEFA Cup would be retained as a feeder competition but the European Cup (including the Champions' League) and the Cup-winners' Cup would be abolished. As initial entry to the ESL would be based on performance in Europe during the previous season, there would be two Italian clubs, two German and two Spanish in the top division but no English clubs. Herein lay an important flaw in the plan. While the champions of Finland qualified, the third-placed team in the English Premier League didn't. Moreover, if a major club missed the cut-off point for the establishment of the ESL by not finishing high enough in its own national league, there would be a lengthy time span before it could join its peers. In an updated version, these problems have been ironed out. The qualifiers would now represent the strength of their own national leagues, with the UEFA Cup enlarged as a counterpoint. Most important of all, the competition would be a moveable feast. Apart from three clubs – the ESL champions, the winners of the regional play-off for promotion, and the UEFA Cup-winners, who would go into the regional division – every club would have to qualify every season, as they do under the current system.

Fynn's plan was taken up by the media across Europe,

particularly in Spain and Portugal, both of which countries would have representatives in the top division. Even UEFA president Lennart Johansson was moved to ask: 'If we are talking about something that should be extended regionally, why not discuss it?' In reality, though, Johansson did nothing of the sort.

In March 1993, Johansson, together with Gerhard Aigner, put forward the most radical official proposals yet seen. They wanted to extend the Champions' League to encompass 128 teams by amalgamating it with the UEFA Cup. This way, all the big European clubs, even those who fail to win their domestic leagues, could have the opportunity to play in the premier competition. The plan was fiercely opposed, however, particularly in Italy, which saw its pre-eminence among European leagues under threat if it were to be allowed. By April the Johansson-Aigner idea was effectively killed off by the UEFA Executive Committee, which instead decided to examine the possibility of bringing together the UEFA Cup and the Cup-winners' Cup in a new knock-out competition. In addition, the Champions' League was altered to allow seeding so that, say, Milan and Marseille would not have to face each other in the group matches.

When he opened a new stand at Liverpool earlier in the season, Johansson was told by former Tottenham chairman Irving Scholar that he should consider adding a semi-final to the Champions' League in order to sustain interest in all group matches until the end. Johansson thought there was enough merit in the idea to ask Sir Bert Millichip to raise it with the Executive Committee. It was the appropriate time: it brought four more money-spinning ties and was instituted for the 1993–94 season.

Lennart Johansson was taken aback by the opposition to his original plan: 'I have never claimed unanimity for such a project and I accept absolutely that reservations have been announced, but I have not heard of other proposals. One must think of the future of football.' The problem identified by Johansson is the one of unanimity (or consensus). For a European league to succeed, a format must be found which not only pleases fans and television, but also all the vested interests within UEFA and the various national associations. As opposition from Italy has shown, any competition which diminishes the importance of the Italian League will be fought. However, the logic of a European league is inexorable. The big clubs want it and television wants it. The only thing that remains is to come up with a formula that can satisfy everyone. Although Johansson now recognises that 'you will go nowhere unless you can take people with you', which means keeping the 'big' countries like Italy happy, he has gone far enough to imagine a scenario of national leagues reducing their top divisions to a maximum of sixteen clubs (perhaps imposed by UEFA) to enable a midweek European league to run concurrently. Such a format may even woo the fans. It might also be the only way to force the recalcitrant British to trim the size of their leagues. So if the big clubs get their wish it may be at the expense of increasing UEFA's power and reducing the capability of smaller clubs to maximise their income. It may, however, be a price the really big clubs of Europe are prepared to pay.

Ownership of the biggest clubs is now inextricably linked to ownership, or at least understanding, of the new media imperatives. The commercialisation of sport is so far advanced that the tide cannot now be rolled back. How football deals with this issue will determine the shape of the world's greatest game in the next century. The World Cup in the USA in 1994 should provide a glimpse of how that future will pan out.

15

American Dream

England are humiliated twice in quick succession while Jack Charlton shows how it should be done. Meanwhile, commercialism rules in the USA but will England learn the lessons? And will English football ever again be able to compete with the best?

> *'The first England football team ever to surrender without a fight was born of the first England manager to consistently seek to save his own pathetic neck by criticising his players in public.'*

Jeff Powell, writing in the Daily Mail *after England's 2–0 defeat by Norway, 1993.*

> *'I am the man for the job. I couldn't do a worse job, could I?'*

Screaming Lord Sutch, after England's 2–0 defeat by the USA, 1993.

> *'Blimey! US boots the Brits.'*

Headline in the Boston Herald *after the same match.*

At the end of the 1992–93 season, the thoroughly inept nature of the whole England set-up was exposed for all to see. The seeds of disaster were sown sixteen months before, on February 20 1992, at a fateful meeting at the Amsterdam Hilton hotel. There, the two Grahams, Kelly and Taylor, met with their counterparts from the other nations in Group 2 of the qualifying tournament for the 1994 World Cup to arrange the dates when the group matches would be played.

Amazingly, the English delegation agreed to play two crucial away games right at the end of the following English season. Moreover, without apparently giving any consideration to the probability of players being exhausted after the climax of the gruelling English campaign, Kelly and Taylor accepted fixture dates against Poland and Norway that required England to play the matches within five days of each other.

As if this wasn't enough, England were under other handicaps as the World Cup games approached. Graham Taylor seemed to have at last decided on the formation he wanted to use – Gascoigne in the free role supported by what were essentially ball-winners in midfield – but never quite convinced observers that he was at ease with the system, and he gave the feeling that he would change it without too much prompting. In addition, having dropped crucial home points against Norway and Holland, the pressure was now on to get at least two, and preferably three points from the two away games. Defeat, as Taylor recognised, 'was unthinkable'.

Nevertheless, the 'unthinkable' almost happened in Poland. In front of an intimidating 60,000 crowd in Chorzow, near Katowice, the scene of a disastrous 2–0 defeat in 1973 which all but killed off hopes of qualifying for the 1974 World Cup, England were comprehensively outplayed by a Poland team missing a number of first-choice players. According to Taylor, England played like 'headless chickens', but the truth was that they were second-best in every department and looked a yard slower than their opponents. That Poland held only a one-goal advantage going into the last ten minutes had more to do with fortune smiling on England and two dreadful misses by Lesniak than any competence in the English defence. Des Walker was again short of pace, while John Barnes and Gazza were anonymous. After seventy minutes, Taylor brought on Ian Wright for Carlton Palmer, and it was Wright who salvaged England's World Cup prospects with his first goal at international level. Only six minutes were left. There were two consolations in what was, in all honesty, an appalling performance. First was the result, which England hardly deserved. Second was the assured performance of new cap, David Bardsley, a late replacement for Lee Dixon in the problem right back position. The game left England still in second place in the group behind Norway. Both teams had nine points but Norway had a game in hand. If England were to keep their destiny in their own hands they needed at least a point from the game in Oslo four days later.

Since the shock of beating England 2–1 in a qualifying match for the 1982 World Cup, memorably described by an emotional television commentator, who screamed, 'Maggie Thatcher, can you hear me? Your boys took a terrible beating,' Norwegian football has improved significantly. A storming start in the qualifying group for the 1994 World Cup had reinforced expectations that they could beat England again, particularly after the mediocre performance at Wembley had seen the Norwegians emerge with a 1–1 draw. Meanwhile, other Scandinavian teams have shown that they also are no longer whipping-boys. Sweden have become a force to be reckoned with, as the team showed when beating England in the European Championships in 1992, and of course Denmark came from nowhere to win that tournament. The progress has not been achieved by accident. The Scandinavians, from the early 1980s, showed English football live on television to whet the public appetite for the game. In addition, new coaching systems were put in place and foreign teams, particularly from Africa, were invited over to play club sides. And whereas most Scandinavian players of the past were semi-professional with the odd gifted individual playing for a foreign club, now, as well as a larger number of the most talented playing their football abroad, full-time professional leagues have been established at home.

Norway's transformation into a team of real substance was completed by the coach who took over in 1990, Egil Olsen. Olsen's record certainly bears comparison with Graham Taylor's – 4 defeats in 26 games before the England encounter. Olsen was himself an international who had become a university lecturer once his playing career was over. He attributes his success as an international manager to the 'direct play' methods of Charles Hughes. Indeed, prior to the game against England he held up a copy of *The Winning Formula* for all his players to see and told them that the way to play was laid out in the book – but, he added, the English don't use it.

Olsen's Norway play to their strengths, which means a consistent tactical approach using a zonal defence (Norway never use man-to-man marking) and a pressure game when the team has lost possession. Counter-attacks at speed, which is how Olsen interprets direct play, are a particular feature of Norway's style, often utilising either the long ball or crosses from the flanks. The long ball is not just a hopeful punt into the penalty area or 'down the channels', but an accurate pass intended to release a forward player. Once the ball has reached an attacker, the midfield pours forward, believing that defensively, they can resist a counter-attack against themselves. 'The most important thing,' Olsen says, 'is that the players know what is expected of them and believe it is the most effective way to play.' Olsen's goalkeeper, Erik Thorstvedt, who plays in England for Tottenham, told how the team reacted to this outlook: 'It's stimulating for the players because they know that as important parts of a well-organised side they have to do their bit.'

Olsen was rightly annoyed to be portrayed by the bellicose wing of the English press as a 'mad professor'. As usual, it was a complete distortion of the truth and if it sowed any complacency in English minds it did a terrible disservice to the team. Erik Thorstvedt was more rigorous in his assessment. 'It's [rare] to find people with such an intellect who decide to use that intellect in football,' he said. 'He almost single-handedly has turned Norwegian football around at international level.' Thorstvedt went on to explain some of Olsen's methods, which are in many ways unique, and the players' reaction to them. Olsen makes a point, for instance, of encouraging each player to assess his own performance after a game. 'Everything you've done,' Thorstvedt revealed, 'is analysed by numbers. He'll look at every player. Players find it interesting to say "Let's see what I did last time." It's enlightening . . . He goes through each player to see what he's done. How many times he's touched the ball, how much he was involved, how many good things, how many bad things. The players love it.' Olsen is not obsessed by such analyses, however, as Thorstvedt made clear. 'He doesn't go on about it, he just brings it up.'

When the England management announced the team to play Norway, which was less than an hour before kick-off due to a ludicrous level of paranoid secrecy which included seclusion at a NATO military base and the removal in handcuffs of a Norwegian photographer (not to mention the exclusion of a representative of the Norwegian FA on the grounds that he might be a spy). This was totally unneccessary as Graham Taylor had revealed his tactical formation to the media, and therefore the opposition, two days previously. It was a formation that stunned everybody, including his own players. A new tactical plan was to be put into operation based mainly on countering the Norwegian right-sided player, Jostein Flo, who at the time wasn't even playing in the country's First Division (although he subsequently went 'up' in the world when he was transferred to Sheffield United). Three centre backs were deployed, no full backs (the two Lees, Sharpe and Dixon, were used as 'wing backs'), with two up front, effectively in a 3–5–2 shape. Having said he couldn't pick Chris Waddle because it would affect the side's style of play, Taylor had now, at a stroke, thrown his tactics of the last six months out of the window.

Olsen, on the other hand, stuck firmly to his game plan. The first match at Wembley had provided a salutary lesson for him because, as Erik Thorstvedt later recalled, 'We were overrun by England and he didn't expect that to happen. It was a good day for England and not such a good day for us, but we still got away with a point which was tremendous. It was the only time he was mistaken in his forecast of how a game would go and he apologised to us for perhaps giving us a false sense of security.' Olsen's low-key methods were in sharp contrast to Taylor's, which appeared ever more agonised. 'When we meet up on the Sunday [before a Wednesday match],' continued Thorstvedt, he [Olsen] always says, "Don't think about the game," which is a very good rule. The good thing about him is that a team meeting lasts only twenty-five minutes. It's never like we sit there for two hours being told how good the opponents are.'

After seeing the Poland game, the Norwegians felt they had nothing to fear. Olsen came to the point, according to Thorstvedt, only on the day of the match itself. 'Just before leaving the hotel, 'he said, "Well guys, I feel we are favourites here today, we should win this one." So . . . he put the pressure on a little bit.'

Taylor's unbelievably naïve plan was completely destroyed within a few minutes of the start. Flo may not have been playing in the First Division in Norway but he could carry out instructions. As soon as it was obvious that England intended to reinforce the left side of their defence and midfield to stop Flo, Olsen moved him to the other side, throwing the England defence into confusion. Like Keown in the Dutch game, Pallister was uncertain about what to do now he had no one to mark, and as a consequence did very little that was of any benefit to his team. Sharpe, who was making his full debut, was asked to fulfil a role totally alien to him, namely patrolling the whole of the left-hand side. In addition to the problems in defence, Taylor had no out-and-out ball winner in midfield. A more complete departure from his earlier tactics would be difficult to imagine. The front players, meanwhile, were isolated and rarely got into the action. When the England players were in proximity to the bench for a throw-in they looked for support, only to find that the bench was just as mystified as they were.

All of this confusion was compounded by a number of poor individual performances. The England players' lack of basic technique was at times horribly exposed and Gazza was unable to provide the kind of spark he had given the team in the Wembley game. It was a side which was simply not up to the task. Time and again the ball was either hoofed forward mindlessly or passed to a red shirt. After forty-two minutes of this Des Walker displayed an uncharacteristic lack of professionalism when he argued with a decision of the referee. While Walker was gesticulating at the official, Halle took a quick free kick, Walker struggled to get back and cover and Norway were one up through Leonhardsen.

English supporters might have felt that Taylor would at least have the chance to rectify matters at half-time. Erik Thorstvedt was worried about the same thing and told his team-mates: 'That team in the other dressing room is the team that always comes back. Let's make sure they don't come back this time.' Thorstvedt need not have worried, as three minutes after the break Norway scored again. This time Chris Woods failed to stand up to Bohinen's shot after the defence had melted away in the face of one of Norway's surging breaks. Norway were now playing with verve and spirit and ran out worthy winners. England, by contrast, appeared to have thrown in the towel long before the final whistle. The Norwegian players certainly thought so. 'I was very surprised they didn't do any more,' Thorstvedt said. 'It felt like when we got to 2–0 it was over . . . It was very easy towards the end of the game. They [the Norwegian players] didn't feel [England] put up a great struggle. I felt it was almost a bit embarrassing for England towards the end because we started to jump over the ball [and] do that kind of stuff. For that to happen was embarrassing.'

Egil Olsen seemed almost shocked at the way England so abjectly played into his hands. 'They gave up in the last twenty minutes,' he said. 'I never thought I would see an England team do that.' Graham Taylor lost no time in blaming the players again. Without taking any responsibility for the way he had introduced his tactical plan at the last minute, Taylor hit the players where it hurt, saying, 'It was a performance way below what was expected. It must have left a lot of people back home angry and frustrated and I feel the same.' (Weeks later he qualified his comments, admitting that the team had not had sufficient time to adapt to the new tactics, but he stopped short of admitting any flaws to the tactical plan itself.) Whatever spin was put upon the débâcle, however, the stark fact remained that it was Taylor's team, Taylor's players, and Taylor's system. The World Cup finals now seemed a very long way away. Moreover, Taylor had undermined his most potent weapon, Paul Gascoigne, by telling the media before the match that Gazza was out of condition and 'must learn how to eat properly and refuel properly'. Such a condescending public remark could not have done anything to improve Gazza's state of mind. 'You can't rip Gazza's head off,' Gary Lineker told Hugh McIlvanney of the *Observer*, 'because he will sulk for a week and won't play for you.' Lineker reiterated his concerns in an interview with Robert Philip in the *Daily Telegraph*, saying, 'Terry Venables was great, [he] handled him brilliantly, and Dino Zoff seems to be doing OK, but at England level he has taken a bit of stick from the manager and if he starts getting that in private, let alone in public, he'll sulk. Things affect him like that.' It was this public slagging-off of the players that added oil to the troubled waters of the relationship between the manager and his former captain. Such was the rift that had been created that Lineker was moved to say: '[There is] something . . . about his approach I can never forgive and that's his readiness to slaughter people in public. I have told him so to his face many times. There has been a lot of talk lately about England players going on the field with bad attitudes, lacking motivation. The real problem is lack of confidence, a little bit of fear, especially fear of failure. Public criticism by their manager has much to do with that. He denied doing it but the evidence is overwhelming.'

The wheel had turned full circle. Having been dumped out of the European Championships in 1992 by Sweden, England were now facing the possibility of elimination from the World Cup by Norway. These were two Scandinavian countries whose players play in the English League and whose fans are fans of English football. It was a defeat by pupils who taught their masters a painful lesson.

Back in England, there was outrage at such a supine performance. Bobby Charlton, just as he had after the Swedish disaster, summed up the feelings of many when he said: 'We were technically naïve, unprofessional in everything we did. It was a performance that really plumbed the depths. What really hurts a lot of people is not that they lost the match but the way that they lost it. We always seem to pride ourselves on being aggressive, tough, professional and brave. Those were all the qualities that were lacking.' What, at the very least, was needed, then, and what Taylor signally failed to provide, were the traditional English virtues. When Taylor took over as England manager, a wall in the England changing room at Wembley was decorated with a mural of Samurai warriors. Taylor had it removed because he said it had nothing to do with England and replaced it with a small plaque of the three England lions. The England team certainly looked as if it needed to regain some of the strengths of those Japanese fighters, let alone of the players who performed alongside Bobby Charlton.

Naturally, the media had a field day. From the reasoned and reasonable editorials in the quality press to the hysterical outpourings of the tabloids (NORSE MANURE – YOU'VE GONE AND DUNG IT AGAIN TAYLOR, said the Sun), it seemed everyone was agreed. Taylor should go. Everyone, that is, except the FA. One leading Premier League chairman sought to raise the matter before the FA's International Committee, which appointed Taylor, on the basis that since the team still stood a chance of making it to the World Cup finals, Taylor should be replaced while that chance still existed. By the following morning, however, Peter Swales, chairman of Manchester City and head of the International Committee, firmly rejected any such notion, giving Taylor a public vote of confidence without reference to his committee. 'Why are you asking me that question now?' Swales replied as if he'd been asked to say who would be manager in the year 2000. 'The World Cup campaign is not over yet. We have three matches left and it is still feasible that we might qualify. Graham Taylor still has our confidence and we know that he is not a quitter.' This was the man who fired Peter Reid after four games of the 1993–94 season, the twelfth managerial change in Swales' twenty-year tenure as chairman of Manchester City. This was the same man who, on an earlier occasion, had said that England would 'easily' qualify for the USA. It was also the same Peter Swales who intimated that it might have been preferable to have been knocked out of Italia '90 at the semi-final stage because to have won it would have saddled the country with another four years of Bobby Robson's stewardship. Robson, according to Swales, could not take the pressure.

In fact, cries for Taylor's removal obscured the real lesson. If Taylor were sacked what would prevent more of the same? The attributes of an effective international manager have never really been analysed in England. Generally speaking, successful managers at this level fall into three categories. First is the great player who has done it all. Recent examples of this are Franz Beckenbauer and Michel Platini. In England Kevin Keegan and Glenn Hoddle come into this category. It is important that those in this group are appointed fairly quickly after their playing careers have ended. Their inexperience is less important than the fact that the players stepping up to international level at this time will probably have hero-worshipped such a manager as a player.

The second kind is the wily old fox, the older man who is nonetheless respected by younger players for his knowledge of the game, his tactical acumen and his achievements, which are generally associated with getting the best out of great players. Rinus Michels, Raymond Goethals and Enzo Bearzot are good examples of this breed. In England, perhaps Bob Paisley could fulfil such a role, but of course he has never been called upon.

The third broad type falls somewhere between these extremes. He will generally be a man who has moulded players to perform to the tactics he wants. More often than not, these are strong, even wilful individuals. The two Scandinavians, Richard Moeller Nielson, who won the European Championships with Denmark and England's tormentor in Oslo, Egil Olsen, fit into this category. But perhaps the most obvious example is an Englishman, and a thorough patriot at that. He is Jack Charlton.

Charlton was never cut out to be a club manager. His spells in charge of Middlesbrough, Newcastle United and Sheffield Wednesday were always punctuated by rumblings of discontent from Big Jack. Quite simply, he often preferred country pursuits like shooting and fishing to the grind of running a club. He was not unsuccessful, however, although his teams, particularly the one he created at Middlesbrough, were not noted for their flair. Nevertheless, Charlton always put out a side which knew what it was supposed to do and at each of the three clubs he managed, all of which were in the doldrums when he arrived, he established foundations which would later be built upon by others to great effect. Eventually, boredom or disillusionment would set in and Charlton would resign, saying that he did not have the time or the inclination to put up with the lot of a club manager.

Charlton's track record should have alerted the FA that here was someone who had won just about every honour as a player, was obviously a good manager, yet was not enamoured of club management. In other words, a potentially ideal mentor for the national team, where the need is to rise to the occasion in just a few games each year. True to form, however, the FA apparently didn't even give Charlton the courtesy of a reply when he applied for the job. Instead, he went to the Republic of Ireland, and the rest is history.

After nine games in their World Cup qualifying group, Ireland had won six and drawn three. They led the group by two points and looked sure-fire certainties to make it to the USA. Around the end of the 1992–93 season, the Irish won three consecutive away games, against Albania, Latvia and Lithuania, to make them the dominant force in the group. Yet Charlton essentially called on the same bunch of tired players from the English Premier League that Graham Taylor had to choose from, which begs the question, why were Charlton's methods so effective while Taylor's were not? The key difference between the two is that Charlton knows exactly what system and method he wants his players to use. They understand it perfectly well and feel confident in carrying out his plans. Charlton chooses his tactics and the players he picks are there to fulfil easily identifiable tasks. It is as simple as that. If Ireland suffer an injury, even to a key player, the tactics do not change, rather, the replacement is expected to slot in. The continuity this produces is the greatest asset an international squad, which only gets together irregularly, can possess.

Moreover, as manager of a small country with limited resources, Charlton had no compunction about exploiting FIFA's qualification rules, which allowed him to select players who had no connection with the Emerald Isle beyond one grandparent having been born there. Charlton had the birth register scoured, then informed the players he wanted that they were qualified to play for the Republic, and were, in fact, 'Irishmen'. In this way he was able to offer quality 'English' and 'Scottish' players, like Andy Townsend and Ray Houghton, the chance to play international football, which they seized upon with relish.

Charlton also recognises the need for evolution within a national team. At first Ireland played like an international version of Wimbledon, but with success came the belief that a passing game could be added to the traditional way. As Liam Brady commented, 'With good players you can vary the options and play the direct game with skill.' By doing this, Charlton has avoided over-reliance on the long ball. Instead, the manager, and therefore the team, has kept one step ahead. It is an indication that Charlton may yet metamorphose into a wily old fox.

There are other differences in the way Charlton approaches his task. He seems happy to accommodate stars and is big enough to make exceptions for players. Paul McGrath was brought back into the fold immediately after he had unexpectedly pulled out of the Albania game for no discernible reason. If there was a valid excuse, it was never publicly revealed. At the same time, the players know that Charlton is a straight-talking man who won't stand any nonsense, and has a vindictive side to his nature as David O'Leary and Liam Brady could testify. He also expects, and gets, loyalty and he is prepared to show it in return. John Aldridge has always been a prolific scorer at club level but this part of his game was not seen to its maximum effect within the Irish system. Charlton persevered with him, however, and Aldridge never complained that his role diminished his stature as a goal-scorer at the highest level, to the benefit of both the team and, eventually, the player. Those on the fringes are constantly kept in mind. Charlton has gone out of his way, for instance, to heap praise on David Kelly, a forward who is not an automatic selection. When Charlton was commentating for ITV on Newcastle's 7–1 victory over Leicester City at the end of the 1992–93 season, you would have thought Kelly was the best striker Charlton had ever seen, such was the eulogy he delivered every time Kelly came within a couple of yards of the ball.

What Charlton is not prepared to tolerate is a player, no matter how gifted, not playing to the system. Liam Brady, one of the greatest Irish players of all time, was both patriotic and realistic enough to admit that 'you play Jack Charlton's way or you don't play at all', Brady, a true ambassador for the game, surely deserved a better fate than to be pulled off in his last international appearance – it was also his benefit game, and a friendly – before half-time. It was Charlton's way, however, of bringing home to everybody exactly who it is who decides how the team plays.

The manager is able to lighten the mood, albeit sometimes unintentionally, with his idiosyncrasies, such as his apparent inability to pronounce any foreign player's name correctly. Such social *faux pas* would never be tolerated at the English FA but they have endeared Charlton to the Irish. He is, in many ways, more Irish than the Irish, and his team is more English than the English, but with one crucial difference: both manager and team are winners. A national team of no-hopers which had never made the final stages of any international competition was taken on the crest of a wave of emotion to the European Championships in Germany in 1988 and to Italia '90, where it performed better than anyone but Charlton had a right to expect. As the season ended in 1993, the Irish looked like the only Premier League players who would be going to the USA in 1994.

The success the Irish team has enjoyed under Charlton has brought invitations to play the top sides in the world, and in the summer of 1993 Ireland were rated sixth in the world in the new FIFA rankings (England were eleventh). In addition, the income to the Irish FA from gate receipts, sponsorship and tournament share-outs during the Charlton era has enabled the governing body to embark on a programme to entrench the game's new-found popularity. The Irish FA's objective is to ensure a strengthened Irish League with clubs playing in modern grounds.

The legacy Jack Charlton will bequeath to Irish football when he eventually moves on will be immense. Beyond mere results, he has single-handedly created the modern Irish supporters, who travel in their droves to away games and tournaments, determined to enjoy themselves and present a friendly face. According to Liam Brady, they have contributed to the excellent team spirit that characterises the Irish squad. 'It was a pleasure to play for them,' he said. 'They are very loyal and would never boo a player the way [the Wembley crowd] booed John Barnes.' Yet just as success is embraced with lightheartedness, so disappointment, like being edged out by England for a place in the European Championship finals in Sweden in 1992, is taken with good grace and dignity by the fans, in contrast to the manager who hates to be defeated at any time.

Charlton is a man who would take a job only on his terms. Such a loose cannon is anathema to the English FA, but the Irish FA, to its credit, and to the benefit of Irish football, was prepared to give him his head. England's loss has been Ireland's gain. Jack Charlton is probably the only living Englishman granted the status, conferred by the adulation of the people, of honorary Irishman.

In 1992, Charlton took his team on a close-season tour of the USA, where they appeared in the USA Cup. Recognising the futility of such tournaments at the end of a long, hard English season; he was adamant that he would never again undertake such a commitment. At least Charlton was two years away from the World Cup finals and at the time the USA Cup was some consolation at least for missing the finals of the European Championships in Sweden. For the 1993 USA Cup, the final dress rehearsal for the World Cup in 1994, the

Americans tempted the world champions, Germany, the most beguiling team of all, Brazil, and Graham Taylor's England. When accepting the invitation, the English response was to claim arrogantly that the tournament would be an excellent acclimatisation exercise for the World Cup.

At the time, it must have seemed like a good idea. The two qualifying games against Poland and Norway would be completed, England would have taken giant strides towards qualification, and it was a way to keep the players together (Club England again) while giving the opportunity for fringe performers to gain valuable international experience. Lazio were reluctant to let Paul Gascoigne go (the Italian League was still in progress), and indeed Gazza did not make the trip. If Ken Bates had had his way, no one would have gone. 'We are lectured by the FA,' he said, 'that we are playing too much football and the very institution that lectures us is going for more and more meaningless friendlies. There was an unwritten agreement between the League and the FA that every other summer we would play either World Cup or European Championships and every other summer we would have a rest. Three years ago they do that stupid Australasian tour only so that certain council members can get a free holiday and this year Taylor's got no more brains. Having played two shitty matches and got one point out of four, instead of coming back and licking his wounds [he] goes off to the stupid USA Cup.'

Quite apart from Bates' criticism, The England camp's reasoning was fatally flawed in another direction. As a key pre-World Cup tournament featuring the world's most prestigious teams, the USA Cup acquired an importance it would not otherwise enjoy. The other three teams, Germany, Brazil and the USA, all had good reasons to take the games seriously and not treat them as friendlies. The Germans, as holders of the World Cup, qualified for USA '94 automatically so were desperate for all the competitive matches they could get, while Brazil had an emerging side of no little talent based on their Olympic team. In addition, a number of their most famous internationals had club commitments in Europe and at home and could not take part so the youngsters had the chance to prove themselves. For the USA, it was important to give a good account of themselves in order to engender support among the public and the media in the run-up to the World Cup. Finally, it was the most important soccer tournament yet staged in the USA. The Americans needed to show they could mount a top-class football event and the plan to lay natural grass on top of the artificial turf in the enclosed Pontiac Silverdome in Michigan would be tested for the first time – in full view of the world. It was never a time to experiment, nor would the tournament provide a bit of light relief from the pressure of qualifying games, as Graham Taylor imagined. The catalogue of errors, so disastrously exposed in Poland and Norway, had one final catastrophe to deliver to the beleaguered England regime.

The 2–0 defeat the Americans inflicted on Taylor's England, a few days after the young Brazilians had beaten the USA at a stroll, was even more humiliating than the result in Oslo. Although it was inexcusable to go down to a small Scandinavian country without a fight, at least Norway possessed a reasonable international record and had defeated Holland. Succumbing to a nation that had only notched up one victory in its previous fourteen games and had not scored a single goal in its last four; a country which had no professional league and where the game is seen as one played primarily by college kids and women (the USA are the current women's world champions), however, was simply beyond belief. The American media recognised this and the *International Herald Tribune* said that 'an English soccer team just doesn't lose to a US team any more than a US basketball team loses to Bahrain or Sri Lanka.' Taylor now seemed like Mr Micawber again, desperately hoping something would turn up. 'There will be a turning-point,' he said.'Something will happen. I don't know what and I don't know when but something will happen.' The *Daily Mirror*, meanwhile, had Taylor's face on a WANTED – DEAD OR ALIVE poster and called him the 'outlaw of English football'.

The English players managed to dredge up some self-respect in the following game against Brazil, a 1–1 draw played in front of 54,000 people in Washington; and the improvement was continued in the final game against Germany in the magnificent Silverdome in Pontiac, Michigan, which became the first football international to be played on real grass in an indoor stadium. The crowd, at over 62,000, was the highest of the tournament. However, England lost the match 2–1 and looked a class below the Germans, who fulfilled their ambition to win the competition having, in true German style, come back from 3–0 down against Brazil in their first game to draw 3–3, and beaten the Americans 4–3 in a crazy match in Chicago.

Throughout the American trip, Graham Taylor appeared increasingly bemused by events on the pitch. After the USA game, he seemed to be saying that the only reason England lost was because of an inspired performance from the American goalkeeper, Tony Meola (the correct result, according to Taylor, should have been 4–2 to England), but Taylor knew as well as anyone else that if an international team concedes two goals in a match it is unlikely to win it. Taylor was at it again after the German game. 'Give us Lothar Mathaus and we win,' he claimed. One might as well say that England would have won the 1970 World Cup if Alf Ramsey could have picked Pele, or the 1986 tournament if Maradona had been English. And while it was perfectly true that Mathaus had given an outstanding performance, Taylor's point was particularly unfair on the rest of the German midfield and one of his own players. Where would England have been without David Platt's 13 goals in his last 22 international games?

The worst aspect of the American experience was that Taylor still seemed to be experimenting and was no nearer a settled side. The absence of first-choice players from the squads of Brazil and Germany was overcome because the replacements had a tried and tested tactical system into which they could fit with ease and they knew what was expected of them (they were also, it must be said, better players). This contrasted sharply with the English, who at times looked to have lost their self-belief, which was hardly surprising given the inconsistent selection policy. As an example of the confusion, the right back situation is instructive. David Bardsley, one of the few successes against Poland, was dropped; Paul Parker, one of the best defenders in the country, was nowhere to be seen; then Taylor went on to pick Earl Barrett for the US tour. And after criticising his demeanour against Poland, the manager made Paul Ince his captain. Ken Bates was characteristically dismissive of the whole tour. 'One thing you learn in life,' he said, 'is you never go into a battle you ain't going to win and there's no way he [Taylor] could have won. If we'd have stuffed the USA 4–0, so bloody what? Anything other than that [and] you're on a hiding to nothing in the press. He could have beaten Brazil and Germany, which was unlikely because morale was at rock bottom, so what? It was a meaningless tournament and now we can't even win a meaningless tournament. He should have gone home, cut the grass, painted the house, taken the kids to Chessington Zoo or something and said, "I'll see you in August."'

Of course the real blame lay with the FA, who picked the wrong man in the first place and then compounded the error by refusing to alter the coaching set-up to accommodate fresh ideas from icons like Glenn Hoddle and Kevin Keegan. The FA was encouraged in its indolence by the scoreless draw Norway obtained against the Dutch in Rotterdam on the day of England's humiliation at the hands of the USA. Following that result, two wins for England against Poland and San Marino and a draw in Holland should see England qualify in second place behind Norway. Anything less will mean Taylor relying on the gods and at least one of the other fancied teams dropping points. Difficulties in the Dutch camp between the players, the manager and administrators (Ruud Gullit stated that he no longer wanted to play for the national team), a perennial problem in the Netherlands, might help Taylor, but what will happen to England if they do make it to the USA is anyone's guess.

Those finals, as we have seen, are tailor-made for even a half-decent English team. The USA, as a nation which instinctively understands the role of top-class sport in society, will do whatever is necessary to ensure the success of the tournament.

Sport looms large in American life and culture. Its influence spreads throughout all levels of society and in a country so large geographically and with such a diverse ethnic mix it has acted as a unifying force for a nation in which individual states guard their autonomy like zealots. The isolationism of the country for large chunks of its history probably accounts for the fact that it felt it had to invent its own sports, a development which took place in the nineteenth and early twentieth centuries. Only popular culture, as exemplified by Hollywood movies, modern music and sport can challenge the divisive nature of American society. It was no accident that the fight to end the second-class status of Afro-Americans, for instance, was first thrust into the consciousness of white America, not by the civil rights movement of the 1960s, but in the late 1940s when the prowess within baseball's 'negro leagues' was obvious to all. This recognition culminated in Jackie Robinson of the Brooklyn Dodgers breaking the ban on black players in Major League baseball, which had been in existence since 1889.

The Americans understood early on that sport is a business and therefore ripe for exploitation. One of the earliest examples of corruption in modern sport came with the infamous attempt by serious gambling and gangster interests to 'fix' baseball's 1919 World Series. In more modern times, the USA was the first country in which television paid huge rights fees and came to be of supreme importance to the success or failure of any spectator sport. This ethos reached its zenith in Los Angeles in 1984, when the Olympic Games, which had left such massive financial burdens on previous host cities and countries that hardly anyone was prepared to bid for them, were transformed into a money-spinner of gigantic proportions.

With its licence to print money, sport in the USA has long ceased to belong to the people. The franchise system of team ownership in the major sports – gridiron football, Major League baseball, basketball and ice hockey, has given owners immense power. They are exempted, for instance, from anti-trust laws, which means they can enjoy monopoly status in a city or state. They are free to uproot teams from their inner-city origins and move to wealthier, more gentrified climes where business and political interests will offer a better financial deal. Thus one of baseball's best-loved teams, the Brooklyn Dodgers, was transported 3,000 miles across the continent to Los Angeles, while the Baltimore Colts went overnight to Indianapolis, leaving fans who had supported the team for decades bereft. No comparable example could ever be envisaged in English football because even if Liverpool were transplanted to more salubrious surroundings, the supporters would still be able to travel to watch them. Anyway, having a football club in town is not seen as the community asset it is in the USA. Instead of a loyal, working-class audience, the new environment gave owners the chance to change the fan base. Escalating ticket prices reflect the search for a new type of fan who can afford to spend copiously on refreshments and merchandising or is the recipient of a corporate entertainment freebee and therefore watches the action with disinterest rather than passion.

While taking money from the paying supporter with one hand, the owners have sold out to television on the other. This explains the proliferation of time outs, half-time contests, entertainment, assorted starting times and saturation coverage, all part of the search for more media dollars, which has taken place at the expense of the traditional fan, who now has to watch on television. Moreover, television's insatiable appetite for stars has seen salaries rise to astronomical levels, over $7 million per year in some cases. It was into this milieu that FIFA plunged when, in 1988, it awarded the biggest sporting tournament of all, the World Cup, to the USA.

Attempts to establish soccer in the USA have always ended in failure. The last great effort in the 1970s tried to impose the game from the top down by importing aging stars such as Pele, Cruyff and Beckenbauer. When they left there was a void which homespun heroes simply could not fill and professional football collapsed. It did, however, leave a legacy of massive interest as a participatory sport, particularly among the young. FIFA president Joao Havelange's hope, when the 1994 finals were awarded to the USA, was that the impact of the tournament would leave the country ready at last for a top-grade league.

More important than this, though, was the fact that Havelange wanted to secure his place in history. He had ousted the Englishman, Sir Stanley Rous, from the FIFA presidency in 1974 by pledging to third-world countries increased representation in the World Cup finals. To achieve this, the number of participating teams would rise from sixteen to twenty-four. It was a laudable aim because it encouraged the worldwide growth of football and increased the numbers who play it at all levels. As long as the World Cup finals were stuck on sixteen teams, the prospects of countries like the USA or Japan reaching them was miniscule. If there was little likelihood of these countries, let alone more African nations, appearing in the finals of football's greatest competition, there was equally little incentive to develop the game in those countries. Moreover, other sports were ready to fill the vacuum. Havelange saw football as being in direct competition with other mega-sports events like the Olympic Games and he wanted to ensure that football remained the world's number one sport by encouraging all nations to play it. The downside of securing the future of the game in ever more countries would be the dropping of standards in the finals themselves, but Havelange thought it was worth it. In order to pay for the increase, Havelange was forced to embrace commercialism. With the help of Horst Dassler, the German owner of Adidas, and his English partner, Patrick Nally, FIFA signed up Coca-Cola and the future of the tournament was promptly underwritten. The increase in the number of games in the finals – up to an overblown fifty-two – brought with it opportunities to raise further commercial income in the form of television and sponsorship fees.

Havelange also realised that football could never be a truly world game unless it cracked the final frontier – the USA. In fact, the 1986 tournament should have gone to America but Havelange allowed his personal relationship with a Mexican television company, Televista, to get the better of him and he swung the vote Mexico's way when the original choice, Colombia, pulled out at a late stage. Mexico gained the finals despite a campaign on behalf of the USA led by the former secretary of state, Henry Kissinger.

For 1994 there were compelling reasons to award the tournament to the USA. First, there was the American love of sporting events and the unrivalled experience the country possesses in putting them on. Such mega-events as the Super Bowl and the World Series meant that the infrastructure – electronic communication, transport and hotels – was already in place. Second, some of the World Cup's major sponsors, including Coca-Cola and Mars, are American companies and a successful US tournament would be a bonus for them in their own backyard. Third, there was a wealth of choice of modern, well-equipped stadia, and modern biotechnology now meant that grass could be laid on top of synthetic surfaces. Lastly, although it may be a minority sport, soccer could count on a loyal base of fans in the urban communities comprising ethnic minorities. By the late 1980s, this had been supplemented by the millions in suburban high schools and on college campuses who were playing the game.

Having seen off feeble bids from Brazil and Morocco, the United States Soccer Federation (USSF), the country's governing body, was in a position to start making demands of its own. With the compliance of Havelange and the FIFA general secretary, Sepp Blatter, crazy notions to make the game more dramatic for television were proposed. These included bigger goals and the division of the match into four quarters. Thankfully, most of these suggestions were laughed out of court. Nonetheless, Blatter continued to pursue his ideas, which he feels will 'stretch' the game, thereby making it more 'exciting'. There is no doubt that the new back-pass law speeds up the game, increasing the chances of goals from defensive errors. What was, perhaps, not foreseen was that it would also mean more offside decisions. More contentious than any of this is Blatter's intention to replace the throw-in with a kick-in, to the horror of purists, who have nightmares about even more fifty-yard balls into the penalty area. On a more enlightened note, Blatter has put forward a number of practical propositions like time restrictions on goalkeepers' possession of the ball, sudden death after extra time and three points for a win, any or all of which might yet be adopted for the 1994 finals.

Of course, one of the big prizes for football, should the World Cup prove to be a success in the USA, is the possibility of further huge riches from television. US TV has always been ambivalent about screening football since it could not stop the game for a commercial break (although that has been tried in the past), and anyway the interest was simply not great enough. The television rating, which is the percentage of the available television audience gained, for the USA-Germany game in 1993, shown live by ABC as a dry run for the World Cup, was two, comparable to the National Hockey League play-offs for the Stanley Cup, and satisfactory for a Sunday lunchtime but nowhere near enough to increase interest from hard-bitten TV executives, who live and die by the ratings they bring in.

In 1990, The USSF struck a deal with one of the three big networks, NBC, to cover the World Cup, but the arrangement was vetoed by FIFA on the grounds that only seven matches would be screened live. However, the other main broadcasters, CBS, ABC and the cable operator ESPN, did not show much interest in bidding for rights. Fearful that they would not only lose a rights fee but also not have any pictures to beam around the world, FIFA went to the European television companies which, through their collective organisation, the European Broadcasting Union, agreed to become the 'host broadcaster'. Later, an agreement was made with ABC and its sister company, ESPN, which between them will carry all fifty-two games in the 1994 tournament. Only eleven will be shown directly on the ABC network – the rest will be available exclusively on subscription. ABC and ESPN have, however, promised uninterrupted transmissions of each half, a period of continuous play which only the Masters golf tournament has previously been able to rival.

ABC was in a position to acquire the rights only because of the support of the World Cup sponsors, Mars, General Motors, Adidas, Fuji and Mastercard, which all agreed to forgo advertising breaks during play in return for exclusive broadcast sponsorship. Each company is guaranteed signage for fifteen minutes alongside the permanent clock on screen. In addition, their time on air will be announced with their slogan. The second half of the US-Germany game began with a voice saying, 'Whatever your colours, choose Fuji Film.' More worrying was the distortion that excessive home bias and an inability to appreciate the finer points of the game might produce. For instance, it was Tony Meola's 'twenty-nine saves' that were trumpeted rather than Karl Heinz Reidle's hat-trick.

It is pretty obvious from the dealings with television in the USA, as well as the evidence from Britain and around the world, that television, rather than the traditional paying spectator, is now the game's most important customer (in fact, fans are not customers in the true sense, since the committed supporter cannot take his custom elsewhere). Tickets for the 1994 World Cup went on sale as the 1993 USA Cup was being played. The response was phenomenal and the indications are that most of the fifty-two games will be played to capacity audiences. Moreover, because there are no exclusive deals with travel companies, it is unlikely that fans will be ripped off as they were during Italia '90 (except, of course, the English, from whom all other fans have to be protected). The

Olympic football tournament of 1984 drew good crowds but that did not stop it from being relegated to second-class status, not just because the world's top players were not there but because it was not shown extensively on television. In fact, with the worst advertising recession in years in the USA, the days of automatic big money are over. Fingers have been badly burned by the downturn in advertising income and sport has not been insulated from the rationalisation that has taken place. Even the NFL has not been immune. In 1993, only NBC's coverage of professional basketball was showing a substantial profit. When baseball, the true national sport of the USA, is affected by these trends then you know something profound is taking place. The latest deal between television and baseball is a revenue-sharing exercise between the sport, NBC and CBS (maybe Ken Bates negotiated it for them). For its last baseball deal in 1989, CBS paid $1.06 billion (£716 million). Its estimated losses on that contract were over $100 million (£67 million).

Despite the hitches with television, it is probable that USA '94 will be a successful, money-spinning endeavour. In expectation of this, the USSF promised to establish a professional league by the time of the finals. So far there is no sign of this happening. Currently, there is a semi-professional league of thirteen teams playing to average attendances of 5,000 (a nine-year high). There is no chance of national television with crowds like these, and with no television contract there is simply no future for a professional league. The USSF hopes to get round this by a part-franchising expansion plan to attract leading European clubs. Milan are said to have expressed an interest, not only in lending their name to another football team but to other sports as well. Needless to say, key Milan personnel are already based in the United States to investigate whether this idea might not only save US soccer but also be the genesis of Silvio Berlusconi's world league.

Elsewhere, those in the medium now understand the audience that football delivers. It brings sponsors, advertisers and massive amounts of money. And the event that brings the greatest opportunity of all is the World Cup. The new Japanese J League, for instance, was brought into existence as a vehicle for Japan's bid to be awarded the World Cup in 2002.

Thus the game in Japan has become – as befits a nation where long-term strategic thinking is instilled into everyone from an early age – a tool of economic and social policy. Whereas the Americans had to abandon what were, in effect, last-minute attempts to set up a professional league, the Japanese started with twelve years to spare. With typical thoroughness, the Japanese also sought to make sure that each club could claim a regional identity and was sponsored by a major corporation (although Tokyo does not, as yet, have a team). When Joao Havelange expressed the wish that the continent of Asia should stage the World Cup by 2002, the Japanese took him at his word. It has often been said that Japan is good at taking other people's inventions and making them better. If they can do this with football who knows what the outcome will be?

For the Japanese corporations backing the fledgling J League, there is another imperative which justifies their involvement beyond supporting their local community (important though that is to Japanese companies). As the world moves towards the rise of new economic blocs and groupings following the collapse of communism, the importance of global media interests is rising. The new multi-nationals are communication- and media-based. Since sport in general and football in particular are major areas of viewer and consumer interest, the companies involved will reap a double reward. As Silvio Berlusconi realised, if they are successful they will be revered in their own heartland and will also make the huge profits that football brings, not necessarily directly (which enables them to claim that they do not make money from football), but through the knock-on effects football can have through the rest of the business.

If the lesson of recent years is that television is becoming ever more powerful, then the reverse, that fans are deemed less important, is also true. Even to Silvio Berlusconi, it is not enough to enjoy the support of the Milanese; his business strategy requires that the whole world supports Milan. And where Berlusconi goes, others, like Bernard Tapie, David Murray and Alan Sugar, will not be far behind. The great march forward of television has happened largely while football has been ignorant of the changes taking place. When a Berlusconi gets involved, the ignorance quota is bound to go down but the developments have still been piecemeal. With

FIFA regulating World Cup television deals and UEFA looking to control more of the television rights to European games (and even, perhaps, imposing limits on the size of national leagues), that situation has at least now been addressed. It remains, however, at a supra-national level. Domestic games remain the property of domestic federations, leagues and clubs, most of which do not have sufficient expertise to realise what the agenda really is. In all the euphoria and self-congratulation that followed the signing of the contract between the English Premier League and BSkyB, touted as the biggest deal in European sport, no one seemed to notice that the English were still one step behind.

For supporters who pay their money week in and week out to watch their favourite teams, the way things are going does not look good. Even in countries where fans are accorded a higher status than in Britain, the cost of attending games is going up all the time. Moreover, as the recession bites hard into European economies, clubs in the wealthiest league of all, Italy, have gone out of business. It was even announced in 1993 that Juventus, once the richest club in the world, was no longer to be a part of the Fiat empire. In England, the situation is much worse. Fans here are used to being treated shabbily but television, with its ability to make alterations, such as changing kick-off times seemingly at will, is only succeeding in alienating many who should be wholehearted supporters. From the record of the last few years, it is clear that the English only do something for fans when forced, as happened with the Taylor Report, and even then can only do it with extreme bad grace. In 1993, a series of 'consultations' were announced, which were to be between the FA, Premier League and Football League on the one hand and supporters on the other. The supporters to be consulted, however, were hand-picked from the Football Supporters Association and the National Federation of Supporters Clubs. There was no guarantee that any views expressed would be acted upon and the exercise could not even be justified on market research grounds. It was better than nothing, though, since every business should canvass the views of those who buy its products. The fact that it has taken football over a hundred years to do so should not blind anyone to the merits of the consultations. It is nevertheless too little, too late, and supporters would be foolish to believe it will do anything to resolve the fundamental conflict between the needs of fans and the needs of clubs which are in hock to television and sponsors.

The real view of the authorities towards the fans can be seen in the fact that when the FA's Blueprint was being organised, the only time supporters came into the equation was under the heading of 'Crowd Control'. Another small, but pertinent example of the way fans are not only treated badly but also prevented from organising matters themselves can be seen in the arrangements the FA made for England supporters travelling to Sweden for the 1992 European Championships. The FA appointed exclusive agents to handle travel and ticket sales and gave the Football Supporters Association no help to make their own arrangements; indeed the FA opposed them at every turn. The same will apply in the USA if England qualify. To change attitudes is not easy, as the FSA has consistently found out.

The fans, however, remain vital to the success of football. They can live with television – indeed, they form part of the combative backdrop without which televised matches would be less entertaining. At other times they are part of the viewing public themselves. They do not like, nor should they have to endure, the incompetence and shady dealings which have characterised the administration of the English game for so long. Of course fans want a successful team but they also want to be taken into account when important decisions are made. With global corporate interests beginning to rule the roost while the FA is more concerned with parochial matters, their wishes are even less likely to be heeded. Kate Hoey, Labour MP for Vauxhall, a confirmed football fan of long standing and a woman who worked as an educational adviser to apprentice players at a number of London clubs, sang a lament for all fans when she wrote in the *Daily Telegraph*: 'In three years, England host the European Championships. This is an opportunity which should be seized upon to restore pride in the team, in the supporters and in the reputation of England as a confident footballing nation. I have no faith in the present FA hierarchy to deliver any of this.'

The week following Hoey's article, Graham Kelly's reply was published. It gave no indication that here was the man to bring back the pride about which Hoey had written. All he could point to was that the future was going to be alright because the infrastructure to oversee the development of young players had been overhauled and the benefits would soon be seen. He also stated that the creation of the Premier League 'will be seen to have reduced the amount of football played by the top players'. This response was lambasted by a *Telegraph* reader, one J.R. Anderson of Wilmslow, Cheshire, who wrote: 'Come off it, Graham Kelly, who do you think you are kidding about a reduction in the number of games? The FA failed completely in their avowed aim to start the Premier League with an eighteen-team format.'

Kelly's disappointing defence to Kate Hoey was in direct contrast to his performance at a special awards ceremony organised by *When Saturday Comes*. Kelly had been voted by readers 'the person who has done the most damage to football in the recent past'. Entering into the spirit of the occasion, Kelly accepted the award, Richard Attenborough-like, thanking everybody he had ever met and shedding copious tears. *WSC* was extremely lucky to have found the FA's chief executive in the country and presumably only did so because, since donning the mantle of Kelly of the Yard, he was needed at home to pursue his investigations religiously. While it showed Kelly's nice line in self-deprecating humour, he was clearly anxious not to receive the award again. He wrote to *WSC*, repeating his defence to Kate Hoey, which will probably ensure his election again next year.

Many attempts have been made to change the nature of football's administration, the most recent of formal proposals being the Football League's idea of a joint board. In fact, there is merit in the concept of a board, but not as the League envisaged it. As Alex Fynn pointed out in an article in *Time Out* in August 1993, the only way a board can be successful is if it acts like the board of directors of a company. Such a board, Fynn maintained, should consist of all of football's interest groups, the FA being only one, albeit the most powerful. Managers, players, referees, supporters, Leagues and clubs should all have representation, and legal, financial and marketing expertise should also be incorporated. A board of directors exists to lay down policy. That policy is then implemented by a managing director or chief executive who has the power to make decisions. Steve Coppell, the England international and former manager of Crystal Palace, went further, writing in the *Independent*, 'A supremo needs to be appointed to run the game. Nearly all the big American sports have grown enormously under the guidance of a single person . . . He would be given the power by the chairmen to make decisions which might be considered contrary to their interests and those of their clubs, but would be for the benefit of the game.' If such a supremo were appointed, though, what guarantee is there, one might ask, that the right person would be given the job? There is, of course, no guarantee, but the holder of the post could be judged on whether clear, well-defined targets were achieved. One of these might be linked to the performance of the England team, which would ensure that the supremo could not be hijacked by forceful club chairmen who pay only lip-service to the needs of the national team.

The first crucial test for a supremo would be to get the size of the Premier League down to manageable proportions, in spite of the views of Ken Bates and Ron Noades. Although it has been agreed that the Premier League will be reduced to twenty in 1995, this is still two clubs more than advocated in the Blueprint, and anyway comes far too late to help England in their preparations for USA '94. After Steve Coppell resigned as manager of Crystal Palace he felt able to put forward his thoughts on this subject, which were in direct contrast to those of his erstwhile employer, Ron Noades. 'Before Italia '90,' Coppell said, 'the First Division had twenty teams, which meant a thirty-eight-game league programme over approximately thirty-six weeks. At that time we had two major cup competitions and no European club games, so even the most successful players had only fifty matches to play. The results were evident, with England knocked out at the semi-final stage by the eventual winners in a penalty shoot-out. I rate this our best performance since 1966 . . . All the European countries who have dominated world football in the last thirty years have had a domestic programme comprising a league of between sixteen and eighteen clubs, plus one cup competition. We ignore this overwhelming evidence only to our future regret.'

All attempts at change have failed in the past because in order to effect real change, the lumbering FA Council would have to vote itself out of existence, which is like asking turkeys to vote for Christmas. Graham Kelly's Blueprint offered hope but this was dashed when it was implemented only in part, with the real benefits, such as the proposed Sports Institute in conjunction with Loughborough University and the National Plan for Stadia, falling by the wayside. Ken Bates once again summed up what any advocate of change is up against. 'It [the FA] is a badly run quagmire of committees,' he said. 'It's a bit like Topsy, it just grew. Precedents have become customs, customs have become rights and rights have become cast in stone. You'll never change football because I don't really think the people at the top want to change it. There isn't the political will to change it.'

Graham Kelly put it more succinctly. As a hostage to the power of the counties, not to mention the clubs, he claimed, perhaps with only half his tongue in his cheek: 'I don't have the authority to change the plug on a kettle.' The fact is that the whole of the football world believed that, at last, with the Blueprint, radical change was going to take place. Instead, the merry-go-round carries on as before, only some of the names have been changed. Since then Kelly has kept a low profile while football's fans have been diverted by an endless succession of court cases. Perhaps it is time to stop attempting the impossible and turn attentions elsewhere.

The English game needs the revolution that was fleetingly offered by the Blueprint then snatched away. Supporters here should now realise that meaningful change will come only if imposed from a higher level, which means by FIFA or UEFA. UEFA is in a state of transition and is looking to take more power to itself, thus a window of opportunity exists. UEFA support for new concepts, including a European league and a reduction in the number of domestic games, is the only route by which the FA can be forced to act. The time is now. If history is anything to go by, the window will not only be closed very soon, it will be bolted shut for a long time to come and we shall be left to live wlth all the old failures repeating themselves, this time from the comfort of our armchair in front of the television screen – if we can afford the cost of pay-TV.

Postscript

The fallout from the Marseille bribery affair rumbled on through 1993. In addition to being thrown out of the 1993–94 European Cup, the club was stripped of its French title and was not allowed to contest the Super Cup or the Intercontinental Cup. Perhaps worse, an anticipated huge financial deficit threatened bankruptcy and automatic relegation to the second division. Bernard Tapie gave notice of his intention to withdraw from the club at the end of the season. The French national team, meanwhile, suffered a complete loss of confidence and were beaten at home in their two final World Cup games, failing in the process to qualify for the USA.

At least the Marseille affair was speedily resolved, thanks to the intervention of UEFA and FIFA. This was in direct contrast with the English authorities' tardy response to the agents' scandal. Kelly of the Yard made little progress in his investigations and the Premier League set up its own committee. Neither inspired much confidence that any wrongdoing would be rooted out.

In Scotland, Rangers began the new season uncertainly and went out of the European Cup in the first round to Levski Sofia of Bulgaria, a serious dent to the club's new European status. Celtic, who replaced Liam Brady with Lou Macari, failed in the second round of the UEFA Cup, beaten by Bobby Robson's Sporting Lisbon, a team Celtic trounced when they had last met in European competition ten years before. What really showed how times have changed was the fact that Sporting were, from the outset, expected to win. By November, no Scottish club had survived in Europe.

The situation in England was little better. In the eight years from 1977 to 1984, English teams won the European Cup seven times. Now, the English champions, for the third year in succession, couldn't get beyond the second round. Manchester United were hailed and hyped so much by the English media that perhaps they began to believe their own publicity. An eleven point lead in the Premiership resulted in an illusion that they were a great side but they deservedly lost on away goals to Galatasaray of Turkey. The fact that it was the unfancied Turks and not one of Europe's big clubs that delivered the blow made the defeat seem that much worse. At the very highest level, United were found wanting and their most influential players failed to impress.

Two key reasons for the demise are easy to identify. First, the ban from Europe. At the best of times, the English fail to heed lessons learned elsewhere and during the years of exile there was no counterweight to balance what became an inexorable slide into mediocrity (Malcolm Allison said that the 1993 Premiership was the worst top division he could recall). Second was the qualification rule imposed by UEFA. Manchester United suffered particularly from the regulation because of the 'foreigner' status in England of the Scots, Welsh and Irish, thus United became the only team in the European Cup which could not field its championship-winning side. This made it almost impossible for Alex Ferguson to avoid selection mistakes. However, Ferguson knew the rules when he began his European campaign, yet he still bought Roy Keane, an Irishman, as his main close-season purchase.

The situation was exacerbated by the disparity between the Premiership's eligibility rules, and those of UEFA. This means that in future either the Premiership will have to fall into line with UEFA (which would cause an outcry) or the likes of Manchester United will have to go the way of clubs like Arsenal and Norwich, who either buy or develop English players (and fared better in Europe as a consequence).

The dangerous delusion still persists that because the English domestic game is popular as entertainment and is admired for its competitiveness, it is still the best, or at least up there with the best. Graham Kelly made just this point in answer to criticism from FIFA general secretary, Sepp Blatter, who proclaimed that English football was thirty years behind the times. The complacency now seems endemic. Take one example. The English have always trumpeted the strength in depth of the English league. But after the second round of Europe in 1993 only two English teams, Arsenal and Norwich, remained. There were still three French teams left (despite Marseille's enforced withdrawal), six Italian, five German, four Spanish and four Portuguese. There may well be fifteen adequate teams in the Premiership but where it matters, at the top, England has been overtaken and is in danger of relegation to the second division of any European league.

Worse than all of this were England's performances in the World Cup qualifying phase, which went from the sublime to the ridiculous. Hopes were falsely raised in September following a 3-0 home win over a demoralised Poland but the crunch came in Rotterdam a month later in a game England had at least to draw to stand any chance of making it to the finals in the USA.

Without the banned and injured Paul Gascoigne, there was still no room in the England side for midfield players of flair. Instead, we saw the same failures which had blighted the whole campaign and England were deservedly beaten 2-0 by the Dutch, some undistinguished refereeing notwithstanding. Graham Taylor, who had become adept at finding others to blame for his own mistakes, felt England were 'cheated' by the referee. A more realistic assessment was that it was the Dutch who had cheated – they passed the ball to each other along the ground.

Graham Kelly gave a feeble answer to the mounting speculation about the manager's future, claiming that he (Kelly) could hear the sound of 'axes grinding'. Too right he could! England's failure was dismal and while Kelly was right to talk about altering the nature of the country's managerial structure, the fact remained that Taylor was patently the wrong man for the job. Quite simply, had Terry Venables been in charge, the team, for all its shortcomings, would have qualified for the USA. Moreover, it was the FA which had failed to implement its own Blueprint. This is hardly surprising since the amateur ethos pervades the running of the professional game. For instance, there are no players' or managers' representatives on the International Committee which appoints the England manager. Instead, there are FA councillors who have never been involved in the professional game and club chairmen whose voting record for the 22-team Premier League shows where their interest really lies (the only leading director who publicly puts the interests of the national team on a par with those of his own club – David Dein of Arsenal – is not even a member of the FA council).

The formalities were completed when Holland beat the Poles in Poznan to secure their place in the USA. England's 7-1 win in Bologna against San Marino could not save them. On the same night Wales lost at home to Romania, which put paid to their chances. With Scotland and Northern Ireland eliminated early on, the UK would be sending no representatives to America. Jack Charlton, on the other hand, steered his side to second place in a tough group, edging out the European champions, Denmark. The Republic of Ireland were now torch bearers for the whole of the British game.

The FIFA hierarchy was annoyed by England's failure as it knew (perhaps better than the English) that England's participation in the USA was extremely important, although the US World Cup committee, fearful of the reputation of English fans, breathed a huge sigh of relief. Sepp Blatter's comments, made more out of sorrow than anger, led to speculation that FIFA and UEFA might force the country to field a Great Britain team in major championships. Also called into question by Blatter's statement was Britain's unique position in having fifty per cent of the votes on the International Board, which decides rule changes.

Sooner or later that situation, along with the many others raised in this book, will have to be addressed. The FA which these days is consistently outmanoeuvred in the corridors of power of world football, may eventually find itself being forced to accept not only a Great Britain side, but one British entrant in the European Cup and one in the Cup Winners Cup, with reduced numbers in the UEFA Cup. It is becoming increasingly obvious that, as Colin Malam put it in the *Daily Telegraph*, 'Football's mother country now exerts an influence out of all proportion to its current standing in the game.' Only one question remains: when will they ever learn?

Graham Taylor and his assistant Lawrie McMenemy resigned on 23rd November, 1993.

Appendices

**Proposed Structure for
English League Football**

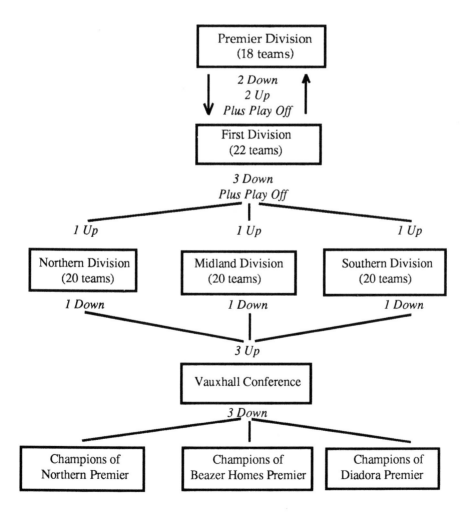

Premier Division
(18 teams)

*2 Down
2 Up
Plus Play Off*

First Division
(22 teams)

*3 Down
Plus Play Off*

1 Up   *1 Up*   *1 Up*

Northern Division
(20 teams)   Midland Division
(20 teams)   Southern Division
(20 teams)

1 Down   *1 Down*   *1 Down*

3 Up

Vauxhall Conference

3 Down

Champions of
Northern Premier   Champions of
Beazer Homes Premier   Champions of
Diadora Premier

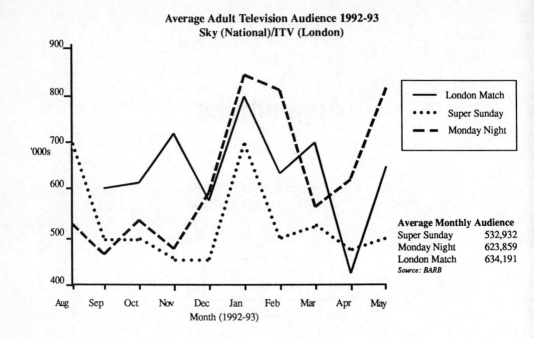

Average Adult Television Audience 1992-93
Sky (National)/ITV (London)

Average Monthly Audience
Super Sunday   532,932
Monday Night   623,859
London Match   634,191
Source: BARB

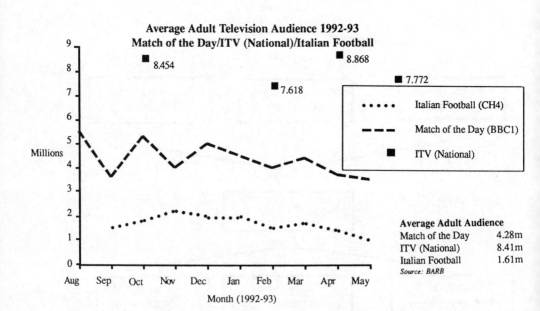

Average Adult Television Audience 1992-93
Match of the Day/ITV (National)/Italian Football

Average Adult Audience
Match of the Day   4.28m
ITV (National)   8.41m
Italian Football   1.61m
Source: BARB

Proposed Structure for
Scottish League Football

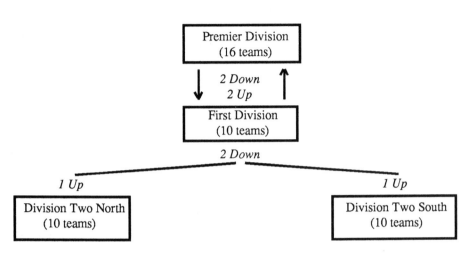

The European Superleague
Proposed Structure

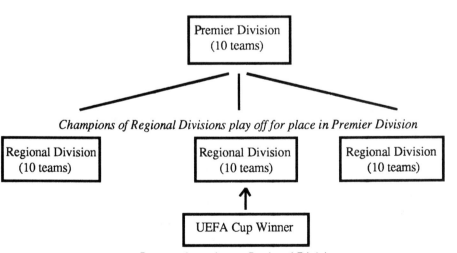

Index